CONFLICT RESOLUTION
The Partnership Way

Barry K. Weinhold, Ph.D.
University of Colorado-Colorado Springs

Janae B. Weinhold, Ph.D.
Licensed Professional Counselor

LOVE PUBLISHING COMPANY®
Denver • London • Sydney

The authors co-direct the Colorado Institute for Conflict Resolution and Creative Leadership in Colorado Springs. Through their Institute, they offer courses in conflict resolution and train professionals in *Developmental Process Work,* a modality for resolving conflict at its source. The Weinholds can be reached at:

1408 Mount View Lane
Colorado Springs, CO 80907
Phone: (719) 264-6626
Fax: (719) 264-6628
E-mail: weinholds@pcisys.net
Web Site: www.weinholds.org

Published by Love Publishing Company
Denver, Colorado 80222

Copyright © 2000 Love Publishing Company
Printed in the United States of America
ISBN 0-89108-264-6
Library of Congress Catalog Card Number 98–67861

CONTENTS

Chapter 15

How Can I Apply The Partnership Way in the Workplace? 159

Chapter 16

How Can I Apply The Partnership Way to the Legal System? 170

Chapter 17

How Can I Apply The Partnership Way in Larger Social Systems? 180

Chapter 18

How Can The Partnership Way Be Applied to the Evolution of the Human Species? 194

Chapter 19

How Can I Integrate the Elements of The Partnership Way? 202

Resources

References...227

Index...233

ACKNOWLEDGMENTS

No one writes a book in isolation, and our twelve-year journey in writing this book clearly attests to that fact. We would like to thank the many students, clients, and workshop participants who contributed to this book. They inspired us by using our ideas and exercises to change their lives and motivated us to keep developing our approach and to write this book.

We also thank the many volunteers who have worked with us at the Colorado Institute for Conflict Resolution and Creative Leadership over the years. They helped us organize seminars, workshops, and two international conferences that helped build our foundation of knowledge in the field of conflict resolution.

We want to thank Jean Houston, who inspired us to become "possible humans" and to work collaboratively on our journey of transformation. We also want to thank Arnold and Amy Mindell and their students for their contributions to our understanding of conflict. Our time studying and living in Zurich deepened our commitment to becoming part of the solution rather than part of the problem. We recognize Valentina Bondarovskaya and her Ukrainian colleagues for their contributions to our study of large social systems and post-Soviet psychology. We also thank our Slovak colleagues, Susan Vranová and Blanka Bajánkova, for their support during our assignment in Bratislava, Slovakia. We also appreciate the support of Henri Sokalski, Eugene Rolfe, and the staff of the United Nations Secretariat for the International Year of the Family at the United Nations Centre in Vienna, Austria.

We thank the members of our respective men's support group and women's support group for providing vessels as we moved toward completion of this manuscript. We also wish to thank Marian Harris and Marla Kay Rose, who helped in the preparation of this manuscript, and reviewers Bill Hornbostel and Judith Light.

Finally, we acknowledge our own relationship, which served as our laboratory for understanding and practicing the resolution of conflicts in a partnership way. We acknowledge the assistance of Claudia Matthews who helped us better understand the mysteries of conflict in our own relationship.

INTRODUCTION

OVERVIEW OF THIS BOOK

Although it has earlier roots in other disciplines, the professional study of conflict resolution is still very new—less than twenty years old. As with any new field of study, it has developed organically due to societal needs and to the personal and professional interests of those who are pioneers in the field. Some aspects of the field, such as alternative dispute resolution (ADR), are more highly advanced, while others are still in their infancy. The organic development of the field of conflict resolution left it with gaps and holes that call for new concepts and models to complete these deficits. For example, the ADR model has no approved methods for dealing with conflicts involving strong feelings.

The general deterioration in the level of civility among people; the growing tendency to use violence or litigation to resolve differences; the increasing polarization between and among religious, economic, social, political, ethnic, and racial groups; the rapid globalization of the planet; and the escalation in social and interpersonal conflict all clearly indicate the need for a new paradigm to resolve conflict. Never before have the stakes been so high.

It is the strong philosophical belief of the authors that the natural state of the universe is peaceful interdependence. Their premise in writing this book is that "peace is inevitable." This new paradigm in the field of conflict resolution transcends the prevalent paradigm that "conflict is inevitable and we must learn to manage it."

The authors view conflict as an unskilled, ineffective attempt by humans to prove their worth and get their needs met. This book identifies unmet developmental needs as a primary cause of the competitive, aggressive nature of humans. It shows how the lack of proper parental support during the first three years of life creates people with undiagnosed developmental trauma that leaves them unable to get their needs met in peaceful, cooperative, nonviolent ways.

The purpose of this book is to help adults recognize their residue of developmental trauma and to teach the psychological tools needed to resolve their conflicts in peaceful ways. The authors believe this is the next leap in evolution for the human species, one that will help people to live peacefully and interdependently.

This book presents a two-part vision for achieving this natural state of peace. The first part focuses on remediating developmental trauma, particularly that which appears in conflict situations. The second part is an optimal model for birthing and rearing children that focuses on the prevention of developmental trauma.

In this optimal model that draws from the latest research in pre- and perinatal psychology, parents conceive, gestate, birth, and parent consciously. They prepare themselves for these tasks prior to conception by consciously clearing the major unresolved conflicts from their own childhood. During all phases of their child's development, the parents focus their attention on the needs of the child. They provide loving encouragement, take the needs of the child seriously and set limits in loving and supportive ways without harming the child mentally, emotionally, physically and spiritually. If the parents find themselves unable to provide constancy in their parenting or experience conflict between them, they use adult resources such as therapy or parent support groups to help them with these issues.

Around this optimal nuclear family unit is a secondary ring of support that comes through an extended family network. The function of this group of individuals, couples, and families is to support the parents so that they can parent the child. This group provides emotional, spiritual, physical, and mental sustenance for the couple so that they can provide constant and consistent attention to the needs of the child. A tertiary ring of help for the nuclear family unit comes through community resources. This ring provides aid via social programs and policies designed to foster strong family units and make the needs of children a priority.

Buoyed by the assistance from these multi-tiered support systems, the child is able to complete the first critical stages of psychological development without lasting trauma. By age three the child is sufficiently self-reliant, self-confident, and capable of getting his or her needs met without having to whine, cry, get angry, or act violently. Able to instinctively trust his/her intuition and natural ways of knowing, the child grows in wisdom and understanding about how the world works.

The parents, who accept the child's natural curiosity and impulses, allow the child to master the tasks of daily living and delight with the child in his or her growing competencies. The child continues to refine his or her skills in getting needs met by direct negotiation and learns to resolve conflicts of wants and needs naturally through cooperative ways. The parents model respectful interpersonal behaviors and honor differences of all kinds.

School experiences are structured so that the child expands his or her skills in living interdependently. Cooperative learning replaces competition and rewards and punishment. Teachers model respectful, cooperative behaviors and reinforce kind, compassionate, humane, and benevolent behaviors. As the child moves into adolescence, the adults in his/her life support the healthy, safe exploration of adult roles and responsibilities and the child becomes more mature in his/her choices.

Children who experience a strong developmental foundation grow up and become mature adults who are capable of directing their lives in responsible ways. They know how to get their needs met in healthy, responsible ways and can effectively resolve their conflicts.

This prevention-based vision of birthing peaceful children and a peaceful world is within the realm of possibilities. Frederic Leboyer (1975), one of the pioneers of this vision, discovered that gently birthed babies were developmentally advanced for their ages, were happier, better adjusted and were more loving and peaceful (Russell, 1979). The significance of the birth experience has been repeatedly correlated with the overall quality of a person's life (Grof, 1985). This research is now influencing public policymaking. After a lengthy investigation into the "roots of crime," the Commission on Crime Control and Violence Prevention in Sacramento, California,

recommended, among other things, childbirth with parental involvement, family intimacy, and a natural delivery (Jones, 1995).

The vision of remediating the effects of traumatic births and early childhood is equally attainable. Research findings on optimal childhood also provide guidelines and interventions coupled with new trauma reduction therapy modalities, comprise a comprehensive model for emancipating adults and children from their residue of developmental trauma. This book describes numerous elements of this vision.

When President Kennedy announced his vision of sending a man to the moon by the end of 1960s, the technology to accomplish this task did not exist. Because his vision caught peoples' imagination, the scientific world quickly created the technology and accomplished the task.

There is now sufficient scientific information and psychological technologies available to make a vision of a peaceful world a reality. The next step is to inspire the imagination of this vision at a collective level. As technology has shrunk the world, the need for cooperation and peaceful interdependency is now an evolutionary necessity. The peaceful resolution of conflicts becomes unequivocally linked to our survival as a species.

Realizing the limitations of existing models of conflict resolution to address the growing evolutionary crisis, the authors set about developing a new paradigm for resolving conflicts. Through field research and a meta-analysis of the research on existing models of conflict resolution, the authors have identified a number of critical components for the creation of a new paradigm that will teach people to:

- simplify the context of conflict,
- simplify the resolution of conflict,
- reframe conflict from a negative to a positive experience,
- utilize the strong feelings that often emerge during conflict situations,
- unify opposites that appear in conflict situations,
- develop reciprocity in relationships,
- infuse conflict situations with compassion and kindness and
- resolve intractable conflicts at their source.

This book, drawn from over a decade of research and development by the authors, presents a new paradigm of conflict resolution that is designed to (1) fill these crucial gaps in existing models of conflict resolution and (2) teach the psychological skills needed to effectively resolve conflicts of all kinds in a cooperative, peaceful manner. The Partnership Way presents proven methods for creating a new paradigm for conflict resolution.

The authors call their model the Partnership Way for several reasons. First, it advocates embracing or "partnering," with both the experience of conflict and the people with whom you have conflict. The goal of embracing conflict is self-discovery. Information discovered during the process of resolving a conflict can be used as an opportunity for personal growth. Second, this book advocates building partnership relationships that facilitate reciprocity, interdependency, unity, mutuality, and cooperation. It facilitates moving people beyond the polarized "us vs. them" splits in thinking into the "both/and" thinking that is essential for partnering.

The theory on which the Partnership Way is based, which is both comprehensive and integrative, represents a cross-disciplinary approach to conflict. The applied aspect of the model, presented through a variety of self-inventories, self-awareness exercises and skill building exercises at the end of each chapter, provides concrete activities designed to bridge the splits in consciousness that cause polarization and escalation in conflict situations.

The authors have not only studied this field for twelve years, but they have tested its validity and applicability with thousands of people around the world. They have presented the Partnership Way at numerous national and international conferences and taught it to thousands of graduate students and professionals in education, psychology, social work, medicine, business, and the military. They have also "lived the paradigm" in the "laboratory" of their personal and professional relationships. The structure of the book is drawn from the current graduate level course in Conflict Resolution Strategies which they have taught for ten years in the Counseling and Human Services M.A. program at the University of Colorado-Colorado Springs.

THE UNIQUE FEATURES OF THE PARTNERSHIP WAY:

The Partnership Way is designed to address the psychological and social conditions that foster conflict. It is unique in several ways:

- *It embraces conflict* and encourages people in conflict to see themselves as "partners" who can help resolve conflicts at their source rather than become "enemies."
- *All adversaries become potential "partners,"* providing an unlimited number of opportunities for resolving conflicts.
- *It identifies parent-child experiences during the first three years of life as the most common source of intractable conflicts.*
- *It extends the definition of trauma to include more subtle developmental issues and deficits.*
- *It correlates trauma with recurring conflicts* and provides tools for identifying and addressing the symptoms of trauma.
- *It helps readers learn how to desensitize themselves* to any traumatic or negative experiences they have had in conflict situations.
- *It helps participants identify and modify their "internal working model of reality"* created during the formative

years of their lives so that they can interact more effectively at both personal and professional levels.
- *It reframes conflict from a pathological emphasis to a growth emphasis,* making it an opportunity for personal transformation and development.
- *It emphasizes kindness and compassion* for one's opponents during conflict situation, using them as doorways to deeper human experiences *(no aggression).*
- *It utilizes a unitive, "partnership" approach* that goes beyond the concept of "compromise."
- *It utilizes the symbol of the "mandorla," the prototype of partnership conflict resolution,* to foster the integration of opposites to help heal internal splits and stop polarized thinking and behaviors during conflict situations.
- *It utilizes a set of core principles for understanding and resolving conflicts that can be applied systemically* to both micro systems such as individuals, couples, and families and to macro systems such as organizations, cultural sub-groups, communities, and nation-states.
- *Its systemic construction helps readers overcome the feelings of hopelessness and powerlessness* that can typically accompany conflict situations in a variety of settings.
- *It provides personally empowering concepts and tools* designed to help the readers utilize the book for both personal and professional development.
- *It presents a multi-tiered approach to conflict resolution* and identifies three levels for resolving conflicts, with each level becoming more complex and more personal. These three levels are: (1) resolving conflicts of wants and needs, (2) resolving conflicts of values and beliefs, and (3) resolving conflicts at their source by examining family of origin issues.
- *Utilizes dialogue and the skills of reflective listening and inquiry* to help resolve intractable conflicts involving values and beliefs.
- *It uses a step-by-step, psycho-educational approach* to break down the process of conflict resolution into its component parts. This helps the reader learn the individual skills needed to master the *Partnership Way.*
- *It utilizes a therapeutic modality, Developmental Process Work,* to help clients resolve conflicts related to developmental trauma.
- *It integrates theory and practice* through a diverse spectrum of written exercises, experiential activities and auxiliary materials designed to help the reader achieve a more personal understanding of the material.

PURPOSE OF THE BOOK

The purpose of this book is to take you on a journey through the mysteries of conflict where you learn to embrace conflict as an opportunity for personal growth. The word "mystery" comes from the Greek word *musein,* which means "to close the eyes or the mouth." Conflicts can open a doorway into less accessible archetypal realms where transformative, life-altering change can occur. Most people, however, feel afraid to open the door to these mysteries. As a result, this major avenue for personal growth remains blocked.

This book can also help reframe conflict in an important way. Most people tend to criticize or judge others when they get into conflict, particularly if they are acting escalated, out of control or slightly crazy. As you discover how past conflicts contaminate current conflicts, the authors hope that you will become more kind, more compassionate toward people in conflict (including yourself) and open yourself to deeper, more reciprocal relationships.

Mastering the skills of the Partnership Way can help open your eyes and mouths to help you solve these mysteries and move forward in your psychological development. Some mastery comes through the use of critical questions throughout the book that are designed to open the door to deeper reflection and stronger action regarding the resolution of conflict. Beginning with Chapter 2, each major section begins with a key question that is then answered by the following text. The authors hope that this "inquiry" method will assist you in breaking conflict down into its component parts and make it easier to assimilate.

ORGANIZATION OF THIS BOOK

This book poses questions that the authors believe are important to answer on your journey into the unknown realms of conflict. It is divided into four parts. The first part provides you with an overview of the Partnership Way. The second part explains how to use this model to resolve less complex personal conflicts. The third part illustrates how to use it to resolve more complex personal conflicts involving unmet needs related to developmental trauma. The fourth part focuses on the professional application of the Partnership Way in a variety of settings. There are suggested writing and experiential exercises at the end of each chapter to help you both personalize the material and deepen your understanding of the mysteries of conflict.

Part One describes the basic components of the Partnership Way for resolving conflict. This section includes information about the history, research and social factors that lead to its development. Part Two describes how to resolve conflicts related to wants and needs and values and beliefs. Here you will identify your own personal style of conflict resolution and use a variety of inventories to (1) critically analyze your personal style, (2) to determine how it developed and (3) understand where it is effective and where it is not.

Part Three focuses on resolving more complex conflicts that tend to recycle in your life. This part focuses on healing the internal "splits" in consciousness at the source of most intractable or difficult to resolve conflicts. In this part, you will learn how to use the skills and information

from Part Two to resolve conflicts in intimate relationships and in your family.

Part Four of the book applies the Partnership Way to various helping professions that utilize conflict resolution —counseling, education, law and mediation and other forms of alternative dispute resolution. Part Four also focuses on the application of the conflict resolution skills in more complex social systems such as intimate relationships, the workplace and racial, religious, and national conflicts. At the end of the book, you will find a resource section containing information on professional associations and training programs, curricular materials, videotapes, and other resources.

FOR WHOM THIS BOOK IS WRITTEN

The primary audience for this book are people who wish to learn more effective methods of resolving conflict. Its highly personal and experiential nature make it an ideal self-instructional tool for individuals, couples, and families, as well as those working in helping professions such as counseling, education, special education, law, business, curriculum and instruction and educational leadership programs. It can also be used as a primary textbook for undergraduate and graduate level elective classes in conflict resolution or as an auxiliary text in communications, psychology, and sociology curricula.

Many experienced teachers need conflict resolution skills, as they are being asked to teach them to elementary and secondary school students. Some large city schools such as New York, Chicago and Kansas City, require all students to take a course in conflict resolution. Kansas City recently developed a required K-12 conflict resolution curriculum. Over 8,500 schools nationwide now teach conflict resolution skills. Many of these schools are also training peer mediators to help resolve conflicts on the playground, the lunchroom and in the hallways.

The National Institute for Dispute Resolution is one of a myriad of organizations focusing on conflict resolution that holds national and regional conferences each year and publishes newsletters to inform about the need for conflict resolution and to publicize new approaches. Other groups such as the Educators for Social Responsibility (ESR) have developed an elementary and secondary school curriculum that is used widely. The Community Board in San Francisco, a community based conflict resolution program, has also developed school curriculum materials that are used in many elementary and secondary schools.

THE VOICE OF THIS BOOK

The personal nature of this book emerges in several ways. First, the authors describe some of their learnings from their twelve year quest for a new approach to conflict resolution. Second, the tone of the book is identical to that which they use when teaching this material to students—warm, authentic and self-disclosing. Third, this book is designed for a conflict resolution class that combines personal and professional development. For this reason, the authors include numerous examples of how they have applied the material in their lives as individuals and as a couple. Chapter 19 describes their own personal journeys through the mysteries of conflict. They hope to "partner" with you as you journey through your own mysteries of conflict via this book.

HOW TO USE THIS BOOK

While the authors present a sequential approach for learning to resolve conflicts, please feel free to start with the chapter or part of the book or workbook that best fits your needs. Your personal needs and learning style should guide you in your study of conflict resolution. At the end of each chapter, you will find exercises designed to personalize and deepen your understanding of conflict. Your personal process can serve as a constant internal guide as you use this book to evolve and grow in your ability to resolve your conflicts from a more enlightened state of awareness.

The authors present four levels of competencies to master in your study of conflict resolution. You can use these levels to assess your own learning about conflict resolution. The four levels are as follows:

- knowledge of the major theories and techniques that make up the Partnership Way for resolving conflict.
- examination of your personal style of conflict resolution and the application of these theories and techniques to help you develop an effective, partnering style of conflict resolution.
- application of these theories and techniques to helping others resolve their conflicts.
- the ability to teach others about conflict resolution.

The first level of competencies includes a basic awareness of the key terms and concepts presented in the textbook and workbook. Reading this book will help you develop some level one competencies. Other level one competencies may be gained from class lectures, class discussions, and by reading some of the other journal articles and books recommended in the textbook and workbook.

The second level of competency is often omitted from many counselor training programs, but is seen by the authors as being very important. To work effectively helping others resolve their conflicts, they believe you need competencies in resolving your own conflicts. Without this skill, you are likely to experience numerous countertransference issues where someone mirrors some of your own unresolved conflicts. When this happens, it is usually difficult to be effective in helping others. In the counseling and human services program at the University of Colorado-Colorado Springs, the motto that emphasizes the need to develop this competency is, "Do unto yourself before doing unto others."

Begin first with an assessment of your own personal style of conflict resolution to identify the strengths and weaknesses. Then you can develop a plan for addressing any weaknesses you might find that interfere with effectively resolving your own conflicts. Through the self-inventories, writing exercises and other suggested experiential exercises you can develop more awareness of your personal style of conflict resolution and how to experience cooperative, partnering resolutions to your conflicts.

The third level of competency involves learning how to apply the knowledge from levels one and two in your profession. The degree to which you have mastered the first two levels of competencies will determine how effectively you can apply this knowledge in your professional life.

The fourth level of competency is teaching this material to others. To teach you must understand the subtle key ideas and concepts of the Partnership Way, have a clear comprehension about the nature of your own conflicts, learned to successfully resolve your major conflicts and mastered these skills in your work with other people. As a final project in the conflict resolution class taught at UCCS, students apply what they have learned in the course to some area of their life. They may teach conflict resolution skills to their colleagues at work or to family members at home or implement a neighborhood or community project.

The following activities can be used to strengthen these four levels of competency:

Level one competencies, broadening and deepening your knowledge of conflict resolution, can be developed and strengthened by some of the following activities:

1. Reading each chapter in the book.
2. Completing the Self-Awareness exercises, Self Inventories and Skill Practice exercises in the book.
3. Completing the Practice Test at the end of the book.
4. Reading some of the books and articles recommended in the book.

Level two competencies related to your personal style of conflict resolution can be accomplished by the following activities:

1. Filling out and scoring the self-inventories in various chapters of the book (especially Chapter 3) designed to help you identify your own personal style of conflict resolution.
2. Discussing the results of your self-assessment with fellow students.
3. Developing new skills to correct any perceived weaknesses or win-lose parts of your personal style and develop an effective partnership approach to resolving your own conflicts.
4. Practice your newly developed skills using fellow students to role play people with whom you have unresolved conflicts.

5. Get feedback from these people as to your effectiveness.
6. Use these newly developed win-win skills to effectively resolve any unresolved conflicts in your life.

Level three competencies related to applying course learning by helping others solve conflicts effectively can be accomplished by the following activities:

1. Studying the case examples in the book.
2. Reviewing the intervention strategies suggested in the book.
3. Practicing your skills by serving as a third party mediator helping fellow students resolving their conflicts.
4. Get feedback from these students on the effectiveness of your work as a third party mediator in the various Skill Practice exercises.
5. Testing your skills with actual clients or in situations where you can serve as a third party mediator or as a counselor.

Level four competencies related to your ability to teach others what you learned can be accomplished by the following activities:

1. Review the content in the book.
2. Review the self-inventories and writing exercises to see if any of them could be used to teach others about conflict resolution.
3. Check the Resources section at the end of the book for resources you can use to teach others about conflict resolution.
4. Utilize the outline for the Application Project that follows to design a project to teach others about conflict resolution.

OUTLINE FOR APPLICATION PROJECT

This outline for the application project can be used to develop third and/or fourth level competencies:

1. Title of the project.
   a. Use a short title that captures the essence of the project.

2. Brief description of the nature of the project.
   a. Include a summary of the "what," "when," "where," "how" and "with whom" aspects of the project.
3. Rationale for the project.
   a. Why is this change needed?
   b. How did you determine this need? (Be specific, i.e., polled 100 students.)
4. Personal rationale.
   a. What do you hope to learn about yourself from this project?
   b. How is this project going to help you be more effective?
   c. How does this project relate to your emerging personal theory of conflict resolution? Be specific.
   d. How does this project relate to your emerging theory of social change?
5. State the behavioral objectives of the project.
   a. What do you hope to accomplish?
   b. State your goals and objectives in specific observable behaviors, i.e. "The members of my family will be able to successfully resolve their conflicts of wants and needs using win-win strategies 80% of the time."
6. Procedures.
   a. What specific steps do you propose for this project to be carried out successfully?
   b. What is the time period for completing each step in your plan?
   c. Develop a flowchart showing the steps you propose to use to carry out this project. (See example in Figure 1 that follows this outline).
7. Evaluation of the project.
   a. Develop a plan to evaluate each of your objectives. Include some follow-up procedures to show longer term outcomes.
   b. Show the results of your evaluation.
   c. Based on your evaluation, was the application project successful? What would you do different if you were starting over with this project?

PROCESS MODEL

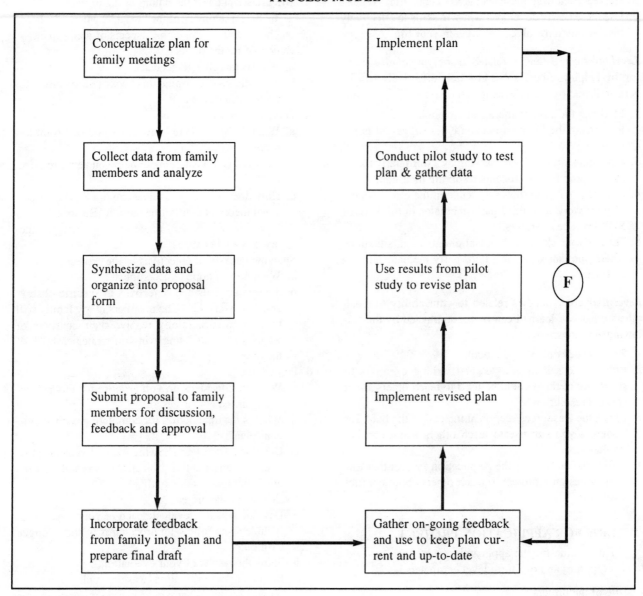

Figure 1
Flowchart Model of a Planned Application Project

CONFLICT RESOLUTION AS TRANSFORMATION

This book is designed not only to teach you conflict resolution skills, but also to facilitate a transformative process for you. As the result of teaching this course to literally thousands of people over the past 10 years, the authors have learned how to help raise the consciousness of the students to where they are able to transform their lives.

The first step is to recognize at what stage of consciousness you are operating. A helpful taxonomy of stages of consciousness has been developed by Harvard psychologist and educator, Robert Kegan, and presented in his book, *In Over Their Heads* (1994). Kegan identifies five distinct stages of consciousness and through a meta-analysis of the research identifies the approximate percentage of the population that is in each stage. The stages are described below:

Stage One: Magical Thinking. The individual lacks good cause and effect thinking and often attributes things that happen to them to magic. These people often act on impulses and engage in fantasy projections. In conflicts, they will likely blame it on coincidence or something about the other person that may have little to do with the conflict.

Stage Two: Concrete Thinking. These people base their reality on what is visible and concrete to them. They do not really understand abstract concepts such as justice or freedom. Everything has to be presented to them in concrete, visible ways. In conflicts they try to deal only with the most visible and obvious affects of the conflict. The rest will seem unimportant to them.

Stage Three: Cross-Relational Thinking. These people are able to deal with abstractions. They can see relationships between categories of information, however they tend to see the world as acting upon them. They often think, act and feel like a victim. In conflict situations they will most likely feel victimized by others.

Stage Four: Systemic Thinking. These people can think holistically and are aware of the underlying patterns of thoughts, feelings and behaviors that repeat themselves over and over and control their lives. In conflict situations, they will be able to relate a current conflict to similar ones from the past. They will be able to understand why this conflict might be occurring because of an unresolved conflict from their past.

Stage Five: Trans-Systemic Thinking. These people see the relationships between their current conflicts and their past unresolved conflicts. In addition, they have the ability to change the patterns that are restricting their lives. This means that they are able to see why they were unable to resolve past conflicts, how these unresolved conflicts are affecting their lives now and how to resolve their intractable conflicts at their source.

From his research and a review of other research of these stages, Kegan estimates that about 70% of the adult population operates at Stage Three or below. Approximately 30% are entering or at Stage Four and less than 1% are entering or at Stage Five.

Our experience in using the material presented in this book in our courses showed us that most students are operating at Stage Three when they begin the course, with many of them being ready to enter Stage Four. The way the book is organized, it helps the reader move into Stages Four and Five. What seems to facilitate this movement is the personal focus of the book. When readers can apply what they are learning about conflict to their own lives, they begin to understand the patterns of intractable conflict that are controlling their lives. Many exercises in the book are designed to help people learn how to resolve intractable conflicts at their source. This facilitates movement into Kegan's Stage Five of Consciousness.

~

PART I

~

WHAT IS
THE PARTNERSHIP WAY?

Chapter 1

~

Why Is There Need
for a New Paradigm
in Conflict Resolution?

Since we began studying conflict over 12 years ago, there has been a significant escalation of conflict and violence around the world. Efforts to peacefully resolve international conflicts have not made the world a safer, more peaceful place. Television and movies contribute by portraying violence as an acceptable option for resolving conflicts. There is more domestic violence, more child abuse, more youth violence, more use of handguns, and a decreasing sense of connection and community in our cities.

The proliferation of violent youth and family conflict is an issue of great social concern. Why do so many of today's youth seem so violent? What is causing the violent conflicts in families? What can be done about these problems as a society? What can we, as individuals, do about it? These are some of the questions that are addressed in this book. Let us begin by examining the history of conflict.

The most serious and attention-getting conflicts throughout history are those that might be described as "intractable." These are the stubborn or persistent conflicts that recycle or recur over and over in people's lives. This seemingly endless cycle of intractable conflict has divided countries, religious and ethnic groups, and families. For individuals, intractable or persistent conflicts occur in their lives around various themes, such as conflicts with people in positions of authority, power struggles in intimate relationships concerning whose needs are most important, or episodes of victimization. Intractable conflicts leave people feeling hopeless, powerless, and helpless.

Many long-standing religious, ethnic, and socioeconomic conflicts that have recycled for centuries are intractable in nature. Examples of intractable international conflicts include wars over the ownership of territory or about which beliefs and values will prevail, such as the religious and ethnic wars in Ireland, the Middle East, Rwanda, and Bosnia. Other intractable conflicts include socioeconomic class struggles between rich and poor, gender conflicts between men and women, and conflicts related to different sexual orientations.

Everyone experiences conflict in different aspects of his or her life—in intimate and family relationships, at work and school, in communities, and within the culture. Conflicts that transcend the realm of the individual and become pervasive in other aspects of one's life are known as "systemic" conflicts. Models for working with conflict therefore, must also be systemic, providing a framework to help people understand how unresolved conflict inside themselves recycles in predictable patterns outside themselves in their relationships, families, schools, workplaces, and nation.

Models for resolving conflicts must also utilize tools that empower people and help them personalize the material and tools so that they can break through the feelings of despair and hopelessness that typically emerge when intractable conflicts are addressed.

The Partnership Way of conflict resolution described in this book satisfies these conditions. It addresses the systemic nature of conflict and can be used by individuals to locate the sources of their intractable conflicts. Its sequential, inquiring approach helps individuals break conflict down into its various components, starting with internal conflicts and then moving to conflicts that occur in one's intimate relationships, inside the family, at work and school, in communities, and within cultures.

WHAT ARE YOUR EXPERIENCES WITH VIOLENCE?

When we present background material about conflict in a class or workshop or speak to a community group about violent youth and family conflicts, we usually ask the following question: "How many of you have personally encountered violence or witnessed violence in some form?" To our surprise, only about one-third to one-half of the people present raise their hands.

When we ask those people who raised their hands for personal examples of their conflict experiences, it becomes clear to those who didn't raise their hands that they had limited their definition of violence. After hearing how others in the larger group defined violence, they realized that they had discounted their feelings and convinced themselves that what they had experienced was not violence. Common examples our students and workshop participants often cite include being bullied in school, being sexually or physically abused as a child, witnessing violence on television and in the movies, and being a spectator at violent sporting events.

In addition, the lack of support in their family, school, workplace, community, and global environments and the rise in frequency and intensity of violence in their lives create an insidious atmosphere of stress that makes people feel overwhelmed. To cope with their experiences of subtle peril, people shut down their senses and become "numb." Numbing is the primary mechanism that humans use to cope with an experience of trauma. Others become hypervigilant and anxious, ready to fight, flee, or freeze at a moment's notice.

WORSENING SOCIAL CONDITIONS

Many complex social, economic, political, and psychological conditions contribute to the widespread occurrence of violent conflicts in this country. A summary of these conditions follows:

The Lack of "Family-Friendly" Government Policies

The United States is not a child- or family-centered country. There are few government policies that support families. Compare our minimal family leave policy (12 weeks of unpaid leave) with those of most other developed countries. Most European countries, for example, allow up to two or three years of paid leave time for family needs related to birth, death, and disability (United Nations, 1992) All western industrialized countries, except the United States and South Africa, also provide free home visitation services for three to five years (Garbarino et al., 1992).

Home visitation services send a volunteer or paraprofessional to support new parents and provide them with information regarding access to community resources. The research (Olds & Henderson, 1994) clearly indicates that the delivery of home visitation services is the most effective means of curbing child abuse and neglect. These early intervention programs, which are inexpensive to operate, save tax money in the long run by helping high-risk families avoid problems that might later require a need for social services. Elected officials in the United States have not generally approved funding for home visitation programs, believing instead that the electorate favors short-term, shortsighted solutions.

The lack of family- and child-friendly government policies in this country adversely affects early bonding and attachment between mother and child, promoting increased child abuse and neglect. Especially hard hit are single parent families without extended family support.

Research on violence in the media findings indicate that 15 years after TV is introduced into a country, the homicide rate doubles (Garbarino et al., 1991). Research has also shown that children, who have less developed defense systems than adults, are more traumatized by the violence on TV and in films than are adults. Garbarino estimates that children typically witness more than 8,000 murders on television by the time they enter secondary school. Violence on television may be a leading cause of trauma in children. Public awareness of this problem has produced media curbs such as a rating system and the "V-chip" that allows parents to block access to television programs containing violence.

Research on increases in public violence indicates that children are directly exposed to violence at younger and younger ages. In recent years, 50% of all killings in Chicago have occurred in public (Garbarino, 1993). A 1991 study showed that 45% of first- and second-graders in Washington, DC, had witnessed muggings, 31% had witnessed shootings, and 39% had seen dead bodies (Garbarino et al., 1991).

Early exposure to violence teaches children two sobering facts. First, they learn that the body is fragile, in contrast to what is depicted in cartoons and computer games. When someone is cut or shot, they see all too well the fragility of life. They learn firsthand, and often traumatically, that a thin layer of skin provides no protection against firearms and other tools of violence to the bones, muscles, blood vessels, and vital organs within. Second, children learn that adults cannot always protect them from violence. Feeling unprotected is a very frightening experience for children and leaves them feeling helpless and hopeless.

A recent survey estimates that as many as 6.9 million children are physically abused each year (Dickstein & Nadelson, 1989). Much of this abuse is still unreported and very few parents are found guilty of child abuse when charges are pressed. Unfortunately, there is no way to estimate the amount of shame-based emotional abuse that takes place in families that later explodes as acts of violence.

The "cycle of violence" contains three primary components: the experience of trauma, subsequent feelings of shame, and the desire for aggressive behaviors such as revenge or retaliation. Traumatic events produce feelings of shame ("I am no good"). Aggressive and violent behaviors are then used to defend against feeling the shame. This is why "dissing" or acting disrespectful to a gang member can cause him to erupt into a violent burst of anger.

Breakdown of the Extended Family

In the transient North American culture, many young parents lack an extended family support system to help them cope with the pressures of isolation, work, and parenting. In addition, new parents receive no training for the most important job in the world—raising children. Studies consistently show that without proper training, many parents do to their children what was done to them. Parents who were abused as children will abuse their own children. Parents who were neglected will neglect. Sadly, abuse or neglect of children early in life creates kids without a conscience. High-risk kids, angry about neglect and/or abuse, often commit revengeful acts of violence. Many other developed countries are ahead of the United States in the area of laws and policies designed to curb violence against children. Six European countries have outlawed corporal punishment of children by their parents. In Sweden, where such legislation has been in effect for 15 years, reported child abuse has been virtually eliminated (Weinhold & Weinhold, 1993).

Lack of Quality Daycare for Children

In the United States a single mother without extended family support who wants to work must find daycare for her children. Most of the time it is either not available or too expensive in relation to her potential income. Welfare and child protection reforms at both the national and state levels are working to address these problems. The results, unfortunately, are mixed. Legislative initiatives to remove people from the public assistance rolls and decrease welfare costs often are in direct opposition to the best interests of children. Indeed, legislation has been passed that

cuts off welfare to children if their mothers cannot find work or requires mothers of young children to work outside the home, forcing children into nonparental care. These kinds of social and family policies coerce mothers to sacrifice the psychological and emotional needs of their children as a trade-off for economic survival. These kinds of social policies ignore repeated research findings that children face significant risks in attachment when they are in nonparental care more than twenty hours per week (Violato & Russell, 1994).

Lack of Affordable Housing

The American dream of owning a home is out of reach for many young families. Finding affordable housing is difficult in some areas of the country because of a limited supply of low-income rentals. The number of homeless families has increased greatly in almost all urban areas. In Colorado Springs, Colorado, a five-year waiting list exists for people wanting to rent low-cost public housing. Working-poor families who have few housing alternatives are left with acute stress.

Breakdown of the Nuclear Family

Over 30% of all children born in this country in 1993 were illegitimate. Among black Americans the rate was over 60%.

The nuclear family has broken down in other ways, as well. For instance, domestic violence is now the leading cause of injury to women between the ages of 15 and 44 (McKay, 1994). Not only women, but children are affected. Children from violent homes are three to four times more likely than children from nonviolent homes to commit illegal acts—vandalism, stealing, alcohol and drug abuse. Over 80% of all prison inmates were neglected and physically/sexually abused as young children (Finkelhor, 1990).

Attachment disorders, a result of developmental trauma, are caused by parental neglect and abuse in early childhood and seriously affect a child's ability to bond. In their book, *High Risk: Children Without a Conscience*, Ken Magid and Carol McKelvey (1989) say that children without proper bonding are likely to grow up to be sociopaths—people without a conscience. They warn that these children require early interventions, with age 16 as the outside limit. After this age, the only remaining option is to "warehouse" them in detention centers and prisons. Magid and McKelvey estimate that 15 to 20% of all children grow up to be adults without consciences.

Another sign of the breakdown of the nuclear family is that the United States has the highest rate of unmarried teen pregnancies in the Western World (Garbarino et al., 1991). Approximately one out of five children live in single-parent families. Many of these children are poorly bonded to their parent. Their needs of belonging and feeling wanted and of feeling powerful are often not met. As a result, many of these children turn to a gang in an attempt to have these needs met outside the family.

Increase in Poverty

In 1970, one in seven children in the United States lived in poverty; in 1993 the ratio was one in five children, and it has continued to grow worse (Garbarino, 1993). For African-American youth, most of whom live in poverty, homicide is the most common cause of death (Garbarino et al., 1992). Economic stress in poor families may get even worse as a result of recent welfare reform legislation that took away a number of the entitlements that were part of the economic and social safety net for the poor.

Violence in Schools

In 1940 U.S. teachers rated the following as the major problems in the schools: gum chewing, cutting in line, littering, talking too loudly, and running in the halls. In 1990, U.S. teachers listed the following as the major problems: suicide, rape, drug abuse, guns, and gang violence. Guns and lethal weapons are being brought to schools in record numbers. Schools are now the largest purchasers of metal detectors (Garbarino, 1993).

Bullying, a rampant form of peer violence involving intimidation of smaller or weaker people, occurs most often in school, at home, and in the neighborhood. Over 50% of all schoolyard bullies end up in prison. Each year over 29 million youth commit one or more acts of violence against a sibling in the family (Straus & Gelles, 1988). Three out of four students report being bullied at school. Each month, over 250,000 students are physically attacked while at school (Garrity et al., 1994). And the average child receives 213 put-downs a week or thirty per day (Fried & Fried, 1996).

Increased Class Size

In the inner city schools, where violence is the worst, the ratio of teachers to students is 1 to 28 or 30. Ideally, it should be 1 to 15 (Garbarino, 1993). With these current conditions, teachers do not have time to help the students who are falling behind and these students eventually get lost in the system. They often stay in school only until they are old enough to drop out.

Reliance on Short-Term, Quick-Fix Solutions

Many adults believe the best answer to violence is to lock up the offenders. Consider what happened in Michigan in the mid-1990s. The governor and the state legislature were elected on a get-tough-on-crime platform, partly the result of public outcries over the recent shootings of a police officer and his family, and legislation was passed to build new prisons. They built so many that a new one was opening every eight weeks. Funding proved inadequate; the state found itself without the money to staff its prison facilities, and several stood empty. When homeless people began breaking into the empty prisons and using them for living quarters, the state had to hire people to guard the prisons against break-ins. The state's quick-fix solution didn't work. It is clear that our focus needs to be on supporting long-term solutions, such as primary prevention and early intervention, and avoid expensive, quick-fix schemes (Fried, 1995).

UNDIAGNOSED POST-TRAUMATIC STRESS DISORDER AS A FACTOR IN PERSONAL AND SOCIAL VIOLENCE

Trauma is defined as "an overwhelming psychological experience that causes changes in the biological stress response" (van der Kolk, McFarlane, & Weisaeth, 1996). This definition means that the body and psyche become connected through the parasympathetic nervous system. For instance, a woman who had an automobile crash experiences a physical reaction every time she hears the screeching tires and the crunching of metal of another crash. She may start trembling, experience a sense of panic and danger, and feel flooded with images of her own crash experience. Even though this woman knows that she is not involved in another crash, she reacts in both her psyche and her body as though she is.

This woman has symptoms of *post-traumatic stress disorder* (PTSD), a disorder with symptoms that range on a continuum between mild and severe. Individuals with less severe or fewer symptoms have what is known as *subclinical* PTSD, meaning that they do not meet all the criteria for a clinical diagnosis, but that they still display some of the main characteristics of the disorder. The following sections describe PTSD and how it plays a role in causing intractable conflicts.

What Is PTSD?

The *Diagnostic and Statistical Manual of Mental Disorders* (*DSM-IV*) (American Psychiatric Association, 1994) defines PTSD as behavior resulting from exposure to an traumatic event and involving any of the following conditions:

1. The person experienced, witnessed, or was confronted with an event or events that involved actual or threatened death or serious injury, or a threat to the physical integrity of self or others.
2. The person has intense fear, helplessness, or horror. In children this can be expressed by disorganized or agitated behavior.
3. The person has clinically significant distress and impairment in social, occupational, or other important areas of functioning.

Vicarious traumatization, covered under condition #1, can also occur if a person witnesses the serious injury or death of others. PTSD can be categorized as acute, delayed, chronic, or intermittent/recurrent.

What Are the Symptoms of PTSD?

The standard clinical symptoms of PTSD, taken from the *DSM-IV* (American Psychiatric Association, 1994) are:

1. *Re-experiencing* the traumatic event in one of the following ways:
   a. Sudden flashbacks of memory of the trauma at unexpected and unwelcome times
   b. Enduring memories of the traumatic event or events
   c. Recurrent distressing dreams or nightmares about traumatic events
   d. Sudden feeling that the event is happening now
   e. Intense distress when exposed to events that symbolize or resemble a part of the traumatic event
2. *Avoidance* of things that remind one of the traumatic event or a general numbing reaction. This symptom can include:
   a. Compulsive efforts to avoid thoughts or feelings of the trauma
   b. Compulsive efforts to avoid activities or situation that remind one of the trauma
   c. Amnesia for an important part of the trauma
   d. Marked disinterest in work, relationships, or recreation
   e. Feelings of detachment or estrangement from others
   f. A restricted range of feelings, including angry and loving feelings
   g. A sense of doom about the future
3. *Hyperarousal* symptoms as evidenced by any of the following:
   a. Difficulty falling or staying asleep
   b. Irritability or outbursts of anger
   c. Difficulty concentrating
   d. Hypervigilance
   e. Exaggerated startle response
   f. Physical symptoms such as sweating, nausea, or an increased pulse rate

What Is the Impact of Traumatic Experiences?

Symptoms of post-traumatic stress often appear in a generalized pattern of response that causes people to feel overwhelmed and helpless. The following categories developed by Meichenbaum (1994) help break these symptoms down into more identifiable components.

Typical responses to trauma include emotional, cognitive, biological, behavioral, and characterological responses.

Emotional responses can be manifested in shock, disbelief, anger, rage, grief, panic, fear, and distrust.

Cognitive responses include impaired concentration, confusion, intrusive thoughts, flashbacks, fear of losing control, and fear of retraumatization.

Biological responses show up as fatigue, insomnia, nightmares, hyperarousal, startle responses, and psychosomatic complaints.

Behavioral responses can include avoidance, alienation, withdrawal, substance abuse, sensation-seeking behavior, regressed behavior, and conduct disorders.

Characterological responses result in changes in personality and deformations of relational skills and self-identity. PTSD has been seen to mimic symptoms of every personality disorder.

Symptomatic responses to trauma include dissociation, anxiety responses, and sexual dysfunction. *Dissociation* is a splitting off from one's sense of self. Symptoms include detachment, depersonalization, and a sense of numbing and amnesia concerning the traumatic event. Included in this category are *anxiety responses* and *sexual dysfunctions*, particularly in cases of rape or childhood sexual abuse.

Phenomenological responses to trauma involve the shattering of survival defenses, including the belief (1) in one's invulnerability, (2) in the predictability and fairness of life events, (3) that life is meaningful, and (4) that one is a worthy person. In addition, a traumatic experience can lead to a sense of loss, feelings of mistrust, fears of being unsafe, and a sense of self-blame.

Neurophysiological and *biochemical responses* to trauma include an abnormal startle response, acute hypersensitivity to stimuli that resemble the traumatic situation, insomnia, long-term elevations of blood pressure, increased adrenal functioning, reduced immune functioning, a lowering of the pain threshold, and increased urinary and digestive functioning.

What Is the Role of the Adrenal Stress Response in Conflict?

The responses to trauma described earlier are often grouped together under the term *adrenal stress response* (ASR), which is an automatic bodily response to situations perceived as dangerous. One of the primary results of the ASR is the secretion of adrenaline and other neuorohormones into the blood stream. The adrenaline causes a state of hyperarousal that stimulates this fight, flight, or freeze response when survival is threatened. These adrenal stress responses to trauma are almost identical to the responses that people report in conflict situations:

1. They become aggressive and fight.
2. Stimuli similar to that of the original trauma recreates the intense fear and they become immobilized by their feelings.
3. They flee any situation that might cause them to reexperience any of the feelings they felt during the original traumatic event.

Unresolved conflicts and traumas from the past cause people to react to reminders of these earlier unresolved conflicts or traumas with emergency responses that perhaps were relevant in the original situation, but may not have any bearing on the current conflict. Because they are unable to put the memories of the previous trauma behind them, people attempt to keep their emotions under control at the expense of paying attention to their current circumstances and problems. They can become unconsciously fixated upon the past, behaving and feeling as though they are being traumatized over and over again without being able to locate the origins of these feelings (van der Kolk & van der Hart, 1989, 1991).

Research by Mary Carlson, quoted in an Associated Press story (1997), about babies in Romanian daycare centers who lacked the loving care for normal physical growth revealed that the babies had higher levels of adrenaline on weekdays when they were in a badly run daycare center than on weekends when they were home with their parents. Carlson summarizes their plight: "When a baby's environment includes reliable parental care, it develops trust. It thinks the world is not such a bad place. But when the environment is not supportive, the message is "the world sucks." Stress research on 10-day-old rats taken from their mothers for 24 hours showed excess production of adrenaline that caused a fear reaction, immobilization, and memory loss (Associated Press, 1997).

While a rush of adrenaline helps mobilize survival behaviors, it is designed only for occasional use in crisis situations. Adrenaline activates all of the organs and glands in the hormonal system involved in the survival response (ovaries, testes, liver, gallbladder, pancreas, thyroid, pituitary, and pineal). Extended exposure to adrenaline harms the organs and glands, gradually toxifying and stressing them so that their function becomes impaired. This eventually causes stress-related illnesses such as premenstrual syndrome, hypo-/hyperthyroidism, ulcers, anxiety, irrational fear, major depression, high blood pressure, and arthritis (Associated Press, 1997).

A recent investigation into the addictive nature of adrenaline led Diamond (1989) to conclude that adrenaline may be one of the most addictive substances there is. He noted the attraction that people in the United States have for "fast-lane" lifestyles that include workaholism; restless, driven behaviors involving speed, shortcuts, fast turnarounds; and the need for increasing stimulation, danger, violence, and thrill-seeking. Diamond identifies these activities, which continually stimulate ASR, as a defense to compensate for deep-seated feelings of inferiority and emptiness. He says that people with this addiction make repeated attempts to demonstrate their physical prowess or intellectual ability (p. 22).

According to Diamond, the addiction to adrenaline is similar to other addictions. The neurochemistry of the brain eventually requires a steady supply of adrenaline in order to avoid any withdrawal symptoms and avoid encountering the deep-seated feelings of inferiority and emptiness covered up by this excessive activity. Adrenaline addiction creates behavioral responses that are socially acceptable in the work culture of this country. As an integral component of affluence and success, this frantic kind of lifestyle can look rather "normal" until the chronic effects of the adrenaline addiction begins to impact physical health.

Another study on the addictive nature of adrenaline, an endogenous opioid or "cousin" to opium, revealed that opiate withdrawal symptoms can occur when a stressful stimuli is terminated. This study found that two decades after the original trauma, people with PTSD symptoms still developed opioid-mediated analgesia or pain-relieving responses to a stimulus resembling the traumatic stressor. The amount of endogenous opioid secreted correlated with 8 mg of morphine, a very potent dose (van der Kolk, Greenberg, Orr, & Pitman, 1989).

At the end of this chapter, are two self-inventories related to trauma. The PTSD Inventory assesses symptoms of PTSD. The Addiction to Adrenaline Inventory will help assess possible addiction to adrenaline.

Traditional definitions of PTSD focus on behavioral symptoms caused by out-of-the-ordinary events, such as accidents, murders, wars, natural catastrophes, and human-made ecological disasters or abuse. Behavioral symptoms of PTSD can be easily correlated to these kinds of more acute experiences. There is growing evidence that many people who exhibit some symptoms of PTSD have not experienced any unusual or extreme events in their background. This has led researchers and clinicians to speculate that ordinary developmental events may have produced traumas for some people.

What Is Developmental Trauma?

By studying clinical research, direct links between seemingly ordinary childhood events and later experiences of post-traumatic stress symptoms in adults can be found. These links, which were particularly evident in our work with hundreds of couples experiencing intense conflict, led us to expand our definition of trauma to include life-imprinting parent-child dynamics during the first three years of life. Developmental trauma is more subtle and more difficult to identify, particularly if it involves neglect. It involves physiological response patterns, a distorted belief or cognition, a split within the child's sense of self and disturbances in self-other relationship dynamics. The following example illustrates the elements of developmental trauma.

A boy's mother had postpartum depression just after his birth. His older siblings and the mother's sisters helped care for him during her convalescence. The mother was never able to meet many of this child's needs, and he described feeling "lost." He developed anxious behaviors when his older siblings began to leave home to attend college, and he suffered a major episode of post-traumatic stress at the age of twelve when his dog died. At some point, he decided that his birth trauma was the cause of his mother's inability to connect with him and began to expect being abandoned. He developed a strong sense of self-blaming related to his experiences of abandonment that lowered his self-esteem. As an adult, he found himself drawn to women who served as mother figures, most of whom suddenly left his life. When his wife decided to enroll in graduate school, he fell into a depression that he could not shake. He finally sought therapy with the hope of getting his wife to reverse her decision about beginning graduate school.

Our clinical research has consistently revealed the presence of developmentally related trauma as the primary source of post-traumatic-stress reactions. We believe that this form of trauma is far more prevalent than the trauma caused by extraordinary events such as sexual or physical abuse that have been recognized extensively in the mental health field. There is, however, a growing recognition of the importance of this more insidious kind of trauma.

Research from the field trials for *DSM-IV* (van der Kolk, Roth, Pelcovitz, & Mandel, 1993) found that people who had been traumatized at an early age tended to have problems that were described as "disorders of extreme stress not otherwise specified" (DESNOS). This kind of trauma affects a whole range of core psychological functions, such as the regulation of feelings; clear thoughts or memories about what has happened in the past; ways in which feelings are expressed in the body; and people's views of themselves, strangers, and intimates. The younger children were at the time of traumatization, the longer the duration of the trauma, and the less protection they had the more pervasive the damage (van der Kolk, McFarlane, & Weisaeth, 1996). Field trial research has also indicated that early and prolonged interpersonal trauma results in psychological problems characteristic of the DESNOS syndrome.

Over the past 30 years researchers and clinicians have started to unravel the differential effects of trauma at various age levels. Clinicians have begun to reconsider the ways in which incomplete attachments and traumatic separations affect the developing organism. A rapidly expanding body of research has shown that disturbances in infant bonding can have long-term neurobiological consequences. A large number of studies have shown that childhood abuse, neglect, and separation can have far-reaching biopsychosocial effects, including lasting biological changes that can adversely affect children's capacity to modulate emotions, make it difficult to learn coping skills, alter their immune competency, and impair their capacity to engage in meaningful social affiliations (Perry, 1996).

Our long-term study of pre- and perinatal psychology, object relations theory, addictions, and developmental psychology has helped us identify the critical needs of young children at different stages of development. These needs must be met before a child can successfully complete the fundamental psychosocial tasks related to bonding and individuation. When these needs are not met, children suffer "developmental traumas." It is now recognized that parental neglect or the lack of proper parental support during the first three years of life creates developmental trauma (Bowlby, 1969, 1973; Bradshaw, 1988, 1990; Miller, 1981, 1983, 1986, 1998, 1991; Weinhold & Weinhold, 1989, 1992). Developmental trauma can even occur in families where parenting is "adequate," meaning that the parents function at a sufficiently high level to meet most of the developmental needs of the child.

One of the unique characteristics of this book is its recognition of the role that unprocessed developmental trauma plays in creating intractable conflicts. Developmental trauma can be subtle, covert, and leave lasting wounds that appear in recycling patterns of intractable conflict.

THE ROLE OF DEVELOPMENTAL TRAUMA IN CREATING CONFLICT

Unmet developmental needs, experiences of neglect, abandonment, and betrayal leave distortions in the relational patterns between parents and child. Bowlby (1969) maintains that these experiences create the child's "internal working model" of reality. Longitudinal research (Krause & Haverkamp, 1996) indicates that the internal working model of reality remains virtually unchanged through a person's lifetime unless conscious interventions such as counseling are used to change it. Developmental trauma is typically inflicted on children unconsciously and without malicious intent by adults who are not aware of the physical, psychological, mental, and physical needs of infants and children. Because they have not been educated regarding these needs and because they did not get their own needs met as children, most adults are unable to effectively meet many of the fundamental needs of their own children. Most parents do not understand that they are inflicting developmental traumas on their children.

This kind of trauma can create symptoms even when a person has no memory of traumatic events. Some children are so sensitive that it takes very little to traumatize them. Other children may not have been directly abused but were traumatized by witnessed abuse. Witnessing trauma is now acknowledged to be just as traumatic as the direct experience of it. In other instances, developmental trauma is more related to neglect. Neglect is very difficult to identify and treat because "nothing happened." The covert nature of neglect often appears in adult behaviors as poor self-care habits such as inadequate eating routines, infrequent bathing, and the inability to manage finances, relationships, and jobs.

Undiagnosed developmental trauma may be the single most significant factor in recycling, intractable conflicts. Through our clinical research with hundreds of people in our private practices, workshops, and classes, we have discovered that the concepts of PTSD and developmental trauma are most helpful to those seeking to both understand the source of their current intractable conflicts and to find effective resolutions to them.

By identifying traumatic events experienced during the first three years of their lives, people can typically find correlations between these early events and the kind of conflicts they are currently experiencing. Once people see this correlation, they typically feel immense relief. Often they say, "Now it all makes perfect sense. I just thought I was crazy!" and "For the first time, I feel compassion for myself when I behave so irrationally. I understand why I do what I do." and "When I see other people doing irrational or crazy things, I just remind myself that they are in a trauma state and can't help themselves."

There is a growing awareness of the significance of developmental trauma within the mental health field, through both clinical practice and research (Belsky & Rovine, 1988; Cole, 1997; Reber, 1996; Sroufe & Rutter, 1984; van der Kolk, McFarlane, & Weisaeth, 1996; Violato & Russell, 1994). Social policy-makers and health care service deliverers, however, are moving in the opposite direction via mandatory managed care services that do not recognize the impact of developmental trauma on the physical and mental health of children and adults. As these two opposing forces grow in strength, mental health professionals will need to increase their efforts to educate the public about the physical and psychological needs of infants and children and the debilitating trauma that often results when these needs are not met.

At the end of this chapter is a self-inventory, the Family-of-Origin Risk Analysis, designed to help you assess the possibility of developmental trauma in your family-of-origin experiences.

THE ROLE OF DEVELOPMENTAL TRAUMA IN INTRACTABLE CONFLICTS

Very few people have correlated developmental trauma and symptoms of post-traumatic stress with intractable conflicts. Our continuing clinical research helping people resolve conflicts at their source repeatedly reveals that undiagnosed and unresolved developmental trauma is a major factor in recycling or recurring conflicts.

Developmental trauma, like all other kinds of trauma, is stored internally in the sensory system as pictures, words, feelings, body sensations, and spontaneous movements. Each traumatic event is stored as sensory modules containing a unique combination of those sensory components. Relationship dynamics, most often related to the interaction between the child and its parents or other bonded caregivers, are another part of the stored memories of each traumatic event.

For example, a child whose mother had frequent bouts of dissociation, becomes sensitized to people who have blank, distant expressions on their faces. The loss of her mother's attention, during an instance of dissociation, simultaneously activates experiences of abandonment. When she sees people with a vacant facial expression, she can be triggered into a post-traumatic state. The visual trigger catapults her into a past memory of a traumatic experience and activates the adrenal stress response, releasing the contents of a memory module containing other sensory components (words, emotions, body sensations, spontaneous movements) and memories of past relational experiences with her mother where she felt abandoned. This phenomenon includes *regression*, a unique post-traumatic symptom involving a feeling of "time distortion." It also includes *reenactment*, which is the experience of replaying some event from the past in the present time, accompanied by feelings similar to "dé-jà vu."

What Is the Role of Regression in Creating Conflicts?

Most conflicts contain elements of invisible spontaneous regression and reenactment related to some unresolved developmental trauma. For example, a conflict erupts in the present when two people mutually trigger a response in each other and activate a complex memory module for each of them containing sensory cues related to earlier traumatic events. This mutual triggering dynamic causes a spontaneous regression in each person into past realities related to previous experiences involving other people. During a reenactment, one person may experience the other person as a parent or a boss. This spontaneous regression prevents both individuals from consciously resolving the current conflict because they have been triggered into a PTSD reaction involving a past conflict or trauma.

A spontaneous regression experience during a conflict makes it very difficult to resolve a current conflict. When both people involved in a conflict are experiencing a spontaneous regression, each believes and reacts as if their past reality is "real" in the current situation. They often try to convince each other that their reality is the "right" one. Bessel van der Kolk states it this way, "When memories of past trauma remain unprocessed, traumatized individuals tend to become like Pavlov's dogs: subtle reminders become conditioned stimuli for the reexperiencing of frightening feelings and perceptions belonging to the past" (van der Kolk, McFarlane, & Weisaeth, 1996, p. 27).

Unraveling the post-traumatic or regressive component of any conflict takes a lot of courage and insight, as it requires both parties in a conflict to identify the activated past conflict or trauma. Many people would rather just blame the other person and try to resolve the problem in the present than look at how past traumatic events might be "bleeding" into their present time realities.

One of the unique features of the Partnership Way of conflict resolution is that it teaches you how to identify the influence of past unresolved conflicts on your present conflict and how to resolve your conflicts at their source. This requires a lot of spiritual courage, because it forces people to face archaic or primitive feelings, to accept the truth about their relational dynamics with their parents, and to change any distortions in their patterns of thinking and behaving that formed as the result of developmental trauma. When people learn to resolve conflicts at their source, they experience fewer intractable conflicts and can more easily resolve conflicts from a peaceful, win-win perspective.

The Role of Culture Denial in Accepting Developmental Trauma

It may take a new level of social consciousness to understand and accept a concept like developmental trauma. The whole field of traumatology is only about ten years old. In spite of the great strides that have been made, much more research is needed to confirm the new discoveries. As a result of the ongoing research on this subject, new information is being discovered daily. For instance, only in the past three to four years have we understood that certain memories are stored in different parts of the brain, which usually don't communicate with each other. This discovery has opened doors to even more research and caused us to change some of our theories about how to treat PTSD.

A brief look at the history of how the traumatology field evolved may illustrate the point. Post-traumatic stress was first identified as "shell shock" in veterans after World Wars I and II, the Korean War, and the Vietnam War. As long as men were found to suffer from delayed retrieval of memories related to atrocities committed by a clearly identifiable enemy, this condition was not a controversial topic and was well-documented in psychological literature. PTSD emerged as a clinical disorder primarily from the treatment of Vietnam veterans, who displayed many of the symptoms now described in the *DSM-IV* (APA, 1994).

When women and girls began revealing delayed recall of traumatic memories related to sexual assault and domestic violence in the mid-1970s, this news was deemed unbelievable and at first was considered highly controversial. Investigations regarding the prevalence of domestic violence, which grew out of the women's movement, validated the existence of post-traumatic stress in women who survived domestic battery, incest, street rape, acquaintance rape, date rape, and rape in their marriage. It became clear to many investigators during the women's movement that the subordinate condition of women was being maintained and enforced by the hidden violence of men. When female victims began seeking justice against their alleged perpetrators, however, the issue came out of the closet and moved from science into politics (Herman, 1992).

Interestingly, the issue of delayed recall of memories related to the traumatization of children, particularly sexual abuse, has now moved to the forefront. The whole idea of "false memories" planted by unscrupulous therapists has currently become one of the most heated debates in psychology and psychiatry. Researchers from the field of traumatology have presented extensive research showing the correlation of post-traumatic stress reactions with child abuse and domestic violence, demonstrating that PTSD is more than shell shock or combat trauma.

Opponents to these theories dismissed a century of clinical observation and scientific investigations from battlefields, emergency rooms, and psychiatric wards and labeled delayed recall of traumatic memories as "false memories." They attribute delayed recall to "memory implantations" by unscrupulous therapists.

This sudden shift in attitude regarding delayed retrieval of memory illustrates how society reacts when scientific discoveries conflict with established values and beliefs that support the cultural denial of a problem. Psychology and psychiatry have traditionally been vulnerable in these cases and often were pressured into giving up the pursuit of science and, instead, conformed to the prevailing societal attitudes. The cultural denial of the impact of trauma is reflected in the paucity of available treatment programs and of academically based training for these programs. It is also visible in the ferocity with which the "false memory" debate is being pursued in both courtrooms and in academic psychiatry and psychology programs (van der Kolk, McFarlane, & Weisaeth, 1996, p. 568).

THE EFFECT OF TRAUMA ON THE BRAIN AND PHYSIOLOGY OF HUMANS

One of the positive outcomes of this heated debate is that it is stimulating a tremendous amount of new research on the brain and how it stores memories. This research is providing a wealth of new information to help us all better understand the psychophysiology of trauma. It is shattering the long-held views about how memory is stored during the first four or five years of life and about how early memory is stored in a different part of the brain than memory stored after the age of five. This new information is helping many people understand more fully both the needs of children and the impact of unmet needs on their own development. The emphasis on the impact of trauma on early brain development is quickly becoming a vital component of prevention programs for infancy and early childhood development.

New information from brain research also indicates that trauma damages the neural wiring of the brain increasing the risk of an individual developing a wide variety of mental and physical illnesses, including aggression, language failure, depression and other mental disorders, asthma, epilepsy, high blood pressure, immune-system dysfunction, and diabetes (Perry, 1996). All of these physical illnesses are on the rise as the forces that generate stress continue to escalate. These include poverty, violence, sexual abuse, family breakup, neglect, drugs, lack of proper infant stimulation, and too much of the improper kind of infant stimulation. These findings have been corroborated in animal research, which indicates that brain cells in infant rats break up and die when they are separated from their mother (Kotulak, 1996).

One of the more astounding findings in the new research is that the stresses caused by trauma can actually affect the genes, switching them on or off at the wrong times, forcing them to build abnormal networks of brain-cell connections. This research shows the impact of parent-child interactions on the way the brain becomes wired, making it important for children to have good parenting from the very beginning of life (Kotulak, 1996).

This research is leading to a growing awareness of the social costs of poor or insufficient parenting practices. A recent nationwide survey showed that one child in five under age eighteen has learning, emotional, behavioral, or developmental problems that researchers correlate with the continuing dissolution of the two-parent family. Forty-two percent of U.S. families with children start out with one, two, or three strikes against them as a result of traumatic family circumstances, including:

• low educational levels of parents
• lack of commitment to parenting
• lack of maternal maturity

All of these conditions cause stress in children that manifests as brain damage (Perry, 1996).

WHAT IS THE CORRELATION BETWEEN PTSD AND PERSONAL STYLE OF CONFLICT RESOLUTION?

The manner in which a person instinctively responds to conflict is important. In the face of conflict, many people flee in a desperate attempt to avoid it. In fact, from our field research, we found that this is still the most common personal style of conflict resolution. Others may fight by using violence or threats of violence to manipulate and control the conflict situation and to ward off the return of feeling states related to previous traumatic events. A third group simply freezes, feeling unable to either speak or act in their own behalf. These survival-based, adrenaline-related responses are designed to help people cope with a fear of being retraumatized by the current conflict. This fear indicates the presence of some historical event that needs to be identified in order to understand and resolve current conflicts.

Given these automatic responses, conflicts often escalate into win-lose or lose-lose resolutions that do cause retraumatization. Rather than preventing the feared experience of retraumatization, the flight/fight/freeze responses instead become part of a unique personal style

of conflict resolution containing characteristic patterns of sensory and relational "triggers" or cues. For example, a person who experienced corporal punishment as a child might fear large or authoritarian people as an adult. They might have a flight/fight/freeze reaction when someone moves quickly toward them or feel regressed when someone speaks to them in a loud voice.

Once a person's sensory system is activated by cues related to current conflicts, time distortional elements from the past are evoked. The current conflict becomes an access point or doorway to a stage where traumatic events from the past can be reenacted via a spontaneous, unconscious regressive state.

This phenomenon was described extensively by Alice Miller (1983) in her book, *For Your Own Good*, where she correlates Adolf Hitler's genocide of the Jewish people with the abusive circumstances of his early childhood. This subtle interlinking of people and conflicts in the present with people and conflicts from the past makes conflict resolution seem difficult, if not impossible. The distortion in each person's time and place realities is a major cause of intractable or persistent conflicts that recycle over and over again.

WHAT IS THE ROLE OF COMPASSION AND KINDNESS IN RESOLVING CONFLICTS?

Kindness affirms the principle of interconnectedness, which is our natural state and one of the things that can easily disappear during a conflict. In a conflict situation it is sometimes difficult to feel that you are in conflict with a kind person. One of the biggest advocates of compassion and kindness is the Dalai Lama (Gyatso, 1997), the temporal and spiritual leader of Tibetan Buddhism. His messages stress that the future of humanity is dependent upon the ability to build relationships and communities that bind people to common aspirations. He describes the 20th century as one of violence and proposes that the 21st century be one of dialogue. He urges people to break free of mass thinking and take individual action in choosing peaceful rather than violent choices. Making this shift requires attention to one's heart and the focus of one's attention on being kind, both of which come with increasing awareness and consciousness.

Feeling compassion and expressing kindness is difficult when people are acting violent, rageful, and out of control. The critical factor we have discovered in making the shift from judgment and criticism to compassion and kindness is the awareness that these escalated people are experiencing symptoms of post-traumatic stress and that their behavior is not driven by conscious forces. Understanding that most people do not want to be angry, that they are regressed and unable to distinguish the past from the present can be a powerful awareness.

Once people understand the role of post-traumatic stress reactions in their conflicts, most can feel compassion and express kindness towards themselves and others even though they may not be feeling that way. The shift that comes from this awareness is almost miraculous. The judgment, criticism, and anger stop. The conflict quickly loses its intensity, the oppositional atmosphere can become cooperative, and a space opens for understanding, cooperation, and caring.

HOW CAN THIS BOOK HELP RESOLVE CONFLICTS INVOLVING PTSD SYMPTOMS?

This book is designed to help individuals understand the relationship between untreated traumas from the past and their current conflicts. It will help identify symptoms of post-traumatic stress and the triggers or cues that may lead to retraumatization from certain kinds of conflict situations.

Throughout this book, kindness and compassion appear as recurring themes. Time and again, you will be asked to have kindness and compassion for yourself when you suffer post-traumatic symptoms in conflict situations. You will also be asked to extend the same compassion to those around you when they slip into unkindness, anger, and even rage. As you do this, you will gradually learn the power of kind and compassionate acts and how they can become a magical elixir transforming conflict into compassion.

One significant clue that post-traumatic stress symptoms are present is an awareness of any intense feelings that seem out of proportion to the events of the moment. Overreactions almost always relate back to some unresolved conflict or traumatic incident from the past. In Chapter 4, you will identify your typical reactions in conflict situations and learn how to restructure your patterned behaviors during conflicts.

Identifying the underlying cause of conflict is often a critical step in preventing conflict and in slowing or stopping it once it has begun. Most people are not aware that they are experiencing symptoms of post-traumatic stress while they are in the midst of a conflict. Just knowing that they are experiencing a post-traumatic stress reaction helps people understand that often a deep psychological process is occurring during conflict situations. They feel less judgmental about their impulses to fight, flee, or freeze and understand that these responses are autonomic and out of their conscious control.

Once people understand that unhealed trauma and unresolved post-traumatic stress are factors in their current intractable conflicts, they are better able to understand and stop this unconscious and seemingly uncontrollable process. The Partnership Way intervention begins by reframing the concept of post-traumatic stress. Rather than using it as a diagnosis for "diseasing" people, it can be used as a prescription or protocol for establishing new behavioral responses.

Resolving conflicts using the Partnership Way requires the use of three different kinds of tools that correlate with three different kinds of conflicts: conflicts related to wants and needs, conflicts related to values and beliefs, and conflicts involving "time distortions" that can only be resolved at the source. All three kinds of conflicts and the tools needed to resolve them are addressed thoroughly in Part 2 of this book.

SELF-INVENTORY: THE PTSD INVENTORY

This inventory is for your benefit, so be as honest as you can in filling it out. Place a number in the blank that precedes each statement to indicate how true that statement is for you.

1 = Almost Never   2 = Occasionally

3 = Usually   4 = Almost Always.

_____ 1. Inside I feel like a tightly coiled spring.

_____ 2. I have trouble falling asleep and staying asleep.

_____ 3. I feel I have to "walk on egg shells."

_____ 4. I have trouble concentrating on what I am doing.

_____ 5. I feel empty and alone.

_____ 6. I feel like I am on an emotional roller-coaster.

_____ 7. I have a hard time telling what I am feeling.

_____ 8. I avoid certain kinds of places that remind me of events from my past.

_____ 9. Certain smells, movements, or behaviors can easily cause a reaction inside of me.

_____10. I feel like a spectator to my life.

_____11. I have recurring bad memories/dreams of my past.

_____12. I overreact to certain kinds of people or in certain situations.

_____13. I feel like other people are in charge of my life.

_____14. My thoughts seem to have a life of their own.

_____15. I feel like I have a huge black hole inside of me.

_____16. When I think about my childhood I draw a blank.

_____17. I experience periodic episodes of rage or of just "losing it."

_____18. I work best when I am under a lot of pressure.

_____19. I have trouble paying attention to what others are saying.

_____20. I am easily bored.

_____21. I have trouble connecting with people.

_____22. I organize my life around the avoidance of conflict.

_____23. I have trouble keeping my weight down.

_____24. I experience big gaps in memory when I think about my childhood.

_____25. It's hard for me to have positive thoughts about my future.

_____ **Total Score**

Scoring and Interpretation

25–35   Your answers indicate that you may have very few PTSD symptoms.

36–50   Your answers indicate that you may have some PTSD symptoms.

51–100   Your answers indicate that you may have many PTSD symptoms.

SELF-INVENTORY: FAMILY-OF-ORIGIN RISK ANALYSIS

In high-risk families there is a greater likelihood that serious developmental trauma involving abuse and/or neglect occurred early in life. You may not know whether or not you grew up in a high-risk family. Below are the criteria that health professionals use to assess the risk factors in families. Circle the number of the ones that describe circumstances in your family of origin during the prenatal and perinatal period (first three years).

Points	Social/Environmental Risks
3	Developmentally delayed parents
3	Parent with clinically diagnosed psychiatric disorder
3	Intergenerational history of child abuse in family
3	Significant maternal infections in the first year after birth of child
2	Age of mother is 16 years or less
2	No prenatal care or less than three prenatal visits during pregnancy
2	Parental substance abuse (type:_____)
2	Parents with sensory impairments
1	Age of mother is between 16 and 18 years
1	Difficulty in parent-infant bonding (prematurity, perinatal illness [mother or child], retardation, deformity)
1	Lack of familial and/or social support
1	Lack of permanent housing for family
1	Maternal education less than 12th grade
1	More than four children in the home
1	Mother with ill health
1	High stress in family
1	Low income
_____	**Total Points**

Scoring and Interpretation

In order to be classified as a high-risk family, only one of the above risks has to be present. Obviously, the greater number the risks, the greater the possibility of developmental traumas being present. For each risk present in your family of origin, reflect on how it might have affected your development and what traumas you might have encountered as a result of its presence. You might also speculate on how these risk factors correlate with the symptoms you identified in the PTSD Inventory.

SELF-INVENTORY: ADDICTION TO ADRENALINE INVENTORY*

Place a number before each question that best indicates the degree to which this is true in your life.

1 = Almost Never 2 = Occasionally
3 = Usually 4 = Almost Always

_____1. Do you talk fast?

_____2. Do you drive fast?

_____3. Do you eat fast?

_____4. Do you read while you eat?

_____5. Do you read in the bathroom?

_____6. Does doing one thing at a time seem like a waste?

_____7. Do you drink more than three cups of coffee a day?

_____8. Do you talk on the phone while preparing meals?

_____9. Are you drawn to "time efficiency" devices such as car phones, fax machines, microwaves, food processors, and computers?

_____10. Are you better at "starting" relationships than "making them work?"

_____11. Do you work more than 60 hours a week?

_____12. Do you find it difficult to leave work at the office?

_____13. Do you smoke cigarettes?

_____14. Do you feel anxious when you are "out of touch" with the work setting?

_____15. Do you feel that sleeping is time wasted?

_____16. Do you find it difficult to relax when the work day is done?

_____17. Does lying on the beach "doing nothing" seem more like torture than relaxation?

_____18. Do you find accomplishing many things at once immensely satisfying?

_____19. Do you feel you don't spend as much time as you'd like with your family?

_____20. Do you find you don't spend as much time alone as you'd like?

_____21. Do you feel "driven" to get more done?

_____22. Do you schedule your time so tightly you are frustrated by the inevitable interruptions?

_____23. Do you get upset when others are late?

_____24. Do you have difficulty waiting in lines?

_____25. Do you get angry when the light changes and the person in front of you takes too much time getting moving?

_____26. Do you get frustrated with slow drivers?

_____27. Do you skip meals because you're too busy with more important things?

_____28. Do you eat "on the run?"

_____29. Do you hurry your children along because they aren't moving fast enough?

_____30. Do you "love" computers because they are fast, efficient, accurate, and obedient?

_____31. Do you "have trouble" with people who are slow, inefficient, inaccurate, or disobedient?

_____32. Do you believe that living faster means living better?

_____33. Do you hate to make two trips carrying in the groceries if it is at all possible to do it in one?

_____34. Do you do things in a hurry, even though doing it quickly may mean you may have to do it again?

_____35. Do you seek out "high intensity" experiences?

_____36. Do you resist reading directions, preferring to jump in and get started?

_____37. Do you find that a level of "danger" is a necessary ingredient for feeling fully alive?

_____38. Do you have trouble slowing down because you fear that something or someone might gain on you?

_____39. Do you feel you must keep yourself "revved up" to keep from becoming bored or depressed?

_____40. Do you find people boring if they don't live high intensity lives?

_____41. Do you find it difficult to take time to "just think and dream?"

_____42. Do you find it difficult to "shut down" your mind, even on your off hours?

_____43. Do you keep a notepad or recording machine with you to jot down important thoughts?

_____44. Do you panic just thinking about the possibility that your computer may "go down?"

_____45. Does the fear of computer viruses rival or surpass your fear of AIDS?

_____46. Do you miss taking time to "enjoy the sunsets and smell the flowers?"

_____47. Do you like the multiplex theaters because you can check out another movie if you get bored with the first?

_____48. Do you like reading *USA Today* because it is quick and easy to learn a little about a lot of things?

_____49. Do you find it difficult to read a book from cover to cover, even when you are enjoying it?

_____50. Do you have many partially read books lying around?

_____51. Do you read mostly "business related" books and feel slightly guilty if you read "just for pleasure?"

_____52. Do you feel dependent on the constant stimulation, pressure, and excitement you get in life?

_____53. Do you find yourself accepting civic and business obligations even after you feel overloaded?

_____54. Do you find you are missing important times with your children because you are "too busy?"

_____55. Are your preferred forms of exercise or recreation demanding and/or competitive?

_____56. Do you become anxious or depressed when you can't "work out?"

_____57. Do you feel your life is moving too fast?

_____58. Have you had stress-related illnesses such as back problems, high blood pressure, ulcers, or "nervous stomach?"

_____59. Do you dream of "hitting the jackpot" via lottery tickets, sports betting (horse or dog racing, weekly football pools, etc.), or playing the slots?

_____60. Do you like to watch scary movies and TV shows?

_____ **Total Score**

Scoring and Interpretation

Add the numbers in the left-hand column and record your total score. Each person must decide for himself or herself just what the score means in analyzing personal lifestyle. For one person, missing their child's first concert may be enough to make a change. For another, it may require a serious heart attack. The following interpretation guidelines will help you in your lifestyle analysis.

60–90	Seemingly low risk of adrenaline addiction.
91–120	Possibly some risk of adrenaline addiction.
121–150	Possibly a high risk of adrenaline addiction.
151–180	Very likely a high risk of adrenaline addiction.
181–240	Danger; likely an extremely high risk of adrenaline addiction.

* Adapted from a similar instrument by Jed Diamond, 1989. Used here with permission.

Chapter 2

~

How Can We Address
the Problem of Conflict?

In 1986 we spent six months in Switzerland studying with Arnold Mindell, a Jungian analyst and theoretician. Mindell was just beginning to study conflict resolution using Jungian psychology, which utilizes the concept of internal polarities. Mindell identified that polarities are often at the source of both internal and external conflicts.

In late April of 1986, we frequently walked around in Zurich during the welcomed spring weather to admire the beautiful flowers and blossoming trees. On April 29, we heard that a nuclear reactor at Chernobyl had exploded three days earlier. We felt shocked to discover that we had been exposed to high levels of radiation during our walks over these three beautiful spring days. We also experienced a sense of horror about the invisible nature of radiation and our inability to protect ourselves from its insidious dangers.

Our experiences during the following weeks were some of the most incredible of our lives. For the first time we saw an abundance of food destroyed. Many Swiss cows had to be killed and none of their milk, butter, or cheese could be eaten. We could only eat canned goods or imported fresh vegetables grown under glass in Spain or other countries that were not in the path of the radioactive fallout. Anyone who lived in the path of the radiation had their lives significantly disrupted. Most of the reindeer in Finland, for example, had to eventually be killed.

This manmade disaster affected not only the people living in the region of the Chernobyl reactor, but most of Eastern and some of Western Europe as far away as England and France. The Soviets, who initially attempted to cover up the disaster, took three days to finally announce it to the world. We personally felt stunned by the realization that this disaster and the ensuing problems were the result of an unresolved conflict between the East and West and that the nations involved were in a Cold War that prevented them from communicating clearly about the disaster.

We were deeply impacted by this experience and saw the inherent danger of neighbors not speaking to each other. We could easily see how conflict between national "neighbors," if not resolved, could eventually escalate into a larger conflict involving many more countries.

We also had another significant experience related to global conflict during our stay in Switzerland. After terrorists bombed a German nightclub killing U.S. servicemen, the United States attempted to retaliate by trying to kill Muammar Kaddafi, whom intelligence sources said had ordered this terrorist act. American planes flew from England over European airspace to drop bombs on Libya. As temporary expatriates, we learned quickly that many Europeans did not appreciate American acts of aggression against one of their volatile neighbors. The Europeans expected Kaddafi to retaliate first by bombing a European site rather than a site in the United States, putting them in imminent danger.

The U.S. planes also accidentally bombed the Swiss Embassy in Tripoli during their attack on Kaddafi. This stirred old resentments among the Swiss, who remembered how the United States had accidentally bombed a Swiss village during World War II. Again we saw how an old unresolved conflict could easily flair up if something in a current conflict was a reminder of a past unresolved conflict. For a while, we felt vulnerable and exposed about being Americans in Switzerland, so we kept a very low profile for several weeks until some of the strong emotions calmed down.

These two experiences jolted us, leaving us feeling helpless and powerless. As we talked between ourselves, with colleagues, and with Mindell, we decided that we wanted to do something to become part of the solution rather than part of the problem—something that would allow us to feel personally empowered about conflict.

RESEARCH AND DEVELOPMENT FOR THE PARTNERSHIP WAY

When we returned to the United States, we began a review of the literature on conflict resolution and felt thoroughly underwhelmed by what we found. Most of the so-called seminal works in the field seemed very shallow, rather mechanical, and lacked inspiration and vision. Then we discovered that many of these books were being used as mediation and conflict resolution textbooks in the hallowed halls of our colleges and universities. One bestselling book, for example, used the premise that "war is inevitable" and then presented detailed strategies for managing, but not resolving regional and global conflict. We felt very disconcerted to discover that these outdated "win-lose" methods were considered to be state-of-the-art approaches in the field of conflict resolution.

We decided, after our literature review, to become proactive. We formed our own nonprofit institute, the Colorado Institute for Conflict Resolution and Creative Leadership, whose basic premise is "peace is inevitable." We believed that beginning with a different set of assumptions might lead to different outcomes. Our first step was to discover what was working in the field of conflict resolution and what was not.

We initiated a field research project to learn more about theories, approaches, and models of conflict resolution. To facilitate our research, we organized two international conferences in 1987 and 1988 focusing on new approaches to conflict resolution. We used these two conferences to speak directly to the leaders of various models of conflict resolution and asked them the following questions: "Under what conditions does your approach work the best? Where does it break down? What do you see as missing from the field of conflict resolution?" The answers we got from these leaders helped us understand the current state of the field of conflict resolution and showed us where to focus our efforts.

RESEARCH FINDINGS

We found from our field research that a number of approaches were successful in resolving conflicts of wants and needs. However, we discovered some major deficits in these approaches that needed to be addressed. For example, none of them effectively addressed the intense feelings that often accompany conflict situations. There also were no successful models for resolving conflicts of values and beliefs. In addition, no one considered that the intractable conflicts that recycle in peoples' lives might contain elements of developmental trauma or that post-traumatic stress might be a factor. The models we initially investigated also did not address the phenomena of splitting and polarization during conflicts. Virtually none of them emphasized the role of compassion and kindness in shifting the attitude of people in conflict. Finally, we did not find any systemic models that could fully explain the relationship between various conflicts in different levels of human systems.

OUR "PARTNERSHIP" APPROACH

From our research, we began to develop our own paradigm for working with conflict and a set of practical tools for resolving conflicts that we call the Partnership Way. As our approach matured, we created a theoretical foundation, Developmental Systems Theory, which we will describe in Chapter 3 and again in Chapter 13, along with a treatment modality that we call Developmental Process Work (DPW). This treatment modality specifically focuses on resolving conflicts at their source through a systemic approach that applies the principles of individual development and dysfunction to increasingly larger human systems.

We have identified seven systemic levels, the developmental tasks for each level, the needs that must be met in order to complete these tasks, and the common dysfunctional behaviors that appear if the needs are not met and the tasks not completed. Each of these levels will be described in detail in Parts III and IV of this book. The seven systemic levels of development are:

- individuals
- couples (intimate partners, friends, coworkers)
- families
- organizations
- cultural subgroups
- nation-states
- humans as a species

Assumptions of the Partnership Way

As we began to work with the concept of partnership during the research and development phase, we found certain critical assumptions that addressed limitations and deficits in other existing approaches. These philosophical assumptions created a specific lens through which we began to view conflict. These assumptions are:

- *Conflict is an opportunity for growth and intimacy.* Many people avoid conflict because they fail to see the inherent opportunities for growth and increased intimacy in conflict situations. Resolving conflicts effectively brings people closer together and helps them work more cooperatively.
- *Individual initiative is critical* in the resolution of the conflict. Each person is responsible for identifying and addressing their contribution to the conflict situation.
- *Unidentified and untreated developmental trauma is a major force in the creation of conflict.* Unresolved effects of early developmental traumas and conflicts cause intrapsychic splitting (dissociation), polarization, and other symptoms of post-traumatic stress that later create intractable, recycling conflicts in relationships, families, organizations, and nation-states.
- *The ability to feel compassion and express kindness helps people bring together polarities* both inside and outside themselves.

As we wove together different tools, exercises, and experiential activities and identified those that were most effective, we began correlating our assumptions and practical tools with various theories.

WHAT IS THE THEORETICAL FOUNDATION OF THE PARTNERSHIP WAY?

We explored cognitive-behavioral theories, humanistic theories, psychodynamic theories, systems theories, transpersonal theories, and chaos theory and found that each of these theoretical approaches had something useful in them that added to our theory. Rather than attempting to compare the theories, we extracted the "gems" from each and synthesized them into a meta-theory that we call Developmental Systems Theory. The components of this theoretical foundation are described in more detail in Chapter 3.

HOW IS THE PARTNERSHIP WAY ORGANIZED?

The structure of the Partnership Way is illustrated in the following flowchart (Fig. 2.1) depicting each step of the process and the five worksheets containing its applied components. You will find each worksheet explained in more detail in subsequent chapters, but a brief overview is provided here. This overview can help you understand the various components of the Partnership Way and the experiential nature of the model used in this book.

Worksheet #1 prepares individuals for a conflict resolution session by helping them understand how they experience conflict internally. It helps identify the first physical and emotional signals of conflict and to recall previous conflicts with similar internal experiences. Worksheet #1 also helps identify typical post-traumatic or adrenal stress responses in conflict situations, offers several options for approaching a conflict, and provides a set of ground rules for resolving a conflict.

Worksheet #2 gives a format for resolving conflicts of wants and needs. Worksheet #3 provides a format for resolving conflicts of values and beliefs. Worksheet #4 helps identify the sources of conflicts. Worksheet #5 is a format for resolving conflicts at their source. These five worksheets provide a sequential course of action for resolving increasingly more complex conflicts. We advise working with the material in each of the worksheets until you feel that you have mastered the skills before going on to the next level.

In this chapter, we shared some of the personal experiences that inspired us to write this book. You can examine the experiences that motivated you to learn more about resolving conflicts by completing the "Self-Awareness Exercise: Personal Experiences with Conflict" at the end of this chapter. It may also help you set some goals for desired outcomes.

One of the unique features of this book, as stated previously, is that it reframes conflict into a positive experience. As you begin to look at your personal style of conflict resolution, you will learn how to reframe your perceptions about conflict. Through the use of metaphor, this chapter focuses on using conflict as a tool for self-discovery. Western culture, with its overemphasis on technology, recently has rediscovered myth and metaphor as tools for finding meaning and deeper connection in life. As part of this search, there has been a growing affinity for the wisdom of indigenous cultures such as Native Americans, who use the Medicine Wheel as a metaphor to guide their lives.

HOW CAN METAPHOR BE USED TO REFRAME CONFLICT?

Metaphors compare two seemingly dissimilar objects to help enhance the understanding of both objects. They help make the familiar strange and the strange familiar (Gladding, 1979). The Partnership Way uses three circular metaphors to explain some of the paradoxes and incongruities encountered in resolving conflicts. Metaphors help uncover underlying feelings, make the unconscious conscious, reveal hidden solutions through insight, and increase feelings of competence and connectedness (Gladding, 1996).

The first metaphor used in the Partnership Way is the *mandorla,* an ancient symbol found in many cultures

THE PARTNERSHIP WAY:
A WIN/WIN APPROACH TO CONFLICT RESOLUTION

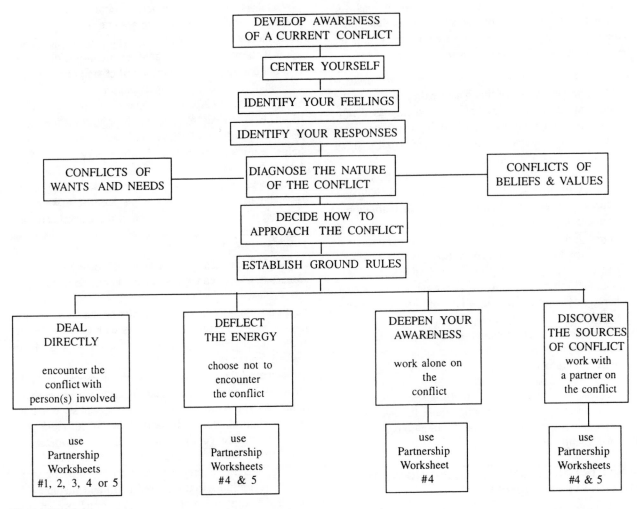

Figure 2.1
Structure of the Partnership Way

around the world. Its two interlocking circles are a prototype of transformation, because they represent the binding together of the opposites often found in conflicts. The elliptical space in the center where the two circles overlap is actually the mandorla, and it represents the art of healing, the place of poetry. The cover art on this book contains a mandorla.

The second metaphor used in the Partnership Way is the Medicine Wheel from Native American traditions. It provides a paradigm or organizing tool for understanding the stages and challenges of life experiences. This chapter draws on the Medicine Wheel as a metaphor for understanding the role of conflict resolution in your life.

The third metaphor used in this book is the Journey of Transformation, found in Chapter 19. It describes a larger circular journey of transformation that covers a person's

lifetime, as well as the numerous mini-journeys within a lifetime. Each stage of development is a step or mini-journey in the lifelong journey of transformation. Each resolution of a conflict is a mini-journey of transformation.

THE MEDICINE WHEEL METAPHOR

The Medicine Wheel teaches people that everything has a place and is meaningful, so they learn to embrace everything that comes to them. This accepting attitude fosters kindness and compassion, rather than judgment and criticism. Many Native American people use the Medicine Wheel as a metaphor to provide meaning in their lives. Figure 2.2 shows the symbolic meanings that some of the Native American people have attributed to the four directions of the Medicine Wheel.

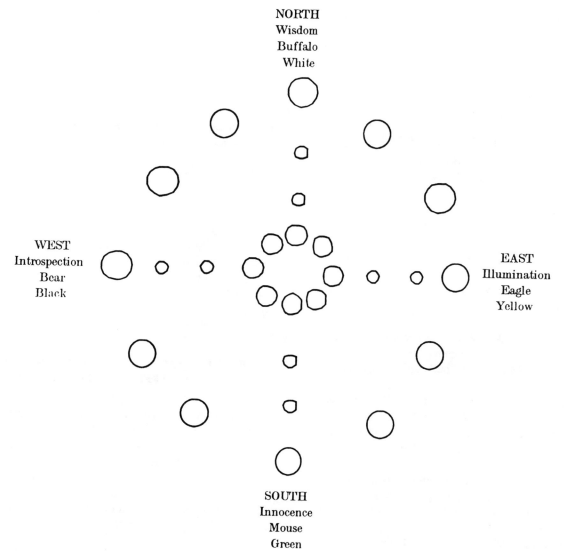

NORTH
Wisdom
Buffalo
White

WEST
Introspection
Bear
Black

EAST
Illumination
Eagle
Yellow

SOUTH
Innocence
Mouse
Green

Figure 2.2
The Medicine Wheel

Many traditional Native American beliefs state that everything that happens in life is significant, that nothing is "an accident." Each life experience was placed on the Medicine Wheel and used as a mirror for self-discovery. The elders assisted the younger members of the tribe in understanding the lessons imbedded in everyday events that might otherwise go unnoticed. The Medicine Wheel metaphor served as an effective psychological and spiritual tool to develop powers of introspection and self-awareness. Any idea, object, animal, person, or event that happened or was seen during the day or night could provide some wisdom, understanding, or insight when the teachings of the Medicine Wheel were applied. The elders taught the youth that the universe is the mirror of the people and that each person is a mirror to every other person.

In this paradigm, the potential for self-awareness is all around us. All we have to do is pay attention. Can you imagine what your life would have been like if you had grown up in a culture in which this perspective had been emphasized? Can you imagine how your life might have been different if you had been taught that everything that happened to you and everything you saw was meaningful and had something to teach you?

In his book *Seven Arrows*, Hyemeyohsts Storm (1972) wrote about how the Sioux and many of the other Plains Indians used the Medicine Wheel as a teaching tool. They created a Medicine Wheel by placing stones in a design similar to the one in Figure 2.2. One stone marked each of the four cardinal directions. Other stones radiated out from within the circle connecting each of the four directions. Each stone symbolized a specific aspect of the universe. If a stone symbolized the winged creatures, for example, they would talk to the young people about what winged creatures could teach them.

Because these native people believed that the Medicine Wheel contained the whole Universe, an important part of their ceremonies was to sit around the wheel while the medicine men and women told stories. They would refer to a certain rock in the wheel and then tell a story about that rock. It was a way of taking very abstract concepts and making them concrete.

The Role of the Wheel in Naming Children

The Medicine Wheel also played an important role in the birth of children. Many Native Americans believed that a child was assigned one of the four directions on the wheel depending on when he or she was born, with the placement determined by the season of the birth. Thus every child was assigned to one of the four great powers (wisdom, illumination, innocence, or introspection) predetermined by his or her birth. The task of this child was to develop his or her powers of the other three directions during the rest of his or her life.

Therefore, the time of the year when the child was born often determined what the child was named. Children born in the summer, for example, were given a name related to the qualities of the South, such as innocence. Then the task would be to balance that innocence with wisdom from the North, introspection from the West, and illumination from the East. Children born in the spring would have the power of illumination as a birthright; while those born in the winter would have the power of wisdom.

Totem animals were also identified with each of the four cardinal directions, each carrying special meaning and gifts. They, too, often played a role in the naming of children. A child born in the south on the wheel, for example, might be called Running Mouse, Jumping Mouse, Quiet Mouse, or some other name with "mouse" in it. A child born in the fall might be given a name including the word "bear," such as Running Bear.

In many Native American cultures, the male child's birth name was temporary and changed at about age 12 or 13, when the child was given a new adult name. Each young male, for example, went alone into the wilderness for a number of days on a vision quest to await a vision, dream, or some important encounter with nature. On returning to the tribe, the young man told his dream or vision to the tribal elders, who then gave him a new name based on their interpretation of his vision quest experience. That adult name stayed with him the rest of his life.

Many Native Americans believed that the journey of life, like the Medicine Wheel, was circular and that no matter when a person was born, during his or her lifetime he or she was expected to fully master the other three powers of the Medicine Wheel. It was presumed that the other three powers would be more difficult to achieve than the one assigned to a person at birth. Names immediately affirmed each child's innate qualities. Each time a

child born in the summer said something out of innocence, people would say, "Oh there's Running Mouse saying another innocent thing. Isn't that wonderful?" They might add, "He is so innocent and so great in his innocence." Thus children received a lot of early mirroring experiences that gave them a strong foundation of self-esteem. The circular quality of the Medicine Wheel emphasized that learning is a lifelong quest. That concept, along with the idea that everything that happens to us teaches us something is important to remember.

The Partnership Way of conflict resolution utilizes a number of principles from the Native American tradition of the Medicine Wheel. They are as follows:

- All life experiences have meaning.
- Kindness, compassion, acceptance, and interconnectedness are important human values.
- Children need many mirroring experiences to build their self-esteem.
- All conflict brings gifts or messages that can be used for self-discovery.

HOW DO PERSONAL ATTITUDES AND BELIEFS ABOUT CONFLICT AFFECT PERSONAL STYLES OF CONFLICT RESOLUTION?

Do you ever look forward to a conflict as an opportunity to learn more about yourself? Probably not, if you are like most people. Because of your prior experiences with conflict, you may view conflict as a win-lose situation and feel afraid you are going to lose, or as a lose-lose situation, in which case we know we'll lose. Consequently, most people have developed a lot of negative beliefs about the experience of conflict.

Releasing Negativity About Conflict

Most people dislike the whole idea of being in conflict. When we ask the questions, "Is conflict positive or negative?" and "Have your experiences with conflict been positive or negative?" most people say "negative." They often share their experiences of hopelessness and helplessness in conflict situations, saying they feel regressed or dependent on somebody else to resolve the conflict for them. Thus, it is extremely important for people to release their negativity about conflict and learn to view it in a more positive way. At the end of this chapter, you will find a self-awareness exercise called "Getting the Negative Out of Conflict" that asks you to list any negative thoughts and feelings you have about conflict.

If a conflict can be resolved in a win-win way, then learning and growth are possible. The Partnership Way should help you develop a more positive attitude toward conflict. With increased skill comes more confidence in your ability to resolve conflicts in a win-win way and more willingness to attempt to resolve conflicts that previously you would have avoided. Be patient with yourself and remember that your experience with conflict will continue to be negative for a while as you learn these new skills.

HOW CAN I IDENTIFY MY PERSONAL STYLE OF CONFLICT RESOLUTION?

Determining Adrenal Stress Response to Conflict Situations

At the end of this chapter, is a series of self-awareness exercises designed to identify whether you tend to fight, freeze, or flee when involved in a conflict. By completing these inventories you will gain a better understanding of what your personal style of conflict resolution is. After you finish reading this chapter, take time to fill out each of the inventories honestly and then score them yourself to determine the role of your adrenal stress responses in conflict situations. This will help you determine whether you typically tend to fight, freeze, or flee when faced with a conflict.

Select a specific context, such as your workplace, family, or a significant intimate relationship, for answering the questions. The more specific the context, the better. If you wish, you can also take the inventories more than once, using different contexts each time. This will help you see how you react to conflict in different situations.

The fight/flight/freeze instinct is wired so automatically into the nervous system that most people do not have to think before using one of these methods. The situation automatically activates the adrenal stress response. The adrenaline flows into the bloodstream, setting off either freeze, fight, or flee responses.

WHAT IS THE ROLE OF PTSD AND THE ASR IN CREATING A PERSONAL STYLE OF CONFLICT RESOLUTION?

Adrenaline is a very addictive substance. Many people become addicted to the adrenaline "rush" they get from stressful exercise, extreme physical risks such as skydiving, activities such as gambling, and the drama of conflict. Without a steady supply of adrenaline, hyperactive individuals may become bored or even depressed.

Trauma is an important factor in activating the adrenal stress response. The response can get triggered not only by present trauma but also by emotional, cognitive, biological, and behavioral responses from past memories of trauma. If you grew up in a family in which violence was an accepted method for resolving conflicts, you may, when faced with conflict today, experience flashbacks to your earlier conflict situations that leave you feeling not only regressed, but caught in fight/flight/freeze responses.

Addiction to adrenaline may also be a factor in rage attacks and spousal abuse. Without being aware of it, men or women who feel stuck in meaningless work or feel unfulfilled in their life can become addicted to the rush of energy and release of negative feelings that they experience by engaging in a fight or conflict. Review the results of "The Addiction to Adrenaline Inventory" at the end of Chapter 1 that assesses your level of addiction to adrenaline.

If you grew up in a family that characteristically displayed "fight" responses to conflict, you likely use fighting today as your favorite response. Your primary coping mechanism in conflict may be related to the person with whom you felt most connected as a child: mother, father, or a sibling. The coping response that person modeled in conflict situations may influence your current reactions and answers on the fight/flight/freeze inventories. Early family experiences related to conflict can have a big effect on which adrenaline-based response patterns you use today to resolve conflicts.

HOW CAN I CHANGE MY PERSONAL STYLE OF CONFLICT RESOLUTION?

After taking the three inventories at the end of this chapter, you should have a good idea of which instinctive response you typically use in conflict situations. If you find that you have a high fight, flight, or freeze style of conflict resolution, it most likely developed from your experiences in your family of origin and the role that you held in the family. The fight response style is more characteristic of the "rebel" role and related more to an experience of abuse. The flight response is more characteristic of the "loner" role and may be associated with an avoidant response to experiences of abuse or neglect. The "lost child" role, frequently associated with the freeze response, may be associated with a dissociative response to neglect or abandonment.

If you have adopted any of these styles, it is likely that you needed to do so to protect yourself in your family of origin. While it probably served as an important defense for you during your childhood, it may not be functional or effective in your adult relationships. It may inhibit your ability to be intimate and even prevent you from finding cooperative, peaceful resolutions to your conflicts. If you find yourself reverting to old behavior patterns in moments of post-traumatic stress, it is important to treat yourself with kindness and compassion. Remember that these behaviors get triggered outside of your conscious awareness and that you do not intentionally act angry or rageful. Develop an accepting attitude toward these old behavior patterns knowing that you are in the process of changing them.

Unfortunately, as mentioned earlier, all fight/flight/freeze responses are win-lose or lose-lose methods for resolving conflicts. If you have adopted one of these styles, you were probably on the losing end of conflicts as a child and still carry the emotional wounds from your encounters. Healing these wounds is vital to having healthy, intimate relationships in the present. Without an awareness of the need to heal these wounds and without the skills to reach win-win conflict resolutions, you will likely continue with the methods for coping with conflict you learned from your family of origin. Current conflicts can retraumatize you and perpetuate the vicious cycle of cruelty.

The first step in changing your personal style of conflict resolution is to compassionately acknowledge any parts of that style that need changing. From taking the self-inventories you should have a better idea of what these parts are. In the remainder of the book, you will learn a new approach to conflict resolution where both parties can win. With practice in using this approach, you can make the changes you probably have wanted to make in your conflict resolution style, but didn't know how. We encourage you to complete the last exercise at the end of this chapter, which is designed to help you develop a plan for changing your personal style of conflict resolution. Take some time to complete that exercise and to develop your personal plan.

TAKING INVENTORY OF A PERSONAL STYLE OF CONFLICT RESOLUTION

The three different self-inventories at the end of this chapter are to help identify a personal style of conflict resolution. Take, score, and interpret the results of each inventory. It is best to focus on a specific context such as work, family, or intimate relationships with your significant other when answering the questions. If you wish, you can also retake the inventories using a different context or situation to see if your answers might change. After you have completed these inventories, at the end of the chapter you will find a concluding self-awareness exercise "Changing My Personal Style of Conflict Resolution." It can help you envision a new style of conflict resolution and to more effectively personalize the material in the remainder of this book.

SELF-AWARENESS EXERCISE: GETTING THE NEGATIVE OUT OF CONFLICT

Most people carry around lots of negative thoughts and feelings about conflict. In order to surface your negative feelings about conflict, in the space provided below or on a separate sheet of paper, make a list of the negative words that you associate with the word conflict. After compiling the list, look at the items and see if you can identify any specific experiences with conflict that you had in mind when you put that item on your list. This can help you connect your past experiences with conflict to your present attitudes, feelings, and behaviors.

My negative experiences about conflicts:

SELF-INVENTORY: IDENTIFYING "DIRTY FIGHTING" RESPONSES TO CONFLICT

Identify your favorite dirty fighting responses and the degree to which you use them to resolve conflicts.

1 = Almost Never 2 = Occasionally
3 = Usually 4 = Almost Always

Note: the items in this inventory are purposely written in a humorous way. It can be healthy to laugh at yourself when you recognize some typical "dirty fighting" responses. Obviously, the actual effects of this style are usually not funny and can be very destructive to the people with whom you are fighting.

_____1. Timing. Pick the right time to begin an argument. Your best options are late at night, during a favorite TV program, after several drinks, or just when your partner least expects it or is least able to respond.

_____2. Escalating. Move quickly from the issue to questioning the other person's worth and/or the worth of the relationship ("these problems are too big to work out"). Interpret your partner's shortcomings as evidence of bad faith and the impossibility of having a happy relationship.

_____3. Brown-bagging. Try to list as many problems in as much detail as possible. Don't stick to the original issue. Throw in all the present, past, and possible future problems you can think of. If your partner can't recall the offenses, so much the better.

_____4. Over-generalizing. Use words like *always* and *never* as in "You are always late." This is likely to distract your partner into discussing the over-generalization rather than the original issue and will insure further misunderstandings.

_____5. Cross-complaining. Respond to any complaint from your partner with the statement: *If it wasn't for the fact that you never have any clean clothes for me..."* If you do it properly, you can balance one complaint against another complaint forever.

_____6. Crucializing. Exaggerate the importance of the issue with statements such as, *"If you really loved me or us, you would never have done it in the first place,"* or *"This proves that you don't care."* Never concede that an issue is not absolutely critical and in need of immediate resolution.

_____7. Asking Why. *Why didn't you clean up?"* or *"Why were you late?"* will imply that there must be something very wrong with your spouse and that something more is wrong with them than a simple problem behavior that he or she might easily resolve.

_____8. Blaming. Make it clear that the fault lies entirely with your partner and that, again, you are simply the innocent victim. Don't admit that your behavior plays any part in the difficulty. Make sure your spouse realizes that you will not change first.

_____9. Pulling rank. Rather than depending on the merits of your argument, pull rank by reminding your partner that you make more money, have more education, are older or younger, or are wiser or more experienced in such matters. Anything that will enhance your status at your partner's expense is acceptable.

_____10. Not listening, dominating. Anytime you appear to be listening, you run the risk of suggesting that you value your partner's opinion. Consider talking while your partner is talking, pretending to read, or falling asleep.

_____11. Listing injustices. This is a great morale builder. By reciting every slight injustice or inequity you have suffered in the relationship, you will experience a renewed sense of self-righteousness. You can use this approach to justify almost any activity you have always wanted to engage in. For example, *"Since you went ahead and bought those new clothes, I am going to buy a new car."*

_____12. Labeling. By labeling someone in a negative manner, you can create the impression that this person is totally at fault. Psychological labels, such as childish, neurotic, insecure, or alcoholic are particularly effective in obscuring issues where you may be vulnerable.

_____13. Mind-reading. By deciding that you know the real reason why someone is acting in a certain way, you can avoid having to debate issues. For example, "You *only said that to set me up,*" or "*You don't really feel that way,*" are particularly effective.

_____14. Fortune-telling. Predicting the future can save you the effort of really trying to resolve conflicts. "*You will never change,*" or "*It would be easy for me to change, but you wouldn't live up to it,*" are statements that can protect you from having to make any effort at all.

_____15. Being sarcastic. This is a great way of saying something without having to take responsibility for it. If you can say, "*You are so smart…*" just right, you can imply that your partner is stupid and deny that you said it at the same time.

_____16. Avoiding responsibility. Although not a very elegant tactic, saying "*I don't remember*" can bring the discussion to an abrupt halt. Alcohol or fatigue can serve the same purpose as in, "*I must have had too much to drink.*"

_____17. Leaving. No problem is so big or important that it can't be ignored. Walk out of the room, leave home, or just refuse to talk. Sometimes just threatening to leave can accomplish the same ends without the inconvenience involved in actually leaving.

_____18. Rejecting compromise. Don't back down. Why settle for compromise when, with a little luck, you can really devastate your partner (and destroy the relationship). Stick with the "one winner" philosophy.

_____19. Personalizing. Anybody can resolve a conflict by sticking to the issue. Shift to personality issues and you should be able to generate enough defensiveness to keep the conflict going forever.

_____20. Playing the martyr. If timed properly, this tactic can completely disorient the opposition. "*You're right, dear, I am hopeless*" can stop your partner cold. An example of a less subtle form is "*How could you say that, after all I've done for you?*" An extreme form is to threaten to kill yourself if your spouse doesn't shape up.

_____21. Using money. "*If you made as much money as…,*" or, "*When you make as much as I do, then you can have an opinion*" are old favorites.

_____22. Using the children. "*If you spent more time with them, they wouldn't be failing,*" or "*Do you want them to grow up like you?*" can always be used unless you are so unfortunate as to have perfect children.

_____23. Using relatives. "*When you do that you are just like your mother or father*" can be used to break your partner's concentration and undermine confidence.

_____24. Giving advice. By telling people how to act, think, and feel, you can maintain a position of superiority while insisting that you are only trying to be helpful.

_____25. Getting even. Don't settle for a compromise or an apology. Hold grudges for as long as possible. You might need those complaints in future arguments.

_____26. Using terminal language. For example, if you happened to get upset by the fact that your partner didn't straighten up his or her room, start with, "*You slob…*" to suggest that it is your partner's existence and not behavior that is in question.

_____27. Threatening. "*If you won't do X, I won't do Y.*"

_____28. Being inconsistent. Keep your partner off balance by changing your position. Try complaining that he/she never talks to you and then ignore whatever your partner says.

_____29. Using oppositional behavior. Whatever the other person says, you take the opposite position. This keeps them off balance and more vulnerable.

_____30. Playing it cool. Nothing upsets the other person quicker than your refusal to get upset at what they are saying or doing to you. Act as if nothing ever bothers you, that you are definitely capable of rising above the other person and are, therefore, superior to them.

_____ **Total Score**

Scoring and Interpretation

Add the numbers in the column to determine your total score. Use the following guide to interpret your score.

30–60 Limited use of dirty fighting to resolve conflicts. You may need to find better ways to resolve conflicts in certain situations.

61–90 Extensive use of dirty fighting to resolve conflicts. You may need to find better ways to resolve all your conflicts.

91–120 Dirty fighting is the primary way you attempt to resolve conflicts. You will need to develop new ways to resolve your conflicts.

SELF-INVENTORY: IDENTIFYING FREEZE RESPONSES TO CONFLICT

Identify your favorite freeze responses and the degree to which you use them to resolve conflicts.

1 = Almost Never 2 = Occasionally
3 = Usually 4 = Almost Always

When I find myself in a conflict, I:

_____1. Don't know what to do to resolve the conflict.

_____2. See the conflict as unsolvable.

_____3. Am afraid I will lose.

_____4. Am not even aware there is a conflict.

_____5. Can't get my mind off the conflict.

_____6. Feel sure that I will be blamed for doing something wrong.

_____7. Feel powerless to change the other person's ideas/perceptions/beliefs.

_____8. Don't know what I want or need to resolve the conflict.

_____9. Do not feel obligated by the terms of the resolution and withdraw emotionally.

_____10. Get confused easily about the details of the conflict.

_____11. See both sides of the conflict and can't decide who is right.

_____12. Get talked out of my ideas, perceptions, and beliefs.

_____13. Get down on myself and criticize myself.

_____14. Can't think of what to say.

_____15. Can't think of how to defend myself.

_____16. Feel overwhelmed by my own feelings.

_____17. Fear the outcome will damage my relationship with those involved.

_____18. Feel that I must adapt or comply with the wishes of the other person.

_____19. Feel controlled by the other person.

_____20. Give up what I think is important in order to keep the peace.

_____ **Total Score**

Scoring and Interpretation

Add the numbers in the column to determine your total score. Use the following guide to interpret your score.

20–40 Limited use of freeze reactions to resolve conflicts. May need to look for better ways to resolve conflicts in certain situations.

41–60 Extensive use of freeze reactions to resolve conflicts. You may need to look for better ways to resolve all your conflicts.

61–80 Freeze reactions are the primary way you attempt to resolve conflicts. You need to find better ways to resolve your conflicts.

SELF-INVENTORY: IDENTIFYING FLIGHT RESPONSES TO CONFLICT

Identify your favorite flight responses and the degree to which you use them to resolve conflicts.

1 = Almost Never 2 = Occasionally
3 = Usually 4 = Almost Always

When I find myself in a conflict, I:

_____1. Avoid the person I have the conflict with as much as possible.

_____2. Change the subject if the person wants to discuss the conflict.

_____3. Try to turn the conflict into a joke and make light of the whole thing.

_____4. Accept the blame, apologize, and leave quickly.

_____5. Postpone dealing with it for as long as possible.

_____6. Admit I was wrong, even if I don't believe I am.

_____7. Do whatever he or she wants, so I don't have to feel bad.

_____8. Do whatever is necessary to avoid hurting the other person's feelings.

_____9. Keep the conflict impersonal and cite rules and regulations that apply.

_____10. Don't reveal my opinions or my feelings.

_____11. Act like I am not interested or am too busy to deal with the conflict.

_____12. Get others to support my side of the conflict before dealing with it.

_____13. Tell a lie, if it will help avoid the conflict.

_____14. Patch things up without dealing with the cause of the conflict.

_____15. Do things I know the other person would like, hoping they will forget about the conflict.

_____16. Try to find an easy way out of the conflict.

_____17. Refuse to discuss the conflict and make it seem unimportant.

_____18. Try to act the opposite of what I am really feeling.

_____19. Let the other person know I am suffering because of their behavior.

_____20. Play "hard to get" and make the other person seek me out to resolve the conflict.

_____ **Total Score**

Scoring and Interpretation

Add the numbers in the column to determine your total score. Use the following guide to interpret your score.

20–40 Limited use of flight reactions to resolve conflicts. You may want to look for better ways to resolve conflicts in specific situations.

41–60 Extensive use of flight reactions to resolve conflicts. You may want to find better ways to resolve your conflicts in general.

61–80 Flight reactions are the primary way you attempt to resolve conflicts. You need to develop better ways to resolve your conflicts.

SKILL PRACTICE EXERCISE: CHANGING YOUR PERSONAL STYLE OF CONFLICT RESOLUTION

The following questions are designed to focus your awareness on what you like and dislike about your personal style of conflict resolution and to identify how you would like to change it.

Part One:

1. What do I like and dislike about my personal style of conflict resolution?

2. What would I like to change about my personal style of conflict resolution?

3. What do I need in order to make these changes?

Note: Consider the following questions that are implied in this exercise. Where does my conflict resolution style work the best for me and where does it not work? Where doesn't it work for me? Where do things break down for me during a conflict? Do they break down in a work-related situations where I have a conflict with someone in authority? Do they break down when I have a conflict with my coworkers or classmates? Do I have more problems resolving conflicts in my personal relationships with a spouse, child, or a loved one?

Part Two: Dialogue with a Partner

One of the main objectives of this book is to give you suggestions and tools so that you can change and strengthen your personal style of conflict resolution. Find a partner and spend ten or fifteen minutes sharing what you've learned from the previous skill-building exercise regarding your personal style of conflict resolution.
Discuss:
• where it works
• where it doesn't work
• what you would like to change about it
• how you would like to go about making those changes

SELF-AWARENESS EXERCISE: PERSONAL EXPERIENCES WITH CONFLICT

Answer the following questions about your personal experiences with conflict. Use them to set some goals for desired outcomes regarding the study of conflict resolution.

1. Identify the critical experiences in your life that motivated you to learn more about conflict.
   a. Incident #1:

   b. Incident #2:

   c. Incident #3:

2. Describe what was most difficult or challenging about these experiences.
   a. Incident #1:

   b. Incident #2:

   c. Incident #3:

3. Describe what you would have liked as different outcomes regarding these experiences.
   a. Incident #1:

   b. Incident #2:

   c. Incident #3:

4. What skills do you believe would have helped you achieve these different outcomes?

Chapter 3

~

What Theories of Conflict Resolution Contribute to the Partnership Way?

This chapter identifies significant contributions from the major counseling and conflict resolution theories to the Partnership Way. As we developed the Partnership Way, we focused our attention on identifying the aspects from our research that seemed most effective in resolving conflicts. Once we identified those components, we saw that they came from a number of psychological theories. One of our most important discoveries was that each of these theories lent something useful to our work. Rather than trying to compare the theories, we extracted the "gem" from each that was useful and synthesized those gems into a meta-theory.

The meta-theory approach deals with more than just the cognitive aspects of human beings. It recognizes that humans have multiple dimensions, including emotional, physical, and spiritual aspects. The Partnership Way of conflict resolution presented in this book provides a comprehensive and integrative approach. It can become a powerful and proactive tool for understanding and in conflict situations.

The theories in the Partnership Way can be molded into a personal theory of conflict resolution that is compatible with your own values and beliefs. It may be somewhat different from the synthesis developed by us. Initially, theory-making must examine the ideas and experiences of others while simultaneously listening to yourself to see how each theory fits your personal worldview.

CONTRIBUTIONS FROM THE COGNITIVE-BEHAVIORAL THEORIES OF CONFLICT RESOLUTION

These theories tend to see intrapersonal and interpersonal conflict as the result of faulty thinking or irrational beliefs. Frequently, the resolution of the conflict involves teaching someone to think about the conflict in a new way or to change certain beliefs, feelings, and behaviors that are seen as part of the cause of the conflict. It also may involve teaching the person steps to follow to resolve conflicts.

There has been a great deal of research and pioneering efforts in the field of conflict resolution from cognitive-behaviorists, including the following people:

Roger Fisher and **William Ury's Harvard Negotiation Project** pioneered the concept of win-win conflict resolution through negotiation. A ground-breaking book, *Getting To Yes* (Fisher & Ury, 1981), outlined a method of "principled negotiation" that involves resolving conflicts from a new perspective. The authors looked at the usual pitfalls with which people deal when approaching a conflict situation and suggested alternative approaches.

Fisher and Ury suggested separating the relationship from the problem so that personal attacks can be removed from the process of resolving conflicts. They also cautioned people not to get locked into a position but to focus instead on reconciling differing interests. Finally, they suggested a process for creating options that involves mutual gain. Their approach avoids the "win at all costs" attitude but is very cognitive and matter-of-fact. The authors saw their attempt to first build a relationship as a useful approach to conflict resolution. In separating the person and the relationship from the conflict or problem, Fisher and Ury suggested that you pay attention to the following principles:

- People are not conflicts. Their needs and your needs are in conflict and these have to be addressed in a relationship way.
- Deal directly with the relationship problem caused by the conflict.
- Do not argue about the truth. People's perception are true for them, and you have to accept perceptions as truth. You may have different perceptions, but trying to claim yours are true and theirs are false does not work. Instead talk about how they reached theirs and you reached yours.
- Put yourself in their shoes and show them you understand their perceptions.
- Be careful not to assume that their intentions are based on your fears.
- Once you know their perceptions of you, look for opportunities to behave counter to what they would expect. This helps them change their perceptions.
- Make sure both of you participate equally in the process of reaching an agreement. If one side gives in too quickly they may not feel bound to honor the agreement.
- As much as possible, make your proposals consistent with their values. This helps the other person "save face."
- Legitimize all feelings, let the other side let off steam if necessary, and don't overreact to emotional outbursts. Listen and show respect for their feelings.
- Use "I" messages, not "you" messages.
- Talk openly about the effect that the conflict has on your relationship.

We adapted some of their ideas and expanded on them in a Self-Awareness Exercise: Separating the Person from the Problem, which can be found at the end of this chapter.

George Bach and **Peter Wyden's Fair Fighting Model** was one of the earliest works in the area of interpersonal conflict. Their book, *The Intimate Enemy* (Bach & Wyden, 1968), focused on teaching couples how to fight fairly. They believe that couples who know how to fight fairly can use their conflicts as a way to increase the level of intimacy in their relationship. We were intrigued by this concept, for we had seen it in action in our own relationship and while facilitating relationship conflicts for our clients and students. We began to explore the idea even more and saw, as Bach and Wyden point out in their book, that conflict does have the potential for changing the status quo of a relationship. We found that couples could be taught to resolve conflicts in a way where both people felt they had won and doing so increased the level of their intimacy.

Albert Ellis' (1995) **Rational Emotive Behavioral Therapy** assumes that an irrational belief is the source of conflict. This irrational belief affects the way people approach others in conflictual situations. To resolve a conflict, Ellis first looks for the underlying irrational belief, such as "I must be liked by everyone I meet. If I am not, there is something wrong with me." According to Ellis' theory, people trying to solve a conflict must look for the irrational belief rather than attacking the other person. Ellis believes that people need to develop more situational values that avoid imposing rigid standards on themselves and others. His theory particularly impacted our search for more effective ways to resolve conflicts of values and beliefs.

A whole new field of cognitive-behavioral research known as "traumatology" (studying the effects of trauma on humans) has emerged in the past several years. A number of individuals involved in this research provided critical theoretical contributions to our approach.

Donald Meichenbaum's PTSD Approach was extremely useful in understanding the role of PTSD in intractable conflicts. Meichenbaum, one of the chief contributors to cognitive-behavioral theory, has also done extensive research on PTSD (Meichenbaum, 1994). It was his research on PTSD that helped us link intractable conflicts with post-traumatic stress. Meichenbaum, who has devoted 30 years of clinical research and study to PTSD, is recognized as one of the leading authorities in the world on this subject. Meichenbaum's book gives a thorough analysis of the elements of trauma and discusses how trauma is stored in the body-mind and later activated as symptoms of post-traumatic stress.

Bessel van der Kolk's Post-Traumatic Stress Approach is summarized in *Traumatic Stress: The Overwhelming Experience on Mind, Body and Society* (van der Kolk, McFarlane, Weisaeth, 1996). His approach also contributed significantly to our understanding of the developmental and biological aspects of human adaptation to trauma, including the nature of traumatic memories. His research and clinical knowledge on the treatment of post-traumatic symptoms, particularly those related to brain function and the mechanisms and processes of traumatic memory, were critical in validating our own clinical experiences. His approach was particularly significant in correlating developmental trauma and regression with experiences of conflict.

Beverly James' Attachment-Trauma Approach was the first book we found that correlated attachment and trauma. In *Handbook for Treatment of Attachment-Trauma Problems in Children* (1994), James provided an integrated blueprint for assessing and working with trauma-related attachment disturbances. She also identified a disturbance in the parent-child relationship that she calls "trauma bonds." Her research and clinical protocols were useful resources for refining the "developmental trauma" component of the Partnership Way.

CONTRIBUTIONS FROM THE HUMANISTIC THEORIES OF CONFLICT RESOLUTION

Humanistic theories of conflict resolution emphasize relationship dynamics and the communication patterns of the individuals in conflict. Interventions, which typically involve helping individuals better understand each other by using clear, straight communication in conflict situations, may involve teaching communications skills as a prerequisite to teaching conflict resolution or problem-solving skills. The main premise is that people who communicate effectively with each other are likely to have fewer conflicts and that the conflicts they do have are more readily resolved because they have a foundation of skills for resolving them. The humanistic theories emphasize communications models, which we found useful to integrate into our meta-model.

Katz and **Lawyer's Communications Model** attempts to integrate conflict resolution with other communication skills. In their book, *Communication and Conflict Resolution Skills*, Katz and Lawyer (1985) teach interpersonal communication skills as a means of resolving conflict. They view conflict resolution skills as just another set of essential interpersonal communication skills. With their method, participants first identify their personal style of conflict resolution and then, armed with this information, become open to new options that facilitate changing that style.

Katz and Lawyer also described several methods for reducing conflict before attempting to resolve it. For example, they suggested that each person use reflective listening before stating his or her own view of the problem when resolving conflicts of wants and needs, as well as conflicts of values and beliefs. We adapted this aspect of their approach into our values and beliefs conflict approach.

While Katz and Lawyer differentiated between conflicts of wants and needs and conflicts of values and beliefs and offered a method for distinguishing them, they proposed a singular method for resolving both kinds of conflicts. We feel the use of different strategies for resolving each kind of conflict situation works better.

Late in his career, **Carl Rogers** became very interested in applying his **Person-Centered Theory** to international conflict resolution. He hypothesized that the negative stereotypes people with long-standing conflicts project on each other might be replaced by caring and empathic relatedness. He successfully demonstrated this in numerous international settings (Rogers & Ryback, 1984).

In the early 1980s, Rogers began to meet with very diverse large international groups (sometimes as large as several thousand people) who had long-standing conflicts. For example, he met with a large group of Irish Catholics and Protestants in Northern Ireland. He also led cross-cultural workshops in Brazil, Dublin, South Africa, and Hungary. One meeting in Austria included a significant number of diplomats and other government officials (Rogers, 1986). At this meeting, he modeled how diplomats could increase their capacity for empathic understanding and genuineness.

As we integrated reflective listening into our approach for resolving conflicts of values and beliefs, we found Rogers' hypothesis to be accurate. When people with conflicts of values and beliefs treated each other with respect and could express some empathy toward each other, they were able to better understand their differences. Reflective listening is now an essential component of resolving conflicts of values and beliefs in the Partnership Way.

Terry Bolton's People Skills Approach also utilizes a communications approach to conflict resolution. In his book, *People Skills*, Bolton (1979) described conflict resolution skills as one of the types of communication proficiencies that people need. He emphasized, as do we, that "conflict is inevitable" and "conflict can be positive." He also stressed the precept that conflict resolution is a process, not just a set of rules to govern interpersonal strife. To address the emotional aspects of a conflict, he suggested the following:

1. Treat the other person with respect.
2. Listen to each other until you are able to enter into the experience of the person on the other side.
3. State your views, needs, and feelings.

Although we agree that emotions are an important part of conflict, we feel that people must use the emotions attached to a conflict constructively rather than resolve them separately from the actual conflict.

CONTRIBUTIONS OF THE PSYCHODYNAMIC THEORIES OF CONFLICT RESOLUTION

Psychodynamic theories of conflict resolution emphasize early antecedents of present intrapersonal or interpersonal conflicts. The core concept is that unresolved conflicts from our past history tend to recur in our lives. Psychodynamic conflict resolution methods, consequently, involve helping people identify the sources of their current conflicts and then find ways in the here and now to resolve issues from the past. This process of self-discovery first involves teaching people understanding about the conditions of optimal development and correlating missing pieces in their early development to current adult conflicts.

Erik Erikson, Robert Havighurst, and **Jean Piaget's Developmental Theories and Research** helped us identify the stages of physical development and the cognitive, emotional, and psychosocial tasks to be mastered at each stage. The work of Erikson (1959), Havighurst (1972), and Piaget (1951) provided us with foundational material for identifying these stages.

Jacqui Schiff, Eric Berne, Dorothy Babcock, Terry Keepers, John Bradshaw, Pam Levin, and **Jean Illsley Clark's Transactional Analysis Approaches** provided many ideas and methods of working with adults who are severely affected by early childhood trauma. In 1970, Schiff published a book titled, *All My Children.* She described a revolutionary therapy approach called "reparenting," which grew out of Eric Berne's work on transactional analysis (TA). Schiff reported a great deal of success with the reparenting therapy she and her husband had used, often with schizophrenic clients. They used a residential treatment program that required 24-hour-a-day care. Most of the people who went through their program went on to become highly functioning adults, many becoming therapists themselves.

Schiff's methods, considered highly controversial at the time, encouraged clients to regress to an infant stage. The interventions were designed to heal clients' developmental deficits related to that babyhood and included diapering them, holding them, and feeding them from bottles, as well as structured anger- and rage-reduction techniques. Their methods were designed to reconnect their clients with the sources of their original trauma, to allow them to express repressed feelings related to the trauma and to provide them with the support, nurturing, and new information needed to heal their early wounds.

Schiff and her colleagues (1976) wrote a sequel book, *The Cathexis Reader,* which described a set of passive or discounting behaviors that kept people stuck in symbiotic or codependent relationships and intractable conflicts. The book outlined effective methods for confronting these dysfunctional behaviors. Passive people, for example, often discount their own needs and focus on the needs of others, hoping to "win" some attention or approval from them. In addition, they discount their ability to ask directly for what they want. Being forced to ask directly to get their needs met has been found to be an effective means for resolving their internal conflicts.

As Schiff and her colleagues studied passivity and discounting, they discovered that these behaviors weren't just part of the pathology of schizophrenics. They were also very much a part of the everyday life of most people. They estimated that as many as two out of every five interactions between people involved some evidence of discounting or passivity. The Schiffs indicated that these behaviors were the major causes of intractable conflicts.

TA practitioners Dorothy Babcock and Terry Keepers (1976) combined the passivity/discounting concept with script analysis in a book for parents called *Raising Kids OK.* Goulding and Goulding (1978) were among those who adapted the concept into other types of TA therapy such as **Redecision Therapy.**

During this period, Schiff became embroiled in political battles over her methods within the International Association of Transactional Analysis and eventually was censured by the organization. The censuring effectively stopped the progress of Schiff's treatment modality, although a few of her former students did continue to develop the theory.

Bowlby, Winnicott, Kernberg, Kohut, Mahler, and **Cashdan's Object Relations Theory and Therapy Approaches** theorize that events during the first year of life dictate the course of human development. Bowlby (1969), Kernberg (1976), Mahler (1968, 1975), and Winnicott (1960) were pioneers in this specialized field of psychodynamic psychology. Of these theorists, we drew most heavily from the research of Margaret Mahler and her colleague, Louise Kaplan, who charted the course of development from the bonding stage of the infant (birth to nine months) through the separation stage (nine to twenty-four months). Kaplan's (1978) book, *Oneness and Separateness,* based on Mahler's research, provided us with a clear narrative description of these two stages, including what might prevent the successful completion of each stage. Cashdan's (1988) book, *Object Relations Therapy,* helped us identify the specific distortions that emerge as a result of traumatic parent-child relationships.

With the onset of the addictions and recovery movement in the late 1980s, object relations theory and therapy began to appear in literature containing a developmental perspective. John Bradshaw utilized many reparenting concepts in his series of books on recovery and inner child therapy (e.g., *Healing the Shame that Binds You,* 1988; *Homecoming: Reclaiming and Championing Your Inner Child,* 1990). Jon and Laurie Weiss described corrective parenting techniques for treating codependency in *Recovery From Co-dependency* (Weiss & Weiss, 1989). Jean Illsley Clarke wrote two important books applying this evolving theory to parenting practices: *Self-esteem: A Family Affair* (Clarke, 1978) and *Growing Up Again: Parenting Ourselves, Parenting Our Children* (Clarke & Dawson, 1989). Pamela Levin (1988a & b) also wrote several books that further developed reparenting theory, including *Becoming the Way We Are* and *Cycles of Power.*

Our books, *Breaking Free of the Co-dependency Trap* (Weinhold & Weinhold, 1989), *Counter-dependency: The*

Flight From Intimacy (Weinhold & Weinhold, 1992), and *Breaking Free of Addictive Family Relationships* (Weinhold, 1991), utilize reparenting techniques and a developmental approach. The last work describes the process of breaking addictive relationship dynamics using many concepts from object relations theory. We eventually integrated many reparenting and developmental concepts into the Partnership Way, as tools to help people recover their "true self" by resolving their conflicts at the source.

Clarke's and Levin's books contributed affirmations designed to assist in the healing of early cognitive trauma. They also created lists of the developmental needs of early childhood to help people locate the sources of their adult conflicts. We found these lists useful in helping clients in their recovery process and incorporated them into the component for resolving conflicts at their source.

We also incorporated **Steven Karpman's** (1968) **Drama Triangle** into the Partnership Way component for resolving conflicts at their source. From Karpman's description of persecutor, rescuer, and victim roles and how the roles rotate around a triangle, we identified an equivalent set of dynamics in the parent-child separation process. We extended his model into an optimal family dynamic we call the functional family triangle. The Partnership Way correlates the interpersonal dynamics of the drama triangle with drama from unresolved developmental trauma containing symptoms of post-traumatic stress.

Alice Miller and **Philip Ney's Intergenerational Theories** taught us much about the psychodynamics of developmental trauma. Much of the reparenting component of our paradigm grew out of the pioneering work of the Swiss analyst Alice Miller (1981, 1983, 1986, 1988, and 1991). Her books helped us examine the role of early narcissistic wounds on later development. Miller's work clearly explained many of the adverse effects of "standard parenting practices" and documented that the same dysfunctional patterns of behavior repeat from one generation to the next. Her work also helped us better understand the causes of intergenerational conflicts.

Philip Ney (1987, 1988) helped increase our understanding of the intergenerational transmission of conflict. Ney based his model of family conflict on three rotating roles: the perpetrator, the victim, and the observer. He proposed that family members repeat the maladaptive parenting practices used on them as a means of better understanding their parents' behavior. Ney also noticed that people who were in an observer role as children remained in that role as adults. Similar to the dynamics of the drama triangle, in Ney's theory the roles rotate between family members. For example, to better understand why he or she was victimized by a parent, the victim can become the perpetrator or the observer.

Ney applied his theory to professionals in the workplace to show how easy it is to get caught up in countertransference behaviors relating to roles from their own family of origin. Professionals can easily slip into the roles of victim, perpetrator, or observer, preventing them from being effective. The Partnership Way draws heavily on Ney's theory, using it to demonstrate the recycling of conflicts through intergenerational structures. Ney's theory reinforced our belief in the importance of helping professionals' identifying the nature and source of their own personal styles of conflict resolution.

Our study in 1985 and 1986 with **Arnold Mindell** and his **Global Process Work** provided a significant contribution to our approach. Mindell, a former Jungian analyst, developed an adaptation of Jungian theory called global process work (1983, 1985a&b, & 1987).

While working as a Jungian analyst in Zurich, Switzerland, Arnold Mindell became ill with a life-threatening disease. After unsuccessfully attempting to cure himself using the standard analytic tools he had in his Jungian toolbox, he began to investigate the relationship between body symptoms and dreams. He realized that he knew much less about his body than he did about his dreams, so he began studying various body-oriented therapies, including yoga, bioenergetics, breath work, Rolfing, massage, movement therapy, psychodrama, neurolinguistic programming, Gestalt therapy, and meditation, in an attempt to heal himself. During his investigation process, he not only healed himself but began to weave together threads from each of these approaches into a new body/mind therapy that he called the "dreambody approach" (Mindell, 1983).

Mindell adapted much of Jung's work, including his ideas about dreams. Mindell began to realize that people are dreaming all the time. Their waking dreams, according to Mindell, are often means of avoiding unpleasant realities or unpleasant memories, while their sleeping dreams provide an outlet for unconscious material to emerge.

The real genius of Mindell's work, however, was his expansion of information theories such as neurolinguistic programming (NLP) into six main channels and his use of Taoist principles in therapy. His form of information theory provided a mechanism the therapist can use to track information as it presents itself through the client's symptoms and problems. Mindell's use of Taoist principles provided a context of "rightness" of all symptoms and problems, as well as the use of client-centered techniques for "following" the client.

In addition, Mindell used the principles of unified field theory from quantum physics to show how problems move from one "field" or system to another. According to his theory, for example, an internal conflict that is not resolved at the individual level will move out into the relationship field and emerge there as a conflict. If not resolved at that level, it would move out into the next level of the system—the family. Using this theory to examine national and international conflicts, he began to hypothesize about how unresolved global conflicts could be the collective manifestation of many unresolved individual, relationship, group, and organizational conflicts.

CONTRIBUTIONS FROM THE SYSTEMS THEORIES OF CONFLICT RESOLUTION

Systems theories view conflict through an entirely different lens. System theorists do not try to find the person or persons in a family system, for example, that are causing the problems or conflicts. Instead, they view the whole system as contributing to the conflict in some important way. Looking at conflict systemically gives a broader perspective for identifying the interacting forces that may be contributing to a conflict. With this approach, there is less of a tendency to label individuals or try to assign blame.

Systems theorists may perceive conflict as a stabilizing force in a dysfunctional family with a lot of conflict. The conflict itself, in this theory, can serve as a force of equilibrium or balance. Systems theorists believe that it is more effective to utilize whole system interventions than to try to change the behavior of just one member of the system. According to this theory, individual interventions can cause disequilibrium and perhaps more conflict within the larger system. We included many of the concepts from general systems and family systems theories in the Partnership Way.

Weiner, Buckley, von Bertalanffy, and **Miller's General Systems Theories** provided an understanding of how conflict operates in all human systems. General systems theory originated in the early 1940s as mathematicians, physicists, and engineers searched for functional and structural rules that could describe all physical (non-human) systems. Norbert Weiner (1954) first applied these principles as he developed the Norden bomb sight during World War II. He coined the term "cybernetics" to describe this emerging field of study. Books by Buckley (1968) and von Bertalanffy (1968) attempted to apply systems concepts to human systems. Ten years later, James Miller (1978) wrote a book applying the concepts of general systems theory to human systems.

Bateson, Bowen, Framo, Jackson, and **Sager's Family Systems Theories** helped us better understand the complexities of how conflict is processed in family systems. As early as the late 1950s, the Palo Alto group, led by Gregory Bateson (see Bateson, Jackson, Haley, & Weakland, 1956), began applying cybernetics to the study of family therapy. Their work eventually led to a major paradigm shift in the field of family therapy; therapists began to view the individual and each successively more complex social group as interacting systems. With this new perspective, family therapists began to treat the family as a system containing various subsystems. The Partnership Way utilizes both the systems language and the concept of family conflicts as a dynamic system that is constantly changing and evolving.

In developing the Partnership Way, we also borrowed from several of the established family systems theories. The work of Bowen (1971, 1978) and Framo (1981, 1982), for example, formed a useful model for helping individuals and families sort out family-of-origin issues that are recycling in the current family dynamic. Bowen also was the first to emphasize the importance of the family therapist doing his or her own family-of-origin work as part of training to become a family therapist.

Structural family therapy contributed useful definitions of the boundaries and rules present in each subsystem in a family. These helped us to better understand and create the interrelated subsystems used in this approach: the individual, the couple, the family, a group or organization, and nation states.

The work of Don Jackson (1965) and of Sager and his associates (Sager et al., 1971) helped us better understand how to bring together intrapsychic and family systems concepts. The basic assumption of their models is that unconscious and conscious aspects of family members' inner conflicts form an important part of the systemic feedback loop that can be observed in the interaction, communication, and behavior patterns of family members. Taub-Bynum (1984) extended the family communication system developed by Jackson and others to include such transpersonal aspects as telepathy and extra sensory perception as ways in which the family's unconscious conflicts are communicated.

We have also borrowed from the strategic approaches to family therapy. Like those approaches, the Partnership Way emphasizes focusing on the resolution of the presenting family conflict. We adhere to the belief that following the family's process is the most useful route for the therapist. Family systems therapy utilizes paradox in much the same way it is used by strategic family therapists.

Bohm, Krishnamurti, and **Senge's Dialogue Process** provided us with important information on how to resolve conflicts of values and beliefs. In our search for a way to create a dialogue rather than a debate or discussion between people experiencing conflicts of values and beliefs, we discovered dialogue master Peter Senge. His book, *The Fifth Discipline* (1990), provided us with the dialogue component of our approach, which became a major component of our method for resolving conflicts of values and beliefs. The dialogue process is ancient, tracing its beginnings back to ancient Greece as well as to native and indigenous peoples.

Senge drew much of his dialogue process from the work of physicist David Bohm. According to Bohm, there are three basic conditions necessary for the dialogue process. First, all participants must suspend their assumptions, opening themselves to observation and questioning. Second, all participants must regard one another as colleagues or equals. Third, there must be either a facilitator or a printed protocol to keep the dialogue from drifting into debate or discussion. Following these conditions, Bohm says people become observers of their own thinking. They begin to see it is their thoughts of the people involved that are engaged in conflict rather than the people themselves.

Bohm learned the principles of dialogue from his spiritual teacher, J. Krishnamurti, from whom he discovered dialogue is an essential tool for advancing science. Bohm discovered that the great ideas of science have come about during conversations among scientists and were not born in isolation in the laboratory as many people believed. Bohm, and later Senge, also argued that the need to "win" or be "right" inhibits the search for the truth. Their perspective helped us see how these needs are counterproductive to resolving conflicts of values and beliefs, and we incorporated that principle into our approach.

Gleick's, Wheatley's, and **Briggs** and **Peat's** interpretations of **Chaos Theory** were important contributions to our approach. We spent over a year studying chaos theory, a branch of quantum physics, with a group of individuals seeking to apply its principles to the helping professions. After working our way through the strange language of chaos theory, we began to see its relevance to the Partnership Way. Gleick's (1987) *Chaos: Making a New Science* and Briggs and Peat's (1989) *The Turbulent Mirror* provided both a language and a conceptual model for understanding chaos theory. Chaos theorists believe that there is always an inherent order in situations that look chaotic. This order, however, is visible only over an extended period of time.

Most people do not look at conflict from a temporal perspective; seldom is conflict viewed over the history of a person's lifetime. When we began to look at singular and clustered conflicts in our own lives and the lives of our students and clients, however, we were able to identify a unifying pattern that ran through the conflicts. Then we looked for the *fractals*, story lines or themes that appear in each conflict situation, searching for the earliest experience, or source, of this patterned behavior. We were pretty amazed to discover that the most common *strange attractor*, an organizing experience for people's life scripts, was related to the circumstances of their birth and their experiences during the first three years of their lives.

We also found that our most successful interventions in changing these life scripts occurred with systems that were seeking to change. According to chaos theory, the more open a system is to change, the more likely it will transform itself into levels of higher and higher order in a search for expanded levels of autonomy and identity. This theory can be particularly helpful in encouraging individuals who try to protect themselves from conflict by closing down to remain as open as possible to each other. Although many of the books on chaos theory are difficult to read, we thoroughly delighted in Margaret Wheatley's (1992) *Leadership and the New Science.*

CONTRIBUTIONS FROM THE TRANSPERSONAL THEORIES OF CONFLICT RESOLUTION

Transpersonal theories of conflict resolution emphasize the need to move around, under, over, and through one's ego defenses in order to resolve conflicts. The basic idea in transpersonal theory is that each person has an essential part of self that is beyond the ego. Ego defenses cause people to become attached to certain ideas, feelings, and activities that can cause conflict. Without a transpersonal perspective, it may be difficult to see the way through certain intrapersonal and interpersonal conflicts. The transpersonal therapist may encourage the people involved in a conflict to look at the conflict from a higher perspective that does not involve ego concerns. Doing so may involve spiritual practices such as meditation, the concept of forgiveness, or spiritual concepts such as karma, past lives, reincarnation, non-attachment, and the Higher Self.

As we synthesized various theories, we realized that our approach needed a solid spiritual foundation. A spiritual component seems to help people move directly into and through core issues in a permanent manner. All of the following transpersonal theorists contributed to our understanding and growth of our approach.

The messages of **Tenzin Gyatso, the 14th Dalai Lama (1997) and temporal and spiritual leader of Tibetan Buddhism,** encourage people to view conflict from a higher perspective, one which does not involve ego concerns, and to change their behavior through the force of consciousness. He urges people to break free of mass thinking and to take individual action in choosing peaceful rather than violent choices. Making this shift requires attention to the focus of one's mind and to one's heart, which requires great awareness and focused intention.

Ken Wilber's Transpersonal Theory of Human Development helped us expand our knowledge of conflict into the spiritual and transpersonal realms. His books *The Atman Project* (1980) and *A Brief History of Everything* (1996) were very helpful in describing the transcendent and spiritual aspects of developmental psychology. Wilber's concepts of the transegoic stages of human development and the superconscious levels of awareness guided us as we integrated the spiritual and transformative elements of human development into our emerging model of conflict resolution. In addition, his work led us to study other transpersonal and spiritual approaches, including Gnosticism, the teachings of spiritual masters from Eastern philosophies such as Integral Yoga, Taoism, Hinduism, Agni Yoga, and other teachings of the so-called ageless wisdom traditions.

Leonard Orr and **Sondra Ray's Rebirthing and Breathwork Theory and Practice** also expanded our knowledge of nonverbal and body-oriented methods for processing unresolved conflicts and traumas. Their book (Orr & Ray, 1977) on rebirthing taught us about the power of the breath in helping people reconnect with and heal early childhood traumas, including the birth trauma. After reading this book, we trained as *rebirthers*, an experience that helped us understand the importance of natural childbirth techniques that respect the sanctity of the birth process and the need of the child to be in charge of his or her own birth.

LeBoyer and **Charkovsky's Nonviolent Birthing Methods** proved to be very useful in understanding how certain patterns can be set in place at birth. The work of Frederick LeBoyer (1975), a French obstetrician; Igor Charkovsky, a Russian physician; and the work of the American midwifery movement helped us develop therapeutic methods for assisting people in recreating an ideal birth. Further, our study of prenatal and perinatal psychology and primal therapy helped us develop a variety of correlations between adult conflicts and unresolved prebirth traumas and birth trauma.

Thomas Crum's Aiki Approach to Conflict Resolution helped us understand conflict from an Eastern perspective. Based on the principles of the Japanese martial art of Aikido, this approach involves a series of six interrelated steps to resolve conflict from a win-win perspective. It taught us how to become centered, to blend with energy, and to create a cooperative, nonviolent context for resolving conflicts. Crum, the chief practitioner of this approach, is one of the cofounders of Windstar, a retreat and learning center near Aspen, Colorado. We studied with Tom and invited him to be a keynote speaker at the two international conferences we organized on conflict resolution.

Christopher Hills' Creative Conflict Resolution approach taught us about self-awareness during conflict resolution. Hills developed this unique approach, which he outlined in *Creative Conflict* (1980). This approach is based on the fundamental spiritual principle that "all is one," and therefore all life is a mirror of oneself. Each conflict provides an opportunity to see oneself more clearly. A big part of this approach is integrity training, which Hills recommends as a group activity. The training method involves the use of aphorisms such as, "You are whatever disturbs you," and "I will examine my own motives for disagreeing before doubting the statements of another." In addition, it involves the use of paradoxical maxims such as, "What we do not see and know as manifested around us is what we really are." Hills' believes it is important to live out of one's Higher Self and view conflict from that perspective. We use this concept in our approach to help people identify and reclaim projections.

Margaret and **Jordan Paul's Intentions Training Approach to Conflict Resolution** was very useful in developing the Partnership Way. The Pauls' approach to conflict resolution also emphasizes viewing conflict from the perspective of the Higher Self. In *From Conflict To Caring* (Paul & Paul, 1989), they identified two pathways through conflict. One is ego-centered and is designed to protect the individual from pain or fear. The other-centered

pathway through our Higher Self uses conflict as an opportunity to learn more about oneself and others. According to the Pauls, the first path leads to negative consequences and the second to positive consequences. They suggest that when in conflict with someone, people should ask themselves, "What is the loving behavior?" These concepts also have been incorporated into the Partnership Way.

Following are several exercises designed to apply some of these theories to your life.

SELF-AWARENESS EXERCISE: SEPARATING THE PERSON FROM THE PROBLEM

1. Divide into groups of three and take turns presenting a current conflict.
2. Using the principle of separating the person from the problem, discuss how you might approach this conflict.
3. Repeat this process until all three people have presented a conflict. If you have trouble remembering a current conflict, use one from the past or create a hypothetical one.

SELF-AWARENESS EXERCISE: MY MOTHER, MYSELF*

1. Make a list of traits that describe your mother and another list that describes your father as you remember them when you were growing up. If you have trouble listing at least ten traits, it could mean that there was a lack of relationship with that parent when you were growing up.
2. Read back over your lists and place a check mark next to those traits that you identify with yourself. It is likely you will find many traits in yourself that you saw in your parents.
3. Now look at your lists and place a (+) for all the traits you listed that were positive, a (0) next to those that were essentially neutral, and a (–) next to those that were negative. This will tell you whether or not your perceptions of your mother or father were positive or negative.
4. Note how many traits of your mother or your father that you identified with and whether these traits are positive or negative. This can help you discover whether you had a positive or negative identification with each one of your parents.
5. Identify people in your adult life who have many of the traits of your parents. Place the initials of the important people in your adult life next to these traits. This exercise can be revealing. You may discover, for example, that you are married to someone who carries many of the negative traits you saw in your mother or your father. It can also help you see the sources of intractable conflicts you have with these people. Later in the book you will learn how to use this information to resolve your intractable conflicts at their source.

*Taken from Weinhold, 1991.

SELF-AWARENESS EXERCISE: ANALYZING A CONFLICT USING RATIONAL EMOTIVE BEHAVIOR THERAPY

Focus on a recent conflict you have not yet resolved and then follow the steps below:

1. A = (Activating Event) Describe a recent conflict situation about which you became angry.
2. B = (Beliefs) What did you tell yourself about the conflict situation?
3. C = (Consequences: behavioral and emotional) Describe the upset feeling and what you did because you were angry.
4. D = (Dispute) Question your angry thoughts, feelings, expectations, and disappointments connected to the conflict. Is there any other way of looking at the conflict?
5. E = (Effect) How would you like to see the conflict resolved? What can you make happen and what do you need to accept?

SELF-AWARENESS EXERCISE: IDENTIFYING THE EFFECTS OF A CONFLICT ON YOUR RELATIONSHIP

One of the most interesting tools that Bach and Wyden (1968) developed is their scoring system designed to assess how a conflict affects the relationship between the two people who are involved. To be successful, according to their theory, a conflict should produce more positive than negative effects.

Use Table 3.1 to determine the effects of a recent conflict that you resolved with someone. It is most effective if you can get both people to use the scoring system. In each column they should indicate their feelings with a plus (+), zero (o), or minus (−). It is possible to connect the marks across the categories to get a profile for both people involved in the conflict. This kind of evaluation can facilitate further discussions about how to improve conflict resolution skills.

Table 3.1
The Fight-Effects Profile*

		+	0	−	
Hurt	decreased				increased
Information	new				old
Positional Movement	ground gained				ground lost
Control	increased				decreased
Fear	decreased				increased
Trust	increased				decreased
Revenge	forgiven				stimulated
Preparation	active				none
Centricity	more central				less central
Self-Value	more				less
Catharsis	released				inhibited
Affection	closer				more distant

*Adapted from Bach and Wyden, 1968

~

PART II

~

HOW CAN THE PARTNERSHIP WAY BE USED TO RESOLVE PERSONAL CONFLICTS?

~

Chapter 4

~

How Can I Prepare Myself to Resolve a Conflict?

The two most common methods used to resolve conflicts are win-lose and lose-lose. Both methods assume that someone will lose. The dynamics that create losing are the result of living in a competitive culture that very early on trains people to win at the cost of the other person rather than to resolve differences in peaceful, cooperate ways. Most win-lose and lose-lose dynamics create games involving victimization, persecution, and rescuing that disempower and separate people.

The prevalence of win-lose and lose-lose methods in our society raises a number of important questions:

- Why are these methods so common if they aren't really very effective?
- Where and how do people learn these methods?
- What are the beliefs and assumptions on which they are based?
- What makes them so difficult to change?

Why Are These Methods So Common?

The most common reasons people use win-lose and lose-lose methods to resolve conflicts of wants and needs are ignorance and a lack of skills. They simply don't know any other way. Formal training in conflict resolution skills is a very recent phenomenon. Fortunately, many schools are now building conflict resolution training into their school curricula from grades K–12. As a result, more and more people now have access to win-win conflict resolution strategies.

Where and How Do People Learn These Methods?

The primary training ground for conflict resolution was your family-of-origin experience. Your parents are the first teachers about conflict, teaching mostly by example. If you saw your parents arguing and using "dirty fighting" techniques, it is likely that you copied their model. The same is true in families where conflict is avoided at all costs. If you saw your parents become immobilized during conflict, it is likely you will do the same. Unfortunately, it is often the "blind leading the blind," because most of today's parents haven't learned effective skills in resolving conflicts. The dysfunctional intergenerational pattern of conflict resolution isn't recognized and therefore is unconsciously repeated.

Perhaps you made a silent vow with yourself: "When I grow up, I will not treat my spouse or my children the way that I am being treated." When you became a parent, you may have felt shocked to find yourself saying and doing the very things you vowed you would never say or do. Chapter 12 explores these intergenerational patterns in more depth, examining how they are transferred from generation to generation.

WHAT ARE THE COMMON ASSUMPTIONS BEHIND WIN-LOSE AND LOSE-LOSE CONFLICT RESOLUTION?

In conflict resolution, as in other areas, your assumptions and beliefs direct your behavior. If you are unaware of your assumptions and beliefs, they will direct your behavior in unconscious ways. Once you become aware of your assumptions and beliefs, you can direct your behavior more consciously. Almost all of the assumptions and beliefs related to win-lose or lose-lose approaches for resolving conflicts involve competitive and comparative thinking. This kind of either/or or black-and-white thinking usually involves seeing only two alternatives to resolving a conflict. Learning to use both/and or cooperative thinking is necessary for creating partnership solutions.

All win-lose and lose-lose conflict resolution methods are based on some of the following assumptions:

- It is difficult or impossible to get my needs met and I will have to engage in a competitive struggle if mine are to prevail.
- I must compete with others to get my needs met because there is a scarcity of what I need.
- I must hide my needs, thoughts, and feelings so others don't take advantage of me or betray me.
- There is a scarcity of love and assistance available to help me meet my needs.
- If someone else gets his or her needs met (wins), I will likely not get my needs met (lose).
- To get my needs met in a conflict, I will need to use power plays to force or manipulate my opponent into meeting them (one-up power).
- I have to be a victim for people to pay attention to my needs (one-down power).
- If I don't win, people will see me as weak and take advantage of me. I must win at all costs (one-up power).

WHAT ARE THE COMMON ASSUMPTIONS OF PARTNERSHIP CONFLICT METHODS?

Win-win approaches to conflict resolution are usually interpreted as compromise, an adversarial situation in which each person involved in a conflict gives up something in order to get something. Win-win really goes beyond compromise. The Partnership Way defines win-win as a mutual desire for each person in the conflict to learn more about themselves as they resolve a conflict. In this way, both parties win no matter how the details of the immediate conflict are resolved.

The Partnership Way of conflict resolution includes the following assumptions:

- We can learn the truth about who we really are and what we need (no secrets).
- We can ask directly for what we want and need from each other (no power plays).
- We agree to seek cooperative solutions to all our conflicts (no competitiveness).
- We focus on kindness and compassion for each other during conflicts and use them as doorways to deeper, more spiritual experiences (no aggression).
- We choose to experience rich and abundant lives with each other on many levels: mental, emotional, spiritual, and physical (no scarcity).
- We negotiate to meet our needs for closeness and separateness, allowing opportunities for varying degrees of both (no games).
- We see each other as complete and separate persons with both positive and negative traits (no splitting).
- We are internally self-sufficient to risk the possible loss of the relationship through direct and honest communications (no victims.)
- We help each other heal old narcissistic wounds through cooperative, reparenting contracts (no power struggles).

WHAT ARE THE DIFFERENCES BETWEEN COMPETITIVE AND COOPERATIVE RELATIONSHIPS?

The differences between win-lose and partnership approaches to conflict resolution can be seen by contrasting competitive and cooperative relationships. Competitive relationships, which foster codependency/counterdependency, are based on dualities such as dominator/dominated, passive/aggressive, and win/lose. Cooperative relationships foster interdependent actions based on unified concepts such as mutuality, inclusiveness, and win-win. Most relationships probably contain some of both elements, but a comparison of the two might look like Table 4.1.

The basic differences in the philosophies and practices of these two types of relationship are apparent in this comparison. More and more people are using books, classes, and therapy to help them create relationships that emphasize kindness, compassion, and cooperation. It is difficult to live cooperatively on a daily basis. Western cultures are so competitively based that those people with cooperative ideals often feel the need to form support groups to help them hold firmly to their vision.

Table 4.1
Comparison of Competitive and Cooperative Relationships

Competitive Relationships	Cooperative Relationships
• win-lose or lose-lose conflict resolution	• win-win conflict resolution
• use force or threats to enforce domination	• use the force of higher consciousness to encourage linking for common good
• treat women and children as property or chattel	• treat women and children as equals and unique individuals
• inequalities in power and decision-making	• equal opportunities in power and decision-making
• use violence and exploitation	• use nurturing qualities such as kindness, compassion, and peaceful dialogue
• utilize rigid sex roles	• utilize fluid sex roles
• use fear to create separation	• use hope and high ideals to create unity
• support codependent and counter-dependent behaviors	• support interdependent behaviors and intimacy
• employ control, manipulation, and deception in communicating	• employ truth, empathy and directness in communicating
• materially oriented	• spiritually oriented
• follow a path of fear and protection	• follow a path of learning and discovery
• value either the needs of the relationship or the needs of the individual	• value both the needs of the individuals and the needs of the relationship

HOW TO CHANGE FROM A WIN-LOSE OR LOSE-LOSE TO A PARTNERSHIP STRATEGY

Changing your approach to conflict resolution may require changing patterns of learned behavior from your childhood. Can you imagine how many times you witnessed or participated in win-lose conflicts in your family or while at school while growing up? This repeated modeling makes it difficult to change your patterns of conflict resolution. In addition to a desire to change your patterns, you need acquire a vision of a new strategy. Win-lose conflict resolution is the only approach most people know.

The Partnership Way provides the vision of a new strategy. It offers you an opportunity to totally change from win-lose or lose-lose to a cooperative strategy. The next several chapters will provide detailed information to help you make this important shift.

WHAT ARE THE STEPS IN PREPARING FOR A CONFLICT RESOLUTION SESSION?

Residue from your unresolved past traumatic conflict experiences affect the way that you respond to conflict in the present. This residue, consisting mostly of post-traumatic responses of fight/flight/freeze, cause you to dread conflict and try to avoid it. This residue of unconscious sensory cues can activate a conflict without warning and snap you into an escalated emotional state where you feel retraumatized.

This chapter is designed to help you identify your residue of post-traumatic responses and to discover why

you have them. This information will help you break your experience of conflict into manageable steps so that you'll no longer feel overwhelmed by post-traumatic symptoms during a conflict situation. This step-by-step approach will not only teach you the specific skills needed to resolve conflicts, but will help desensitize you to the experience of conflict. It also helps you break free of critical, judgmental self-talk and become kinder and more compassionate towards yourself. We have broken the inner experience of conflict into seven component parts:

1. Become aware of your inner experience of conflict.
2. Center yourself.
3. Identify your feelings involved in the conflict.
4. Identify your typical responses in conflict situations.
5. Diagnose the nature of the conflict.
6. Decide how to approach the conflict.
7. Establish ground rules for dealing with the conflict.

Step 1:
Become Aware of Your Inner Experience of Conflict

When we asked students and workshop participants how they know when they are in a conflict, they consistently respond with descriptions of physical symptoms such as a tight stomach, sweaty palms, dizziness, or rapid breathing. The discovery that conflict begins inside them with physical symptoms is an important awareness for most people, particularly since they believed that conflict begins "out there" and do not realize they are disconnected from their internal experiences. As soon as they perceive a conflict in progress their focus immediately shifts into a defense mode such as fight, flight, or freeze, which takes them further away from their inner experience of conflict. The first skill learned to repattern this autonomic response mechanism is centering. Use Step 1 of Worksheet #1 at the end of this chapter to help you become aware of your inner experience during conflict situations.

Step 2: Center Yourself

Centering is a concept drawn from Eastern philosophies, particularly martial arts such as kung fu, tai chi chuan, and aikido. It is a mental process used to focus your energy so you can "stop the world" for a moment and relax. Centering will enable you to stay calm while resolving a conflict and allows for a moment to explore the options before taking action. It is especially useful in interrupting the autonomic fight/flight/freeze responses. Step 2 of Worksheet #1 is useful in learning how to center yourself in conflict situations.

Step 3:
Identify Your Feelings Involved in the Conflict

Most people categorize feelings as "good" and "bad." In fact, all feelings are useful and serve important functions in maintaining your mental health. If you can determine what you are feeling, you will know more about what you need in a conflict situation. Teaching people to identify the functions of different feelings is an important part of conflict resolution, yet it has been overlooked by many professionals. Understanding that each

feeling has a purpose helps eliminate self-destructive thinking when "bad" feelings erupt.

Most people do not understand the true function of feelings. Let's look at the function of each of the six basic feelings: anger, fear, sadness, shame, excitement, and happiness. Table 4.2 describes the function of each of these feelings. Bear in mind that there are gradations of each of these feelings, such as frustration, which is a form of anger; despair, which is a form of sadness; embarrassment, which is a form of shame; and panic, which is an extreme form of fear. The following discussion is adapted from Weinhold & Weinhold (1989).

Once you understand the function of these feelings and their critical role in understanding your internal experiences, it is easy to see how feelings function in conflicts. This helps you shift into an attitude of compassion and kindness toward yourself and others in conflict situations.

Anger is the most common feeling people have during a conflict. The function of anger is to tell you that there is something you feel you need that you don't have. When someone is angry with you, you can assume that the other person needs something from you. You can de-escalate a conflict by simply asking the other person what they need from you. This can be a very powerful response. People don't consciously know what they need or want. When asked what they need, they must think about it. This often shifts them out of their feelings and into a more cognitive state. This question can help them identify their needs and integrate their thinking and feeling states.

Table 4.2
Basic Feelings and Their Functions

Feeling	Function
1. Anger	This is a natural response to not getting your wants or needs met. People who feel afraid to ask directly for what they need may act angry instead. Through intimidation, they may be able to get what they want without asking directly. When you are feeling angry, it is important to ask yourself, "What am I wanting or needing?"
2. Fear	This is a natural response to perceived danger or the anticipated loss of something important. When a person feels afraid, it is important to determine if the perceived danger is real. People also use fear to cover up their anger because they were punished for expressing it when they were children.
3. Sadness	This is a natural response to the loss of a person, object, or relationship (real or fantasized). It is the result of giving up something to which you were attached. You may also feel anger with the experience of loss because some of your needs and wants may no longer get met.
4. Shame	This is a natural response to violating some personal or social limit about what is appropriate. Healthy shame helps us monitor our behavior in public situations and also helps form our ethical code. Toxic shame is different from guilt. Guilt means having done something wrong, while shame means that there is something intrinsically wrong with us.
5. Excitement	This is a natural response to anticipating that something good will happen to you. Fear and excitement are often closely related. Some people never received permission as children to show excitement and instead feel embarrassed at their own excitement.
6. Happiness/Joy	These are natural responses to getting what you want or need, or for doing something effectively. Some people do not know it is okay to be happy. They may be addicted to struggle.

One of us (Barry) had an experience that really reinforced this principle:

> I had a conflict with a colleague who was teaching the course that was a prerequisite for one of my courses. Without telling me, he decided to change textbooks and the structure of the class. When I came to my first class, I told the students how this course would build on the material they had learned in the prerequisite course. The students all looked at me with puzzlement and said, "We never learned any of that." I felt really foolish.
>
> I called my colleague the next morning and asked him if what the students had told me was true. He said it was. Then I explained how I expected students to have a certain foundation of information when they began my course and that I would have to provide this material before I could teach my course. I asked him why he didn't tell me he had changed his course content, and he said he forgot. I said, "I'm really angry at you." He replied, "Well, what do you need from me?" This question stopped me cold. I thought for a minute and said, "First of all, I'd like to just be angry a little longer (as I hadn't yet gotten all the anger out of my system)." He said, "I could probably handle a few more minutes of your anger, if you need to stay angry a little longer."
>
> I thought about what I needed and said, "First, I'd like an apology for not telling me about changing your course, and second, I want you to promise that you won't do this again." He apologized and promised that he wouldn't. I noticed that after I had gotten what I needed, it was difficult for me to stay angry. Our conflict was over in less than 10 minutes. Had he not asked me what I needed from him or gotten defensive, the conflict could have easily escalated.

In a conflict situation in which someone is angry with you, it's really important to remember that the person's anger means she or he needs something from you. Don't try to guess what it is. Just ask them directly, "What do you need from me?" Conversely, when you feel angry at another person, ask yourself, "What do I need from this person?" This allows you to process your anger before engaging a conflict. You not only have a much better possibility of getting your needs met this way but have a better chance of a peaceful, win-win resolution to the conflict.

Another feeling commonly encountered in a conflict situation is sadness. You can process your feelings of sadness during a conflict by asking, "What have I lost or expect to lose in this conflict?" or "Does this conflict have a post-traumatic aspect to it? Does it remind me of something I lost in the past?"

The third feeling during conflict is fear. The function of fear is to tell you that you are anticipating the loss of something that you now have or that you have already lost something. If the fear is associated with an anticipated loss, it may be related to post-traumatic symptoms from earlier conflicts where you did lose something. You might fear the loss of freedom, respect, a relationship, or even your life.

Sometimes you may feel a mixture of sadness and anger in a conflict situation. The anger comes from not getting a need met, while the sadness tells you that something you once had is gone. When these two feelings become intertwined in a conflict situation, you need to separate them before you can effectively deal with them.

Excitement helps you anticipate getting something that you want or need, while happiness lets you know that you have gotten it. These two feelings may also be difficult to experience. They kindle feelings of hope, particularly that the unpleasant experiences of the past will not return. Having the feeling of hope dashed is very painful, so painful that many people would rather not hope for something better and feel hopeless about the future.

Understanding the functions of these primary feelings, both in yourself and in other people, will enable you to resolve conflicts more easily and more peacefully. Most other models of conflict resolution address intense feelings by advising people to take time and calm down. The opposite is often true. Feelings can open people to deeper states of awareness, particularly those containing post-traumatic memories.

Use Step 3 of Worksheet #1 to identify your typical feeling responses in conflict situations. It is important to determine how the feelings you currently experience in a conflict are related to past conflict situations. Post-traumatic stress symptoms from a previous conflict may be playing a role in your present conflict. If this is the case, remember to feel kindness and compassion for yourself. This will help you return to center so that you can determine your options in the conflict.

Step 4: Identify Your Post-Traumatic Responses in Conflict Situations

This step helps identify the presence of post-traumatic responses during conflict situations: fight, flight, or freeze. What is your typical response to conflict and might it influence how you approach a conflict? Does your typical response catapult you into post-traumatic states in which you repeat or reexperience conflicts from the past? If you find any such connections, you might consider seeking out trauma reduction therapy to help desensitize yourself to the cues or signals that activate these feelings and responses. Step 4 of Worksheet #1 will help you identify your post-traumatic responses in conflict situations.

Step 5: Diagnose the Nature of the Conflict

Identifying the nature of a conflict is critical, as there are two distinctly different methods for resolving conflicts. One works best with conflicts of wants and needs and the other works best with conflicts of values and beliefs. How do you tell the difference between a conflict of wants and needs and a conflict of values and beliefs?

Generally, you can tell the difference by determining if the conflict has tangible effects on you. If you can identify some concrete or tangible effects, then you are probably dealing with a conflict of wants and needs. If you cannot find any tangible effects of the conflict on you or the effects are minimal, it is likely that you are involved in a conflict of values and beliefs. If, for example, someone commits to do something and then does not do it, this has a tangible effect on your relationship. If someone else values orderliness, while you are comfortable with clutter, you may have a conflict of values and beliefs. Chapter 5 describes the Eight-Step Process for Resolving Conflicts of Wants and Needs. Chapter 6 describes the Seven-Step Process for Resolving Conflicts of Values and Beliefs. Use Step 5 of Worksheet #1 to help determine the nature of a conflict.

Step 6: Decide How to Approach the Conflict

There are four effective options for approaching conflict. The option you choose should depend on the nature of the conflict, the situation in which the conflict occurs, and the willingness of the other person to resolve it in a cooperative, partnership way. To make this determination, you must first engage the energy of the other person(s). Then you can assess the situation and choose an appropriate course of action. Remember to consider each option from an attitude of kindness and compassion, which will have a powerful influence on the outcome you experience. The four options are:

Option 1: Deal directly with the person(s) with whom you have conflict. Attempt first to resolve it as a conflict of wants and needs. If the conflict does not seem completely resolved when you have finished using Worksheet #2, then attempt to resolve it as a conflict of values and beliefs. If the conflict still does not feel resolved, particularly if it is a conflict with an intimate partner, then attempt to resolve it at the source using Worksheets #4 and #5.

Option 2: Deflect the conflict by stepping aside and deciding not to encounter it. You may experience the other person as over-reactive, aggressive, too escalated, or unsafe to resolve conflict with. This person gives you reason to believe they are unwilling or unable to seek out a partnership solution to the conflict. Sometimes these people are like "freight trains." The smart thing to do when being approached by a freight train is get off the tracks. Rather than engaging out-of-control people, move to Option #3.

Option 3: Deepen your self-awareness by working alone on the conflict. When the other person is unwilling or unable to work cooperatively and peacefully to resolve a conflict, you can deepen your own awareness by asking yourself questions such as: "What can I learn about myself from this conflict? What is this person bringing to me that can help me heal some aspect of a past trauma or can show me some part of myself that I have difficulty seeing?"

There seems to be a mythical place called "Central Casting," an agency with an unlimited supply of actors who are sent into people's lives as often as needed until they learn their lessons. If, for example, you never learned how to deal with people in authority, the director at Central Casting will continue to send authoritarian people into your life until you learn how to effectively deal with them.

Central Casting's supply of authoritarian actors is unlimited. If the current version comes and you say, "No thanks, I don't want to deal with this guy—he's a jerk," other jerks will continue to appear you until you learn to deal with them. Then you may move to a new unresolved issue and they will send another kind of person. For example, if you don't know how to deal with passive people, you may find a series of passive people coming into your life. The important thing is to transform your conflict into an opportunity to discover the "gift" this person is bringing you.

With this option, it isn't necessary to have direct conflicts with people. You can just look at your reactions to people and learn something about yourself. You can ask yourself compassionately, "What is it about this person that is creating my response? What does my reaction tell me about myself?" You can, of course, think to yourself, "Isn't she an awful person? Why doesn't he stop doing that? Don't they know better?" Choosing these critical and judgmental responses helps you focus on what the other person is doing or not doing and prevents you from learning much about yourself.

Using this option, the whole world can become your mirror. Your internal reactions, judgments, biases, prejudices, overreactions, and conflicts become metaphors similar to those described earlier in the medicine wheel teachings. Everything that happens becomes an opportunity for self-discovery.

Option 4: Discover the sources of your conflicts by looking at elements of past traumatic events that might be recycling in your present conflict experiences. Finding a partner who is equally committed to identifying the sources of a current conflict is extremely helpful, but you can also work alone, looking for patterns in your conflicts, such as betrayal, abandonment, abuse, or neglect. These feelings, beliefs, and dynamics fit into a theme or story containing dramatic or life-threatening elements.

For example, your best friend turns your partner against you and you lose your relationship with them both. This kind of pattern may be a replay of an abandonment dynamic between you and your parents. Perhaps you had a really close relationship with your mother until your parents got divorced. When your mother remarried and focused her attention on her new husband, you lost the love of both your parents. Whatever the source, remember that post-traumatic stress responses are out of your conscious control. Develop compassion for yourself while you are changing your behaviors and becoming conscious of your actions.

Step 7: Establish Ground Rules for Dealing with the Conflict Situation

It is important to make some agreements with your partner in a conflict situation regarding the procedures you will use to resolve your conflict. Effective ground rules at the end of this chapter can help you create safety and structure during the resolution of a conflict. In most instances, you will have more skills in resolving conflicts than the other person(s). This can be a challenge, because you hold both the intention of resolving the conflict in a peaceful, cooperative way while simultaneously guiding the process. If the other person is open to learning these skills, then it is a bit easier.

Having a set of prescribed protocols and procedures such as the Worksheets can make conflict resolution easier. Couples and students who get into conflict after learning the Partnership Way often report saying to each other, "Okay, let's get out the worksheets." Using the ground rules and the appropriate worksheets, they guide themselves through the conflict.

PARTNERSHIP WORKSHEET #1: HOW TO PREPARE FOR A CONFLICT

Step 1: The Inner Experience of Conflict

Using a current conflict, fill in the blanks below to help you better prepare for entering a conflict resolution session.

I know that I am in a conflict because _____
(the signals I experience internally: tight stomach, mind goes blank, sweaty palms, dizziness, rapid breathing).

Where I feel this conflict in my body is _____
(place where I feel the conflict)

The feelings which go with these internal responses are _____
(anger, fear, sadness, shame, guilt, hurt).

Identify the aspects of this current conflict that have evoked these feelings. _____

I remember feeling this way before when _____
(identify aspects of previous conflict situations that may indicate symptoms of post traumatic-stress).

Step 2: Centering

Physical centering involves a mental refocusing of your energy. The concept can be demonstrated with a simple activity involving two people. The first person, who is learning to be centered, stands with his or her feet about shoulder-width apart and knees slightly bent but not locked. This person then focuses his or her thoughts on a conflict situation. The second person stands facing the side of the first person so that they make a 90-degree angle. The second person gently uses the right hand to gently apply pressure on the first person's back. As the second person gradually applies more pressure on the first person's back, the first person will feel uncentered and begin to fall forward. Now the second person repeats this process by gently using the left hand to apply pressure to the other person's upper chest to see if they will begin to fall backwards as well. Notice if there are any differences between the way the person learning to be centered responds when pushed from the back versus being pushed from the front.

Next, the person learning to be centered focuses his or her thoughts on about two inches below the navel near the physical center of gravity. To assist in this focusing, it is useful for the first person to place one hand on this area of the abdomen while the other person again applies pressure on the upper back and then the upper chest of the first person. Both people should see a noticeable difference. The person who is centered should feel very solid and strong without having to exert any extra energy. The person who is pushing with one hand should find that their partner is no longer a "push over."

Taking part in this activity helps people physically feel an experience of centering. Once this state of awareness is physically anchored in the body, it is easy to return to by taking a deep breath and focusing on the center of gravity in the abdomen. If you return to this state during conflict situations, you'll find it easier to think quickly and flow with the unfolding elements of the conflict.

Centering can be useful even when you are not in a conflict. You can take a deep breath and direct your breath into an area of your body where you feel some tension. As you breathe into this tense place, visualize the tension lessening. When it releases, place the palm of your hand at your center of gravity two inches below your navel and then refocus your attention. Breathe into this area of your belly area while simultaneously visualizing your energy going down toward your feet to firmly anchor them in the Earth. Let yourself feel the flow of energy between the Earth's core and your whole body. Notice how your body feels when you breathe and visualize in this way so that you can train yourself to quickly move to your body's natural center when you are about to enter a conflict.

Step 3: Identifying Your Feelings Involved in the Conflict

Using the same conflict as before, fill in the blanks with the appropriate feeling that you identified in the "How to Identify Feelings in a Conflict" exercise.

When I think of this conflict, I feel _____
(name of feeling).

When I identify this feeling, it tells me _____
(identify the function of this feeling).

Step 4: Identifying Post-Traumatic Responses in Conflict Situations

Using the same current conflict, fill in the blanks below to identify your typical responses in a conflict situation.

The way that I typically deal with these feelings and body symptoms is _____
(describe your usual response in a conflict situation, noting any symptoms of post-traumatic stress).

Step 5: Diagnosing the Nature of the Conflict

Using the same current conflict, fill in the blanks below to help you diagnose the nature of the conflict.

The way that this conflict affects me is _____
(more tangible effects of conflict on me = needs/wants conflict;
few or no tangible effects of conflict on me = values/belief conflict).

This conflict reminds me of other conflicts from the past in the following ways: _____

Step 6: Deciding How to Approach the Conflict

There are four main options for approaching a conflict. Decide which option best fits the conflict situation with which you have been working.

Option 1: Deal directly with the person with whom you have the conflict.

- Use Worksheet #1 (Chapter 4) to get yourself ready to approach the conflict.
- Use Worksheet #2 (Chapter 5) for conflicts of wants and needs.
- Use Worksheet #3 (Chapter 6) for conflicts of values and beliefs.
- If these Worksheets do not help resolve the conflict, go to Option #4 and use Worksheets #4 and #5 (Chapters 7, 8, 9, 10, and 12).

Option 2: Deflect the conflict by stepping aside and deciding not to encounter the conflict. The opponent is too powerful, is overreacting, or aggressive or someone you feel unsafe to work with on conflicts.

- Use Worksheets #4 and #5 to determine what in you draws you into conflict with this kind of person(s) so that you can identify the source of the conflict and resolve it.

Option 3: Deepen your awareness. Work alone on the conflict because the other person is unwilling or unable to work on it with you.

- Use Worksheets #4 and #5 to deepen your awareness of your part in the conflict.

Option 4: Discover the sources of your conflict by looking at your past and your unfinished business in previous relationships. Work with a partner who will help you get to the sources of the conflict.

- Use Worksheets #4 and #5 to help you discover the sources of your conflict and deal with the unresolved elements of the conflict at its source.

Step 7: Establish Ground Rules for Dealing with the Conflict Situation

- Agree on a time frame for the conflict resolution session. If a resolution has not been reached in the allotted time, renegotiate for more time or reschedule.
- Each person states his or her perceptions of the conflict. Get an agreement on what the conflict is before trying to resolve it.
- Each person shares a desired outcome. Ask: "How would you like to have this conflict resolved?"
- Take turns presenting the problem according to the instructions on Worksheets #2, #3, #4, or #5.
- Avoid complaining and ask for what you want directly from the other person(s) involved. If someone seems to be complaining, ask them what they want from you.
- If there are obvious projections present, deal with those first. Using the instructions on Worksheet #5, have each person directly address the person(s) with whom they had the original conflict (usually parents) and have another person role-play them. Then deal with any present-time elements of the conflict that are left over, if any.
- Agree to test any new agreements for a specified time to see if they will work.
- Learn to accept relapses. The old behaviors that caused the conflict may not change immediately. If that happens, ask the person who has a relapse what she/he wants or needs to be successful in changing his/her behavior.
- Agree to get back together at the earliest possible time if the agreement needs to be modified.

Chapter 5
~
How Can I Use the Partnership Way to Resolve Conflicts of Wants and Needs?

If the issue about which you are in conflict has a tangible, concrete effect on you, then it is likely you are having a conflict of wants and needs. For example, if you have scheduled a lunch with a friend and you set a date for noon, you expect to meet her at 12:00. You arrive at 12:00 and she has not, so you wait. You only have an hour for lunch and begin to feel angry by 12:15 p.m. By 12:30, you feel uncertain about whether to order or to wait for her to show up. She doesn't call, doesn't let you know why she is late, she just doesn't show up. This is a conflict of wants and needs, because you wanted to have lunch with her. You wanted to have your lunch and be back at work on time at 1:00 p.m. You ended up gulping down your lunch and being late getting back to your workplace. This experience causes a conflict with tangible effects on you.

Returning to the same scenario, depending on the nature of your relationship, you may question whether it is worthwhile to try to reschedule lunch with her. You might not want to. You may consider the tangible long-term effects of this lunch experience on your relationship with her. You may not feel as close to her. You may not want to do things with her after she broke your agreement without renegotiating. Until you determine why she was late and did not call, these thoughts may run through your mind.

Maybe she had an unforeseen delay, such as a traffic accident, that kept her from calling. When she does call she may say, "Gee, I'm very sorry, I wish I could have called. I wasn't in a position to call. I don't have a cell phone, and I was caught in traffic. I'm really sorry; I know this inconvenienced you. Let's try it again, and lunch will be on me." Such circumstances may make the conflict less serious than you originally thought.

Your friend may not call and just "blow off" your appointment. This may indicate your conflict involves values and beliefs. Perhaps she does not value friendships or keeping agreements as much as you do. This conflict may qualify as one of both wants and needs and values and beliefs. If it is not resolved at these levels, it may be necessary to resolve it "at the source," an even deeper kind of resolution.

HOW CAN I DETERMINE IF IT IS A CONFLICT OF WANTS AND NEEDS OR VALUES AND BELIEFS?

Unlike conflicts of wants and needs, conflicts of values and beliefs have less immediate and less tangible effects. An issue that often causes conflicts of values and beliefs is cleanliness. Conflict over cleanliness typically occurs between roommates, couples, or parents and children. Consider the following scenario: A mother and her teenage son are in conflict because the son does not want to clean his room. Mom walks down the hall and sees through the open door of her son's room that it is a disaster—clothing and food all over the floor, the bed unmade. She walks into the room and trips over a pair of shoes. She tells her son he's grounded until he cleans up his room! The son responds, "But Mom, it's my room! I think I have the right to keep it the way I want it." They get into a power struggle over who is right or has the most authority over the son's room.

Now imagine yourself as the mother in this scenario. What are the tangible consequences for you if your son doesn't clean up his room? There could be bugs or ants if there's old food left in the room. That's a tangible consequence. Let's suppose things haven't gone that far, but you fear that food will be left there. That is not a tangible consequence. The fact is, your son has a different standard of cleanliness for his room than you do. As the mother, you would need to ask yourself, "Does my son's messy room really affect me in a tangible way? I can close the door and not see it, and if I don't have to clean it up, it doesn't tangibly affect me. It is his room." In reality, there are no tangible effects on the mother in this situation. The conflict is one of values and beliefs.

Early in a conflict, you need to diagnose its nature to determine if it is a conflict of wants and needs or values and beliefs. Be aware that the diagnosis may not be as clear as in the scenarios presented here. A situation may have elements of both kinds of conflicts. When you suspect that both types of elements are present, it is useful to approach the conflict initially as a conflict of wants and needs because it is usually a little easier to resolve. If you have any doubt as to whether the conflict has been resolved, look to see if there's a conflict of values and beliefs beneath the conflict of wants and needs. Conflicts are often complex, frequently having hidden layers that only emerge when you search deeply. Determining the tangibility of effects is a useful guidelines

HOW CAN I USE A PARTNERSHIP APPROACH TO RESOLVE MY CONFLICTS OF WANTS AND NEEDS?

The remainder of this chapter describes an effective process for resolving conflicts of wants and needs using the Partnership Way. Usually the person feeling in conflict should initiate its resolution. If that person doesn't have win-win skills in conflict resolution and the other person

does, the latter should take the lead. You can begin to prepare for a face-to-face conflict resolution session by first completing Worksheet #1 at the end of Chapter 4.

The success or failure of your efforts to find a cooperative resolution to your conflict of wants and needs will depend on how well you completed Worksheet #1. It will help you clarify your inner experience of conflict, center yourself, identify your feelings involved in the conflict, and determine your typical responses to conflict situations. Following completion of the worksheet, you will need to decide if the conflict involves wants and needs or values and beliefs. Once you have taken these steps, you must decide how to approach the conflict. Worksheet #2 at the end of this chapter will guide you through a direct encounter with the person or persons involved in a conflict of wants and needs, should you decide to approach the conflict in that way. Chapter 6 presents a method for resolving conflicts of values and beliefs. Note that before you begin any conflict resolution session, it is important to set some ground rules before you start, including time limits and general agreements about avoiding "blame and complain" strategies.

THE CONFLICT RESOLUTION SESSION: A REVIEW OF AN EIGHT-STEP METHOD FOR RESOLVING CONFLICTS OF WANTS AND NEEDS

Step 1: Objective Description of the Conflict

Worksheet #2 asks you to objectively describe your perception of the problem or conflict to the other person. It is important to avoid any inflammatory statements or name calling such as, "You are such a slob for not cleaning up your dishes," or black-and-white statements such as, "You are *always* leaving your dishes for me to clean up, and you *never* lift a hand to clean up after yourself."

Focus your description of the problem on the other person's *behavior* rather than on him or her as a person: "I notice that your dishes from last night are still in the sink" versus "I guess your arms must be broken or something because you didn't clean up your dishes again last night." Focusing on the problem can be difficult when you are having strong feelings, which is why it is important to center yourself before the conflict resolution session. Remember that you both may be experiencing symptoms of post-traumatic stress and need to develop an attitude of kindness toward yourself and the other person. It may also be difficult for the person you are confronting to perceive you objectively. If you notice that the other person becomes immediately defensive, you may have to shift to Step Six and reflect his or her feelings ("You seem pretty upset that I would mention this problem that I am having"). If the person relaxes a bit after you say that, you may be able to return to Step One. If the other person does not relax immediately, continue giving reflective feedback until he or she does or postpone resolving the conflict until they have calmed down.

Step 2: State Your Feelings

Worksheet #2 asks you to express your feelings regarding the behavior of the other person that is preventing you from meeting your needs. It is important to remember the functions of different feelings and to express those feelings in a functional way It is more effective to say, "I feel unvalued when you don't keep your agreements with me" than to either escalate your feelings or express them critically or accusingly. Saying "I hate you" or "I feel that you don't love me" would be escalation, a form of "dirty fighting."

Step 3: Describe the Tangible Effects

Describe how the other person's behavior tangibly keeps you from getting your need(s) met. Your description should be objective and straightforward. In the example given in Worksheet #2, the tangible effect would be having to clean and remove the other person's dishes in order to use the sink. This effect, in addition to being quite tangible, would be visible to the other person. Other effects such as damage to your trust or to your feelings of closeness would not be as visible and would therefore be less effective.

Step 4: State What You Want in Order to Resolve the Conflict

It is important to take responsibility by telling the other person what you need in order to resolve the conflict. Without this step, you might imply that it is the other person's responsibility to suggest a resolution to your part of the conflict, therefore taking care of your needs. Such a transaction would invite inappropriate caretaking and win-lose or lose-lose conflict resolution. When you tell the other person what you want as a resolution, you are giving that person the choice of either accepting your resolution, if it meets his or her needs as well, or coming up with an alternative resolution.

Step 5: Ask for What You Want

Even though you have stated what you want or need, you still have to ask the other person directly for what you want and need. These first five steps provide the other person with all the information he or she needs to respond to your request. By asking directly for what you want and need from the other person, you make it possible for him or her to directly respond to your needs. This person then has the responsibility to decide if your request meets his or her needs. This kind of exchange conveys a clear message that says, "I am willing to take responsibility for meeting my needs and I invite you to do the same."

Step 6: Use Reflective Listening, if Necessary

This step may not be necessary if the first five steps of this process are clearly communicated. At sometime during the process, however, it may be useful to stop and check with your partner to see how he or she is feeling. Some people may "over adapt" when involved in this kind of structured session. People who do so may not tell you until much later that they didn't like what was happening and didn't feel strong or courageous enough to say so at the time. Even if the process seems to be moving along with ease, it is good to stop at Step Six and check in with your partner. It is important to listen to the other person's side of the conflict, even if they have agreed to your request. If your partner does not agree with your suggested resolution, it is essential that you listen to your partner's feelings and perceptions, asking for a resolution that meets his or her needs, too. Avoid getting defensive if the other person does not like your suggested resolution. Ask in an attitude of kindness and compassion, "What would better meet your needs? I'm open to your suggestions."

Step 7: Negotiate, if Necessary

This step involves a negotiation process in which each person is free to state his or her needs and suggest resolutions that would effectively meet those needs. If the earlier steps were completed effectively, you will likely find a mutually agreeable win-win resolution to your conflict and not need to negotiate. Sometimes the conflict resolution process may bog down here. You may need to take a break or schedule another session so you can have an opportunity to think about other options before finally resolving the conflict.

Step 8: Agree to Disagree, if Necessary, or Move to Other Worksheets

This step is necessary only if you and/or your partner gets into an, "I'd rather be right than win" position. If you become unable to find a win-win resolution to your conflict, you have a couple of choices. First, you can agree to disagree and talk about how your lack of agreement might create barriers in your relationship. Understanding the impact of these barriers on your relationship may activate a shift that makes it possible for both of you to seek a win-win resolution.

Another choice is for you to shift focus. If you seem stuck in your attempts to resolve the conflict as one of wants and needs, continue on to Worksheet #3 to see if your conflict might involve values and beliefs. If you do not resolve your conflict at that level, you can go even deeper into the conflict and use Worksheets # 4 and # 5 to help find the sources of your conflict.

SKILL PRACTICE EXERCISE: RESOLVING CONFLICTS OF WANTS AND NEEDS THE PARTNERSHIP WAY

1. Choose a partner with whom to role-play a current conflict of wants and needs that you are experiencing. This experience will give you a chance to rehearse before you actually confront the person with whom you are in conflict.

2. Use a current conflict that is not resolved. It doesn't have to be the biggest conflict you've ever had in your life, but one that seems to have some tangible effects on you. Your role-play conflict needs to be one you can use when you go to the other person to resolve the conflict. If the person doesn't have the same information or skills that you have, you will have to take the lead. Also, don't pick a conflict where you're sure the person wouldn't sit down with you to resolve it or one where you're sure that they would roll right over you like a freight train.

3. Briefly describe your conflict to your role-play partner so that they can get into the role.

4. Follow the step-by-step process described below to role-play a resolution to your conflict. In role-playing the conflict, you may develop some new skills and insights that are useful when you work directly with the person with whom you have the real conflict.

5. Debrief the role-playing session. Discuss what new insights you gained by doing the rehearsal. Plan a strategy with your partner for dealing with the actual person involved in the conflict.

   Alternate Step: You may want to include a third person as a mediator to help you follow the worksheet correctly. The mediator's task is to help you stay on track with the steps.

6. Now reverse roles. The person with the conflict now becomes the partner and the partner now works on his or her own conflict.

7. Make plans to apply your learning in a real conflict situation by preparing for an anticipated conflict of wants and needs or by confronting someone with whom you have a current conflict of wants and needs.

PARTNERSHIP WORKSHEET #2:
EIGHT-STEP METHOD FOR RESOLVING CONFLICTS OF WANTS AND NEEDS

Step 1: Describe objectively your perception of the problem or behavior. Begin with "I" statements. Avoid using harsh or judgmental language, "you" statements, threatening body language, or a strident voice. For example, you might begin with, "I noticed that you didn't clean up your dishes after you ate last night."

Step 2: Share the way you feel toward the person or problem. Keep your focus internally, specifically on your inner experience of the conflict to help you stay centered so that you do not escalate or lose your objectivity. Continuing with the above example, you might say, "I felt angry with you when I saw the dishes sitting there."

Step 3: Describe the tangible effects or results of the problem or issue on you and/or your relationship. Speak authentically in such a way that helps the other person realize that their behavior has created a consequence for them that affects the bond or connection you feel toward him or her. Here you tell the other person how what they did affected you by saying, "When I had to clean up your dishes in order to use the sink, I didn't feel close to you and I didn't look forward to being with you tonight."

Step 4: State directly what it is you want from the other person. Formulate this request ahead of time in your mind so that you can speak precisely. Be prepared to enter into a negotiation process, if necessary, to get your need met by having a series of options or solutions that might be acceptable. Emphasize how much you value and care for the other person by saying, "What I want is to be able to feel close to you and in order to do that, I want you to keep your agreement to clean up your dishes after you eat."

Step 5: Ask the person directly for what you want. Asking directly gives the other person a choice. When people have choice, they are more likely to act cooperatively and be willing to negotiate with you if your initial suggestion is not acceptable to them. You need to ask directly, "Would you be willing to do that?" Be prepared for a refusal of cooperation with the question, "Well, what would you be willing to do?"

Step 6: Use reflective listening. At this point, the other person will likely give you an explanation for their behavior. Repeat back what you hear them say so that they feel heard and understood before you go onto the next step. Avoid getting bogged down here by defending yourself, blaming them, complaining about them, or escalating by bringing in other issues. Focus on your feelings of compassion and caring for the other person as you reflect back what you think they are feeling. You can say to them, "When I get angry about these things, you look like you are feeling hurt and angry. Is this true?" Once you have reflected back their statement, you may want to return to your original question: "Would you be willing to do that?"

Step 7: Negotiate if there are differences between what you want and what the other person is willing to give. If the other person refuses to cooperate with your initial request, ask them, "What would you be willing to do?"

Step 8: If you are unable to negotiate the differences, look for other sources of the conflict. In this case, you may have to agree to disagree and invite the other person to join you in exploring the conflict further. You might say, "I see that we just don't agree on this issue, and I accept our disagreement. Would you also agree that we can't find a win-win solution at this time?" Or you might say to the other person, "Would you be willing to explore our differences further by looking for possible conflicts of values or beliefs or other possible sources of this conflict?" This would involve using Worksheets #3, #4, and #5 to help explore the deeper elements of the conflict.

Chapter 6

~

How Can I Use the Partnership Way to Resolve Conflicts of Values and Beliefs?

Finding a Partnership Way to resolve conflicts of values and beliefs seemed like an impossible task when we began our study of conflict resolution. When we asked the leading experts on conflict resolution how they resolved conflicts of values and beliefs, they usually shrugged their shoulders or shook their heads indicating that they couldn't help us. When we searched the literature seeking ideas for resolving conflicts of values and beliefs from a win-win perspective, our search came up empty. Most wars and intractable conflicts throughout history have been fought over differences of values and beliefs, so we knew how important our search was. In spite of our lack of success, we persisted in searching for an answer.

Finally, we found the missing key. Barry was once asked to mediate a conflict between two men who were serving as volunteers in our Institute at that time. In the process, he found the missing key. Barry recalls this critical event:

David and Eldon (not their real names) were co-chairs of the planning committee for our second international conference on conflict resolution. During one of our executive committee meetings, these two men got into a conflict that quickly escalated into a shouting match. I offered to mediate the conflict. As they continued in their conflict, I saw that their argument appeared to center on a disagreement regarding leadership styles. David wanted to organize the steering committee by assigning tasks to the members, while Eldon wanted the committee members to volunteer for their tasks.

They both seemed very upset over this issue, which I didn't perceive as a big deal. Mostly out of curiosity, I asked each to reflect for a moment on the conflict. As they reflected, I asked them to see if the other person reminded them of someone from their past. This question seemed to spark a new awareness in David. He said, "Eldon reminds me of my mother, who always seemed to be telling me that I wasn't doing it right." He looked very sad as he recounted several incidents where she had undermined his attempts to do something effectively. This revelation apparently touched Eldon. He began to remember a boss who was very controlling and replied, "David reminds me of my former college dean, who always demanded that I do everything his way." Then he lowered his head and began to sob. Between sobs, Eldon said, "And that is the way my dad treated me as well. I had forgotten how painful it was for me to assert myself with him."

This new information caused an immediate shift in both men. They seemed more compassionate toward each other and wanted to know how the other had dealt with these situations in the past. Both reported feeling powerless to change the outcome of the situations involving their parents. They saw how and why they had gotten triggered but decided that their present situation was different and began searching for a win-win solution. As they talked further, they agreed to structure the tasks as David had suggested, but they would present them to the committee as options that could be changed and give committee members an opportunity to change their assigned task if they so desired. This resolution was satisfactory to both men, and they hugged each other as they left the meeting. It was amazing to see their adversarial behaviors change so quickly into kindness and cooperation.

As I watched their dialogue unfold in this unexpected way, I began to wonder if most of our values and beliefs are tied to past experiences that continue to influence us in the present. These past experiences may have been traumatic, leaving some mark on our memory. Any values and beliefs formed out of these highly emotional experiences may also carry some of our unmet needs. In the situation with these two men, neither had confronted the persons involved in his conflicts from the past, leaving him feeling helpless and hopeless. Without an awareness of how earlier experiences might be connected to forming a belief or value, it would be very hard, if not impossible, to change that value or belief.

We began further experiments with this idea and found that in a safe environment many people can identify the previous experiences that helped them form their values and beliefs. This awareness was the breakthrough for which we had been looking. It led directly to the development of our partnership process for resolving conflicts of values and beliefs.

Values and beliefs have a collective aspect. They are formed during childhood through experiences in our family of origin, neighborhood, school, church, community, culture, and nation and help us locate our niche in the larger world. They are often used as tools for creating an identity related to membership in particular groups, such as male/female, adults/children, Caucasians/people of color, North Americans/Europeans, old/young, and rich/poor. Values and beliefs can also be used to create separation, conflict, and even wars about whose beliefs are "right" and whose are "wrong." Because of the universal nature of values and beliefs within each one of us, it is difficult to both identify and change our values and beliefs. Changing our values and beliefs raises the risk of feeling outside or excluded from social and professional peers. The formative experiences that led to the development of values and beliefs may be less difficult to uncover.

Conflicts involving values and beliefs are some of the most difficult to resolve and require a very different approach than that for resolving conflicts of wants and needs. Resolving conflicts of values and beliefs requires a shift in perception and the ability to understand another person without attempting to change his/her value or belief. We found that this shift in perception and this capacity for understanding emerges most quickly when the people in the conflict can identify the foundational experiences that helped them form their values and beliefs. When these two criteria are met, the power struggles over who is "right" and who is "wrong" diminish.

HOW CAN I DISTINGUISH BETWEEN VALUES, BELIEFS, AND PREFERENCES?

Many interpersonal conflicts are about values and beliefs. In the Partnership Way, a different approach is used for resolving conflicts of wants and needs than for resolving conflicts of values and beliefs. We may know what needs are, but the meanings of values, beliefs, or preferences are more abstract. In this approach, we adhere to the following definitions.

A *value* is discerned or evident in your behavior, is freely chosen and acted on after considering viable alternatives, and brings possible meaning and purpose to your life. Values are usually formed over time as a result of testing out your ideas, preferences, and beliefs. Some values are imposed upon you or are learned as the result of negative or conflictual personal experiences. A value must meet the following criteria:

- It is recognizable in one's behavior.
- It is freely chosen from among one or more viable alternatives.
- It provides the person with positive meaning or purpose in his or her life.
- It is always prioritized, so some values are more important to a person than others.
- It is formed out of experiences from the person's past.

A *belief* is a choice or a decision to accept a statement, truth, or fact without direct personal experience or observation, based upon the testimony or work of another person or a source that you trust. Common sources of beliefs are gossip, secondhand information, and parental stories. Beliefs also come from cultural myths or from religious texts such as the Koran, Bible, or Torah. Beliefs usually create a philosophical foundation that people use for moral guidance and direction in their lives (Katz & Lawyer, 1985).

A *preference* is also a choice, but it doesn't imply a certain value or belief. Preferences are everyday choices; people may, for example, prefer chicken to steak, blue to red, or baseball to basketball. Although preferences bring some satisfaction and order to life, they do not usually bring profound meaning and purpose. They are easier to change than are values and beliefs.

Common so-called value conflicts between teenagers and parents often involve different preferences about the cleanliness of the teenager's room, how teens dress, or how they wear their hair. This kind of conflict can some-times escalate into a family power struggle. When helping families resolve these kind of conflicts, it becomes clear that the teenager's dirty room, dress, or hairstyle fre-quently has little or no tangible effect on the parents other than they would prefer that their son or daughter would do as they specify.

The parents' preferences around cleanliness, dress, and hairstyles simply are different from those of their teenage son or daughter. When a son or daughter asks why they have to behave according to parental preferences, often the parents say, "Do it because I said so." To create a major power struggle over these kind of differences in preferences may not be wise. The important questions that parents must ask themselves in such a situation is, "How important is it that I impose this preference on my chil-dren?" and "What cost will it have on our relationship?" One the other hand, if your son or daughter tells you he or she wants to sell illegal drugs to friends, this is a situation that is more likely to involve a clash of values.

Both values and beliefs are formed very early in life, usually by the age of 10 or 12. Value formation, particu-larly if it is imposed in some overt or covert way, can be connected to intense emotional experiences or traumatic events that leave a powerful imprint on the psyche. As a result, values and beliefs often have an irrational quality that makes it difficult to change them through cognitive and rational discussions. Neither values or beliefs can be truly changed without examining the experiences and cir-cumstances that helped shape or form the value or belief. Conflicts involving differences in preferences are often easier to resolve than those where long-standing values and beliefs are involved. The Partnership Way can be used to resolve conflicts of values, beliefs, and preferences. At the end of this chapter there is a self-inventory to help you distinguish between values, beliefs, and preferences.

WHAT CAUSES PEOPLE TO BECOME TRUE BELIEVERS?

Some people get stuck defending their values, beliefs, and preferences without bothering to examine the sources of them. These people often hold very rigid reli-gious beliefs and act as if they have the moral higher ground. They become true believers and zealots. They also often lack interest in dialoguing or questioning why they believe what they do. In *A Different Drum*, Scott Peck (1987) explained how people form their spiritual beliefs and discussed how some people eventually reach a stage of spiritual development in which they change some of their beliefs.

Peck identified four stages that people usually go through in developing mature spiritual beliefs. According to Peck, all children and about one in five adults are in Stage 1, which is characterized by chaos and asocial or antisocial behaviors. People who remain in this stage as adults are unprincipled, self-serving, and manipulative. Some end up in jail; others become quite disciplined in the service of their own ambition. These people may rise to positions of considerable prestige and power.

People in Stage 2 have submitted themselves to the rules of an institution like the military or the church to help them overcome their chaos. Most churchgoers, according to Peck, fall into this stage. The canons, liturgy, and formalized discipline of the church provide structure to their lives. People in this stage often become quite upset if anyone tries to change the forms that create their structure. Once people integrate the external forms and structures into their behaviors, however, they may start to question the forms. This is a sign that they are ready to move into Stage 3. People in Stage 3 want to explore the sources of their values and beliefs. Unfortunately, they may find that their inquisitiveness is unpopular in tradi-tional institutions and as a result may decide to leave.

This truth-seeking moves many people into Stage 4, which Peck called the mystical, communal stage of spiri-tuality. In this stage, people often change their values and beliefs as a result of their questioning and tend to adopt more altruistic, global values, seeing the whole world as a family or a community. They are able to see beyond prej-udice, pride, nationalism, and regionalism.

Stage 4 has some similarities in both language and behavior to Stage 2 but with one critical difference. In Stage 2, people are directed by strong external forces or have what is known as "an external locus of control." This locus of control generally rests in strict rules or dogma associated with an institution such as a religious organi-zation or a military institution. People living in Stage 2 often need an external reinforcer to maintain the desired behaviors. In Stage 4, the locus of control is internalized and an integral part of the individual. People living in Stage 4 are able to police their own behavior via active self-awareness and a strong conscience. Thus people can avoid the tyranny of true believers by remaining open to dialogue about their beliefs, by questioning their beliefs, and by examining how and why they formed these beliefs in the first place.

HOW CAN I USE DIALOGUE AS A TOOL FOR BUILDING COMMON GROUND RELATED TO VALUE DIFFERENCES?

The conflict of ideologies represented in conflicts of values and beliefs as well as conflicts of wants and needs is a lot about fear. We believe that fear of being dominated or persecuted activates a quest for power, which is at the heart of the drama triangle. It is not possible to resolve the problems inherent in the drama triangle by the persecutor using more power or force against those designated as victims. Yet the person or group in power (persecutor) feels more insecure as the conflict escalates and must con-stantly increase the aggression to avoid a loss of power.

Dialogue, rather than force, is required to stop the escalating conflict.

The Need for Peaceful Dialogue

On a global as well as personal level, people must manage power without resorting to triangulation, aggression, and violence. The principles and practices set forth in the U.S. Constitution support this notion, promoting the use of dialogue and the rule of law for resolving conflicts. While far from perfect, our democratic tradition gives us hope for a better world. This better world may not be without conflict, but it can utilize peaceful dialogue processes to replace war and violence as a method of resolving conflicts.

In 1985 John Murray wrote, "A republic is made up of people locked in civil argument. And the point of the argument is neither to win nor to end the diversity of opinion and power. Peace means keeping the argument going, ad infinitum" (p. 96). In this context, peace becomes as Sam Keen (1991) put it, "fierce men, women and nations struggling together to define their boundaries and enhance self-respect with love and politics as a playing field. I see rivals facing each other not as incarnations of evil, but as worthy opponents" (p. 115).

Albert Camus (1980), possibly one of the most unsentimental minds of the twentieth century, wrote, "It would be completely Utopian to wish that men should no longer kill each other. Skeptical though we are, realism forces us to this Utopian alternative. When our Utopia has become part of history men will find themselves unable to conceive of reality without it. For history is simply man's desperate attempt to give body to his most clairvoyant dreams" (p. 51).

Arnold Mindell (1985a) wrote, "If you cannot dream it, it cannot happen. If you dare to dream it, it is already happening." (p. 9). According to his theory, if you can see a better, more peaceful world, then it already exists.

Dialogue Is the Key

For a more peaceful world, however, we need more than a common vision of peace. We need to acquire the skills that will help us achieve our common goals and realize our dreams. One of the most important skills in this regard is that of dialoguing.

Dialogue, in our opinion, is the key not only to peace but to scientific achievements and all other cooperative efforts. Werner Heisenberg, one of the greatest minds of the twentieth century, argued, "Science is rooted in conversations. The cooperation of different people may culminate in scientific results of the utmost importance" (quoted in Senge, 1990, p. 238). Heisenberg recalled that his dialogues with Wolfgang Pauli, Albert Einstein, and Niels Bohr led directly to the theories that literally reshaped our understanding of the physical world (Senge, 1990, pp. 238-239).

Dialogue is actually a very old idea. It was revered by the ancient Greeks and practiced by many primitive societies, such as the American Indians. Physicist David Bohm developed our contemporary theory and practice of dialogue. He believed that the purpose of science is not the accumulation of knowledge but rather the creation of mental maps that guide and shape our perception and action. These mental maps, Bohm said, are best created by groups who have learned the skill of dialogue.

Dialogue vs. Debate

Dialogue and debate are very different forms of conversation. The purpose of a debate is to have one's views, beliefs, or values accepted as correct by the other person or group. While you might accept part of another person's perspective during a debate in order to strengthen your own position, the basic goal is to be "right," or win the debate. This often leads people to stretch the truth and disregard certain facts. Debate is necessary when a group is trying to reach some agreement on a course of action to be taken. Other times it can stifle creative input for solving a problem.

The goal of dialogue is different. Dialogue does not seek to promote agreement but rather to uncover new possible courses of action. The word dialogue comes from the Greek word *dialogos,* which is defined as "meaning." Senge (1990) wrote that Bohm saw the purpose of dialogue as helping a group of people access a larger pool of common meaning that could not be accessed individually. In a dialogue, people participate in the discovery of this pool of common meaning. At the same time, they become more aware of the assumptions that shape their actions and the events from their pasts that have shaped those assumptions.

Table 6.1 is a summary of the main differences between dialogue and debate. As you read this list, think about how the skill of dialogue could be used to help resolve conflicts of values and beliefs.

What Is Necessary for Dialogue to Be Effective?

For dialogue to be effective, three basic conditions must be met (Bohm, 1987).

- All participants must be willing to suspend their assumptions, reveal them to others, and open them to examination.
- All participants must be willing to regard each other as equals or as colleagues.
- In a group there has to be a facilitator who keeps the dialogue process moving or the group needs to use a written protocol for everyone to follow.

According to Bohm (1987), once an individual "digs in his or her heels" and decides "this is the way it is," the flow of dialogue stops. In a dialogue, different assumptions can be presented as a means for discovering a new idea or enhancing the understanding of other people's

Table 6.1
Comparison of Dialogue and Debate*

Dialogue	Debate
Dialogue is collaborative: two or more sides work together toward common understanding.	Debate is oppositional: two sides oppose each other and attempt to prove each other wrong.
Finding common ground is the goal.	Winning is the goal.
One listens to the other side(s) in order to understand, find meaning, and find agreement.	One listens to the other side(s) in order to find flaws and to counter its arguments.
Dialogue enlarges and possibly changes a participant's point of view.	Debate affirms a participant's point of view.
Dialogue reveals assumptions for reevaluation.	Debate defends assumptions as truth.
Dialogue causes introspection on one's own position.	Debate causes critique of the other person's position.
Dialogue calls for temporally suspending one's beliefs.	Debate calls for investing wholeheartedly in one's beliefs.
With dialogue one searches for basic agreements.	With debate one searches for glaring differences.
Dialogue involves a real concern for the other person and seeks to not alienate or offend.	Debate involves a countering of the other position without focusing on feelings or relationships and often belittles or deprecates the other person.

*Adapted from a paper prepared by Shelley Berman, which was based on discussions of the Dialogue Group of the Boston Chapter of Educators for Social Responsibility (ESR), *A Guide to Training Study Circle Leaders* (1993), Pomfret, CT: Topsfield Foundation, Study Circles Resource Center.

assumptions. Because of the dire need for dialogue to help resolve conflicts at all levels, the Dalai Lama (Gyatso, 1997) proposed that the 21st century be named the century of dialogue.

Dialogue utilizes the skills of reflective listening and inquiry, which are important components of the Partnership Way. You will have an opportunity to practice these skills by completing the skill practice exercises at the end of this chapter.

HOW CAN I USE THE PARTNERSHIP WAY TO RESOLVE CONFLICTS OF VALUES AND BELIEFS?

The seven-step method for resolving conflicts of values and beliefs contained in the Partnership Way is examined in the following paragraphs. Remember that conflicts of values and beliefs sometimes underlie, and are masked by, conflicts of wants and needs. If you completed Worksheet #2 in Chapter 5 and were not satisfied that the conflict was resolved, the next step is to complete Worksheet #3.

There are some important differences in both the processes and the intentions of the two methods for resolving conflicts. The intention in resolving conflicts of

wants and needs is to reach a mutually agreeable resolution. The intention in resolving conflicts of values and beliefs is much broader. It includes discovering more about the other person and developing and communicating respect, compassion, and acceptance (not agreement) for the other person's values. It also involves identifying the source of the other person's values and beliefs, and noting any shifts in those values and beliefs that come as a result of the dialogue process. Through dialogue, the people involved have the opportunity to get beyond any labels or stereotypes and get to know each other in important ways.

The following paragraphs contain a review of the main points to keep in mind when you are attempting to resolve a conflict of values and beliefs using the Partnership Way. Remember to demonstrate compassion, respect, and understanding of the other person's values and beliefs. This helps create a safe context for both of you to explore and possibly change your values and beliefs.

Step 1: Take Turns Listening to Each Other's View of the Conflict Using Reflective Listening

Be sure to identify the feelings as well as the content of each others values or beliefs. Follow the rule that you cannot state your opinion or position until you have first restated what the other person has said and reached agreement that you understand their view. For example, you might say, "You seem to be saying that you think I am trying to control you, and you also seem a little angry and scared. Do I understand accurately what you are saying and feeling?"

Typically, in discussions or debates about a value-laden subject, the people involved spend much more time thinking about what they are going to say in response to the other person than listening carefully to what that person is saying. The reflective listening step requires you to accurately restate what you have heard before you can say anything in response. In addition, you must listen for any unstated feelings. When the second person states his or her view, the first person reflects back the values or beliefs he or she stated. To be able to meet these requirements, each partner must listen carefully instead of thinking about what he or she will say next.

Kind, reflective listening helps to create an atmosphere of trust and respect. Most people are not used to being listened to so carefully, and they usually feel honored that the other person cares enough to actually listen to them. This step helps set the tone for the conflict resolution process and makes it possible for true dialogue to occur.

It also sets the stage for the next step, which requires that the participants look at how they may have formed the values or beliefs around which the conflict is centered. Without some trust, created through the mutual respect displayed in the first step, this next step would be difficult.

Step 2: Take Turns Finding the Sources of the Value or Belief Conflict

Again, it is important for each person to listen to and restate the feelings and content the other expresses before going on. Asking questions such as, "What experiences have you had earlier in your life where you have felt people were trying to control you?" can lead to much new awareness and exciting discoveries. The goal is for each person to get underneath the surface of the conflict and explore the personal experiences that may have influenced the formation of the value or belief. When people examine the sources of their values and beliefs, they often uncover traumatic or unusual experiences that helped to form them. Once the source of a particular value or belief is located, it is possible to change that value or belief.

For example, a client told us about an incident that occurred when she was 10 years old and she saw her mother fall down a flight of stairs in a drunken stupor. She remembered deciding at that time to never again allow herself to get close to anyone. This woman formed the belief that it was too frightening to risk losing someone you were close to and that the only safe choice was to avoid getting close to anyone. Many lonely years passed before she remembered this incident and was able to

change her belief. The key to changing a value or belief is to first remember how and why you formed it and to then express the feelings connected to the causal events. This step is an excellent exercise in developing kindness and compassion toward yourself regarding the way you formed your values and beliefs.

Step 3: Take Turns Finding the Sources of the Feelings

The focus here is on the feelings attached to the values or beliefs expressed. Each person states his or her feelings and reflects back what the other person said. Asking questions like, "What other times in your life have you felt this way?" can get the dialogue started.

When a person has intense feelings about a value or belief, it is almost certain that these feelings relate back to some traumatic conflict or incident from the past that is not resolved. It is usually impossible for the person to change the value or belief until he or she can identify the source of the attached feelings. If, for example, you get very angry when you feel someone is treating you unfairly or when you see someone else being treated unfairly, your anger may be related to times when as a child you felt you were treated unfairly.

Once you remember the incidents you experienced, you can decide what is unresolved about them. In Chapters 8 and 9, you will look for the source of your conflicts. Perhaps as a child you never got to express your feelings directly to those who treated you unfairly. By having your partner role-play a parent who treated you unfairly, you can release those repressed feelings. Finding the source of your feelings and coming to terms with the earlier incident will help you reframe the way you look at this conflict and may cause a shift in awareness that causes you to change your value or belief.

Step 4: Determine Any Shifts in Awareness

This step enables both people to reflect on whether their values have changed as a result of what they have uncovered regarding the sources of their values or beliefs. Asking a question like, "Based on what you have discovered about the sources of your values or beliefs and your feelings, do you have any new perceptions of your value or belief?" is a good way to start the dialogue. The participants should take turns restating any new perceptions expressed by the other person.

Indeed, each of the prior steps can lead to new awareness, and it is important to check how this awareness may have affected the conflict or perceptions of values and beliefs. Although people at this stage of the process are not usually ready to change their value or belief completely, they may have softened their position and often feel more compassionate toward each other's views. It is useful to spend some time exploring these shifts in perception before moving on to the next step.

Step 5: Determine Areas of Agreement and Disagreement

If the dialogue has been successful, it may now be possible to explore areas of mutual agreement and disagreement. For example, in a scenario centered around the issue of control, one partner might say, "I think we now can agree that what we identified as control was really a desire for more directness in our relationship. Because of our past history of having had people try to control us, we are prone to be indirect with each other. Do you agree that this could be a problem for us?"

Armed with the knowledge of the sources of their values or beliefs, the partners can work to sort out the various parts of the conflict. They may find that they are now closer to agreement on many of the aspects. They may also uncover any core disagreements that remain. They also will likely have a better understanding of why such disagreements exist. When one partner can see that the other has formed his or her value or belief out of unique or traumatic experiences, then it is easier to accept that partner and the value or belief he or she holds even if it differs from that of the first partner.

It is unlikely that the partners in a conflict of values or beliefs will reach complete agreement, even when important shifts in perception have occurred as a result of their dialogue. However, from the dialogue they may have acquired enough mutual understanding and compassion to feel closer to each other.

When areas of disagreement remain, it is useful for the partners to identify kind and compassionate ways to handle these disagreements in their relationship. One may say, for example, "I think if either of us is feeling controlled by the other in any way, that person should raise the issue and we can talk about it again."

Step 6: Make Plans to Handle Any Areas of Disagreement

If the partners have successfully completed the previous steps, they will probably be able to agree to disagree, if that is still necessary. The process will inevitably create more intimacy, understanding, compassion, and trust between the two. It is likely that the areas of disagreement that still exist no longer pose a major conflict in their relationship. Even though they did not agree completely, they did reach a more complete understanding of the areas of disagreement. Such understanding leads to more tolerance, acceptance, and compassion for different values and beliefs and allows partners to develop a mutually acceptable plan for handling these differences.

Learning to understand, accept, and welcome differences of values and beliefs in others can be an unexpectedly positive experience. Many people learn to fear differences and avoid people whose values or beliefs are different from their own. By engaging in the dialogue process described here, you can learn to better understand and accept such differences and may even, in the process, change some of your own values and beliefs. If a conflict brings up strong feelings and reactions that the dialogue does not resolve, the source of those strong feelings and reactions should be located to allow the partners to deal with them.

Step 7: Make Plans to Handle Any Strong Feelings or Reactions

Strong feelings or reactions at this stage of the conflict resolution are usually a good indicator that the conflict comes from some unresolved conflict from the past, which is being activated by the current conflict. Any leftover elements of the conflict that have not been adequately explored so far (Step 3) should be addressed at this time. Worksheets #4 and #5 (Chapters 9 and 10, respectively) can provide help in exploring these feeling and reactions and developing a plan to handle them.

WORKSHEET # 3: THE SEVEN-STEP METHOD FOR RESOLVING CONFLICTS OF VALUES AND BELIEFS

Identify a conflict of values and beliefs that you want to resolve with a partner. This exercise will not be a role-play, but a dialogue between two people who differ on some value or belief.

Step 1: Take Turns Listening to Each Other's Views of the Conflict Using Reflective Listening

Be sure to identify the feelings as well as the content. Agree not to state your own opinion or position until you reach agreement that you have reflected back what the other person has said. For example you might say, "You seem to be saying that you think I am trying to control you and you also seem a little angry and scared to me. Do I understand accurately what you are saying and feeling?" When the other person indicates his or her feelings have been heard, then move to Step 2.

Step 2: Take Turns Finding the Sources of the Value or Belief Conflict

Each person talks about personal experiences that may have led to the formation of this value or belief. You might ask your partner, "What experiences have you had in your life where you have felt people were trying to control you?" Again, listen and reflect back the feelings and content for each other before moving forward to the next step.

Step 3: Take Turns Finding the Sources of the Feelings

Focus on the feelings and reflect back what you hear from the other. Ask, "What other times in your life have you felt this way?"

Step 4: Determine Any Shifts in Awareness

Take turns restating any new perceptions. You might say, "Based on your exploration of the sources of your values or beliefs and your feelings, do you have any new perceptions of your value or belief? Are you feeling kinder or more compassionate toward my views?"

Step 5: Explore Areas of Agreement and Disagreement

One way to do this is to say, "I think we can now agree that what we originally identified as control was really a desire for more directness in our relationship. Because of our past history where other people tried to control us, we are indirect in our communication with each other. Do you agree that this could be a problem for us?"

Step 6: Make Plans to Handle Any Areas of Disagreement

This might take the form of saying, "If either of us feels controlled by the other in any way, can we agree to bring it directly to the other so that we can talk about it again?"

Step 7: Make Plans to Handle Any Strong Feelings or Reactions

If this conflict brings up strong feelings and reactions in either one of you, you will need to consult Worksheet #4 in Chapter 9 to help locate the source of these strong feelings and reactions. After that, you may want to use Worksheet #5 in Chapter 10 to deal with these feelings and reactions.

SELF-AWARENESS EXERCISE: IS IT A VALUE, A BELIEF, OR A PREFERENCE?

Next to the following items place a V if you think it is a value, a B if you think it is a belief, and a P if you think it is a preference.

_____	1.	Being married.
_____	2.	Joining a certain church.
_____	3.	Wearing loafer-style shoes.
_____	4.	Witnessing a miracle.
_____	5.	Becoming a vegetarian.
_____	6.	Becoming a mediator.
_____	7.	Car-pooling to work.
_____	8.	Lifting weights.
_____	9.	Watching a television news show.
_____	10.	Coloring your hair blonde.
_____	11.	Drinking Coors beer.
_____	12.	Taking vitamin supplements.
_____	13.	Fly fishing.
_____	14.	Driving a Subaru automobile.
_____	15.	Seeing a UFO.

_____	16.	Owning a red dress/shirt.
_____	17.	Contributing money to a political campaign.
_____	18.	Volunteering at your children's school.
_____	19.	Picking up wastepaper from the sidewalk.
_____	20.	Visiting your parents.

The answers to this exercise are located upside-down below.

Answers to "Is It a Value, a Belief, or a Preference?"

1 = v, 2 = v, 3 = p, 4 = b, 5 = v, 6 = v, 7 = v, 8 = v, 9 = p,
10 = p, 11 = p, 12 = v, 13 = v, 14 = p, 15 = b, 16 = p,
17 = v, 18 = v, 19 = v, 20 = v.

SELF-AWARENESS EXERCISE: DO YOU AGREE OR DISAGREE?

By each of the statements below, place a number from 1 to 10 to indicate your level of agreement or disagreement with the statement (1 = Strongly Disagree to 10 = Strongly Agree). When finished, go through the questions again and mark them the way you think your partner would mark them (use numbers 1 to 10 again).

You   Partner

____   ____   1. Women should have the right to choose an abortion.
____   ____   2. Other than physical sex characteristics, men and women are basically the same.
____   ____   3. Men are better money managers than women.
____   ____   4. Women are inherently smarter than men.
____   ____   5. Women are better at being intimate than men.
____   ____   6. A woman's greatest contribution to society is her ability to raise healthy, effective children.
____   ____   7. Men are better lovers than women.
____   ____   8. Women are better parents than men.
____   ____   9. Women are better conversationalists than men.
____   ____   10. Men have stronger sex drives than women.
____   ____   11. Women are better nurturers than men.
____   ____   12. Women are more self-conscious about their bodies than men.
____   ____   13. Generally speaking, I feel positive about myself.
____   ____   14. Overall, I feel positive about my primary relationship.
____   ____   15. It is important that both people in a couple relationship have similar world views.
____   ____   16. Both people should have equal power in a relationship.
____   ____   17. The success of a primary relationship is more important than the careers of the couple.
____   ____   18. The most important ingredient in a primary relationship is security.
____   ____   19. Women need to be told they are loved more than men do.
____   ____   20. Conflict should be avoided at all costs in a relationship.
____   ____   21. Men are more responsible than women for the environmental damage to the Earth.
____   ____   22. Sexual fidelity is more important for women than for men.
____   ____   23. Men are more likely than women to abuse drugs and alcohol.
____   ____   24. Women are more oppressed by society than are men.
____   ____   25. Women are better at expressing their feelings than are men.

SKILL PRACTICE EXERCISE: A DIALOGUE
ABOUT YOUR CONFLICTS OF VALUES AND BELIEFS

After you and your partner have completed the above inventory, compare your results. Check to see where your perceptions of each other matched and where they didn't. Then pick one of the statements where you have wide differences of values or beliefs and engage in a dialogue using Worksheet #3. After you have had a chance to dialogue about a value conflict and have attempted to resolve it, spend some time talking about the process. Use the following questions to help focus your discussion.

- What seemed to make the biggest difference in causing you to make any shifts?
- What did you like best about the process?
- What did you like least about it?
- What changes would you make to resolve with each other the next time you had a value conflict?

SELF AWARENESS EXERCISE: WHAT IS MY POSITION ON THESE MAJOR VALUES AND BELIEFS ISSUES?

By each item listed below, place a number from 1 to 10 to indicate your level of agreement or disagreement with the statement (1 = Strongly Disagree to 10 = Strongly Agree).

_____ 1. Abortion is murder.

_____ 2. Abortion on demand should be legal.

_____ 3. It's a woman's right to choose whether or not to have an abortion.

_____ 4. Prayer should be allowed in public schools.

_____ 5. The death penalty should be used to punish all murderers.

_____ 6. Homosexuals are a special class whose rights need to be protected.

_____ 7. The federal government intrudes too much into the lives of the citizens of this country.

_____ 8. People have the right to choose to die.

_____ 9. Parents should be given vouchers so they can send their children to the schools of their choice.

_____ 10. Parents should have the right to spank their child to get them to behave.

_____ 11. Marijuana should be legalized.

_____ 12. Drugs should be legalized.

_____ 13. Global warming is a reality.

_____ 14. Our political system needs to be reformed.

_____ 15. Balancing the federal budget is necessary.

_____ 16. Military spending is too high.

_____ 17. We spend too much on welfare programs.

_____ 18. Youth crime is out of control.

_____ 19. Campaign spending must be limited or regulated.

_____ 20. Environmental protection laws need to be strengthened.

SKILL PRACTICE EXERCISE: THE VALUES TANGO

Select one of the issues from the above two inventories where there was the most polarization or differences in values or beliefs, and have one person from each side of the issue dialogue. The rules are as follows:

1. Stand facing each other about four to five feet apart. Decide who is willing to start off and each of you agree to follow the steps outlined in Worksheet #3 as you dialogue about this issue.

2. If the person who starts off feels understood or accepted, they can take a step forward. If they feel more neutral, they can stand fast and not move. If they do not feel understood or accepted, they can take a step backwards to illustrate that they do not feel understood.

3. As you follow the steps in Worksheet #3, continue to step forward, backwards, or stand fast, depending on how understood you feel.

4. After you complete the steps in Worksheet #3, talk together about this process. Look at what were the most difficult parts of the process and where you need to upgrade your skills. Notice whether or not you are standing any closer to each other. This can be one indication of any shifts in understanding or acceptance of each other's views.

~

PART III

~

HOW CAN I USE THE PARTNERSHIP WAY TO RESOLVE MY INTRACTABLE PERSONAL CONFLICTS?

~

Chapter 7

~

What Are Intractable Conflicts and What Causes Them?

Have you ever noticed how certain kinds of conflicts consistently repeat in your life? You might have conflicts with several different people in a short period of time over the same issue. Perhaps you have a fight with your intimate partner about who is right. You find yourself in a similar conflict at work with a colleague or your boss. There may also be certain conflicts that seem to happen over and over in your life. Perhaps you had a domineering father or mother while you were growing up and later have a series of domineering bosses or relationships where you felt dominated. These are known as *intractable* conflicts.

Intractable conflicts are defined in Chapter 1 as the stubborn or persistent conflicts that don't go away. Often at the source of these conflicts is some unresolved conflict or trauma from childhood that may have disappeared from conscious memory. These conflicts usually cannot be resolved by using the worksheets prescribed for resolving conflicts of wants and needs or values and beliefs. Resolving intractable or recurring conflicts requires identifying the source in the past. This necessitates some detective work to locate the original conflict or trauma. The next step is to identify your part of what isn't finished from this old conflict or trauma and then complete it. Once the issues from the past have been resolved, you can see what is left to resolve in the present-time conflict.

HOW CAN I FIND THE SOURCES OF INTRACTABLE CONFLICTS?

The natural learning style of humans is to repeat something until it is learned or understood. Did you ever watch a toddler exploring her environment? If she touches a light bulb that is turned on, for example, she will quickly pull her hand away. What is the very next thing she will usually do? She will touch the light bulb again. She stops touching the hot bulb after the connection is made in her brain that links the heat of the light bulb with the physical pain and the word "hot." This is how all humans learn. We keep repeating, reenacting, and replaying the events of our lives until we figure them out.

If you had a conflict or trauma in childhood involving specific relationship dynamics, you will likely be unconsciously drawn to situations with similar circumstances in order to finally understand and change these dynamics. Even the normal experiences that shaped your personality, such as family and classroom dynamics, can be sufficiently conflictual or traumatic that you find them repeating in your adult life. Ney (1992) showed how this leads to the transgenerational patterns of conflict and violence. He says that,

"...families will reenact violence similar to that of their forebears, hoping to both see and understand how and why it happens."

Ney (1988) found high correlations between the way a mother parents her child and the way she was parented as a child. He also found that women select abusive husbands who treat them exactly the way their fathers treated their mothers. Even when parents vowed not to treat their children like they were treated, he found that they reverted to the old patterns under stress. Ney also found that when rational discussion during a conflict fails to bring any resolution "...people create the opportunity to reexamine their part in conflicts, by reenacting them." Finally, Ney also learned that "any individual who needs to reenact conflicts from which he hopes to learn, will carefully select others to help him enact the unresolved conflict." He added, "In this way many relationships are conflicts looking for an occasion" (Ney, 1992, pp. 15-25).

WHAT IS THE ROLE OF TRAUMA IN INTRACTABLE CONFLICTS?

In our clinical studies of intractable conflicts, particularly our work with couples, we consistently found unresolved trauma to be a critical factor. While developing methods for resolving intractable conflicts, we began to see how they paralleled the protocols for treating trauma. Effectively resolving intractable conflicts requires addressing the following areas:

- Identifying and disconnecting the physiological aspects of the trauma. This includes desensitizing the sensory system to trigger cues or signals, which activate the adrenal stress response and the fight/flight/freeze mechanism.
- Identifying and changing the negative cognition associated with the trauma. This belief is typically a major component of a self-fulfilling prophecy that directs the person's life.
- Identifying the split within the self that occurred during the trauma, and reclaiming this dissociated aspect of self in present time. Split-off or dissociated parts of the self are often related to behaviors that were not accepted in the family or social environment.
- Identifying the distortion in relationship dynamics that occurred as a result of the trauma, and repatterning it. Relational distortions fall into specific categories that create personality disorders later in life.

The correlation of intractable conflicts with unresolved trauma opened a larger door of research related to the study of memory and the operation of the brain. Some of the most exciting contributions to our Partnership Way come from new research on the brain.

HOW DOES THE BRAIN STORE MEMORIES OF CHILDHOOD TRAUMA?

New discoveries from brain research are overturning the concept of the brain as an inaccessible organ. No longer seen as a self-contained unit with a preset, unchangeable set of rules, the brain is now perceived as a flexible, malleable instrument capable of adapting to a broad range of physical, emotional, cognitive, and environmental stimuli. A new area of brain research is focusing on prenatal development and on the treatment of post-traumatic stress symptoms. From this research, the correlation between childhood trauma and violent behavior is now becoming more accepted.

Trauma is stored primarily in the limbic system of the mammalian brain, which is related to relationships and processing emotions. The limbic system is comprised of the *hypothalamus*, the *amygdala*, and the *hippocampus*. Early emotional memories are stored in the amygdala as icons or fixed visual representations. For example, if you were traumatized as an infant or toddler, memories of these experiences will be stored as pictures or symbols rather than language. Severe trauma from wars and natural catastrophes are also stored symbolically. These visual symbols or icons emerge as flashbacks in episodes of PTSD and hold memory traces containing certain scenes that seem to be burned in the brain. Iconic memories are unavailable to the conscious mind, but emerge in dreams, art work, body memories, and events that cause a reenactment of earlier events (van der Kolk, 1988).

A second kind of memory, called narrative memory, consists of words and the meanings created from words. Narrative memory, which begins being stored in the hippocampus around age four or five, forms the memory of the conscious mind (LeDoux, 1994). In order to discharge a traumatic memory from the amygdala, it is necessary to transfer the memory traces stored as pictures or symbols from the amygdala into a narrative memory trace in the hippocampus that uses words and meanings. Developmental trauma can disrupt the circuitry between the cognitive and emotional parts of the brain. This can impair the ability to recognize feelings, as well as the ability to express them. This impairment creates *alexithymia*, or the lack of words to express feelings (Goleman, 1997).

The amygdala is functional at birth. The hippocampus, however, does not completely develop until between three and five years of age. This maturational difference between the amygdala and the hippocampus is a factor in the inability of most people to recall memories prior to the age of three or four. The memories are there, but they are in symbolic rather than narrative form. This maturational factor is critical in understanding the role of early trauma in intractable conflicts.

WHAT IS THE ROLE OF DISSOCIATED MEMORY INTRACTABLE CONFLICTS?

Trauma leaves people vulnerable to arousal by specific sensory cues such as smells, pictures, sounds, and to specific kinds of relational dynamics. When a cue that emerges in the environment correlates with a sensory cue related to a previous traumatic memory, the adrenal stress response activates the fight/flight/freeze response. This immediately causes the person to experience an inner sense of loss of reality. If a war veteran, for example, is crossing a busy city street when a car backfires, he may immediately access dissociated memories from a traumatic war scene. His body reacts as though he were in the past, causing him to fight, flee, or freeze. The memories of that traumatic war scene may also correlate with an earlier layer of memories related to abuse or trauma during his childhood.

A person in the midst of conflict reacts in a similar way. When another person says or does something that reminds them of an unresolved traumatic conflict from the past, the dissociated memories related to the past conflict flood the present conflict situation and cloud one's awareness. The experience of being regressed or spontaneously transported to the past can be very frightening. It can lead into immediate disconnection from the current moment and a shift of awareness into conflicts from the past. Participants may be pulled into each others' unresolved traumas, connected by common sensory elements related to past events. This phenomenon is known as *mutual reenactment*.

Group reenactments of traumatic experiences have been studied extensively by psychohistorian Lloyd deMause (1982). He describes these group reenactments as "group fantasies" or group psychodramas that get played out through wars and ethnic and religious conflicts. This phenomenon is examined more closely in Chapter 17.

WHAT ARE THE COMPONENTS OF TRAUMA-REDUCTION THERAPY?

The treatment of trauma utilizes the same procedures as resolving intractable conflicts described earlier:

- Identifying and disconnecting the physiological aspects of the trauma.
- Identifying and changing the negative cognition associated with the trauma.
- Identifying the distortion in relationship dynamics that occurred as a result of the trauma and repatterning it. Relational distortions fall into four main categories that help create specific kinds of personality disorders later in life.
- Identifying the split within the self that occurred during the trauma and reclaiming this dissociated aspect in the present time.

A growing number of new modalities for treating physiological aspects and negative cognitions have proven to be highly effective. Charles Figley, a professor from the Traumatology Department at Florida State University, conducted a double-blind research project to identify the techniques that might offer a "cure" for PTSD (Carbonell & Figley, 1996). Dr. Figley found that the methods traditionally used to treat PTSD were the least effective and sometimes retraumatized the client. One traditional method for

PTSD, for example, uses flooding to desensitize clients to traumatic associations. This requires them to relive the event over and over until the painful associations no longer cause arousal. Another treatment involves placing clients on psychiatric medications in addition to long-term individual and group therapy. According to Figley, the recovery rate for PTSD using traditional modalities is about 25%.

Figley's project identified four leading approaches to trauma reduction. He found that these four approaches offer quick and relatively painless techniques for reducing post-traumatic symptoms. All four approaches generated impressive results.

Thought-Field Therapy (TFT)

Thought Field Therapy (TFT), developed by Roger Callahan (1997), draws on principles of quantum physics and Eastern or "energy" medicine and utilizes treatment protocols involving meridian points used in applied kinesiology and acupuncture. According to Callahan, it works by disconnecting the wiring of the nervous system that activates the adrenal stress response and creates symptoms of post-traumatic stress. TFT does not delete traumatic memories but eliminates the negative charge related to them.

TFT is sometimes referred to as a "tapping" modality because it involves the client tapping on various meridian points of the body. The TFT trained clinician utilizes some procedures involving applied kinesiology, and the client does the tapping on his or her meridian points involved in the trauma reduction protocol. After treatment, clients receive an instruction sheet that illustrates some of the meridian points and offers ongoing self-treatment protocols to extend the effects of the therapy session.

Preliminary research on TFT shows that psychotherapists trained in Levels I and II have about an 85% level of resolution to trauma. Further research trials on are now underway to determine its long-term effectiveness (Sheets, 1997).

Eye Movement Desensitization and Reprocessing (EMDR)

Eye Movement Desensitization and Reprocessing (EMDR), developed by Francine Shapiro (1995), involves bilateral stimulation of the eyes, ears, or body to help traumatized individuals reprocess traumatic memories. The bilateral stimulation is believed to stimulate a state similar to the rapid eye movement (REM) experienced during deep sleep states. EMDR can only be administered by professionals who have been trained through the EMDR Institute. Clients are not encouraged to treat themselves following their treatment sessions. Treatment involves three specific components:

1. Addressing the original traumatic event that created the client's cognitive/affective framework.
2. Eliciting the internal and environmental triggers that stimulate maladaptive behaviors in the present.

3. Identifying and instilling in the client a more effective, functional cognitive/behavioral response.

The early research results in EMDR are promising; it appears to offer substantial relief from the suffering of post-traumatic symptoms (Carbonell & Figley, 1996). More research on the long-term effectiveness of this modality is currently being conducted.

Visual Kinesthetic Dissociation (VKD)

Visual Kinesthetic Dissociation (VKD), a specialized form of neurolinguistic programming (Cameron-Bandler, 1978), uses a deliberate state of dissociation to treat trauma. VKD creates an "outside observer" position that helps the client shift from being "in" the memory to being "outside" looking at it. This shift stimulates the acquisition of other understandings while emotional coloring is reduced. The distinction between inside and outside becomes clearer as the traumatic event is reviewed on a "screen" that is outside, or separate from it. This perceptual shift is believed to be the primary factor in reducing the impact of the event. This dissociation, a temporarily induced aspect of the VKD protocol, is followed by a guided re-association procedure and instructions designed to maintain the learning acquired during the dissociation phase. The treatment protocol focuses on changing the sensory experience in different sensory channels such as visual, auditory, and kinesthetic. Working in submodalities of the visual channel might change a memory from a "movie" into a "snapshot," from colorful to achromatic, and from clear to fuzzy.

Traumatic Incident Reduction (TIR)

Traumatic Incident Reduction (TIR), developed by psychiatrist Frank Gerbode, grew mainly out of the work of Carl Rogers and Sigmund Freud (Metnick, 1966). It is a brief, one-on-one, nonhypnotic, person-centered, and highly structured method for eliminating the negative effects of past traumas. It involves repeated viewing of a traumatic memory under conditions designed to enhance safety and minimize distractions. In this treatment modality, the client does all the work. The counselor offers no interpretations and no negative or positive evaluations. The client is encouraged to visualize the traumatic incident thoroughly from beginning to end. The therapist serves as a facilitator, providing structure for the session.

The treatment itself utilizes the metaphor of a "videotape." The facilitator encourages the client to review and describe a traumatic event and then "rewind the videotape" and rerun it again. The facilitator does not prescribe the degree of detail, sensory modalities, or content clients are to use in each run-through, but encourages them to view as much as is relatively comfortable. After several viewings, clients become more courageous. They risk encountering emotions and uncomfortable details more and more thoroughly. After several viewings, clients

typically reach an emotional peak until the emotions eventually diminish. At this point, the client reaches a thoughtful, contemplative state where the trauma is reprocessed cognitively and given new meaning related to the trauma itself, life, or him- or herself. This is known as the "end point," the place where the facilitator stops the procedure.

In addition to the research by Figley and Carbonell, the effectiveness of TIR has been researched in a few controlled studies that found it more effective than "Direct Therapeutic Exposure," a tool long used by the Veterans Administration to treat PTSD (Metnick, 1966).

Modalities Used to Treat the Relational Components of Trauma

All trauma happens in a context of relationship. People exist in couple, family, and social relationships that are often the source of traumatic experiences. These systems are also affected by the fallout of their members' traumatic experiences. Trauma literature identifies three specific kinds of relational trauma.

The first is *betrayal trauma* (Freyd, 1994), which involves amnesia or the inability to recall painful or disturbing events related to a betrayal by someone on whom a person depends for survival, such as a child on a parent. It can involve physical and/or sexual abuse. It can also be related to betrayal subordinates suffer at the hands of their superiors, such as the betrayal soldiers in the Vietnam war felt at the lack of support from government leaders and the American people. Psychogenic amnesia becomes necessary to maintain the attachment and improve chances for survival.

The second kind of relational trauma is known as *attachment trauma* (James, 1994). It involves the absence or loss of a protective, nurturing adult relationship, which may leave a child unable to bond or attach appropriately to others. Disturbed attachment behaviors manifest in symptoms of avoidance of intimacy, dissociation, and hyperactivity as well as intrusive, high-risk behaviors and impaired capacities for forming new relationships.

The third kind of relational trauma is known as *developmental trauma* (Weinhold & Weinhold, 1992). It is the result of unmet developmental needs and incomplete psychosocial tasks during the first three years of life. It impairs the process of individuation or the completion of the "psychological birth" that leads to the full expression of human potential and creative capacities needed for interdependent relationships.

Treating the social or relational aspect of trauma requires object relations therapies. Extreme trauma, such as rape, damages the quality of interpersonal relationships. Developmental, attachment, and betrayal traumas create wounds to the self that impair a person's ability to interact effectively in future interpersonal relationships.

Treating trauma via object relations therapy involves reconstellating the relational distortion in the therapeutic relationship. Here it is identified, articulated by the counselor, confronted, and repatterned through kind, compassionate interactions between the counselor and client. The precise way in which the therapist confronts the distortion differs with each kind of relationship distortion and unspoken demand in the relational distortion. The counselor challenges the legitimacy of the distortion as a basis for relationships.

Object relations therapy identifies four specific relationship distortions that involve self-sacrifice, dependency, sexuality, and power (Cashdan, 1988). Each distortion has a specific belief or cognition that will emerge in clinical relationships.

power: "I want to control our relationship. You need my help in order to succeed as a clinician."
sexuality: "I am afraid that you will not like me. I want to have sex with you so that you will like me."
dependency: "I am afraid to be responsible. Please tell me how to live my life."
self-sacrifice: "I want to obligate you in order to solidify our relationship."

Each of these distortions in relationship dynamics must be countered in a respectful, caring way by the clinician with the following opposing cognitions and accompanying congruent behaviors:

power: "I do not need your help to succeed as a clinician,"
sexuality: "I am not going to have sex with you."
dependency: "I am not going to lead your life."
self-sacrifice: "I do not owe you anything."

Object relations therapy views the client-therapist relationship itself as the focus of treatment. Interventions are designed to meet clients' unmet developmental needs and to help them complete the psychosocial tasks that were delayed as the result of trauma from abuse, abandonment, betrayal, and neglect. This kind of therapy focuses on creating compassionate environments for clients where they can consciously recall dissociated or trauma-related memories. The clinician helps clients reprocess their traumatic memories in a safe, protected environment while simultaneously providing the empathic relational components missing during the original traumatic event. Compassionate clinical environments provide nurturing, protection, and support for the client to complete the psychological birth or individuation process.

In Chapter 13 we will discuss Developmental Process Work, an integrative therapy modality for treating developmental trauma that utilizes a number of principles from object relations therapy. These multifaceted approaches offer great hope for treating the symptoms of PTSD. Consult with your local mental health associations to find therapists in your area who are trained in these specialized modalities.

WHAT ARE SOME COMMON SOURCES OF INTRACTABLE CONFLICTS?

The process of identifying the sources of conflicts can seem mysterious. In reality, unresolved conflicts may continue to operate in your life but are outside of your awareness. Remembering them requires identifying the current feelings and thoughts and then correlating them to a situation from the past. At the end of this chapter are a number of self-inventories and writing exercises that are designed to help begin this process. Once you know what to look for, you can begin to trace your intractable conflicts back to their source. The sources of unresolved conflicts can be divided into four main categories.

1. Family patterns source.
2. Split-off parts of self source.
3. Unfinished business source.
4. Developmental sources.

This chapter examines the first three sources; Chapter 8 examines the developmental sources of conflict.

The Family Patterns Source of Conflict

There are patterns of thoughts, feelings, and behaviors that are passed from one generation to another. These intergenerational family patterns get passed on unconsciously through the everyday interactions between family members. Much of this transmission process occurs when the children watch the adults in the family act out unconscious patterns. Without any awareness of the sources and impact of these dysfunctional patterns on children, the adults pass them on to their children (Ney, 1992).

Conflicts often occur when a child or spouse refuses to cooperate with some kind of family "program" and wants to change it. For example, if you had to go to bed at 9 p.m. when you were ten years old, you will likely expect your ten-year-old child to do the same. When your child complains, you may not remember that you also didn't like going to bed that early. If you were forced to, then it is likely you will force your child to do the same. As a parent, you may have forgotten the original circumstances that instigated this rule, such as the need for people in the family to get up early to go to work or school. It is easy to forget the circumstances of the rule and just impose it. If you were not allowed to question rules such as this one when you were a child, you may get upset when your child questions your rules.

At the end of this chapter is a self-inventory, Identifying Family Patterns, designed to help you recognize any patterns you may be reenacting from your family of origin. Following this inventory are descriptions and questions related to 12 common family patterns.

The Split-Off Parts of Self Source of Conflict

It is not possible for you to live separately from your environment. Intimate relationships, family dynamics, work situations, cultural customs, and ecological conditions all influence your behavior. Just as the external world has many aspects, so does the internal world. You are a multifaceted being with many "parts" or roles such as parent, lover, coworker, child, athlete, swimmer, student, practitioner of yoga, baseball fan, and world traveler. If you grew up in a healthy family, you were able to stay more connected to the various parts of yourself. If you grew up in an unhealthy family, you may have had to split off aspects of yourself that your parents deemed unacceptable. Perhaps you were labeled as too loud, too assertive, too energetic, or too inquisitive.

The concept of "split-off parts" comes from a number of different theoretical orientations. Family systems pioneer Virginia Satir (1988) drew heavily on it in her theory and practice of family therapy. "Parts" is also an element of the theory and practice of Jungian psychology and other psychodynamic theories (Mindell, 1985a). The language of quantum physics and chaos theory are sometimes used to explain the dynamic interplay between both internal and external parts of a system.

Split-off parts is a useful concept for understanding that many internal or intrapsychic parts of the self can suddenly show up during a conflict. Those parts inside your awareness are known as "the conscious mind," while the unaware parts reside in "the unconscious mind."

This fracture in perception between the conscious and unconscious mind begins as a child, when you learned to survive by splitting off or dissociating from aspects of yourself during traumatic events or when your family of origin labeled parts of you as unacceptable. These split-off intrapsychic parts, often related to neediness, truthfulness, power, dependency, sexuality, liveliness, or playfulness, are deposited in your unconscious mind where they develop strength and power as the "shadow" part of your personality. Typically repressed, they rush out in force when stimulated with the appropriate sensory cue related to unresolved conflict from the past. This cue or cues activates the adrenal stress response and creates fight/flight/freeze behaviors.

Concepts from quantum field theory and chaos theory are useful in explaining exactly how the parts stored in your unconscious are activated. According to these theories, you have a field of energy surrounding you. This field contains not only the energy that radiates from your conscious parts but from your split-off or unconscious parts. They create a force that organizes your life toward wholeness.

You may have learned to split-off parts of yourself as a child because someone did not like them. Your joyous, effervescent, energetic part may have been too much for some adults. They may have said to you, "Don't be so active or so enthusiastic!" or "Don't be so rambunctious. Sit and be quiet because your excessive energy bothers me." What may have upset these adults is that you were

acting out a part that matched a split-off part of themselves. You suddenly became a pain-evoking mirror that made your parents or other adults uncomfortable. This put you in a dilemma—either split off this part of yourself or risk the loss of your parents' love.

Once a part of your self is split off and hidden in the unconscious, it is no longer possible for you to see it in yourself. The only way to see and experience this part is for you to project it onto another person. Through a resonant field of energy, you send out signals that draw others to you who carry the complementary split-off part. This phenomenon allows people to be mirrors for each other.

For example, if you walk into a room emanating energy from your split-off parts, this energy will immediately interact with the energy of those people in the room who carry complementary split-off parts. You may feel attracted to certain people, repulsed by others, and fail to notice a third person. The people to whom you feel the most attracted and the most repelled indicate those with whom you have created a form of conscious and unconscious communication. You tend to form interlocking relationships based on a "fit" between your conscious and unconscious parts, as illustrated in Figure 7.1 below.

Most long-term relationships with dynamics like that shown in Figure 7.1 are a mixture of the "best of conscious minds" and the "worst of unconscious minds." The unspoken dream is that the interplay between these parts will help you and your partner become more personally aware of and responsible for your hidden aspects. At the end of this chapter you will find questions to help you identify your split-off parts.

The Unfinished Business Source of Conflict

The central premise of this approach is that certain conflicts become intractable because something related to the original conflict or trauma is still unfinished or incomplete. This means there is something that is unsaid, unfelt, or undone. Here are some common elements of unfinished conflicts and traumas:

"I didn't get to express my feelings in this situation. I was too afraid to speak the truth."

"I didn't get my feelings and perceptions validated by anyone. As a result I wasn't even sure my experience really happened."

"I wanted to run away, but I felt trapped."

"I needed my dad to tell me it wasn't my fault that he was leaving."

"I wanted my mother to tell me that she loved me."

Once you have identified unfinished business in your life, you have two choices: (1) you can go directly to the person involved and ask for what you need or (2) complete it for yourself. If the other person is unwilling or deceased, then you can role-play the situation with your spouse, friend, or therapist in order to finish it. Role-playing or

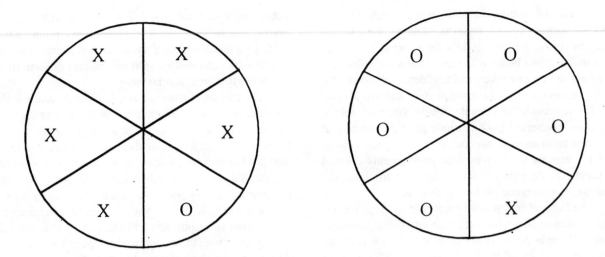

Figure 7.1
Interblocking Relationships Based on the Fit Between Conscious and Unconscious Parts

using Gestalt techniques such as the "empty chair" can be as effective in completing the unfinished elements of a trauma or conflict as directly encountering the person involved in the earlier conflict.

The self-inventories and self-awareness exercises that follow can help you identify the sources of your intractable conflicts. As you take these inventories and score them, use this information to determine the impact of unresolved conflicts on your development and how they may contribute to current conflicts that are recycling in your life.

Developing an awareness of your family dynamics is important, as awareness can consciously redirect your behaviors. Developing compassion for yourself and your family of origin is also important. Your parents did the best that they could in providing for you. Many times they were probably caught in the reenactment of their own developmental traumas and really wanted to be good parents. It may be difficult for you to feel or express compassion toward your parents, but it is an important long-term goal.

Developing compassion for yourself is also important. The coping behaviors you developed in your family of origin enabled you to survive traumatic experiences during your childhood. It is only now that they are becoming dysfunctional and no longer serve you. Allow yourself to see these behaviors in a kind and caring way, without shaming yourself or projecting them onto others. With a kind and caring attitude, move forward in your journey of healing.

SELF INVENTORY: IDENTIFYING FAMILY PATTERNS (WEINHOLD, 1991)

Directions: Complete this self-inventory by placing a number in the blank that precedes each statement to indicate how true that is for you.

1 = almost never   2 = occasionally
3 = usually   4 = almost always

_____   1.   My current relationship conflicts remind me of conflicts I had as a child.
_____   2.   My partner says or does some things that irritate me and reminds me of the way my parents treated me.
_____   3.   My partner disapproves of some things I say or do just the way my parents did.
_____   4.   I criticize myself and others the way I was criticized as a child.
_____   5.   Even though I don't want to, I find myself saying and doing things that hurt my children or partner the same way people hurt me while I was growing up.
_____   6.   When I get upset at myself, I say some of the same critical things to myself that my parents or others said to me when I was a child.
_____   7.   The way my partner relates to me reminds me of the way my parents related to me when I was a child.
_____   8.   I find myself acting weak and helpless so others will feel sorry for me or help me out.
_____   9.   I can see similarities between the kind of intimate relationships I now have and the kind of relationship my parents had or still have with each other.
_____   10. I tend to feel uneasy when everything seems to be going well in my relationships.
_____   11. When I have conflicts with others, I tend to focus on what they did to cause the conflict.
_____   12. I tend to give more than I receive in my relationships.
_____   13. I have trouble enjoying sex the way I would like.
_____   14. I am afraid to be "too successful."
_____   15. I don't like to take risks and prefer to stay with what is familiar.
_____   16. I feel like I am treated unfairly by my intimate partner.
_____   17. When asked, I have trouble thinking about or listing positive traits about myself.
_____   18. I cannot express my feelings the way I would like.
_____   19. I encounter people who tend to treat me like my parents treated me.
_____   20. I feel controlled by the expectations of others.

_____   **Total Score.** (Add the numbers in the column to the left of the statements to get your total score)

Interpretation

Use the following guidelines to help you interpret the possible meaning of your score.

20–40	A few family patterns are likely sources of your present conflicts.
41–60	Many family patterns are the likely sources of your present conflicts.
61–80	Almost all of your present conflicts have their source in unprocessed family patterns.

SELF INVENTORY: ASSESSING THE LEVEL OF DYSFUNCTION IN YOUR FAMILY OF ORIGIN*

Using the list of twenty-five dysfunctional elements of families, rate your own family of origin. Use the following rating scale:

1 = not present at all   2 = present to a small degree
3 = present sometimes   4 = present most of the time
5 = present all of the time

_____ 1. The family promotes competition rather than cooperation. This means that children are compared with each other and sibling rivalry is actually promoted.

_____ 2. There is a misuse of parental power. Parents may use their power to threaten, intimidate, control, and subjugate their children to obey their will. This usually involves a deliberate, but often unconscious, attempt to break the will of the child, often while the child is still an infant. It is often justified as necessary "for their own good."

_____ 3. There is no respect for the basic human rights of children or women. Women and children are treated like chattel or property, without basic human rights. Children are expected to be seen and not heard and have no needs or wants of their own.

_____ 4. There are rigid, compulsive rules. There is an attempt to overcontrol or overregulate the behavior of family members through the use of rigidly enforced rules. Reasons for rules are usually not provided and obedience is mandatory.

_____ 5. There are rigid gender roles. The boys or men are supposed to follow their traditional roles and the girls or women theirs. No exceptions are allowed. People tend to interact with each other through their roles rather than through their individual interests and needs.

_____ 6. There is no sharing of housework or household chores. Women and girls are expected to handle the household chores; the boys and men are exempt from these duties. Boys growing up in this type of family often expect to be waited on by their spouse when they get married.

_____ 7. There are no joint family activities planned. This type of family is very fragmented, and there are no structures or planned activities like family outings that promote unity and family bonding.

_____ 8. The economic condition of the family is kept secret from family members. In these families, children are not told about the family's income and little or no financial responsibility is shared appropriately with other family members.

_____ 9. There is no respect for personal privacy. Children do not have their own personal space or property. Toys, clothing, bedrooms, furniture, and personal items belong to the family not individuals. Parents do not respect their children's needs for privacy or boundaries.

_____ 10. There is no shared decision-making in the family. The head of the household makes all the major decisions, and other family members have very little say in these decisions.

_____ 11. There is no shared parenting. In these families almost all of the parenting is done by one parent, usually the mother. The father is absent or not involved in the day-to-day parenting, perhaps is only involved occasionally in disciplining the children.

_____ 12. There is no support for the expression of feelings. Family members are taught to hide their feelings or are punished for their attempts to express normal feelings such as anger, sadness, fear, or even joy.

_____ 13. The main forms of discipline utilized are spanking, threats, or shaming. The level of physical or emotional violence is high in these families. Usually there is abuse of alcohol or drugs by one or both parents.

_____ 14. Win-lose conflict resolution methods are utilized. Whenever there is a conflict, someone wins and someone loses, instead of finding a solution where both parties can win. Win-win resolutions require a set of problem-solving skills that most parents don't have.

_____ 15. No one admits making a mistake or apologizes for their actions. Parents are always right in these families, and they present themselves as infallible. If they make a mistake, they try to hide it or explain it away instead of owning it and apologizing to those who were affected by the mistake.

_____ 16. Problems are blamed on others. There is a defensiveness in the family; when something bad happens, there is a quick attempt to blame it on someone else. There is no personal accountability or responsibility for one's own actions.

_____ 17. There is resistance to outsiders. There is a "we versus them" attitude toward anyone outside the family. The family is not opened to guests coming in or to sharing with others outside the family.

_____ 18. Loyalty to the family is seen as a duty. Children are expected to defend the family against outside criticism, even when the family is in the wrong. Protecting the family name is overemphasized .

_____ 19. There is resistance to change. Even though there are obvious dysfunctional elements in the family, there is strong resistance to changing them. There seems to be a fear that any change may bring about something worse. Sometimes people have lived for generations with these dysfunctional elements and have become comfortable with their "familiarity." To change them means going into unfamiliar territory.

_____ 20. There is no family unity. In this type of family "two against one" triangles develop to create some unity or safety. There is often a lot of indirect communication where one person may communicate to another through a third person.

_____ 21. There is no protection from abusive acts. In this type of family every conflict is "swept under the rug." Children may be emotionally, physically, or sexually abused by one parent, and the other parent does nothing to protect the child from this abuse. This can also be true in sibling abuse, where an older sibling abuses a younger one and nothing is done by either parent to stop it or protect the younger child.

_____ 22. Conflicts in the family are often ignored. In this type of family every conflict is "swept under the rug" rather than resolved effectively. This often causes a heavy, oppressive family atmosphere where there is conflict in the air and no one is talking about it.

_____ 23. There are a large number of family secrets. Almost every family has some secret they don't want people outside the family to know. The children are admonished not to reveal these secrets. However, many times the children are not told these secrets and the presence of these secrets colors relationships among family members. Often some know the secret and others don't, creating "unholy alliances" in the family.

_____ 24. There is little joy or laughter in the family. In these families, parents often feel overburdened or overwhelmed by the job of parenting, so they can't have fun or allow laughter in the family. In some families, the only laughter that is permitted is when someone is teased or made the butt of some joke. This is a dysfunctional form of humor.

_____ 25. The children are unplanned or unwanted. Over 50% of all children born in this country are either unplanned or unwanted. Children often know they are unplanned or unwanted, even though no one ever tells them. An illegitimate birth is often kept as a family secret.

_____ Total Score

Scoring and Interpretation

Add the points for each item to get an overall rating of how you perceive the level of dysfunction present in your family of origin. Below is a suggested interpretation of your overall rating. If your overall score was between:

0–25	There was almost no evidence of dysfunctional elements present in your family. Caution: Too "rosy" a picture of your family of origin could indicate some denial of these dysfunctional elements and their possible effects on you.
26–75	There is some evidence of dysfunctional elements present in your family of origin.
76–125	There is considerable evidence of dysfunctional elements present in your family or origin.

*From Weinhold, 1991.

SELF-INVENTORY: THE VALUES AND BELIEFS OF DYSFUNCTIONAL FAMILIES

Parents teach their children their values and beliefs. In dysfunctional families, some of the values and beliefs can have negative consequences for children who adopt them without question. The list below identifies some of the social values that are often taught in families. Check any of the following things that you learned as a child that now affect you in negative or dysfunctional ways.

1 = not present at all   2 = present some of the time
3 = present most of the time   4 = present all of the time

_____   1. Have respect for your elders at all times.

_____   2. Have a low or humble opinion of yourself, always appearing modest.

_____   3. See your parents as always right; don't question their actions.

_____   4. Never express any strong feelings; it is bad to be angry.

_____   5. Always act nice (even when you don't feel nice).

_____   6. Pretend to be grateful, even when you don't feel that way.

_____   7. Be strong, tough, and able to take a joke or punishment.

_____   8. Feel duty-bound to always love your parents no matter what they do to you.

_____   9. Do not be strong-willed or obstinate.

_____   10. Children have to earn respect by their good behavior.

_____   11. Always put the needs of your parents and others before your own.

_____   12. Tenderness is a sign of weakness; people will take advantage of you.

_____   13. Sex is dirty; anything pertaining to sex should not be discussed in public.

_____   14. Don't do or say anything that might damage your family's name or reputation.

_____   15. Others (specify)_____

_____   Total Score

Scoring and Interpretation

Use the following guidelines to help you interpret the possible meaning of your total score.

14–28   Very few dysfunctional values or beliefs present.

29–42   Some dysfunctional values or beliefs present.

43–56   Many dysfunctional values and beliefs present.

SELF-AWARENESS EXERCISE: HOW DO DYSFUNCTIONAL FAMILY ELEMENTS AFFECT YOU?

This activity helps you review the list of dysfunctional elements that might have been present in your family and examine the possible effects these elements still have on you. List all the possible effects that each of the dysfunctional elements you identified in the previous activity might have on your thinking, feelings, values, beliefs, and behavior. Items with a rating of "3" or more from the previous two inventories are probably worth examining.

The possible effects of these elements on my present thinking:

The possible effects of these elements on my present feelings:

The possible effects of these elements on my present values:

The possible effects of these elements on my present beliefs:

The possible effects of these elements on my present behaviors:

SELF-AWARENESS EXERCISE: WHAT FAMILY-RELATED PROBLEMS WERE PRESENT IN YOUR FAMILY OF ORIGIN?

It is important to inventory your family-of-origin problems to see how they might have affected you. This may help you locate some sources of unresolved or intractable conflicts. Below is a problem checklist that asks you to identify the problems that were present in your family of origin. These are grouped according to the problem areas discussed in this chapter. Place a checkmark next to each of the questions that indicate that this problem was present in your family of origin. In this activity you are only to determine the presence or absence of the problem and not the degree to which the problem might have been present.

Two-Career Family

_____ 1. Did both of your parents work or spend considerable time outside of the home while you were growing up?

_____ 2. Did you come home from school to an empty house or without a parent there to greet you?

_____ 3. Did the absence of one or both of your parents cause you any problems while you were growing up?

_____ 4. Did you receive less care than you needed from your parents because one or both were working or away from your home a considerable amount of time?

Marital Dysfunction

_____ 5. Was there marital discord present between your parents while you were growing up?

_____ 6. Were you forced to take sides in any marital disputes?

_____ 7. Did the marital discord in your family lead to divorce or legal separation?

_____ 8. Did you feel that any of your important needs were neglected as a result of marital discord?

Single-Parent Family

_____ 9. Did you spend some time growing up in a single-parent family?

_____ 10. Did you spend some time growing up in a step-family?

_____ 11. Did you feel in the middle between divorcing or separating parents?

Drug and Alcohol Abuse

_____ 12. Was there abuse of drugs or alcohol present in your family of origin?

_____ 13. Did you develop codependent behaviors as a result of growing up in your family?

_____ 14. Were there other addictions (food, work, sex, etc.) present in your family of origin?

School-Related Problems

_____ 15. Did you have difficulties in school?

_____ 16. Did you not receive the support you needed from the school or your parents to handle the difficulties effectively?

_____ 17. Was your self-esteem adversely affected by these school-related problems?

Child-Management Problems

_____ 18. Did your parents have difficulty disciplining you effectively as a child?

_____ 19. Were you a family scapegoat who was blamed for problems that were not of your making?

_____ 20. Did you rebel against parental authority?

_____ 21. Did you try to take care of your parents by never causing them any problems?

Adolescent Depression and/or Suicide

_____ 22. Were you depressed for extended periods of time as an adolescent?

_____ 23. Did you ever contemplate or attempt suicide?

_____ 24. Did you ever feel that you were unable to live up to parental expectations?

_____ 25. Was one or both of your parents depressed or suicidal while you were growing up?

Adult Children Leaving Home

_____ 26. Was your departure from home in late adolescence full of conflict?

_____ 27. Did your parents make it hard for you to leave home?

_____ 28. Did you ever have to return to live with your parents after you left home?

Grandparents Live with Family

_____ 29. Did one or more of your grandparents live with your family while you were growing up?

_____ 30. Did problems over the care of your grandparents cause discord in your family while you were growing up?

SELF-AWARENESS EXERCISE: HOW DID FAMILY PROBLEMS AFFECT YOU?

This self-awareness exercise asks you to focus on the effects the problems in the previous list had on you and how they affected your thought, feelings, values, beliefs, and behaviors. Go back to the items you checked and examine the possible effects these problems had on you.

The possible effects of these problems on your present behavior:

The possible effects of these problems on your present feelings:

The possible effects of these problems on your present values:

The possible effects of these problems on your present beliefs:

Chapter 8

~

What Are the Developmental Sources of Intractable Conflicts?

This chapter presents an optimal model for parenting children and identifies critical developmental issues and experiences from the first three years of life that are commonly found at the source of intractable conflicts. We find intractable conflicts often correlate with traumatic events related to abandonment, abuse, and/or neglect during the first three years of life. Early developmental experiences create an internal working model of reality (Bowlby, 1969), which is learned through parent-child dynamics, that colors all adult relationships. When you seek to resolve intractable conflicts at their source, you are likely to discover early traumatic experiences that include betrayal trauma, attachment trauma, and other kinds of developmental trauma related to unmet developmental needs, as well as defense mechanisms that were developed in order to survive these traumatic experiences.

Positive, reciprocal parent-child experiences create adults with a secure, optimistic, cooperative internal working model of reality, while traumatic experiences involving abandonment, neglect, and abuse can create adults with anxious, negative, avoidant, ambivalent, or nonreciprocal model of reality. Most people's internal working model of reality falls somewhere on a continuum between these two extremes. The character of a person's internal working model of reality is most visible in adult patterns of conflict.

As you read about optimal parenting, keep in mind that this information has emerged in the last 10 to 15 years and very little of it has entered the training programs for educators, physicians, and mental health professionals. Remember to hold a kind and compassionate attitude toward your parents and health care professionals regarding the quality of your own early developmental experiences. They have done their best, as you did if you have children, with the information and training that was available. It is also important to remember that developmental deficiencies can be remedied at any time in your life. Once you know what you really needed as an infant, for example, you can make a plan to get it.

WHAT ARE THE STAGES OF HUMAN DEVELOPMENT?

The Partnership Way divides human development into four stages: the *codependent* stage, the *counter-dependent* stage, the *independent* stage, and the *interdependent* stage, and then identifies the critical developmental tasks to be completed in each stage. These stages are illustrated in Table 8.1.

Table 8.1
The Development of an Individual

Stage of Development	Primary Developmental Tasks
Codependent *(0–8 months)*	Bonding with yourself Bonding with your parents Bonding with your immediate family Establishing primal trust with your parents
Counter-dependent *(8–36 months)*	Separating psychologically from your parents Bonding with your extended family Resolving your internal conflicts between oneness and separateness
Independent *(3–6 years)*	Mastering your ability to care for yourself Developing autonomy from your parents Developing your core personal values and beliefs Achieving object constancy as an individual Bonding with nature
Interdependent *(6–28 years)*	Cooperating with others Negotiating to get your needs met Bonding with culture Bonding with a person of the opposite/same sex

Like most people, you may not know about these stages and tasks and the critical role they play in shaping your adult life. Unless there was obvious physical abuse or neglect, you may believe you had a "normal" childhood. Because this information about the early developmental needs of children has not yet reached mainstream, many adults may not be aware of what they missed. From this perspective, virtually everyone alive today has experienced some degree of trauma related to abandonment, neglect, and/or abuse.

Many adults who experience difficulty with intimacy in their relationships also have addictions to substances or activities and experience depression, anxiety, and dissociation related to early trauma. They may also have difficulty tracing these problems to deficits related to developmental trauma. Without knowledge of how things got broken, it is often impossible to fix them. Blaming difficult or traumatic childhood experiences on parents is not useful, as most parents do the best they can with the resources they have available. It is useful, however, to identify childhood antecedents to current conflicts and problems that recycle through life so that active plans can be developed to mediate their influence.

WHAT ARE SOME OF THE CRITICAL FACTORS THAT AFFECT EARLY HUMAN DEVELOPMENT?

Conflicts that produce intense feelings often indicate the presence of developmental trauma from the first year or two of life. These include:

- maternal drug and/or alcohol use during gestation
- premature birth and separation from the mother

- chronic maternal depression
- premature and/or repeated separation or abandonment by the mother or primary caregiver
- coldness or remoteness from the mother or primary caregiver
- undiagnosed and/or chronic or recurring painful illnesses such as colic or ear infections
- betrayal by trusted caregivers
- inconsistent or inadequate daycare
- neglect
- abuse

These traumatic experiences create defensive or protective responses that emerge whenever you experience stress, ranging on a continuum between mild and severe. Research findings on bonding and attachment between parents and children, a new area of investigation, indicate the long-lasting impact of early developmental trauma. As new information on optimal parenting emerges, parents often find themselves feeling negligent, guilty, and remorseful. The truth is that few, if any, people have been perfectly parented. The new trauma reduction therapy modalities bring hope, as it is now possible to remediate much of the residue of developmental trauma.

The Myth of the Perfect Parent

No one need feel guilty for giving or receiving less than perfect parenting. Most parents were not parented optimally and therefore could not provide it for their children. Winnicott (1965, 1975) talks about the "good enough" mother, who is not expected to be perfect but just to provide adequate mothering. Child custody cases sometimes utilize this concept to determine if a child might be more damaged by being left with the mother or by being removed to foster care.

Everyone is responsible, however, for identifying the missing pieces of their parenting that contribute to intractable conflicts and for seeking remedies to them. Present generations may be the first in the history of the human species with sufficient information to reparent themselves and parent their children in ways that approach optimal rather than good enough.

Unresolved conflicts from your childhood will activate when your children reach the same age you were when you experienced a trauma. This phenomenon, known as *regression-progression*, was first identified by Lloyd DeMause (1982, p. 135). He uses this concept to trace the evolution of parenting practices.

The concept of unconscious regression-progression makes it essential that you attempt to fill your own developmental holes before you have children of your own. It isn't enough just to identify these deficits. Unless they are remedied via trauma-reduction therapies, they will likely interfere with your ability to parent children in an optimal manner. You can't truly be present as a parent if you are busy reacting to post-traumatic symptoms related to your own wounds and unmet needs. This concept advocates the necessity of parents healing their own developmental trauma prior to having children or resolving them through therapy to avoid passing them on to their children. For example, if you are the second child in your family, you may be particularly affected by the conflicts, challenges, and experiences of your own second child. You may find yourself identifying and replaying your own patterns more with this child.

If you already have children, it is possible to stop the regression-progression dynamic at any time. Avoid judging yourself or being critical or discouraged about any trauma that you may have inflicted on your children. You have done the best you could as a parent with the tools and awareness you brought from your family of origin. Begin by clearing any residue of your own developmental trauma with trauma-reduction therapies. As you become healthier and clearer, you will be able to help your children clear the residue of developmental trauma they are accumulating. Again, kindness and compassion for yourself, your parents, and your children will help you tremendously in parenting more optimally.

Development Is Continuous

One of the most significant concepts in developmental psychology is that human development is continuous. If something gets missed, development does not pause. It continues, with each task or need building on the next. Any trauma, unmet need, incomplete psychosocial task, or unresolved conflict becomes a developmental hole or gap. A child with few holes is more resilient and able to tolerate stress and trauma later in life.

Because of the natural learning style of humans, your unmet needs and incomplete developmental tasks will recycle and press for completion. At every transition in your subsequent development, these incomplete tasks and unmet needs appear, seeking completion. They emerge as conflicts in your intimate relationships with partners, children, friends, and coworkers and contribute to conflicts in your neighborhood, community, and nation.

You, like most people, probably left childhood still missing some important developmental pieces, which now appear in intractable conflicts. Humans, fortunately, have many built-in defense mechanisms that help them survive. Unfortunately, these defense systems divert life energy from self-actualization.

The next sections of this chapter present an overview of optimal parenting practices. They also show the correlation between developmental trauma and conflict. Before reading the next section, please take the Self-Awareness Inventory: How to Identify Your Codependent Behaviors at the end of this chapter. It may help you personalize the information about the codependent stage of development. After scoring and interpreting this inventory, return here and continue reading.

WHAT ARE THE SOURCES OF TRAUMA AND CONFLICT RELATED TO THE CODEPENDENT STAGE OF DEVELOPMENT?

The codependent stage of development covers the period from zero to about eight months of age. First, let us look at the definition of zero. This varies according to your belief about when psychological life begins. While there is controversy on this topic, some research from pre- and perinatal psychology seems to indicate that it begins at conception. Other studies show that memory and interactive response patterns have begun by the third month of gestation. There is now an impressive body of research that describes prenatal development in considerable detail.

The Importance of Prenatal Development

The ground-breaking research in pre-and perinatal development began with Thomas Verny's (1981) book, *The Secret Life of the Unborn Child.* He summarized all the relevant research in this field. Since this book's publication, the Association for Pre- and Perinatal Psychology and Health has continued collecting and disseminating new research findings in this area. One of the important findings from pre- and perinatal research is the correlation between birth traumas and difficulties in adult relationships. Because of the significance of pre- and perinatal experiences in forming a person's internal working model, it is often a factor in intractable conflicts.

Pre- and perinatal psychology validates many of the things once considered old wives' tales, such as the importance of talking, singing, and playing music to an unborn child. These are now recognized as some of the first steps in parent-child bonding.

Sound can affect the activity of the fetus. In an experiment using ultrasound pictures, the fetus was shown to react to different types of music. From this experiment, researchers found that the largo movements from classical music quieted the fetus. Largo music has about 60 beats per minute, which is about the same as the mother's resting heartbeat. Music with a faster beat takes the child out of harmony with the mother's heartbeat.

There are other conditions during pregnancy that also affect the bonding process between mother and child. Prenatal studies, for example, indicate that the presence of conflict in the family disturbs the fetus. The presence of adrenaline in the mother's blood stresses the fetus and can cause both physical and psychological delays as the child develops. Families with little or no conflict and families with significant conflict were studied for five to ten years. These longitudinal studies found significant differences in growth rates, development rates, and psychological problems of the children. Verny's research shows that babies remember everything and are deeply impacted by the events around them. Unfortunately, they are not able to communicate this at the time.

Our rebirthing therapy with clients supports this research. Many remember exact conversations adults present at their birth had with each other, while others knew what the adults were thinking. After their rebirthing therapy, several clients were able to verify the accuracy of these birth memories with their parents. This anecdotal information indicates that newborns are able to tune into the thoughts and feelings of those around them.

Home Birthing vs. Hospital Birthing

Prior to World War II, almost everyone in the United States was born at home. Since World War II, almost everyone has been born in a hospital, which means that everyone born since then was subjected to modern obstetrical techniques. It is now recognized that these techniques significantly interfere with the parent-child bonding process. When the midwife movement began to gain momentum over the last fifteen years, hospitals began changing their birthing facilities and procedures in order to prevent financial losses. Most hospitals, however, still provide less than optimal birthing procedures.

Traditional hospital birthing procedures tend to disempower parents. When a woman walks into the hospital to give birth, she is immediately placed in a wheelchair. This places the mother lower than other adults, and she must look up to speak. Then the parents-to-be are asked to sign documents that virtually declare the baby as the property of the hospital until baby and mother go home.

The message from traditional medicine is clear: "We're in charge of your baby. We know better than you do what is best for your baby." The best way to avoid this loss of personal power is to draft your own agreement prior to the birth, specifying exactly what procedures you want used and those which you do not wish used, unless you give explicit permission. This agreement should be signed by all birth personnel, including the physician, attending nurse, and birth assistant prior to the birth. If they refuse, you may want to seek another physician and/or hospital.

The Birth Process

The birthing process itself can have profound effects on the development of a child. The research of Klaus and Kennell (1976), who popularized the word "bonding," created the first scenario for optimal birthing conditions. According to their findings, the nude child should be placed on the mother's chest near her breast immediately after birth. Then the child should be allowed to find the breast on its own and begin nursing. Klaus (1995) found that babies who were placed on their mother's chest and received extended eye contact could find their mother's breast and begin nursing within twenty-five minutes. The newborn's sense of smell helps them accomplish this important task.

The umbilical cord should not be cut until the umbilical blood separates, with part flowing into the mother and the other part into the child. Of course, the mother should be awake enough to participate in this first event of separation. Many mothers, however, are drugged and cannot actively participate. Premature cutting of the umbilical cord is now recognized as a contributing factor in newborn jaundice (Dunn, 1985).

For many years, a factor in the premature cutting of the umbilical cord was an economic issue. Prior to concerns about HIV-contaminated blood, placentas were refrigerated in the hospital and sold after the departure of the baby to companies that used their unique substances in research, cosmetics, and commercial products. The value of placentas depends on the amount of blood they contain. Current hospital policies encourage the refrigeration of the placenta in case the child needs a transfusion during the perinatal period (Jeffries, 1997).

More recent research by Marshall Klaus (1995) and his colleagues regarding conditions for optimal maternal/infant bonding calls for extended skin-to-skin contact during the first 36 hours after birth, suckling during the first hour following birth, and "rooming in" arrangements that keep the parents and child together. When these conditions were present at birth, Klaus found a marked drop in early child abuse. One study from a hospital in Thailand, quoted by Klaus (1995), indicated that the presence of these procedures at birth reduced the number of abandoned babies from 33 to 1. Klaus also found that babies cry when they are taken away from their mothers during the first 90 minutes after birth, but do not cry if kept together during this time period.

The Father's Role in the Birthing Process

Klaus and Kennell (1976) also found that it was very important for the father to be present for the birth and participate in it as much as possible. In follow-up studies, they found fathers who were present at the birth were less likely to abuse that child. Once the child has nursed initially, then the baby should be passed to the father and put on his chest. Klaus and Kennell believe that the optimal human-bonding period is the first 12 to 36 hours after birth. During this period, it is best if mother and father spend time in bed together holding the baby. During this time, they should pass the baby back and forth so there is extensive skin-to-skin contact between the mother and the child and the father and the child.

Few individuals got this kind of bonding experience. If you were born in a hospital, you were probably whisked away to the nursery after only minimal contact with your mother and had little or no contact with your father. If there were any complications, you may have been separated from your mother for hours, days, or even weeks. If this is true, you probably still carry imprints of abandonment from your birth experience that impact your adult behaviors. Pre- and perinatal research is just discovering the immense power of these first life experiences in creating internal working models of reality that direct an individual's life.

The Role of Siblings in the Birthing Process

Until recently, young siblings were not allowed to visit the hospital after a birth, and most are still prohibited from being physically present at the birth of a brother or sister. In home births, all members of the nuclear and extended family are frequently present. Research indicates that people who attend a childbirth automatically bond with the child, reducing both sibling rivalry and child abuse. Hospitals may have to change their policies again as a result of the home-birthing movement and new research findings (Klaus, Kennell, & Klaus, 1993, 1995).

Birthing Positions

Some hospitals are now installing water tanks so that mothers can give birth underwater. This is a remarkable innovation. Underwater birthing has been practiced for twenty-five years in France and Russia; it has appeared more recently in California. This procedure makes sense because a child lives in water while in the womb. Water birth is also a natural way to give birth, as it allows the mother to deliver in a squatting position. This allows the forces of gravity and support of the water to assist in the birth process. The worst possible delivery position for a mother is on her back with her feet up in the air. In most "primitive" societies, women squat to give birth.

Research from pre- and perinatal psychology indicates that the parent's unprocessed birth trauma often emerges during the delivery of their own child. Most parents, unfortunately, do not have the opportunity to heal their own birth trauma before having their children. Perhaps this is why so many mothers request to be knocked out with drugs, why fathers often choose not to be present, and why doctors want to get the whole thing over with as quickly as possible. These avoidant behaviors indicate the presence of post-traumatic stress symptoms that prevent adults from being totally present for the miracle of birth. These symptoms may be a factor in the steady rise in the number of Cesarean births since 1947, as well as the use of other so-called timesaving procedures such as episiotomies and forceps.

The context of the birth experience affects all subsequent development of the child, particularly those involving the development of trust. Birth circumstances become part of a trauma syndrome that organizes people's lives. If the birth was traumatic, this trauma gets repeated through a life psychodrama, or story that gets replayed or reenacted through recurring problems and intractable conflicts. Most people, unfortunately, are never able to identify birth trauma as a source of these psychodramas.

The Overuse of Drugs During the Birth Process

Another undesirable birthing practice is the use of epidural or spinal-block anesthesia, which automatically increases the fetal temperature. Doctors may think the child is ill, separate it from the mother, and administer a battery of invasive tests that are necessary only because of the epidural-induced fever. Seventy-five percent of birthing mothers in this country are now given epidural anesthetics (Leiva, 1995).

If physicians expect any complications, they routinely give an epidural. Birth complications are often due to the emergence of the mother's own unprocessed birth trauma, preventing her from being a full participant (Klaus, Kennell, & Klaus, 1995). Many doctors like anesthetizing the mother because it speeds up the birth. They are often more concerned about the danger of malpractice suits than the long-term welfare of the mother and child. All drugs administered to the mother during labor are directly transferred to the fetus. The fetus is also drugged and can't participate fully in the birthing process, necessitating a forceps delivery. There is now mounting evidence correlating drugged births with drug use and abuse during adolescence and adulthood (Leiva, 1995).

Many physicians routinely use drugs to induce labor so that delivery better accommodates their busy schedules. Again, these policies focus more on the physician's needs than the welfare of the child. Drugged births disempower both the mother and the child, so birthing is "done to them." It is little wonder people believe they cannot get their needs met unless they act like a passive victim. Traumatic birth experiences imprint those unlucky enough to be born in hospitals with modern obstetrical methods.

All prospective mothers should have periodic prenatal care, including information on diet and nutrition, if babies are to get a good start. Yet, far too many expectant mothers get no prenatal care. There is a lot of good information available that has been researched and tested. Yet the medical establishment is slow to change. Prenatal education needs to be one of the highest national public health awareness issues. It should be taught in all schools, and the media should be providing constant reminders to the general public through public service announcements.

The Role of Circumcision in Infant Trauma

The United States is the only country in the world that circumcises its male infants for nonreligious reasons. Somewhere between 60% and 80% of all newborn males are still being circumcised in this country, even though in 1983 the American Academy of Pediatrics stated that there is no known medical justification for this practice (Wallenstein, 1985). Estimates are that between 78% and 90% of the present population of 125 million American men have had this painful initiation to life (Slotkowski & King, 1982). Even more sad, most had this procedure done without any anesthetic. Circumcision causes incredible trauma to male infants and must be eliminated. If required for religious reasons, it should be done with a local anesthetic and not just the customary wine that is given during many circumcision rituals. Female circumcision is not practiced as much in this country, but is widely practiced for religious reasons in many Moslem countries, usually before the girl reaches adolescence.

The French obstetrician, Frederic LeBoyer, said:

> Once we remember that all that takes place during the first days of life, on an emotional level, shapes the pattern of all future reactions, we cannot but wonder why such a torture (circumcision) has been inflicted on the child. How could a being who has been so aggressed in this way while totally helpless, develop into a relaxed, loving, trusting person. Indeed, he will never be able to trust anyone in life. He will always be on the defensive, unable to open up to others into life. (Diamond, 1994)

The Care of the Mother During the Birthing Process

A doula is a birth assistant whose job is to take care of the mother during the labor and delivery (Klaus, Kennell, & Klaus, 1993). These trained birth assistants provide support to the mother while the midwife or medical assistants focus on the infant's needs. Doulas typically begin their work with the family during the prenatal period, preparing everyone for the birth process. Doulas provide emotional support for mothers during the labor period if they get discouraged or scared and physical support through massage and holding. Doulas are trained to help the mother stay focused on the child and attend to the signals the child is sending to the mother so that she can harmonize with the child during the birthing process.

Doulas are trained to help parents maximize the bonding period immediately following birth. Every mother should have a doula before, during, and immediately after the birth of their child.

In Great Britain, for example, each mother is automatically assigned a personal doula when she checks into the birthing clinic. This became an accepted practice because it reduced the mother's hospital stay. The research revealed fewer Cesarean births and fewer birth complications, making the use of doulas an economic issue in Britain's socialized medical system.

Other Essentials for Strong Bonding

There are other significant components of bonding, such as eye contact between the mother and child. Until recently, adults assumed that newborn infants couldn't see. In fact, infants are myopic, or nearsighted, and able to see optimally at a distance of about 12 inches. Interestingly, this is the distance from the breast to the mother's face. Nursing newborns or infants held close to the breast can focus their eyes on the faces of their mothers. Everything else they see is out of focus. Mother Nature is pretty intelligent. She creates newborns with the kind of eyesight needed for good bonding.

The initial eye contact between parent and child is very important for bonding. Ideally, your parents could see your essence and feel a sense of anticipation and discovery about your unique unfolding as an individual. If your parents looked at you and were unable to really see your essence, this impacted your ability to bond. Perhaps your mother thought, "I want you to grow up to be a beautiful actress" or your father thought, "I want you to grow up to be a doctor." Parents often project their own unfulfilled wishes and dreams onto their children. Children, even newborns, are so attuned to their parents that they can perceive when they are being received unconditionally and when they are not.

In addition to the extended skin-to-skin contact recommended during the first 12 to 36 hours after birth, research indicates that a full body massage given immediately after birth, with the infant lying in a tub of warm water, can enhance the bonding process. It is best if the mother or father does this massage, although someone with formal massage training is next best. Head-to-toe touch activates the infant's nervous system and releases chemicals that activate brain cells. Repeated infant massages by the mother and/or father during the first several months after birth can also facilitate deeper bonding.

Singing to the young infant is also very important. Infants can recognize tunes they heard while they were in the womb. Michael Odent (1984) is famous for having groups of parents and prospective parents sing together around a piano. Maintaining eye contact while speaking to the infant in soft, loving tones is also very important.

As the child begins to respond with smiles and laughter, the positive effects of early bonding emerge. Mirroring infants' sounds and smiles helps build early communication. Well-bonded infants naturally respond with curiosity to other friends and family. The poorly bonded infant will be fearful of others and cling to known objects.

Creating Optimal Birth Bonding

A group of dedicated professionals, calling themselves the Coalition for Improving Maternity Services, formed a powerful alliance in the summer of 1996 to promote a wellness model of maternity care. They outlined a set of ten principles they call "The Mother-Friendly Childbirth Initiative: Ten Steps to Mother-Friendly Hospitals, Birth Centers, and Home Birth Services" (1996). When all ten steps are achieved, the institution is designated as "Mother-Friendly." The ten requirements are as follows:

1. Offering unrestricted access to birth companions (doulas) to provide continuous emotional and physical support during labor.
2. Access to midwifery care.
3. Provision of accurate descriptions and statistical information to the public about its birth practices, procedures, and outcomes.
4. Freedom to walk, move about, and assume positions of choice during labor and birth.
5. Policies of cooperation with other caregivers providing maternity services to this family.
6. Dropping routine practices not supported by scientific evidence such as withholding nourishment, early rupture of membranes, electronic fetal monitoring, and IV drips.
7. Educating staff in non-drug methods of pain relief.
8. Breast-feeding encouragement and follow-up support.
9. Discouraging nonreligious circumcision of newborn children.
10. To strive to include another ten-step initiative already designed by the World Health Organization/UNESCO called "The Baby-Friendly Hospital Initiative." This initiative is currently being revised by the Coalition for inclusion with its "Mother-Friendly" program to educate all those involved in the birthing industry on the needs and conditions that promote optimal birth bonding.

Before reading about the counter-dependent stage of development described below, please take the Self-Awareness Inventory: How to Identify Your Counter-Dependent Behaviors at the end of the chapter to identify any counter-dependent behaviors that might be causing conflicts in your life. This will give you a personal framework for understanding the following material.

WHAT ARE THE SOURCES OF TRAUMA AND CONFLICT FROM THE COUNTER-DEPENDENT STAGE OF DEVELOPMENT?

This developmental stage begins around eight months of age when the child's attention gradually shifts away from the oneness of bonding to exploration and separation. The primary task of the counter-dependent stage is psychological separation from the parents. During this stage, children learn to experience themselves as separate from their primary caregivers and to develop the capacity for both/and ways of thinking.

As the counter-dependent stage of development unfolds, the child ventures further and further from the bonded safety of the codependent stage into more and more separateness. An exploring child who falls down or gets frightened, quickly runs back to the parents for comfort. This separation process, known as the "terrible twos," can be a rocky period. It contains several substages that are characteristically punctuated by explosive episodes related to an emerging sense of self and the desire for autonomy. During this period, between 18 and 24 months, the child experiences high levels of conflict between the desire for oneness and the drive to explore and become separate.

Oppositional behavior, typical of this splitting substage, also keeps the child trapped in this terrible conflict between the desire for oneness and the desire for separateness. During this critical substage, the child's perception becomes divided into "good" and "bad." Parents who are not immediately available to comfort the child or take care of its needs become "bad parents" who magically convert to "good parents" when they become available. The degree to which the parent is available to meet the child's needs determines the child's perception of the parent's goodness and badness during this stage of development.

Because the child is not separate from the parents, any judgment of badness against the mother or father is also a judgment of badness against the child's self. In other words, the good/bad split is experienced both internally and externally. These splits can take various forms that assign the badness internally within the child or externally to the parents: "I'm not okay and you're not okay," "You're okay and I'm not okay," or "You're not okay and I'm not okay." If these early splitting patterns are not resolved, they become a foundation for lose-lose, win-lose, and lose-win styles of conflict resolution in adulthood. Splitting behavior can become a permanent part of the child's behavior repertoire if it is not successfully resolved by the age of three. We believe that most people are still stuck in the splitting substage of development and still struggle with unresolved internal splits.

Splitting reactions remaining from the counter-dependent stage emerge later in adulthood as black/white, all/nothing, either-or thinking; oppositional behaviors, and one-up/one-down relationship dynamics. If you state that something is one way, oppositional people will argue that it is the other way. Pervasive splitting behaviors in adulthood indicate the probability of developmental trauma between the ages of 18 and 24 months.

Evidence of resolving the splitting stage is the presence of both/and thinking, such as "I'm okay and you're okay." It indicates the child is moving out of the counter-dependent stage of development and into the independent stage of development. At the completion of this process, known as the psychological birth, the child is emotionally and psychologically separate from the parents and can operate from an ever-increasing internal locus of control.

Parents and other bonded caregivers play a critical role in helping the child move through the splitting sub-stage of development toward object constancy. This is the child's ability to maintain a sense of equanimity when people are saying or doing bad things to him or her. Parents' most difficult task is to avoid participation in the child's perceptual split. Behaviorally, this split manifests as the two-against-one game in which the child allies with one parent against the other via some kind of secret, or taking sides. Here, the child tests the strength of the bond between the parents or caregivers, as well as the adults' psychological maturity.

Adults who have not completed their own psychological birth will display splitting behaviors in the midst of a conflict with the child and get into power struggles. When this happens, the adults will find it difficult to validate the child's reality and reflect the child's feelings, making the child's separation process even more difficult. A father with unresolved abandonment issues, for example, may reveal his split by criticizing his wife and making her bad in some way when she pays more attention to the child's needs than she does to his needs. It is no surprise, therefore, that the most common time for fathers to leave a marriage or file for divorce is when the first child is about two years old.

The primary responsibilities of parents during the counter-dependent stage of development are to:

- avoid participating in the child's good-bad splits in perception
- give twice as many yes as no answers
- set appropriate and safe limits without shaming or physically punishing the child
- show respect and compassion for the feelings of the child
- take the child's needs seriously
- make sure the child's needs get met appropriately

If managed properly, the counter-dependent stage of development culminates successfully between ages two and three with the full psychological birth. This is visible by the child's ability to maintain object constancy and the presence of "I'm okay, you're okay" thinking.

The Functional Family Triangle

Resolving the conflicts of the counter-dependent stage of development requires very specific protocols related to splitting and separation on the part of the parents and/or caregivers:

- When one parent is not available to the child, the other parent or another bonded caregiver needs to be available to physically and verbally support the child's feelings of anger, grief, fear, and sadness: "I can see that you are upset because your daddy left."
- The available parent or caregiver needs to assure the child that the absent or unavailable parent will return: "I'm here to take care of you while your daddy is gone tonight."
- Avoid making anyone bad during conflicts and support the child's feelings: "You seem angry because your daddy left. You don't like daddy when he leaves. It is okay to feel angry when daddy leaves."
- Both parents or caregivers must create clear communication patterns between both themselves and between themselves and the child to prevent two-against-one or triangulation dynamics: "I can see that you are angry at Mommy because she asked you to put your toys away. Perhaps you want to go to her and tell her how you feel. Would you like me to go with you to talk to her?"

These protocols help create the *functional family triangle*. Through repeated successful trials, the child eventually learns that neither mother or father is all bad and eventually adopts "I'm okay; you're okay" or both/and thinking. The child is then more free to use feelings and inner knowledge to direct his or her life. The child is emotionally prepared to handle frustration and to move forward to independence, the next stage of development.

When functional family dynamics are not present in the parent-child structure, a dysfunctional family triangle known as the drama triangle develops instead. The dynamics of the drama triangle represent unresolved conflicts stemming originally from the counter-dependent stage of development. These recycling developmental dynamics, which will be discussed in detail in Chapter 9, interfere with people getting their basic needs met in subsequent relationships and are a major factor in the creation of intractable conflicts.

WHAT ARE THE SOURCES OF CONFLICT AND TRAUMA FROM THE INDEPENDENT STAGE OF DEVELOPMENT?

Once the developmental tasks of the previous stages have been successfully completed, the child can focus on mastering self-care activities. Three-year-old children are now ready to feed, dress, and toilet themselves. They continue to have an intense drive to learn and understand how everything in their environment works. This is the "why" stage of development, which usually lasts until about age six.

Another part of the independent stage is a fascination with fantasy. Children's imaginary friends and psychic or other full-sensory abilities can frighten adults. Because there is a fine line between the real and the imagined at this age, some grounding in everyday reality is necessary. At the same time, it is important that adults indulge the child's fantasies, such as listening to their reports of conversations with an imaginary friend, in order to nurture the full development of the child's senses.

Because much of the child's environment is adult-centered rather than child-centered, children may need considerable parental support in mastering their immediate world. Moving the cereal box to a lower shelf where the child can reach it, buying quarts of milk instead of half-gallons, and placing food on the bottom shelf in the refrigerator will not only help support the child's mastery-building process, it will also reduce the amount of frustration in the child's life.

Children who are not supported in developing autonomous behavior during this period grow up without the ability to direct their adult lives. They may exhibit dependent behaviors such as the inability to provide financial support for themselves, hold a steady job, manage their time and/or money, and lack individual initiative. These kinds of passive behaviors make them ideal candidates for the victim role in the drama triangle and to be the object of aggressive acts from others. These children also are candidates for authoritarian organizations seeking compliant and/or obedient members. Adults with deficits from the independent stage of development may also lack critical thinking skills necessary for evaluating information and problem-solving. These skill deficits can also cause intractable conflicts, as these individuals are not able to assume full responsibility for their lives.

WHAT ARE THE SOURCES OF CONFLICT AND TRAUMA FROM THE INTERDEPENDENT STAGE OF DEVELOPMENT?

This stage naturally builds on the three previous stages. Interdependence, which typically develops between 6 and 18 years of age, has two primary tasks: learning cooperative behaviors and learning to resolve conflicts from a win-win position. The first task is, of course, necessary for the development of the second. Most of the skills in the interdependent stage are learned in formal education settings, such as daycare and schools.

It is a challenge for students to develop interdependence skills in a school atmosphere that has an exclusively competitive orientation. If a first-grader helps a classmate with homework, for example, the students will be applauded for being kind and cooperative. If this same student helps a classmate with his homework in fifth grade, their cooperation might be considered cheating.

When students in the first grade are asked if they feel good about themselves, almost all of them say yes. By fifth grade, the yes answers drop to about 20%. By twelfth grade, the percentage is down to about 5% (Weinhold, 1996a). Barry comments on this point:

> This drop in self-esteem and emphasis on negative behavior is visible when I visit schools to promote the Kindness Campaign (discussed in Chapter 14). When I ask students if it is easier for students to get noticed in school for doing something positive or something negative, almost 100% of them say "something negative."

Children who enter school with a high level of completed developmental tasks from the codependent, counter-dependent, and independent stages are more able to maneuver their way through this minimally supportive environment. Some schools have begun to utilize cooperative education in the classroom to balance the overly competitive structure of the schools and to foster development of cooperative skills and win-win conflict resolution. If students reach the age of 18 with most of their developmental tasks completed, they have the foundation they need for a functional adulthood.

Children who do not have support in developing interdependent behaviors grow up without the ability to negotiate to get their needs met. Lacking this critical skill, it is more likely they will use drama triangle dynamics, indirect communication, and victimization to get their needs met. These children also have difficulty in establishing and maintaining cooperative relationships. Without these assertive communication and effective relationship skills, they are also more likely to resort to dirty fighting, litigation, and even violence to resolve their conflicts.

HOW CAN I CHANGE MY INTERNAL WORKING MODEL OF REALITY?

The exercises and activities included in this book are excellent tools for changing your internal working model of reality. While it may seem risky and scary, our experiences and that of many of our clients and students prove it is possible. You can do it, too, by examining the first years of life to see how these experiences might have patterned your life and then using the exercises and activities in the Partnership Way to help you.

To identify how developmental issues and other kinds of unfinished business might be influencing your internal working model, go to the end of this chapter and complete the Skill-Practice Partnership Exercise, Worksheet #4: How to Work on a Conflict by Yourself to Discover the Source. If you wish to identify additional developmental issues, you can complete the Self-Awareness Exercise: The Two Lists as well. This exercise is particularly useful if you are having difficulty locating possible developmental issues.

SELF-AWARENESS EXERCISE: THE TWO LISTS*

Use the exercise below to identify any aspects of unfinished business you may have. Fill out the charts below using information from your childhood related to your mother and father. When filling out List #1, include those things you believe would have made your life not only different but probably easier. When filling out List #2, include those things you believe have been hurtful or even harmful and still affect you today.

Look back to your childhood prior to age 18 and make a list of all the things that you wish your mother or father had done for you or said to you while you were growing up. These are the things that you believe had you gotten them, your life as an adult would now be easier. These are the things you feel may have held you back. For example, "I wish they had told me directly that they loved me" or "I wish they had given me birthday parties and helped me celebrate my birthday." Place these items on the mother or father list, as appropriate, in the first column: *"What I Wanted That I Did Not Get."*

Then look back to your childhood and make a list of all the things you can remember that you wish had not been done or said to you while you were growing up. This list represents the things that hurt or damaged you in some important way and interfered with your adult life. For example, "I wish they hadn't humiliated me when I got pregnant in high school" or "I wish they hadn't punished me by calling me names and hitting me." Place these items on the mother or father list, as appropriate, in the second column: *"What I Got That I Did Not Want."*

If you had a primary caregiver in addition to or in place of one or both of your parents, use these experiences as well. Write just enough to help you identify relevant experiences, such as "Éthe time Mother yelled at me when I got hurt in the second grade." At the end of this exercise, you will find an explanation for the meaning of each column.

Mother

#1 *"What I Wanted That I Did Not Get"*	#2 *"What I Got That I Did Not Want"*

Father

#1 *"What I Wanted That I Did Not Get"*	#2 *"What I Got That I Did Not Want"*

Scoring and Interpretation

List #1: *"What I Wanted That I Did Not Get."* These lists are related to unresolved codependency issues. Unresolved codependency issues indicate that you may still have unmet needs from your early childhood development. These unmet needs are usually caused by incidents of abandonment and neglect. The items on this list are needs that you unconsciously fantasize about getting in your adult relationships, without having to ask for them. You may try to manipulate or control others in order to get them. Initially, the hope may be that you will find someone who will function as the "perfect parent" you never had who can fill your unmet needs. This kind of unconscious passivity usually brings disappointment. People also use codependent or victim body language to attract rescuers who will give them what they need.

Use Column #1 to identify where you can get each need met. Beside each item, place the name of a person who could meet this need. Perhaps you still feel angry and resentful toward your mother or father or are fantasizing they will offer you what you need without you initiating. Grudges and illusions cause stuckness, which is waiting for somebody else to change so you can feel better. Maybe you fear asking for what you want because you might get refused or rejected. These strategies usually don't work. They just keep you locked in anger, resentment, and rejection and feeling hopeless, helpless, and victimized.

List #2: *"What I Got That I Did Not Want."* These lists are related to unresolved issues from the counter-dependent stage of development. The items on this list come from abuse and things that were hurtful and/or harmful to you while you were growing up. They make it difficult to be close to other people. People exhibiting counter-dependent body language say, "I have built a wall around me and I'm not going to let you see who I really am. I'm not going to let you get close to me because I don't want to get hurt again." They engage in defensive behaviors that hide their vulnerability. The dilemma is that people must face the risk of being hurt again in order to get their needs met.

If you have a lot of items in Column #2, you have probably erected barriers to prevent closeness and vulnerability. This puts your in a bind. You may want to get close so that you can get your needs met, but, because of abuse-related defenses, you refuse to take the risk. To break through this, you must penetrate your defenses in order to receive what you need.

Working with this list also often requires the tool of forgiveness (discussed in Chapter 11). You may also need to do completion work with your parents in person or using empty chair techniques to help you clear your feelings of fear, anger, and resentment. Here you can dialogue with your parents about your experiences as their child. Many people who do this find it to be highly transformative.

Sharing the two lists is also a useful activity for a couple to do together. They often find that speaking the truth about these hidden issues can be both healing and freeing. This may provide a structure for working cooperatively to get their needs met and to release their fear, anger, and resentment.

It is likely that you, like most people, have both codependent behaviors and counter-dependent behaviors, depending on the particular set of dynamics that are present in the moment. It is easy to gauge how much you have of each by looking at which of these two lists is longer or seems to have more emotional charge.

*From Weinhold, 1991

SELF-INVENTORY: HOW TO IDENTIFY YOUR CODEPENDENT BEHAVIORS

Place a number from 1 to 4 in the space before each question to indicate the degree of your response.

1 = Never 2 = Occasionally
3 = Frequently 4 = Almost always

_____ 1. I tend to assume responsibility for others' feelings and/or behaviors.

_____ 2. I have difficulty in identifying my feelings.

_____ 3. I have difficulty in expressing my feelings.

_____ 4. I tend to fear or worry how others may respond to my feelings or the behavior of others.

_____ 5. I minimize problems and deny or alter truth about the feelings or behavior of others.

_____ 6. I have difficulty in forming and/or maintaining close relationships.

_____ 7. I am afraid of rejection.

_____ 8. I am a perfectionist and judge myself harshly.

_____ 9. I have difficulty in making decisions.

_____ 10. I tend to be reactive to others rather than to act on my own.

_____ 11. I tend to put other people's wants and needs first.

_____ 12. I tend to value the opinions of others more than my own.

_____ 13. My feelings of worth come from outside myself, through the opinions of other people or from activities that seem to validate my worth.

_____ 14. I find it difficult to be vulnerable and to ask for help.

_____ 15. I deal with issues of control by attempting to always be in control or, the opposite, by being careful never to be in a position of responsibility.

_____ 16. I am extremely loyal to others, even when that loyalty is unjustified.

_____ 17. I tend to view situations with "all or nothing" thinking.

_____ 18. I have a high tolerance for inconsistency and mixed messages.

_____ 19. I have emotional crises and chaos in my life.

_____ 20. I tend to find relationships in which I feel needed and attempt to keep it that way.

_____ **Total Score**

Scoring and Interpretation

Add the numbers to get a total score. Use the following ranges to help interpret your level of codependency.

20–29 A few codependent and/or a high degree of counter-dependent patterns.

30–39 Some degree of codependent patterns.

40–59 A high degree of codependent patterns.

100–80 A very high degree of codependent patterns.

SELF-INVENTORY: HOW TO IDENTIFY YOUR COUNTER-DEPENDENT BEHAVIORS

Place a number before each statement to indicate the degree to which this statement is true in your life.

1 = Never 2 = Occasionally
3 = Frequently 4 = Almost always

_____ 1. I feel a kind of free-floating anxiety when I have nothing to do.
_____ 2. I look to other people, substances, or activities to make me feel good.
_____ 3. I have a difficult time knowing what I want or need.
_____ 4. I feel smothered when I get intimate with my spouse or a friend.
_____ 5. I have difficulty in knowing how I really feel inside.
_____ 6. I exaggerate my accomplishments a bit when I meet someone new.
_____ 7. I get anxious when my partner wants to be intimate with me.
_____ 8. I'm afraid people will find out that I'm not who they think I am.
_____ 9. I demand perfection of myself and others.
_____ 10. I work long hours and never seem to get finished with my work.
_____ 11. I don't like to ask other people for help, even if I need it.
_____ 12. I prefer to work alone rather than with others.
_____ 13. I feel controlled by what others expect of me.
_____ 14. I feel it is really important to have the "right answers."
_____ 15. I get afraid of being consumed by the needs of others.
_____ 16. I function best in structured situations where I am in charge.
_____ 17. I feel important when someone asks me for my opinion.
_____ 18. I find it difficult to form and maintain intimate relationships.
_____ 19. I have trouble deciding if I want sex or nurturing touch.
_____ 20. I have trouble relaxing and have chronic tension in my body.
_____ 21. I enjoy being the center of attention at social gatherings.
_____ 22. I don't like to admit to a mistake.
_____ 23. I reject offers of help from others, even if I need it.
_____ 24. I have many thoughts about sex each day.
_____ 25. I see myself and others as either all good or all bad.
_____ 26. I compare myself to others, feeling either one-up or one-down.
_____ 27. I am told that I am not aware of the needs or concerns of others.
_____ 28. I feel rebellious and fear being controlled by others.
_____ 29. I feel hurt when an accomplishment of mine is not recognized.
_____ 30. I deny my problems or discount the importance of my problems.
_____ **Total Score**

Scoring and Interpretation

Add your score and use the following guidelines to interpret it.

30–39   Some degree of codependent pattern.
56–78   Some counter-dependent behavior patterns; few effects on your functioning level.
79–101   A high number of counter-dependent behavior patterns; can have moderate effects on your functioning level.
102-120   Very high number of counter-dependent behavior patterns; can have serious effects on your functioning level.

PARTNERSHIP WORKSHEET #4:
HOW TO WORK ON A CONFLICT BY YOURSELF TO DISCOVER THE SOURCE

Answer the following questions regarding your conflict using a checkmark for each of the four sources. At the end of this exercise, you will score it so that you can identify where to look for the source of your conflict.

Source #1: Family Patterns Source

_____ Am I afraid of being abandoned or afraid of not getting my needs met?

_____ Am I having trouble trusting this person? Who does s/he remind me of?

_____ Am I feeling like a victim in this conflict? Did I feel like a victim as a child?

_____ Am I clinging to or trying to control this person by manipulating her or him? If so, where did I learn to do that?

_____ Do I have trouble asking for what I want? Was that true when I was a child?

Source #2: Systemic Sources

_____ Does this conflict remind me of any violations or abuse I experienced as a child?

_____ Am I treating the other person in the conflict the same way I was treated as a child?

_____ Am I acting like a persecutor in this conflict?

_____ Am I gathering evidence to make myself totally right and the other person totally wrong in this conflict?

_____ Do I feel like I am being placed in the middle of other people's conflicts like I was when I was growing up?

Source #3: The Unfinished Business Source

_____ What is it about this person that reminds me of some part of myself I don't like?

_____ Am I seeing someone as all bad or wrong in this conflict?

_____ Do I have the urge to split and leave this person alone rather than work out our conflict?

_____ Does this relationship conflict reflect an internal conflict of my own?

_____ Does this conflict force me to look at my shortcomings?

Source #4: Developmental Sources

_____ What didn't I get to say or do in this conflict?

_____ What did I want others to say or do to or for me during this conflict?

_____ What behaviors am I not able to carry out in this conflict?

_____ What feelings did I not get to express in this conflict?

_____ What feelings did others not express to me in this conflict?

Scoring

Add up the number of checkmarks for each source and write it in the blanks below.

Source #1 Score: _____ Look at unresolved codependency issues for the source of these issues.

Source #2 Score: _____ Look at unresolved counter-dependency issues for the source of these issues.

Source #3 Score: _____ Look at how you might be splitting off parts of self and projecting them onto the other person in your conflicts.

Source #4 Score: _____ Look for unfinished business from past relationships to see what is not completed and is recycling in your current conflicts.

Chapter 9

~

How Can I Resolve Intractable Conflicts at Their Source?

Any time you feel yourself overreacting during conflict situations, you know that you're in an intractable conflict containing unidentified and unprocessed material from the past. You know when you are overreacting because your adrenal stress response activates physiological symptoms and you have the urge to fight, flee, or freeze.

For example, your spouse or best friend makes plans for dinner for the two of you without consulting you. Your immediate reaction is to lash out at your spouse or friend, saying how thoughtless he or she is for not first consulting you. You get so angry and irate that you yell, call him or her hurtful names, slam the door, and leave in a huff. In fact, your spouse or friend had assumed that you would want to go and that you might feel relieved to have plans made so simply. Underneath this furor, you might feel like a small child whose parents made plans for you without your consent, leaving you feeling powerless and unimportant.

This chapter is designed to help you identify these kinds of splits in your awareness and how they get played out in relationship dynamics as you strive to complete your psychological birth.

HOW DO SPLITTING BEHAVIORS CAUSE INTRACTABLE CONFLICTS?

It became clear to us during the development of the Partnership Way that most people experience a split in consciousness during a conflict that contains unidentified and/or unprocessed elements of unresolved past conflicts. This split, which typically contains polarized components of good and bad, involves both an internal split against parts of the self and an external split against another person or persons. The relationship between splitting and intractable conflicts seems to correlate with developmental trauma during the splitting subphase of the counter-dependent stage of development. As discussed in Chapter 8, unresolved issues related to splitting in the counter-dependent stage later emerge as black-white, either-or thinking, oppositional behaviors, and one-up/one-down relationship dynamics.

Trauma during the splitting phase of the counter-dependent stage of development distorts thinking patterns during conflicts. One person is perceived as "good/okay" and the other as "bad/not okay." These two splits can then be combined into a variety of relational dynamics, such as:

- I'm not okay/you're not okay (we are both bad)
- You're okay/I'm not okay (you're good and I'm bad)
- I'm okay/you're not okay (I'm good and you're bad)

The timing of trauma during the first three years of life plays a significant role in determining which splitting defense system a person chooses. Individuals who experienced major trauma during the codependent stage of development often gravitate to "you're okay, I'm not okay" dynamics. This happens because an infant has not yet developed a sense of self and cannot determine ownership of the problem.

A mother and child, for example, are separated for several days or weeks when the mother is forced to return to the hospital with postnatal birth complications. The infant has no internal resources for understanding this abandonment. The child is not able to say, "She will be back soon. My grandmother will take good care of me while she is gone." Instead, the child just experiences the pain of abandonment that seems to have no end. The child will likely identify him- or herself as "bad," use "one-down" defenses that reinforce low self-esteem and support victim responses, and later exhibit controlling defenses as adults.

Caregivers can help bridge a child's internal splits in perception by presenting a united front in their care of the child. This provides the child with the experience of solid unity that is essential for developing object constancy. One critical condition in the family structure that can prevent dysfunctional triangulation dynamics from entering the parent/child relationship is a strong bond between the parents or caregivers. Predictable and consistent communication between the adults can help them avoid splitting and subsequently may help the child move successfully through the splitting stage of development. If the parents are unable to avoid splitting, it is likely that a *drama triangle*, or dysfunctional triangle dynamics, will be established.

HOW DOES THE DRAMA TRIANGLE CAUSE INTRACTABLE CONFLICTS?

The drama triangle is one of the core dynamics that must be understood to master conflict. For that reason, it has been stressed several times in this book. A common form of win-lose conflict, known as the Karpman Triangle (Karpman, 1968), contains three roles or positions: *persecutor*, *rescuer*, and *victim*. The drama triangle serves one primary function: It helps people get their needs met by being a victim. As shown in Figure 9.1, there is often no direct communication link between the persecutor and the rescuer.

The dynamics of the drama triangle is a primary source of trauma in families. A child who is victimized repeatedly during family conflicts or witnesses others being victimized, internalizes these experiences. Specific pictures, words, and feelings related to drama triangle conflicts create modules of traumatic memories. The sensory triggers or cures related to these traumatic experiences can quickly catapult people from present time into

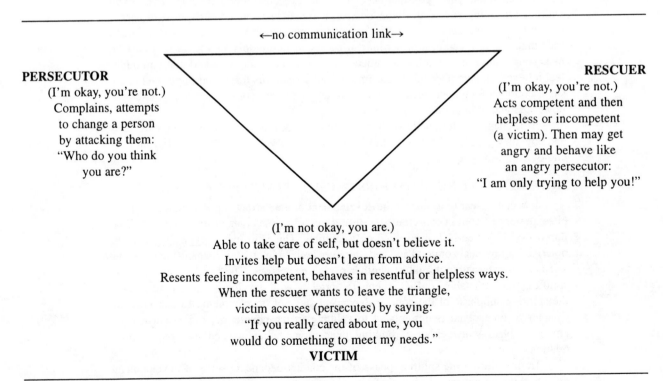

←no communication link→

PERSECUTOR
(I'm okay, you're not.)
Complains, attempts
to change a person
by attacking them:
"Who do you think
you are?"

RESCUER
(I'm okay, you're not.)
Acts competent and then
helpless or incompetent
(a victim). Then may get
angry and behave like
an angry persecutor:
"I am only trying to help you!"

(I'm not okay, you are.)
Able to take care of self, but doesn't believe it.
Invites help but doesn't learn from advice.
Resents feeling incompetent, behaves in resentful or helpless ways.
When the rescuer wants to leave the triangle,
victim accuses (persecutes) by saying:
"If you really cared about me, you
would do something to meet my needs."
VICTIM

Figure 9.1
The Drama Triangle and Its Correlations with Three Types of Internal Splits

a flashback or regressive experience related to past traumatic events. This description parallels the phenomenon of PTSD.

Dysfunctional drama triangle experiences also imprint children cognitively, creating the belief that they can only get their needs met by becoming victims. If a child's parents cannot prevent splitting inside themselves or between them, it is almost impossible for a child to complete the splitting subphase of the counter-dependent stage of development. If this dual dynamic of splitting is repeatedly played out in parent/child interactions, the child finds it impossible to complete the task of separation. Rather than developing a strong sense of internal power and self-directedness, the child takes cues from others and displays the passive and "other-directed" behaviors characteristic of the victim role. Ostensibly, the child remains developmentally stuck, moving back and forth between the codependent and counter-dependent stages of development.

An Example of the Drama Triangle

This example of drama triangle dynamics in a family involves two parents and three children. The father comes home from work to find his children watching television and eating snacks and his wife in the kitchen drinking a cup of coffee and reading the newspaper. This scene does not match the one he fantasized as he was driving home, in which the children were doing homework in their rooms and his wife had dinner waiting. When he opens the front door and finds things are not as he fantasized, he lets the feelings of frustration he had accumulated from problems during the workday erupt.

His frustration comes flying out at the children: "Why aren't you in your rooms doing your homework? You all know this is the rule!" His children look up from the television, stunned by his sharp words. They look cautiously at their mother when she comes into the living room. At this point in the conflict, the father is in the persecutor role and the children are victims. Mother picks up the rescuer role when she defends the children against what she perceives as an attack on them and addresses the father. "Why do you have to come home every night and yell at the children? They were just relaxing after being at school all day!"

Like theater, the next scene of the drama soon emerges. When the mother attacks the father in defense of the children, she assumes the role of persecutor and the father rotates to the victim role. Then the children quickly take up the rescuer role. They turn off the television and say, "We're going to our rooms now to do our homework." This is the end of the second act of the family drama.

In the next scene, the father attacks the mother, "Why don't you have dinner ready? I'm starved!" Father again plays the persecutor and the mother becomes the victim. When the daughter hears her mother and father arguing in the kitchen, she comes running in as the rescuer: "I'll help you get dinner, Mom." This is the end of the third act.

The merry-go-round nature of the drama triangle allows the game to go on forever. Even though the dynamics seem benign, this communication style can be very difficult to eliminate. The first step requires making a commitment to stop getting your needs met by being a victim and to ask directly for what you want and need. The second step is refusing to rescue others. When you do these two things, you can eliminate the drama triangle from your relationships.

HOW CAN I RECOGNIZE A RESCUE?

As shown in the example above, the drama triangle can begin from any of the three positions or roles. Individuals who work in the helping or healing professions typically act out the rescuer role. Counselors tend to attract clients whose issues match their own. The counselor's own post-traumatic cues create a drama that both the client and the counselor can act out together. This professional pitfall is known as *countertransference*.

Counselors and other professional helpers can easily become engaged in mutual dramas that can traumatize the client. For this reason, it is critical that those in the helping professions work diligently to clear themselves of their own unresolved issues.

The behavioral dynamics of the drama triangle relating to the rescue position are:

- Doing something for someone that you really don't want to do.
- Trying to meet other people's needs without being asked.
- Consistently doing more than your fair share of the work in a counseling or helping situation.
- Feeling so uncomfortable with receiving that it is possible to be only in giving relationships with others.
- Trying to fix other people's feelings or talk them out of their feelings.
- Speaking up for another person instead of letting them speak for themselves.
- Not asking for what you need while attending only to the needs of others.
- Feeling rejected when your help is graciously refused.
- Trying to help others without an explicit contract. (This does not include acts of kindness and compassion where help is legitimately needed.)

Children who experience trauma during the counter-dependent stage have a more developed sense of self than those who experience trauma during the codependent stage of development. Older children, who have more defenses for protecting themselves, are more likely to use the "I'm good" identity and "one-up" defenses. Let's use an example of a two-year-old child whose mother goes to the hospital to have another child. The two-year-old decides that the mother is not trustworthy and refuses to bond with her when she returns home several days later. This "I'm okay/you're not okay" or "one-up" defense encourages inflated self-esteem and supports the persecutor and rescuer roles in the drama triangle. The diagram in Figure 9.1 illustrates how these three types of intrapsychic splits correlate with the dynamics of the drama triangle.

Splitting behaviors indicate that a person lacks object constancy, or the ability to hold one's self as an object of worth when feeling rejected or unworthy or when someone says unkind or unpleasant things. Splitting behaviors also form the foundation for "lose-lose" and "win-lose" styles of conflict resolution in adulthood.

HOW DO I BREAK FREE OF THE DRAMA TRIANGLE?

One of the critical factors in the drama triangle is a differential in power between the victim and the persecutor and the victim and the rescuer. Individuals or groups who get dominated typically play victim roles, while those who dominate play the persecutor. Some of the characteristics of drama triangle dynamics include:

- Strong dominating the weaker
- Unequal rights
- Lack of clear boundaries
- Belief in scarcity
- Indirect communication
- Use of drama triangle (persecutor, rescuer, victim)
- Secrets
- Win-lose conflict resolution
- Suppression of feelings

Drama triangle dynamics get reinforced through power plays that are designed to intimidate those perceived as weaker. Some common power plays are:

- Shaming others
- Escalating ("rage-aholic" behavior)
- Sandbagging (dragging in old issues)
- Asking why instead of how
- Blaming others
- Pulling rank
- Labeling and name calling
- Leaving in the middle of conflict
- Avoiding responsibility for a conflict
- Playing martyr
- Using money or sex to control others

Changing the power balance in drama triangle dynamics can be difficult because much of the industrialized world operates on this dominator/dominated system. Individuals who are highly committed to changing this cultural system risk being viewed as strange or weird. Before they can become change agents in macro, or

larger, systems, they must clear their own patterns related to dominating and being dominated. In order to transform systems to partnership models of relationship, the following conditions are necessary:

- Attitude of abundance
- Legislated equal rights
- Social systems constructed to share power
- Skills in negotiation
- Direct lines of communication
- Open expression of feelings
- Cooperative, win-win approaches for resolving conflicts
- Commitment to tell the truth and to seek intimacy
- Respect for the boundaries of others

HOW CAN I IDENTIFY THE SPLITS IN MY CONSCIOUSNESS?

Identifying the splits in your consciousness is the first step in resolving intractable conflicts at their source. Many of these splits are likely the result of traumatic experiences from your childhood and exist outside your awareness. Sometimes it is easier to identify your internal splits by looking at outside events.

The O.J. Simpson trials during 1995 and 1996 and the investigation of President Clinton in 1998 have served as a collective drama for this country that helped many people process their internal splits. They revealed splits such as a victim/perpetrator, black/white, male/female, rich/poor, and good/bad government. As such, this collective event presented a wonderful mirror to help people identify some of the underlying splits in their thinking.

The widespread television coverage of these social dramas provided a stage, similar to those of Shakespeare and the Greek tragedies, where people could experience their internal splits. These events served as a kind of collective therapy. Witnesses became collective projective objects, activating post-traumatic memories of unresolved conflicts and carrying split-off parts of large groups of people. The nature of people's splits determined their beliefs about the guilt or innocence of Simpson and Clinton.

Similar phenomena occurred after the deaths of Mother Teresa and Diana, Princess of Wales, in a two-week period. A collective wave of grief and disbelief, particularly related to Princess Diana's death, swept the world. For the week between her death and her funeral, television stations produced a constant stream of shows memorializing her life and her work. Many people felt distraught, depressed, angry, and immobilized during this period and were somewhat embarrassed about their strong reactions. Most were unable to explain their strong feelings about the loss of these two famous women. Reactions to the death of Princess Diana included splits involving victim/perpetrator, male/female, rich/poor, and good/bad government.

The Simpson trials, the death of Princess Diana, and the Clinton investigation revealed another pervasive split between good and bad. Do you believe that people are basically good or basically bad? Some religions teach that people are inherently evil, that they are born that way and will never escape it. Other religions teach that humans are inherently good and learn evil ways as a result of their experiences, such as growing up in dysfunctional families or in dysfunctional societies. They teach that once people recover their innocence, they will not do evil things anymore.

The question of people's inherent goodness and badness is important for counselors, teachers, attorneys, social service agents, and other human service providers. Personal perspective regarding the innate goodness and evil of people colors both your attitudes and behaviors toward clients, students, and others whose welfare you serve. If you believe that people are basically bad and cannot be trusted, you may feel justified in manipulating and controlling them. If you believe that your clients or students are basically good, even though they may behave in dysfunctional or negative ways, you are more likely to treat them with compassion and understanding. You can empathetically enter their world and help them heal wounds related to past traumas, effectively resolve conflicts, and make new and better choices.

The other significant split that emerged from the O.J. Simpson trials, the death of Princess Diana, and the investigation of President Clinton is the gender split between men and women. The imbalance between masculine and feminine ways of thinking and behaving has been growing for about 5,000 years. Much of this particular split is being acted out in intimate relationships, as evidenced by the rise in domestic violence. Chapter Twelve addresses this particular split in detail.

HOW CAN I UNIFY THE SPLITS IN MY CONSCIOUSNESS?

When you find yourself in conflict, you can immediately ask yourself: "What did I do to draw this person into my life?" "What is incomplete in my development that drew this conflict to me?" "What can this conflict teach me about myself?" Like the followers of the native teachings of the Medicine Wheel, you can use every experience in your life as an opportunity for personal growth.

In order to effectively use the Simpson trials as a therapeutic tool for your own healing, go to the end of this chapter and complete the Self-Awareness Exercise: Seeing Myself More Clearly. Use these activities to help identify your splits, looking specifically for a pattern in your splitting behaviors. Do you more frequently use the "I'm okay/you're not okay" or one-up defenses and find yourself acting out the persecutor and rescuer roles in the drama triangle? Or do you typically choose the "I'm not okay/you're okay" or one-down defenses and find yourself acting out the victim role? Remember, the kind of defense mechanisms you typically use in the drama triangle indicates where to look for developmental trauma.

Unifying the splits in your consciousness identified through these exercises will require several steps. The first is a tool known as *perception checks*. When you get caught in a reenactment of a past trauma and feel regressed, you may find yourself hearing or believing things that are more related to the past than what is happening in the moment. When some sensory cue sets off an overreaction and you feel ready to mount an assault on someone who has offended you, center yourself and ask the other person if your perceptions are true. If you feel criticized or judged in some way, ask this person if they are actually feeling critical or judgmental. Perception checks are an excellent way of diffusing a conflict situation and providing information that is real in the moment. They can also help prevent escalating, overreacting, and hurting innocent individuals for behaviors that were incorrectly perceived.

The second step is to identify early traumatic events that affected your psychological development. If you have more one-down behavioral responses in conflict, look for developmental trauma during the first year of life. If you have more one-up responses, then research the events of your second and third years of life. If you have some of both, which most people do, look for developmental trauma during the first three years of your life.

The third step in healing splits involves desensitizing and reprocessing the elements of your developmental traumas using the trauma reduction modalities described in Chapter 7.

The last step in healing splits is identifying incomplete developmental tasks and unmet needs still present as the result of developmental trauma during the codependent and counter-dependent stages of development and implementing a self-improvement program to remedy these deficiencies. This step includes eliminating one-up/one-down behavioral responses and learning effective relational dynamics that preclude participation in the drama triangle. A primary goal of this program would be the development of *object constancy* or the ability to hold an inner duality of goodness-and-badness even when feeling rejected or unworthy. This goal is best accomplished through individual or group therapy where the therapist uses principles of object relations therapy to help you experience your internal splits, meet your unmet developmental needs, and complete psychosocial tasks.

Most people exhibit a combination of both one-up and one-down behaviors, depending on where they are in the power structure in a conflict. Individuals in positions of authority typically assume the one-up or counter-dependent role while those in a subordinate position generally assume the one-down or codependent role. Use Table 9.1 to help understand and identify the splits in your consciousness and behaviors in conflict situations. The

Table 9.1
Contrasting Codependent and Counter-Dependent Behaviors

Codependent Behaviors	Counter-Dependent Behaviors
Uses "I'm not okay/you're okay" defenses in conflict situations	Uses "I'm okay/you're not okay" defenses in conflict situations
Plays victim and/or rescuer roles in the psychodrama triangle	Plays persecutor and/or rescuer roles in the psychodrama triangle
Lacks structure and boundaries to contain self	Has artificial structure containing false self
Immobilized by feeling states	Cut off from feelings
Other-directed	Self-centered
Uses oral and downer addictions	Uses anal and upper addictions
Exhibits poor self-esteem	Inflated self-esteem
Acts dependent	Acts counter-dependent
Has depressed behaviors	Has manic behaviors
Feels ashamed of having needs	Feels guilty about having needs
Is a people pleaser	Is a people controller
Accepts responsibility for everything	Accepts responsibility for nothing
Blames self	Blames others

question is how to move beyond socially reinforced victim/persecutor roles and other kinds of codependent/counter-dependent splits. Table 9.2 describes behavioral responses for combating these patterns.

At this point in human evolution, very few people have been able to completely heal their splits in consciousness. Those who do typically complete it in their late adulthood long after their children have left home. This means that most young children live with parents who still exhibit splitting behaviors. The obvious outcome for people who have not healed their splits in consciousness is recurring or intractable conflicts.

The prevalence of splitting and hierarchical ranking in social structures makes it difficult to break free of codependent/counter-dependent roles. These roles are reinforced in subtle but powerful ways, such as through commercial ads on television and popular music. The country and western music song titles in Figure 9.2 are excellent examples of codependent and counter-dependent stereotypes.

HOW DO I RESOLVE AN INTRACTABLE CONFLICT?

Janae uses judgments as a barometer for identifying splits in her consciousness:

> I have learned to observe myself enough to know when I am either feeling judged or judging someone else.

When I feel judged, I feel one-down. When I am judging someone else, I feel one-up. In both instances, I want to pull away from the other person and think negative things about myself, about the other person, or think bad things about both myself and the other person. I experience myself obsessing about the other person and the "bad" thing they have done. I either get more angry and escalated or feel helpless and hopeless. When I get into the escalated mode, I usually perceive that I am the one who is good and they are bad. When I fall into feeling helpless and hopeless, I am usually the one who is bad and the other person is good. The cue I use to help me know at the beginning of a conflict that I am splitting my consciousness is an intense over-reaction to the conflict that is happening in the moment.

When you become aware of a split in your consciousness during an intractable conflict, you can use Worksheet #5 at the end of Chapter 10 to help you identify the source of the unresolved conflict from your past. Even if the other person in the current conflict isn't willing to be part of the resolution process, you can still use this worksheet to help you identify your part of the conflict. While the experience of resolving a conflict with a partner feels more complete, it is important to know that you can work on it alone and change your part of the conflict so that it does not recycle.

Table 9.2

How to Heal the Splits Related to Codependent and Counter-Dependent Behaviors

Codependent Behaviors	Counter-Dependent Behaviors
Confront your dependent behaviors by identifying the unmet needs behind them and then getting these needs met.	Ask a trusted person to describe their experiences with your defense mechanisms.
Identify self-defeating behaviors and problem-solve ways to overcome them.	Empathize with the wound under your defenses and reflect on how you use them to protect yourself.
Get support, empathy, and truth to mobilize yourself out of feeling states and into action.	Find someone who can mirror your vulnerability to help you gain access to your feelings.
Develop skills in autonomy.	Develop skills in intimacy.
Develop problem-solving skills needed to mobilize out of intense feeling states.	Identify body signals related to experiencing and expressing feelings.
Move quickly to create structure for yourself.	Move slowly to remove your defenses.
Master the outer world of work and self-care.	Master the inner world of relationships.
Set behavioral limits for yourself.	Expand your behavioral responses.
Develop effective protective defenses against others' beliefs that you are "not okay."	Notice when you place yourself above others and/or make others "not okay."
Reduce overcommitting yourself to meet others' needs.	Expand range of personal commitments to the needs of others.
Separate nurturing and sexuality.	Separate power and sexuality.
Develop compassion for wounds to the self.	Develop compassion for other people's wounds.

How Can I Miss You If You Won't Go Away?
I Hate Every Bone in Your Body Except Mine
Guess My Eyes Were Bigger Than My Heart
How Can You Believe Me When I Say I Love You When You Know I've Been a Liar All My Life?
I'm So Miserable Without You, It's Like Having You Here
I've Been Flushed From the Bathroom of Your Heart
I've Got Red Eyes From Your White Lies and I'm Blue All The Time
If Drinkin' Don't Kill Me, Her Memory Will
If Love Were Oil, I'd Be a Quart Low
If the Phone Don't Ring, Baby, You'll Know It's Me
My John Deere Was Breaking Your Field, While Your Dear John Was Breaking My Heart
She Got the Gold Mine and I Got the Shaft
Thank God and Greyhound She's Gone
Velcro Arms, Teflon Heart
When You Leave Walk Out Backwards, So I'll Think You're Walking In
If I Can't Be Number One In Your Life, Then Number Two On You
Pardon Me, I've Got Somebody to Kill
The Last Word in Lonesome is Me
You Can't Have Your Kate and Edith Too
You Done Tore Out My Heart and Stomped That Sucker Flat

Figure 9.2

Codependent and Counter-Dependent Song Titles

SELF-AWARENESS EXERCISE: SEEING MYSELF MORE CLEARLY

Answer each question as honestly as possible, noting any questions that activate feelings of repulsion or any other internal reactions that may be indications of an internal split. Each group of questions reflects a different perspective reminiscent of the groups and individuals who participated in the O.J. Simpson trial.

Have I ever felt unjustly accused of anything in my life?

Do I have some kind of privilege that allows me to do something that other people don't get away with?

How have I tried to control my kids, my spouse, or my friends?

How do I feel about one person's attempts to control another?

How do I act powerless and identify myself as a victim?

Where do I feel trapped in my life?

Have I ever been trapped in an abusive relationship?

Have I ever allowed someone to dominate or control me?

Have I ever consciously or unconsciously provoked someone to abuse me?

How could I be considered a racist in my words or my actions?

Have I ever lied to protect myself or make myself look good?

Who do I hate or fear in my life?

Where in my life am I feeling sequestered?

Have I looked objectively at the evidence of my own guilt or innocence regarding some conflict?

How have I put people in categories and then judged them according to the category that I assigned them?

What categories do I use to identify myself?

Are they based on my gender, race, religion, or profession?

Now go back through your answers to this exercise and review them regarding the nature of your responses. Count and record in the blanks below the total number of items that reflect a more one-up or more one-down attitude. Your answers will likely reflect the kinds of defense mechanisms you use to avoid dealing with your split-off parts. What people typically do is project these parts onto others. The O. J. Simpson trial provided collective images for us to project our split-off parts rather than see them in ourselves. The first step in reconnecting with our split-off parts is to recognize how you are projecting them onto others. The kind of defense mechanism you typically used in answering these questions also indicates roles you might play in the psychodrama triangle. This also helps to indicate where to look for developmental trauma.

_____ "I'm not okay/you're okay" or one-down defenses
(victim/rescuer roles in the drama triangle)
Look for trauma during the codependent stage of development.

_____ "I'm okay/you're not okay" or one-up defenses
(persecutor/rescuer roles in the drama triangle)
Look for trauma during counter-dependent stage of development.

Chapter 10

~

How Can I Use the Partnership Way to Resolve Intractable Conflicts in Intimate Relationships?

The Partnership Way can be applied to relationships between any two people, whether they be friends, coworkers, or a committed couple. A committed relationship can also consist of sisters, a parent and child, a boss and an employee, or two friends. The commitment is that both people will stay engaged during a conflict and attempt to find a resolution. This kind of commitment is essential for resolving intractable relationship conflicts. When two people work cooperatively to resolve their conflicts, they can develop a tremendous amount of intimacy in their relationship, resolve their own internal conflicts, and deepen their relationship.

The evolution of intimate relationships follows a developmental sequence similar to that of individual relationships. Relationships undergo a series of predictable changes as the relationship and the people involved grow and mature. When you enter an intimate relationship you carry with you the residue of your unrecognized and unhealed developmental traumas. Any unmet developmental needs and issues related to incomplete psychosocial tasks will eventually surface during conflicts in the relationship. Generally, these issues will surface in an intimate relationship when it is safe enough for conflicts to occur. Many couples avoid conflicts in order to maintain some false sense of harmony.

Your experiences in a couple relationship provide you with opportunities for completing not only the psychosocial tasks of your relationship but also the tasks related to your individual development. Intimate relationships are a wonderful crucible for helping you move to a higher stage of development. The four stages of relationship development are *codependent, counter-dependent, independent*, and *interdependent*. The psychosocial tasks of each stage and methods for completing these tasks are listed in Table 10.1.

When couples seek therapy, they are usually in conflict. Their stories have various versions but the main theme is similar: "We had a wonderful relationship in the beginning. We got along so well. Then we started to get on each other's nerves and began

Table 10.1
The Four Stages of Relationships

Stage of Development	Psychosocial Tasks of an Intimate Relationship	Methods for Completing These Tasks
Codependent	• Bonding with each other • Establishing primal trust in the relationship • Creating a relationship identity • Establishing parameters regarding the expression of sexual energy	• Establishing friendship as a quality of the relationship • Recognizing and acknowledging each other's spiritual essence • Exchanging nurturing touch and talk • Respecting and validating each other's needs and feelings • Giving and receiving unconditional love • Creating common interests, values, beliefs, and goals
Counter-Dependent	• Separating psychologically from each other • Resolving internal conflicts between needs of self and needs of other	• Exploring interests outside of the relationship • Separating nurturing touch from sexual touch • Establishing individual goals, values, and beliefs within the relationship • Establishing and receiving respect for individual boundaries • Identifying self-needs vs. other-needs • Negotiating directly to get needs met
Independent	• Mastering self-sufficiency within the relationship • Establishing an equal, egalitarian form of autonomy within the relationship • Achieving object constancy as a couple	• Achieving equality in the relationship (financial, professional, educational, and spiritual) • Achieving a balance between individual and relational needs and interests • Maintaining individual goals, values, and beliefs within the couple relationship • Experiencing mutual constancy in spite of conflicting needs and/or wants
Interdependent	• Partnering with each other • Developing an experience of synergy in the relationship • Utilizing couple synergy in service to the community or world	• Using partnership conflict resolution methods • Sustaining a spiritual dimension in the relationship • Utilizing the relationship as a tool for individuation and mutual spiritual evolution • Mutually affirming spiritual values and goals and acting from them • Identifying situations where couple devotion can be extended to others outside the relationship

having fights." Sometimes the two people have been in conflict long enough to create a reservoir of ill-will between them by holding onto grudges and resentment.

This dramatic change in the course of the relationship indicates that the relationship is maturing, that it is moving from the codependent stage to the counter-dependent stage of development. In the codependent stage, also known as the honeymoon stage, personal conflicts are usually ignored to preserve the good feelings and harmony. Some relationships can stay in this stage for a long time, particularly if the individuals involved are skilled at avoiding conflict.

When the relationship moves into the counter-dependent stage, the disharmony once ignored or avoided comes to the forefront. This may be very frightening at first, as it activates fears that the relationship might end. As in individual development, the shift from the codependent to the counter-dependent stage of development is often triggered by one person's desire to explore interests outside the relationship.

In a relationship, this does not usually happen simultaneously. One person usually wants to become more separate and seek out individual activities before the other person is ready to do this. This creates an imbalance between one person's need for separateness and the other person's need to maintain oneness. The shift into the counter-dependent stage of relationship development may erupt quite innocently and end up as a conflict that feels catastrophic. For example, he wants to take a long trip without her, or she decides to enroll in night classes to get an advanced degree. These kinds of relational changes may activate the other person's fears of abandonment or suffocation and undiscovered symptoms of post-traumatic stress related to developmental trauma.

HOW CAN I REFRAME MY RELATIONSHIP CONFLICTS?

You may feel angry, depressed, or ashamed if your relationship reaches the counter-dependent stage of development before you are ready for this change. When a couple seeks therapy, they need feedback to reframe the problems in their marriage. The counselor can say, "Congratulations! Your relationship is maturing. It is now strong enough and safe enough for conflict to emerge." This kind of feedback may seem strange and confusing. The couple may say, "This is the dumbest thing we ever heard of."

However, when couples understand that relationships go through developmental stages, they can often reframe their perceptions and see their conflict as a sign of growth, challenging though it may be. Working from a developmental perspective can also help partners understand that the sources of their conflicts were present from the very beginning of the relationship and that they needed time together and feelings of safety for them to surface.

Most relationships also contain invisible elements that can cause conflict. You may become aware of subtle differences between you and your partner related to energy levels; the need for change, freedom, or novelty; and contrasting levels of perceptiveness and sensitivity. These kinds of subtle differences can cause imbalances in the levels of your awareness, can affect your sense of timing, and can complicate your communication patterns.

If you are a sensitive person, for example, you may be able to perceive a potential conflict when it is just a spark, while your partner may not be able to perceive it until it ignites into flames. If you are a person who needs more freedom or wants to change the relationship, you

may feel controlled by a partner who wants to maintain the status quo. The control issue may be expressed in subtle messages that say, "I'm scared that you will leave me or abandon me." If the partner who fears being left behind has any unresolved abandonment traumas or conflicts, the other partner's desire for more freedom will eventually activate these issues.

These more subtle elements in your relationship can often cause more disruption than the more obvious differences such as age, religion, parenting styles, or basic values and beliefs. It is important to recognize the potential power of these subtle differences and to look for them as possible sources of relational friction.

Reaching the counter-dependent stage of development is an important milestone for couples. This passage truly is an affirmation of the strength of the relationship and can be a source of empowerment to help you and your partner see the positive aspects of this shift. What couples need most to help them through this crisis is a cooperative context for understanding the nature of their conflicts and tools for resolving them.

A cooperative arrangement is essential for redefining the context of a relationship into one that is "transformative." It provides you with opportunities for reframing your negative perceptions into more positive perceptions that are essential for mutual growth and development. At the end of this chapter are three exercises to help you assess and transform your relationships: (1) How Evolved Is Our Relationship? (2) A Self-Inventory for Identifying Barriers to a Partnership Relationship, and (3) Locating Unresolved Developmental Issues in Your Relationships.

When a couple seeks therapy to resolve their intractable conflicts, the first step usually is to help them create a more cooperative framework for their relationship. This helps them to see that a competitive, fear-based battle over whose needs are going to prevail, or who is "right" and who is "wrong," is a win-lose framework that can only escalate and continually fill the reservoir of ill will between them.

It is also useful to help people expand their concept of intimacy, as there is a tendency for them to include only those times during the bonding stage when everything is wonderful. There is another form of intimacy that occurs when two people are able to sit down together and resolve an intractable conflict at its source. If you and your partner were able to be aware and really honest at the beginning of your relationship, this is probably what you would have hoped for in your relationship.

You may have noticed that you have an unconscious radar system that is activated when you come into a room filled with strangers. Your intuitive perception says to you, "He looks like an interesting person" or "I'd like to get to know her." Most people don't consciously think, "Oh, there's somebody who's going to help me with my unresolved conflicts with my mother." At the beginning of a relationship the honest thing to do is to talk with your partner about the issues you bring with you to the relationship. If your partner refuses to do this, then it is likely that you will have difficulty in resolving conflicts in ways that promote intimacy between you.

HOW CAN I SHIFT FROM WIN-LOSE TO PARTNERSHIP STRATEGIES?

The shift into a cooperative or partnership framework that supports you and your partner is a critical factor in resolving intractable relationship conflicts. If you can make this shift, it is likely that you will not only learn a lot about yourself and your partner, but you will feel closer when the conflict is resolved.

Individuals who seem most able to transform their perceptions of intractable conflict and shift into a cooperative framework are typically those who have had several significant long-term relationships where the same or similar issues and conflicts occurred. These individuals initially believed that other people were at the source of their conflicts. However, after the same kind of conflicts kept reappearing with different partners, bosses, or coworkers, they began to understand that the real source of the problem was inside themselves. Once you reach this awareness, you are ready to take responsibility for your part of the problem.

WHAT IF THERE IS A NEED FOR INDIVIDUAL THERAPY?

Sometimes it becomes apparent that one or both individuals in a relationship need individual counseling. This may be necessary if the issues in the new conflicts have been avoided for a long time or if one person is not yet ready or able to work cooperatively with a partner.

Your level of individual development is critical in resolving relationship conflicts. If you and your partner have reached the independent stage of development, it may be easier for you to use negotiation to get your needs met. Negotiating can be very difficult if you or your partner still feel involved in life-and-death power struggles related to the codependent stage of development or are acting out oppositional issues stemming from the counter-dependent stage of development. People in intimate relationships who have achieved *object constancy* can engage in "I'm okay, you're okay" thinking and can hold themselves as objects of worth during a relationship conflict. When they are not able to do this, it may be an indication of unresolved developmental traumas from the counter-dependent stage of individual development that can best be resolved through individual therapy.

While we are usually optimistic people, the more we study human development the more we believe that the consciousness of the human species is developmentally stalled. Most people still seem to be struggling with unresolved conflicts related to the events of the first three years of their lives that dominate their thinking and behavior. We estimate that less than five percent of the people in the world have reached the independent stage of individual development and can consistently sustain it; even fewer have reached the interdependent stage of development.

What seems most important in helping people to move forward in their evolution is a cooperative framework for resolving relationship conflicts. Developmental trauma, the most common source of relationship conflict, began with your relationship with your parents. If you didn't get these early conflicts resolved, there is still an opportunity to resolve them through your current relationships, be they friendships, coworker relationships, or an intimate relationship with a significant other. Review the developmental chart at the beginning of this chapter to determine the evolution of your most intimate relationships. You can also use it as a road map for moving toward interdependence.

HOW DO I BREAK FREE OF THE DRAMA TRIANGLE IN INTIMATE RELATIONSHIPS?

One of the factors that fosters drama triangle dynamics is a dominator relationship where there are inequities in power. The most dominant or most powerful person or group acts out the Persecutor role, the second most dominant person or group acts out the Rescuer role, and the weakest person or group acts out the Victim role. Use the following criteria to help you recognize dominator relationships.

Characteristics of Dominator Relationships

- Strong partner dominates the weaker
- Unequal rights regarding the use of power, money, sexuality
- Lack of clear psychological boundaries
- Belief in scarcity
- Indirect communication dynamics
- Use of drama triangle (Persecutor, Rescuer, Victim) to resolve conflicts
- Secrets between the partners
- Win-lose or lose-lose conflict resolution strategies
- Suppression of feelings
- Unsafe atmosphere

THE DIFFERENCES BETWEEN DOMINATOR AND PARTNERSHIP RELATIONSHIPS?

Dominator relationships involve splitting and polarization, such as dominator/dominated, passive/aggressive, and win/lose, in order to create hierarchical structures. Partnership relationships involve interdependent actions based on unity, mutuality, and cooperation, in order to create nonhierarchical structures. A comparison of the two kinds of relationships are presented in Table 10.2. From this comparison, you can see some of the basic differences

Table 10.2

Characteristics of Dominator and Partnership Relationships

CHARACTERISTICS OF DOMINATOR AND PARTNERSHIP RELATIONSHIPS	
Dominator Relationships	**Partnership Relationships**
Use force or threat to enforce domination	Use the vision of higher consciousness to encourage linking for common good
Create inequalities in power and decision-making	Create equal opportunities or money and use knowledge as shared power for joint decision-making
Utilize rigid gender roles	Utilize flexible gender roles
Value violence and exploitation	Value negotiation and harmony
Competitive	Cooperative
Use fear to create separation	Use hope and high ideals to create unity
Are materially oriented	Are spiritually oriented
See women and children as property or chattel	See women and children as equal and unique individuals
Support codependent and counter-dependent behaviors	Support independent and interdependent behaviors
Follow a path of fear and protection	Follow a path of learning and discovery
Use control, manipulation, and deception in communicating	Use truth, empathy, and directness in communicating
Value either the needs of the individual or the needs of the relationship	Value both the needs of the individuals and the needs of the relationship

in philosophy and practice of these two models of relationships. Most relationships do not exhibit all of either set of characteristics, but the dominator form of relationship is still by far the most prevalent form of relationship in the world today.

GUIDELINES FOR CREATING A PARTNERSHIP RELATIONSHIP

The most important step in transforming your relationship is recognizing and acknowledging that you each have unresolved conflicts and unmet developmental needs that you have brought to your relationship. Then it is possible to determine which of your conflicts are related to the past and which are related to the present. Once you have identified this, you can contract with each other to cooperate on completing the part from the past. This includes resolving old conflicts, processing current conflicts that contain developmental traumas, and getting any needs met now that you didn't get met while you were growing up. The following guidelines can help you expand an intimate relationship into one that supports mutual growth and development.

1. *Recognize and acknowledge each other's unmet needs.* At the beginning of a romantic relationship you are usually on your best behavior, trying to impress your new partner about how lovable and capable you are. It requires

spiritual courage to reveal your weaknesses to this person after you have worked so hard trying to impress him or her with your strengths. Acknowledging that you both bring unfinished business to your relationship brings an element of truthfulness to your relationship that prevents posturing, denial, and other defense mechanisms. It encourages more empathic and compassionate responses to each other when your weaknesses and unmet needs surface. Without a framework for helping each other heal your wounds from the past, it can be risky to expose your vulnerabilities and deficits. Including this higher purpose in your relationship makes it more possible to develop a partnership relationship. The sooner you risk acknowledging to your partner that you bring unmet needs to your relationship, the better the chance of getting them met.

2. *Help each other meet your unmet needs.* This can shift your relationship from a competitive to a cooperative model where real healing can happen. This step, which calls for understanding and compassion, can create a larger context for your relationship. Then you can each remove your projections and see the wounded child inside each of you.

3. *Be willing to ask for what you want and need 100% of the time.* Rather than being indirect or complaining, be willing to ask your partner directly for what you want. This doesn't mean that you must ask 100% of the

time, only that you are willing. This agreement is essential if you are going to break through your old unresolved conflicts and the ineffective ways you have tried to resolve them.

4. *Tell the truth about your behavior, feelings, and needs 100% of the time.* This requires taking big risks. Telling the truth frees you mentally, emotionally, physiologically, and spiritually and also removes the barriers to intimacy. The best policy, although not the easiest, is to tell the truth even if it creates a conflict. Only when you develop this kind of trust in each other will your relationship evolve.

5. *Close all the exits.* You must both agree to stay together during the counter-dependent stage of the relationship when you are encountering a lot of conflict. A no-exit agreement can help hidden fears surface, as it eliminates responses such as running away or blaming your partner. Neither person can threaten to end the relationship in the middle of a conflict or avoid the issues by using addictions or by seeking out another relationship. If your partner refuses to accept a no-exit agreement, then it really is not safe for you to attempt resolving your deepest conflicts. In these situations, you can only work alone on your part of the conflict or with a trusted friend or counselor. You are not dependent on your partner's cooperation to learn more about yourself and to resolve conflicts from the past.

6. *Practice equality of power, opportunity, and responsibility.* Partners can mutually evolve only if there is a firm foundation of sharing at all levels in the relationship. Relationships with equality as a component create a spirit of cooperation, as well as mutual trust and respect. In a world with economic, social, political, and psychological inequalities, equality is difficult to create without a conscious commitment. Partners also must commit to using cooperative, partnership conflict resolution methods.

7. *Redefine intimacy to include all of your mutual experiences, including conflict.* Choose to define everything you do as intimacy: the intimacy of recreation, the intimacy of regressing and having post-traumatic symptoms, the intimacy of being separate, the intimacy of yelling, the intimacy of holding and comforting, the intimacy of being sexual, and the intimacy of mutual healing.

8. *Respect each other's boundaries.* Communicate clearly to your partner how you wish to share your environment. You can create a great deal of freedom and respect for each other's space if you agree to identify your boundaries and to negotiate clear agreements about sharing your psychological space. This is where the agreement to tell the truth 100% of the time is essential.

9. *Develop regular common spiritual practices.* These practices can take many forms. They may vary from formal activities such as prayer, meditation, or church attendance to informal practices involving walks in the park together or exercising together. The intention behind common spiritual practices is deepening your sense of partnership. Moments of quiet, deep connection can become important islands of intimacy. The outer world stops and you are in touch with each other in that place of timeless connection and eternal love. Such moments nourish your souls and can support you in coping with the stresses of daily living.

10. *Keep all relationship agreements and negotiate any changes.* Whenever circumstances around your agreements change, it is important to go back and renegotiate a new agreement. Broken agreements quickly undermine the trust and good will of a relationship, especially if they are broken unilaterally without direct negotiations with those involved.

11. *Work together to help each other resolve conflicts at their source.* One of the most powerful and affirming parts of a partnership relationship is helping each other resolve conflicts at their source. This kind of cooperative work brings tremendous intimacy to the relationship. This kind of support and help by a partner is what everyone wants but is afraid to ask for. There is a skill practice exercise at the end of this chapter, Partnership Worksheet #5, that will provide assistance in learning how to help each other do this important healing work.

SELF-INVENTORY: HOW EVOLVED IS YOUR RELATIONSHIP?

Place a number from 1 to 10 (1 = never; 10 = always) in the column that best represents your current perception of your primary relationship(s). Use this form for each relationship you wish to assess. You and your partner may want to fill it out separately and then compare your answers.

In this relationship we:

_____ 1. Acknowledge each other's spiritual essence.

_____ 2. Accept and validate each other's feelings and needs.

_____ 3. Have emotional intimacy.

_____ 4. Show our appreciation for each other.

_____ 5. Have mutual trust and love.

_____ 6. Share common values, beliefs, and interests.

_____ 7. Separate nurturing touch from sexual touch.

_____ 8. Show respect and tolerance for any differences of values and beliefs.

_____ 9. Support each other's need to separately explore new ideas and activities.

_____ 10. Show respect for each other's psychological boundaries.

_____ 11. Negotiate directly to meet our wants and needs.

_____ 12. Attempt to identify the underlying sources of our current unresolved conflicts.

_____ 13. Develop ways to fulfill individual needs that do not involve your partner.

_____ 14. Do things that break down cultural gender-role stereotypes regarding career and housekeeping activities.

_____ 15. Are able to tolerate ambiguity and role diffusion in the relationship.

_____ 17. Encourage the development of individual self-identity.

_____ 18. Support each other's independent ideas and actions.

_____ 19. Use win/win methods to resolve our conflicts.

_____ 20. Shift from oneness to separateness without conflict.

_____ 21. Keep our relationship agreements.

_____ 22. Help each other resolve unresolved conflicts from our respective childhoods.

_____ 23. Make the relationship a priority over our careers.

_____ 24. Design and use regular spiritual practices with each other.

Scoring and Interpretation

This inventory yields four sub-scores and a total relationship score. The scoring procedures to obtain each sub-score are explained below, along with an interpretation of each sub-score and the total relationship score.

Codependent Stage (Items 1 through 6)

Add the numbers preceding these items to get the sub-score: _____

Counter-dependent Stage (Items 7 through 12)

Add the numbers preceding these items to get the sub-score: _____

Independent Stage (Items 13 through 18)

Add the numbers preceding these items to get the sub-score: _____

Interdependent Stage (Items 19 through 24)

Add the numbers preceding these items to get the sub-score: _____

_____ Total Relationship Score (Add the four sub-scores to get a total relationship score.)

Interpretation of Sub-Scores. Check your sub-scores for each of these stages and refer to the interpretation below.

6–18	Major problems exist because important developmental tasks for this relationship stage have not been completed.
19–30	A few major developmental tasks for this relationship stage have been completed.
31–42	Some important developmental tasks for this relationship stage have been completed.
43–60	Most of the important developmental tasks for this relationship stage have been completed.

Interpretation of the Total Relationship Score. If you and your partner filled this out separately, you may want to compare your answers and discuss any changes you might want to consider.

24 – 72	Evidence of major barriers to the creation of a partnership relationship.
73–144	Major problems and unresolved conflicts prevent the creation of a partnership relationship.
145–192	Good progress underway toward the creation of a partnership relationship.
193–240	Clear evidence of a partnership relationship.

SELF-INVENTORY: IDENTIFYING BARRIERS TO A PARTNERSHIP RELATIONSHIP

This self-inventory can help you identify intrapersonal and interpersonal barriers to a partnership relationship. Please read each statement below and indicate the degree to which the statement is true of you in your primary relationship. Place a number from 1 to 10 (1 = not present at all; 10 = present all the time) indicating your choice in the blank before each statement. Complete the self-inventory, ask your partner to do the same, and then discuss what each of you have discovered. Make cooperative plans to address and eliminate these barriers.

_____ 1. I have very little time, money, or energy left to improve my relationship.

_____ 2. Work and career concerns tend to come before my relationship.

_____ 3. I do not have enough time or energy left at the end of the day to enjoy sex.

_____ 4. I get more excited about my work than about my relationship.

_____ 5. I have trouble getting out of work on time.

_____ 6. I have to work more than 40 hours per week to get my job done.

_____ 7. I bring work home at night or on weekends.

_____ 8. I think about work while I am driving, before falling asleep at night, and/or when others are talking about some other topic.

_____ 9. I believe that making more money will solve the other problems I have.

_____ 10. I feel a kind of free-floating anxiety when I have nothing to do.

_____ 11. I get anxious when my partner wants to be intimate with me.

_____ 12. I don't like to ask other people for help, even if I need it.

_____ 13. I find my partner's needs overwhelming.

_____ 14. I feel smothered by my partner when we are close and intimate.

_____ 15. I tend to think other people have more satisfying relationships than I do.

_____ 16. I prefer to work alone on a project rather than with others.

_____ 17. I am afraid if people find out who I really am, they will reject me.

_____ 18. I find it difficult to have a close relationship and still maintain my personal freedom.

_____ 19. I feel I give more than I get in my relationship.

_____ 20. I feel like I have to do and say the right things to make my partner happy.

_____ 21. I find it is easier to try to avoid a conflict than to talk about it.

_____ 22. I fear that in the end, I will be abandoned by my partner.

_____ 23. I have difficulty taking care of my own needs while also meeting the needs of my partner.

_____ 24. I let my partner take the lead in making changes in our relationship.

_____ 25. I feel like I'm to blame if there are problems in our relationship.

_____ 26. I use sex to try to smooth over arguments with my partner.

_____ 27. Making changes in my relationship takes too much time and energy.

_____ 28. I don't seem to know what I want to change about myself.

_____ 29. I have trouble doing something new because I am afraid I will fail.

_____ 30. I am afraid to really be myself when I am making love.

_____ **Total Score** (Add the numbers in the left column.)

Scoring and Interpretation:

30 – 90   A few barriers to overcome in creating a partnership relationship.

91–180   Many barriers to overcome that may require lots of work and cooperation. Therapeutic intervention may be useful.

181–300   A partnership relationship may not be possible without therapeutic intervention.

SELF-INVENTORY:
LOCATING UNRESOLVED DEVELOPMENTAL TRAUMAS IN YOUR RELATIONSHIP(S)

Look over Table 10.3 and indicate with a number from 1 to 10 (1 = not at all; 10 = all the time) how much that issue is present in your primary relationship(s). You might ask your partner to complete this separately and then compare and discuss your answers and scores. Then contract with your partner to resolve this issue.

Table 10.3
Common Developmental Conflicts That Emerge in the Counter-Dependent Stage of Relationships and How to Resolve Them at Their Source

Common Issue	*Possible Developmental Trauma*	*How to Cooperatively Resolve the Issue at Its Source*
_____ 1. Fear of intimacy	Emotional, sexual, physical abuse, or invasion of boundaries by caregivers	Have your partner role-play the perpetrator and express any unexpressed feelings.
_____ 2. Addiction to activity	Possible abuse or neglect of basic needs	Learn relaxation and meditation techniques. Have partner do them with you.
_____ 3. Passivity, letting others lead	Little support for independent thoughts and/or actions	Ask partner to role-play parents and give you supporting messages for independent thoughts and actions.
_____ 4. Fear of trying new things	Received more "no" than yes" messages	Ask your partner to role-play a parent and give you lots of "yes" messages.
_____ 5. Fear of touch combined with compulsive eating	Experienced sexual and/or physical abuse	Identify possible perpetrators and have your partner be with you while you express your feelings. Ask for nonsexual touch from your partner.
_____ 6. Bored easily, needing others to keep yourself stimulated	Experienced lack of support for the development of exploration behavior, may have been a "play-pen baby"	Ask your partner to give you support for exploring new ideas and activities.
_____ 7. Help from others rejected even when needed	Shaming discipline used to set limits	Ask your partner to support you as you express your feelings about being shamed.
_____ 8. Strives for perfection	Shame and/or other abusive methods of discipline used to control and set limits	Ask for unconditional strokes from your partner.
_____ 9. Unable to admit mistakes	Punished for mistakes with either shame or hitting	Have your partner role-play a parent, giving you understanding when you make a mistake. Ask for positive messages about mistakes being the way to learn.
_____10. Low tolerance for frustration and/or ambiguity	Efforts to become separate either overtly or covertly sabotaged; failures were punished	Sign up for a wilderness experience to develop risk-building skills.

	Common Issue	*Possible Developmental Trauma*	*How to Cooperatively Resolve the Issue at Its Source*
_____ 11.	Inability to follow through with agreements	Self-management skills were not taught effectively; personal boundaries not respected	Structure regular relationship meetings where agreements are considered contracts and written down. Each person decides on consequence for breaking an agreement and implements it, if necessary.
_____ 12.	Inability to handle time and money effectively	Little support for self-care	Invest in a time-management tool where all time is structured. Hire a financial advisor to teach you how to manage finances.
_____ 13.	Intimidation or manipulation used to resolve conflicts	Not allowed to make own age-appropriate decisions	Create and enforce a "no-power-plays" contract. Learn to express feelings of shame directly.
_____ 14.	Over-personalization of conflicts and other issues; moody behavior	Shame used to prevent development of independent ideas or actions	Use journaling to recover early memories of experiences. Contract with partner to witness the feelings and to speak any unfinished conversations.
_____ 15.	Difficulty in giving and receiving compliments	Lack of support and positive feedback for independent efforts	Contract with partner to give you a specific kind and amount of positive feedback every day. Write positive affirmations.
_____ 16.	Unwillingness to assume responsibility for actions	Lacked effective limit setting; raised with permissive discipline	Use limit-setting structures in your life (time, money, energy) as a focus for structuring realistic limits.
_____ 17.	Follows the direction of others rather than trusting own wisdom and intuition	Received messages that it was not safe to be a separate person; attempts to separate were punished	Take a public speaking or leadership development class. Explore some new activity that pushes you to risk.
_____ 18.	Fear of the future, fears of being left behind, feelings of inadequacy, low self-esteem	Possible unprocessed birth trauma or early abandonment experiences where bonding needs were not met	Use breathwork techniques with your partner present. Ask your partner to hold you and affirm you by offering unconditional love.
_____ 19.	Difficulty relaxing; chronic body tension	Early deprivation and a lack of constant care as an infant	Give each other body massages and other nonsexual touch.
_____ 20.	Compulsive eating, smoking, drinking, or sex	Deprivation of nourishment and/or love; basic needs may have been neglected	Ask your partner to hold you and rock you, perhaps feed you a bottle.
_____ 21.	Feeling unconnected or isolated in the relationship	Early abandonment by those charged with caring for you	Identify your unmet needs and ask your partner to role-play a caregiver providing you with those needs.
_____ 22.	Trouble trusting others, suspicious of the motives of other people	Birth trauma and lack of attention to your needs at birth	Ask your partner to bathe you in a quiet room filled with soft lights and soothing music. Have your partner lead you on a trust walk.

Common Issue	Possible Developmental Trauma	How to Cooperatively Resolve the Issue at Its Source
_____23. Feeling unloved by your partner	Insufficient loving messages from parents and/or other caretakers; criticism rather than praise used to teach socialization	Ask for reassurance from your partner in times of doubt or fear. Identify all the things you wish your parents had said and done during childhood and then ask your partner for them.
_____24. Unable to define wants and needs; expect others to just know how these needs should be met	Needs were anticipated and met prior to caretakers receiving cues for feeding, affection, changing diapers; parent(s) may have hovered and not waited for needs signals to emerge	Ask your partner to role-play your parents and give you permission to identify your needs and affirm your night to get them met. Ask directly for things you want and need.
_____25. Unwillingness to negotiate to get needs met	Subjected to win/lose methods of conflict resolution, negotiation interpreted as "losing"	Enroll in a class in conflict resolution and learn win/win methods for conflict resolution. Express past feelings about situations where loss was experienced.
_____26. Inability to shift from oneness to separateness without difficulty	Rigid atmosphere where everything was either black or white; sometimes a traumatic experience between the age of one and two	Identify instances of trauma or repression and ask partner to witness your expression of feelings about these experiences.
_____27. Avoidance of intimacy through workaholism or other compulsive activity	Abusive or invasive relationship with an adult during childhood that made intimacy unsafe	Identify instances of abuse or invasion and ask partner to support your expression of feelings about these experiences.
_____28. Fear of abandonment	Removed from mother at birth and taken to nursery; abrupt or extended separation from mother during the first year of life reinforced by later experiences of traumatic separation	Contract with partner for "I'm leaving now and I'll be back at _____" messages at times of separation. Do inner child work to validate and release the feelings of loss and trauma during early childhood.
_____29. Resistance to developing spiritual practices	Spiritual trauma between the age of four and twelve; religious abuse	Identify instances of spiritual trauma and ask partner to support your expression of feelings about these experiences.
_____30. Breaking or forgetting relationship agreements	Unpredictability used as a way of avoiding abuse; invasion or punishment from caregivers	Create a commitment contract with partner about keeping agreements, with consequences for breaking them.
_____31. Unwilling to accept past conflicts as the source of current conflicts	Unprocessed rage from abusive and/or shame-based discipline and limit setting	Identify instances of abusive and/or shame-based discipline and ask partner to support your expression of feelings about these experiences

Scoring and Interpretation

30– 90	A few unresolved developmental traumas in your relationship
91–180	Many unresolved developmental traumas in your relationship. Therapeutic intervention may be useful.
181–310	A high level of unresolved developmental traumas in your relationship. Therapeutic intervention is essential for creating a partnership relationship.

PARTNERSHIP WORKSHEET #5: RESOLVING INTRACTABLE CONFLICTS AT THEIR SOURCE

After you have identified the developmental source of your conflict, the incomplete developmental task(s), and unmet developmental needs, contract with your partner to help you complete these elements.

Step 1: Ask your partner to role-play the person with whom you had the original unresolved conflict. Ask your partner to participate by saying something like, "Would you be willing to play my father and listen while I express the anger I felt toward him when he divorced my mother and left our family?"

Step 2: Identify the element in the conflict that is unfinished or unresolved. In order to inform your partner about what you will be needing, you can set the stage by saying something like, "I never got to express my anger at my father and to feel him acknowledge and accept my feelings."

Step 3: Make a contract with your partner. It is important to make a specific request such as, "Will you role-play my 'functional father' and accept my feelings of anger and really hear my feelings? After I have expressed my anger, I want you to tell me I have a right to be angry and that you still love me and won't abandon me. Will you do that?"

Step 4: Complete the contract. Sit across from your partner to do this. You will need to express your anger at your "father." Your partner, role-playing your father, replies, "You have a perfect right to be angry at me. What I did changed your life and made life difficult for you. I'm glad you have the courage to tell me how you feel. I still love you and will not abandon you."

Step 5: Allow yourself to feel the full impact of the role-play. The impact may be dramatic or subtle, so allow enough time to fully feel the changes in awareness that might occur. You might report, "I am feeling much lighter and freer. My jaw seems looser and I notice I am feeling a little sad. I must be grieving the loss of my dad's presence in our family for the first time since he left. My anger must have blocked me from feeling the sadness."

Step 6: Ask for any additional support. If you need support or feedback from your partner after taking this risk, ask for it by saying, "Will you hold me or comfort me while I experience my sadness and grief?" If you do want to be held, it is important to clarify if it is your father or your partner who is doing the holding. If you need to be held by your father, then you must renegotiate with your partner to role-play him. It is important to always keep the roles and relationships clear and separate.

Step 7: Allow your partner to leave the role. Use a direct statement to acknowledge that your partner has completed the role-play so that you can re-enter the present. Say to your partner, "I feel complete now in our role-play. We can return to the present time." Thank your partner for helping you complete this unfinished business with your father.

Step 8: Return to the current conflict. After completing the unresolved elements from your past conflict, return to the current conflict to see if it can now be resolved. It is usually easy to resolve the current issues once the issues from the past have been resolved.

Chapter 11
~
What Is the Role of Betrayal in Intractable Conflicts?

One of the most universal of human experiences is that of betrayal trauma. Betrayal experiences are a special kind of developmental trauma. They often begin in early childhood when you placed all your trust in your parents and other adults, anticipating that they would be perfect caregivers, see your essence, honor your innocence, appreciate your uniqueness, and meet your needs in a timely manner. When your parents were unable to do so, you felt betrayed.

Children are born with the innate potential to become a "Stradivarius," filled with a nuclear divinity that radiates like precious jewels. Bubbling with the rich harvest of millions of years of evoluation, they contain the latent programs needed to express God in Action. Because this abundant potential for divinity is unrecognized and unsupported by parents, grandparents, teachers and representatives of social institutions who are focused on maintaining to status quo, our children's precocious talents gradually disappear. First, they are informed of their smallness in relation to that which is larger, more important and greater, so that they learn quickly of their ignorance, ineptitude, insufficiencies and inconsequentiality. Their connections to Nature, experienced through their physical body, their feelings and their intuition, are systematically discounted as unimportant. Little by little their awareness of their divinity and their ability to express the gifts of evolution they brought with them are extinguished. Finally, they are deemed acceptable to meet society's standards and instead of becoming a "Stradivarius," they become a plastic fiddle.

The research on human potential indicates that most people use only five to eight percent of their inherent capacities. They are so richly overendowed that very few even begin to understand how much unused potential they really have at their disposal. In fact, Einstein, often thought of as the epitome of mental giants, reportedly wept before his death when he contemplated the fact that he had used so little of his own potential.

Betrayal trauma plays a major role in the loss of human potential, particularly the loss of innocence in early childhood. Each time a parent or adult fails to see and understand a child, they chip away at his or her sense of self. The children, rather than knowing themselves as the Stradivariuses that they are, are left feeling like plastic fiddles. It is helpful to look at the when, how, where, and by whom of betrayal experiences to recover split-off parts, restore the connection to essence, and reclaim the vision of true potential.

WHAT IS THE ROLE OF BETRAYAL IN INTRACTABLE CONFLICTS?

When parents fail to follow their children's natural instincts or punish them for their natural spontaneous actions, children feel shame about their inherent nature. As a result of these experiences of shame, they create negative beliefs about themselves. The pertinent dynamics of betrayal trauma get reenacted later in conflicts that contain the critical elements of the original betrayal experience. The reenactment of this earlier experience involves post-traumatic stress symptoms that stimulate the avoidant, obsessive, or compulsive behaviors characteristic of PTSD.

Betrayal traumas can be a source of great learning if you know how to use your betrayal experiences effectively. First, they can provide a lot of information about your developmental traumas, as your current or recent betrayals usually contain the elements of your original or early traumas. Betrayals usually involve a loss of primal trust with another person, which can be easily traced back to earlier traumatic events where you first lost that same sense of primal trust.

If you are not aware that you are reenacting an early betrayal trauma involving the loss of primal trust, you will likely replay it and experience a similar outcome. You may feel very disappointed with a trusted friend or partner who says and does things that open an unhealed wound related to an earlier loss of primal trust in a relationship. After a number of years, betrayal experiences can create predictable patterns of relational dynamics. Until the dynamics and events of previous betrayal traumas have been identified, it may be difficult or even impossible to resolve intractable conflicts in present time.

Most people go through life, however, unconsciously recreating the dynamics that they hope will heal the wounds from earlier betrayals. If you can understand that your current betrayals provide doorways to help you heal past betrayals, it is possible to grow and expand your consciousness as a result of the betrayal process. While it is possible to work on a current betrayal without referencing past betrayals, we have found that current betrayals are almost always related in some way to unhealed past betrayals.

The Role of Betrayal in Christianity

The whole theme of betrayal is woven into the fabric of the Judeo-Christian tradition. Betrayal is one of the most prominent themes in the Christian story of the death and resurrection of Jesus Christ. Most Christians, unfortunately, have focused more on the resurrection theme of the story rather than the betrayal theme.

One group of Christians, known as the Maundy Thursday Movement, now identify betrayal as the most important theme in this story (Houston, 1980). This group says Christian theology missed an important theme of the story that could help Westerners cope more effectively with betrayal. When Jesus was first brought before Pontius Pilate, he was still pretty self-confident. He declared, "I'm the Son of God and you can't hurt me. You can't do anything to me." He had what appears to be primal trust in God, his father. Then came a series of betrayals, some of which he predicted. For example, he reportedly said to Peter, his disciple, "You will betray me three times before the cock crows." The betrayal of the Messiah was actually prophesied by Jewish religious leaders in the Old Testament.

Some suggest that Jesus actually created the betrayal in order to fulfill the ancient prophesies. There could be another reason, however, for his betrayal. Perhaps he was healing earlier betrayals by reenacting them. Jesus' demeanor changed drastically after the series of betrayals that led to his capture and conviction. He was no longer the confident son, trusting his father to protect him. On the cross he uttered a long lament, which began, "Father, why has thou forsaken me?" He felt betrayed by God, his father, and said so. By this time, he was not focusing on the betrayals by Peter and other people close to him. He focused instead on the loss of his primal trust in God. This lament ends with his surrender to his fate and asking for God's forgiveness of his enemies.

What is the hidden meaning in this story? Why is betrayal a main theme in it? What was Jesus trying to teach about betrayal in this scenario? Is it that people must heal their betrayals at their source rather than focusing on those who are betraying them in the moment? These are interesting questions that suggest ways of dealing effectively with betrayals. It is also interesting that most of the people who betrayed Jesus were men. This suggests he may have been reenacting an earlier betrayal trauma that involved his earthly father or other men from his childhood. The story of Jesus' death and resurrection emphasizes the devotion of the women around him, particularly at the cross and the tomb. In the last hours of the crucifixion he does not mention the presence of any of the men in his life, including his earthly father, Joseph.

WHAT ARE UNHEALTHY RESPONSES TO BETRAYAL?

James Hillman (1975) wrote a very penetrating article about betrayal that talks about the choices people make when they are betrayed. His belief is that most people usually make what he calls "sterile choices" that prevent them from learning much from their betrayals. According to Hillman, these sterile choices are how people typically respond to betrayal.

Revenge

People often feel a very strong desire to get even with the person or persons who betrayed them. When someone says or does something hurtful, the immediate impulse may be to get revenge. Hillman says that this choice is the most common response and the one that creates the least amount of growth in consciousness. Seeking revenge and getting even means placing the focus on what other people did or didn't do or say and allows you to avoid looking at yourself in order to expand your awareness.

Splitting

People in intimate relationships who are unable to maintain their internal object constancy or sense of self often resort to splitting. Triggered by post-traumatic stimuli from the past they may feel regressed, and then make either themselves or the other person the "bad guy." This kind of split immediately activates automatic fight/flight/flee behavioral responses. Splitting responses to betrayal may indicate a need for trauma reduction therapies and/or individual counseling that focuses on developmental trauma during the first three years of life.

Denial

A third choice in a betrayal situation is to deny the value of the other person. This choice may involve splitting, or making a person once perceived as "all good" into someone "all bad." It's surprising how quickly this defense mechanism can be activated, often with little awareness.

Cynicism

This easy choice may be the disease of contemporary times. It is easy for someone to get cynical because of their inability to stop reenacting or predicting their betrayal traumas and the subsequent lack of understanding of the patterns inherent in them. Cynicism, unfortunately, doesn't lead to much growth or awareness.

Paranoia

Paranoia, or not trusting the betrayer, is another common response to betrayal. Someone who was betrayed in a loving, trusting relationship may require that people pass a lot of tests before they are allowed to get close. Paranoia also leads to very little growth. It requires a lot of time to constantly monitor the other person's behavior to determine if he or she is passing trustworthiness tests. Rather than focusing on the source of the betrayal or the patterns being reenacted in the relationship, paranoia is a way of avoiding self-scrutiny.

Self-Betrayal

The final sterile choice, according to Hillman, involves the betrayal of one's own self. The inner response to a betrayal might be, "How could I have been so stupid!" Such responses often include a self-judgment about the risks that were taken. Rather than seeing the

risk-taking as a potential for learning, it becomes classified as a mistake that is used for self-judgment and disempowerment.

WHAT ARE SOME HEALTHY RESPONSES TO BETRAYAL?

None of the above sterile choices leads to the effective resolution of intractable conflicts involving betrayals. Only by understanding the patterns of betrayal can behavior really be changed. Being willing to see betrayers as players sent from central casting to act in a betrayal drama, casts them as allies or friends helping to clear earlier betrayal traumas. Betrayal can be used to learn more about yourself and to increase consciousness. Rather than splitting or making another sterile choice, ask, "What other options were available in that situation? Is it still possible to use them?"

The first choice to begin making healthier responses to betrayal involves a perception check with the assumed betrayer. Ask this person, "Are you intending to do _____ (their behavior) to hurt me? Are you aware that I am experiencing your behavior as a betrayal?" This person will likely not recognize his or her behavior as a betrayal, so your question can provide him or her with new awareness about both of you. This direct communication is critical, as it can stop the unfolding of drama triangle dynamics in your relationship.

The second healthy choice is to look for patterns of betrayal. Barry describes how this was helpful for him:

> One day I made a chronological list of my major betrayals. Three or four pages later I began to see a pattern of betrayals involving certain kinds of women, and I identified the recurring themes. I thought, "Oh my God! This has been going on most of my life." These patterns had been there much longer than I realized. Then I looked at what was not finished about each betrayal. In each instance, I was able to identify the unlearned lesson that kept recycling.

You may want to complete the betrayal writing exercise at the end of the chapter to help you recognize your patterns of betrayal.

The third step is learning compassion for yourself and others during a betrayal trauma. Betrayal usually involves some misperception about the other person or distorted perceptions related to your own unmet developmental needs. If you have not done a perception check with the other person, your misperceptions may be creating a narrowly focused picture that allows you to disregard significant information about a person. A betrayal tells you that your image of this person was too narrow and that you overlooked things in order to maintain some illusion of him or her. This critical step will help you move beyond any internal splits and open yourself to connection and reciprocity with this person again.

The fourth healthy choice is to redefine betrayal as an opportunity to expand your consciousness. The real question is, "Who is the betrayer in this situation?" The truth is, you probably betrayed yourself by creating too narrow a view of the other person. Perhaps you wanted to see him or her a certain way, hoping to heal wounds related to an earlier betrayal. People are usually not the way you think they are, or sometimes the way you would like them to be. They have some qualities that you like and some that you don't like. They are trustworthy in some situations and may not be so in others. Barry remembers confronting this in a therapy group:

> A group member said to me, "I really trust you." I recognized the presence of a positive projection and challenged the statement: "I may not be totally trustworthy. What makes you so sure that I'm totally trustworthy?" This question got the person thinking. Then I said to this person, "Don't expect me to be totally trustworthy. You may end up disappointed and then angry because I didn't live up to your expectations. I want a relationship with you where I have permission to be human. While I strive to do my best, I know that I am not perfect. I feel this is more realistic than you expecting me to be a perfect therapist."

By reframing your experiences of betrayal, you may be able to return to the person who has betrayed you and say to them, "I now realize that I gave you a lot of power by making you totally responsible for betraying me. I see that I also had some responsibility in creating the betrayal. I had unrealistic expectations of you because I did not want to see all of you. I want to acknowledge that you're not all bad and that I can see your good qualities as well." Toxic shame or feelings of pride often prevent people from making these kinds of amends. Pride is a defense against feeling shame. If you see a person exhibiting a lot of pride, know that underneath the pride is a lot of hidden shame.

IS IT POSSIBLE TO FORGIVE SOMEONE WHO HAS BETRAYED ME?

In the throes of betrayal, forgiveness may seem impossible. You may feel as though you have been mortally wounded and that you can never be close to your betrayer again. This initial reaction is a normal part of the grief process that accompanies betrayal experiences. Once the anger stage of the grief process passes and you move toward acceptance of the betrayal, you can begin to think about forgiveness.

Compassionate forgiveness can help you heal accumulations of past physical, emotional, psychological, and spiritual wounds from previous betrayals and other kinds of developmental trauma. It can also help you open your heart again so that you can begin rebuilding the fracture in your relationship. The goal is to repair the trust, empathy, reciprocity, and love you once had with this person.

Weinhold and Andresen (1979) wrote, "Forgiveness is basic to all change and growth." The tension from self-judgment and judging others produces a chronic level of stress in your body that depresses your immune system and causes illness (Borysenko, 1996). You have the power to end this kind of destructive cycle by moving beyond the acceptance stage of grieving and work toward forgiving your betrayer.

The healthiest choice in a betrayal trauma is to forgive yourself and the other person for creating the betrayal situation. The word forgive is often misunderstood. To some people, it means to rise above your feelings or to deny or passively condone the act of betrayal. Forgiveness actually means to "give back, give before, or for-give." What are you willing to give back or take back in a betrayal situation? What responsibility do you have in this betrayal? This approach will help you "give back" your projections and misperceptions about the other person's behavior. You may find the other person feels shocked to hear your perceptions about them or the situation.

Perhaps you were not fully truthful with the other person in ways that contributed to his or her misperceptions about you. Perhaps you need to give back the full truth. You may also have unconsciously set up the betrayal by pretending to like something the other person said or did, when in truth you didn't like it.

Compassion is a companion tool to forgiveness. Both are necessary for clearing betrayal traumas. Compassion doesn't necessarily help the person who betrayed you, but it will surely help you heal your own wounds. If you cannot feel compassion for those who betray you, you may continue to draw people into your life who play into your pattern of betrayal.

To be an effective counselor or helper, it is important to practice compassion toward yourself. An excellent way to develop self-compassion is to eliminate the word mistake from your vocabulary. Mistake implies judgment and failure, that something went wrong, and that you or someone else is bad, all of which create intrapsychic splitting. A more compassionate framework is to see everything, including your betrayal traumas, as learning experiences.

Learning has a connotation of discovery, exploration, and adventure, all of which are fun and exciting. When you try something new and it turns out the way that you expected, you probably didn't learn anything. Rather, it reinforced your previous learning. When you try something new and it turns out differently from what you expected, you probably learned something. This unexpected turn of events stimulates your thinking, activates your curiosity, and promotes more exploration and discovery. An attitude of learning fosters synthesis or unitive thinking and increased self-esteem.

What Is Forgiveness Not?

Below is a description of what forgiveness is not. Because of all the misconceptions about forgiveness, it is necessary first to clarify what it is not.

1. *It does not involve ego gratification.* For example, someone might forgive you for doing something that they

didn't like (a judgment on their part) and imply, "Oh, I forgive you because I am so great, and you are not so hot." This is an inappropriate use of forgiveness and does little to resolve the conflict. This approach is more about arrogance than forgiveness.

2. *It does not condone the other person's ignorant or deceitful behavior.* This is the most common misunderstanding of forgiveness. Forgiveness is not letting someone off the hook. They still have to address their own behavior. People who have been grievously wronged by someone else, however, may need to release their anger or rage toward that person before they're ready to even begin to think about forgiving them.

3. *It is not associated with any specific behaviors.* Perhaps someone was abused by their father as a child. The form of forgiveness depends on the situation. This person might forgive their father and never speak to him again. They also could forgive and then develop a good relationship with their father.

4. *It is not a "spiritual bypass."* Forgiveness is not a way to avoid doing your own emotional and psychological work. Even if you are able to forgive someone, you still have to resolve the issues related to your deep grief and anger. You still have to find ways to heal your developmental traumas and move forward in your personal growth. Some people use meditation, prayer, or affirmations in order to bypass doing this deeper kind of spiritual work. It generally isn't very effective. Emotional and psychological work can be difficult and painful, so it is understandable why people want to avoid it. If you try to avoid it, it is likely that you will drive the energy of the wounds deeper into your body where the tension from them can somaticize into life-threatening illnesses.

What Is True Forgiveness?

Forgiveness is a very deep psychophysical process that can hone your wisdom and raise your consciousness.

> Forgiveness is a complex act of consciousness, one that liberates the psyche and soul from the need for personal vengeance and the perception of oneself as a victim. More than releasing from blame the people who caused our wounds, forgiveness means releasing the control that the perception of victimhood has over our psyches. The liberation that forgiveness generates comes in the transition to a higher state of consciousness—not just in theory, but energetically and biologically. (Myss, 1996, p. 215)

Unless you can develop compassionate forgiveness, the original trauma or betrayal will follow you everywhere, continuing to draw new people into your life to help you reenact the betrayal trauma. Why? Because your unconscious knows it is not good for you to hold onto the energy of that trauma and seeks to help you to recreate the trauma in order to finally heal it. Remember, it is the natural learning style of humans to repeat a behavior or

situation until it is completely understood and integrated into your consciousness.

Where Do I Begin in Forgiving Others?

The process of forgiving others begins with developing compassionate forgiveness for yourself. If you blame your betrayals on other people without looking at your contribution, you will find it difficult to forgive the other person. When you can clearly identify your part in the betrayal, you have the potential for real forgiveness. People who judge themselves usually judge others. Below is a listing of the steps in self-forgiveness, followed by a description of each step.

WHAT ARE THE STEPS IN THE PROCESS OF SELF-FORGIVENESS?

Self-forgiveness is a process that includes the following steps:

1. *Take responsibility for what you did.* Taking responsibility means admitting you contributed to the betrayal rather than blaming it all on someone else. Borysenko (1996) quotes Emmanuel on this, saying, "If you deny what is your nature, you become deeply attached to that denial. When you accept what is there in its truth, then you are released. One does not release through rejection, one releases through love." It is truly an act of love to say "I learned something important, and I will accept responsibility for what I did."

2. *Confess to another person(s) the truth about how you contributed to the creation of an event that hurt yourself.* Mind-body studies show that when you confess a perceived wrong, it reduces the stress stored in your body. This stored stress can make you physically ill. Borysenko (1996) cites research involving students who confessed to a shower curtain (no one on was behind the curtain, although the students were not told this). The researcher followed up with these students and found they had better health (fewer colds and illnesses) than did a comparison group who didn't confess. The Catholic church has known about the power of confession for many centuries. Therapy certainly plays a similar role in helping people become less depressed or guilt-ridden.

3. *Look compassionately at yourself, seeing how past betrayals are contaminating your experiences in the present.* Identify how this betrayal correlates with other betrayals you have experienced. This will help you see the other person as "an actor from central casting" who is helping you work on your betrayal pattern. Avoid feeling guilty or depressed about the betrayal and reinforcing feelings of unworthiness. Borysenko (1996) says that the mind always takes the shape of what it dwells upon. If you dwell on your perceived failures or unworthiness, you may find it difficult to remember the good things about

you. In order to balance this self-critical tendency, dwell also on some of your innocence and what is right about this particular betrayal experience.

4. Look compassionately at the other person and be willing to make amends. Barry remembers learning an important lesson in compassion many years ago:

> I was working as a university administrator and had a trusted university colleague and friend in whom I confided periodically regarding my misgivings about certain university policies and the actions of some of my superiors. Without my knowledge, he shared all this information with my superiors. One day my colleague informed me that I had been fired from my administrative position and that it had been given to him. I felt devastated and hated this man for his act of betrayal.

> I sought the advice of a counselor who helped me deal with my self-judgments, as I was really critical of myself for trusting this man. I was also not coping well with the aftermath of the betrayal because my betrayer was now my boss rather than my colleague. This prospect brought up intense shame. The counselor helped me see that I had done nothing wrong or shameful. I managed to keep my object constancy each day when I went to work over the following four months.

> Later that year, I left that job for a much better one. In my new environment, I could see the situation more objectively. Because my job situation had improved and I felt happier, I began to consider forgiving this man. I was able to release my need to see myself as a victim in this situation, while also acknowledging my part in setting up the betrayal. I saw that unhealed abuse issues from childhood were behind my blind trust in this colleague. Because I couldn't see this shadow part of myself, it was difficult for me to see it in others.

> This story had a very interesting ending for me. About five years after I left this university, I returned to visit some friends who still lived in the community. They suggested that we take a drive out to the campus so they could show me the new buildings and how the campus had grown. While we were walking through the building where I formerly worked, I suddenly came face to face with my betrayer. He recognized me and came toward me. At first, I felt a rush of the old anger I had held toward him and felt my fist clench. My anger passed immediately as he began to speak to me.

> He said, "I am so glad to see you. Many times I have tried unsuccessfully to write you a letter and thought of calling you to say how sorry I am about what I did to you. I have had trouble sleeping and have had many nightmares. I want to resolve this. Will you forgive me for what I did? I really need your forgiveness, so I can get on with my life." I thought for a minute, seeing the distress in his eyes. Then I said, "I forgave you a long time ago. I needed to do that for me, not for you. I urge you to forgive yourself, because that is what is holding you back, not my lack of forgiveness."

> He looked at me and seemed to take in what I was saying. Then he said, "Thank you for forgiving me. I will now try to forgive myself." Then he told me that what he had done to me had also happened to him. He had been fired as well. He said that he normally would not have been at the office that day, but he was there packing his things to leave the university. Our chance meeting may not have been chance at all. I had the feeling that this meeting was arranged by someone wiser than us in order to give this man a chance to remove the burden he had carried for the past five years. It also gave me a chance to make amends in a way that I didn't even know I needed to do. It was a profound lesson in forgiveness that I will never forget.

5. Ask for help from spiritual realms (as you define them) in developing compassionate forgiveness. There are numerous spiritual lessons that can be learned from a betrayal. One of the most intriguing spiritual concepts is the concept of surrender. Surrender has to do with letting go of judgments toward self and others. It takes two forms, a masculine form and a feminine form. Men and women need to exhibit both forms. If you are good at one form but not the other, you may find it difficult to heal betrayals.

The masculine form of surrender involves the ability to take charge of your life without guilt. Many people often would rather feel guilty than be responsible and face their shortcomings. Guilt is usually teamed with resentment. If you feel guilty about something you have done to someone, you may also resent this person in some way. It is your responsibility to take charge of your guilt. This is the message I gave the colleague who was unable to take charge of his guilt and was waiting for me to forgive him so he could forgive himself.

The feminine form of surrender involves the ability to receive without resistance. Perhaps you remember a time when someone said or did something that hurt you. It may have been difficult for you to experience what this person did or said. Perhaps you denied the truth of their words or deeds by verbally or physically erecting barriers against their message. Perhaps you responded with some sterile choices, deflecting the impact of the betrayal. In order to learn from the betrayal and achieve some level of spiritual healing, you will need to experience its impact and full meaning.

Men seem to have more difficulty in learning to receive than women do. On the other hand, women seem to have more problems in taking charge without guilt. If a man can't receive without resistance, his capacity for learning from a betrayal situation can be greatly diminished. A woman who cannot take charge without guilt but is good at receiving without resistance may end up being overpowered and victimized. These twin concepts are very important in helping you learn from and heal the trauma you experience from betrayals.

WHAT ARE THE STEPS IN THE PROCESS OF FORGIVING OTHERS?

The process of forgiving others also has a number of steps:

1. Take responsibility for your part of the betrayal or conflict. Recognize that you do not have complete control over all your life events. The only thing you can control is your response to those events. Therefore, you are responsible for any residual feelings from a betrayal. Your attitude is under your direct control. Ask yourself: "Do I want to revictimize myself for the rest of my life? Do I want to continue disempowering myself because of a desire to hold onto an ancient betrayal? Do I want to store the energy of these old resentments in my body? Am I willing to risk making myself ill over this?" By identifying your role in the betrayal, you can take responsibility for it.

Strangely, people seem more willing to feel guilty, angry, or blame someone rather than to experience feelings of helplessness. This fact is behind the question "Why do bad things happen to good people?" The world is a place where both good and bad things happen to everyone. People in the United States need to blame other people, groups, or cultures for the bad things that happen to them. Rather than recognizing their limitations in controlling random events, they either feel guilty and blame themselves or blame others. These sterile choices give people the illusion of control over the randomness of life. While you may never know exactly why a certain betrayal occurred, you can accept responsibility for the feelings it evokes in you. You can also choose to find meaning in a betrayal event that will help you heal wounds from past betrayals, with the hope of ending this betrayal pattern.

2. Confess your role in creating the trauma or betrayal. The prescription for healing any ensuing symptoms of post-traumatic stress related to a betrayal is to move deeper into the experience. This is where many people would rather opt for a spiritual bypass. They say, "I'll get rid of the feelings I have toward the man who beat me or the father who abused me by adopting a spiritual point of view." This will not work. You have to remember the trauma sufficiently to stop its influence on your life. This includes dealing with any anger that is involved. In spiritual circles, anger often is considered a negative emotion. In fact, anger is a very useful and important emotion. It helps you define your boundaries and helps you to get your needs met. Anger only becomes negative when it turns into resentment or when it becomes abusive. You must contact your old anger sufficiently to release it. This often opens the doorway into your grief.

3. Look compassionately at others, seeing how your betrayal pattern fits into theirs. To eliminate splitting responses to a betrayal, focus on the mutuality of your betrayal experiences. Know that your patterns must interlock in some way that is drawing you to see the deeper realms of yourself. See the other person as innocent in this situation and having both positive and negative qualities. As long as you perceive the betrayer as malevolent and all bad, you remain trapped in the victim role. Identify the innocent and positive aspects of yourself to heal your internal splits. Try to unhook from the trauma and reframe it as an opportunity for deeper intimacy with yourself and with the other person.

4. Take specific action to heal your wounds. Take appropriate action in the situation. Some action might be more active and involve the masculine form of surrender. You may take charge without guilt by reporting your abuser to the police with the intention of preventing this person from abusing someone else. Other action may be more receptive and involve the feminine form of surrender. Perhaps you choose to receive your betrayer without resistance by acknowledging how you unconsciously contributed to the betrayal.

Many people come to therapy to heal wounds inflicted on them by their parents or other adults. When adult children are able to feel compassion for their parents, they often experience a breakthrough in their relationship with them. As noted earlier in the book, the only thing that parents owe their children is the truth about what happened during their childhood and how it might be affecting them now. What children want from their parents is to admit they weren't perfect and to apologize for any pain they caused.

5. Look to God or Spirit for help. If you feel reluctant to forgive yourself or others, it may be necessary to use prayer or meditation to seek a deeper understanding of a betrayal. You can pray for help to open you to compassion or you can meditate on the theme of forgiveness to seek insights. You may also think about how feeling compassion for yourself or another person might change your life. If you believe in divine intervention, you can ask for it directly to help you move forward in the forgiveness process.

6. Reflect on what you have learned. This may be the most important step. You may want to review the positive outcomes of a major betrayal. For example, as a result of Barry's betrayal with his university colleague, he found a much better job and lifestyle. It actually changed his life in so many positive ways that it is hard for him now to think of it as a bad experience. Reframing is an important tool for forgiveness, as it provides a new perspective or slant on the problem. A review and reframing of all your betrayals through the forgiveness process can have a profoundly positive effect on your life. This is called harvesting your betrayals.

While betrayals happen to everyone, not everyone learns from them. Some people must endure many betrayals before any learning occurs. The point where you no longer need to repeat negative experiences is known as *grace*. The next time you encounter a betrayal, ask: "What lesson do I need to learn here? How can this betrayal help me expand my consciousness?" If you are able to quickly identify the lesson, then the experience can move through your life in an affirming way.

SKILL PRACTICE EXERCISE: LOCATING YOUR PATTERNS OF BETRAYAL

Make a list of the significant betrayals in your life. You can make the list chronological, starting with the earliest one you can remember, or you can arrange your list from the most significant down to the least significant. After you have listed all these events (you only need a few words to describe the event: "The time when _____ happened"), go back and examine each betrayal using the following questions.

- What were the predominant feelings you had then and have now?
- Which sterile choices did you make in dealing with this betrayal?
- What illusions, misperceptions, or expectations contributed to the betrayal?
- What other choices could you have made in this betrayal situation?
- What new choices still exist for you in this betrayal situation?
- What lessons did you learn as a result of this betrayal?
- What, if any, important benefits came out of this betrayal experience?
- Have you had similar kinds of betrayals? What were the common elements in these betrayals? How do they form a pattern?
- Which betrayals do you feel you have successfully resolved? How did you do that?
- Which betrayals have you not healed? What opportunities still exist to heal or resolve these?

After you have answered the above questions, make a second list of the times when you were the betrayer. Answer the following questions as honestly as possible.

- What were the most prevalent feelings involved in your betrayals?
- How did you deal with each betrayal?
- What were the short-term and long-term effects of the betrayal on you?
- What were the short-term and long-term effects of the betrayal on the other person(s) involved?
- What could you have done instead of betraying the other person?
- What, if any, benefits did you receive as a result of the betrayal?
- What, if any, unfinished business do you think still exists with each of your betrayals?
- What actions do you still need to take to clear any unfinished business left over from any of your betrayals?

SKILL PRACTICE EXERCISE: FORGIVING MYSELF

Using your list of betrayal experiences from the previous exercise, take them one at a time and complete the following self-forgiveness process. Write down your responses for each step.

1. *Take responsibility for your part in the betrayal.* Identify the illusions, misperceptions, projections, and expectations you held that contributed to creating the betrayal. This can be difficult, but without taking full responsibility for your part in setting up the betrayal trauma, you will not be able to clear the issue, risking further betrayals.

   The ways I helped set up this betrayal situation are:

2. *Confess what you did to set up the betrayal.* This step helps you assume complete responsibly for your part by telling another person about what you did. When you do that there is a healing response in the body.

   To whom do I want to confess and why:

3. *Identify good points in yourself.* It is important that you don't split in reverse and blame the whole thing on yourself. Identify your good points to maintain a sense of object constancy.

   The good points I want to remember about myself are:

4. *Be willing to make amends.* When possible, go to the people involved and make amends with them in person. This can involve telling them about your part in setting up the betrayal and telling them you forgive them for their part.

   I plan to make amends in this betrayal situation in the following ways:

5. *Ask for help from God or other spiritual realms.* The last step is to ask for guidance from your higher self or God. The spiritual lessons that you can learn from a betrayal are important to look at and build upon.

   The spiritual lessons I learned from this betrayal are:

SKILL PRACTICE EXERCISE: FORGIVING OTHERS

Using the lists of betrayals you generated previously, determine which still need spiritual forgiveness. Use this exercise to help release any feelings of anger and resentment in an act of self-care. Write down your responses for each step.

1. *Take responsibility for your feelings and reactions.* You are responsible for your feelings and reactions when you are betrayed. If a betrayal happened at an early age when you couldn't deal effectively with your feelings, you can deal with them now that you are older. The choice is to take care of your feelings and move on to avoid being revictimized and giving away your power to potential betrayers.

   I am going to take responsibility for my feelings and reactions in this betrayal situation by:

2. *Confess your role in setting up the betrayal.* This is an important requirement for healing betrayal trauma. This is not the time to choose a spiritual bypass to help you rise above the trauma. While spiritual practices can be helpful, there is no substitute for feeling and expressing the hurt, pain, anger, and grief. This often requires the presence of a guide who has been there. The body and brain simply will not release the trauma unless you do your deep-feeling work.

   To heal the trauma from by this betrayal I am going to:

3. *Look for the good points in yourself and the other person.* This will help you move beyond the good/bad split so common in betrayals. Misperceptions and illusions need to be corrected and seen in the context of opportunities to learn.

   To heal any good/bad splits involved in this betrayal I am going to:

4. *Look for specific action to take.* Consider what actions are appropriate for you to take toward the person who betrayed you. Search your soul to find the answer to this question: What actions do you believe are necessary for you to be healed of the adverse effects of the betrayal trauma?

   The specific actions I am going to take in order to move past this betrayal trauma are:

5. *Ask for spiritual help.* You might use prayer and meditation to help clear any remaining feelings and reactions from your body and brain. Sometimes answers to your prayers come in your dreams. Some people keep a dream journal to work with their spiritual thoughts and feelings. One sign that you are completely through this is if you can feel genuine love and compassion for yourself and the other person.

   The specific spiritual actions that I am going to take to heal the effects of this betrayal situation are:

6. *Determine what you learned from your betrayals.* In retrospect, a betrayal can lead to many positive experiences. This step involves taking a longer view of the betrayal to locate any positive outcomes. Adversity and enemies often are powerful teachers.

   The positive outcomes for me from this betrayal are:

Chapter 12

~

How Can I Use
the Partnership Way
to Resolve Intractable
Family Conflicts?

The evolution of family relationships follows a developmental model similar to that for individual and couple relationships. Adult members of a family carry with them into their family system all the unresolved conflicts and issues related to developmental trauma from both the individual and couple stages of development. This "baggage" eventually surfaces as drama triangle conflicts within the family system.

The principles of the family component of the Partnership Way apply to relationships of three or more individuals, whether they be parents and a child, three friends, or three coworkers. Most people do not understand that a dramatic shift occurs in relational dynamics when the system shifts from two people to three people. You may notice that the word "dramatic" contains the word "drama." This is no coincidence. As soon as there are three people in a relationship, there are sufficient players to fill all the roles in the drama triangle. These dynamics appear only after sufficient trust and intimacy have been established over a period of time. Once this foundation of security is in place, the unfinished business of all three people will surface. For this reason, conflicts involving relationships of three tend to be some of the most intractable.

Staying conscious and clear in a family can be quite difficult, as members' unprocessed trauma can effortlessly trigger conflict. The success of family or three-way relationships depends on the degree to which each person has resolved any developmental trauma, is able to abstain from the dynamics of the drama triangle, and has completed the splitting phase of the counter-dependent stage of development. Trained professionals have difficulty in navigating relationships with two or more people for the same reasons.

The four stages of family development, like those of individuals and couples, are *codependent, counter-dependent, independent,* and *interdependent.* The psychosocial tasks for each stage are illustrated in Table 12.1. If effective methods are provided for each individual member of the system, including the parents in their couple relationship, to complete their psychosocial tasks, the family system can proceed to a higher stage of development.

Table 12.1
Stages of Family Development

Stage of Development	Psychosocial Tasks of a Family	Methods for Completing These Tasks
Codependent	Establish bond between parents and children Establish primal trust in family Establish family identity	Establish a constant environment for parenting the children Recognize and acknowledge each other's spiritual essence Exchange nurturing touch and talk between parents and children and between siblings Give and receive unconditional love between parents and children and between siblings Create common interests, values, beliefs, and goals among family members
Counter-dependent	Psychological separation between parents and children Resolve conflicts between needs of parents and needs of children	Parents and children individually explore interests outside the family Recognize the unique characteristics and life path of each child Build appropriate boundaries between children and parents Identify parents' needs vs. children's needs Seek win/win solutions to conflicts between children's needs and parents' needs
Independent	Develop individual initiative Develop individual and couple autonomy within the family structure Achieve object constancy as a family	Provide children with independence training in managing time, money, school, and extracurricular activities Develop a consequence-based method of discipline for children Maintain boundaries between adult activities and interests and parenting activities Achieve a balance between adults' and children's needs Experience constancy of family relationships and structure during times of stress and/or conflict
Interdependent	Build consensus in decision-making Develop equitable and equal relationships Develop each meiiibcr's fullest potential as a human being	Manage family affairs through family meetings Valuing and keeping agreements between family members Use power equitably between adults and adults, adults and children, and children and children Provide a high level of physical, mental, emotional, and spiritual resources for all members

WHAT IS THE SOURCE OF FAMILY CONFLICT?

The birth of the first child usually causes the shift from couple to family dynamics. The change in dynamics becomes more visible when the child begins separating from the mother or primary caregiver during the counter-dependent stage of development. This stage, characterized by splitting and consequently a lot of conflict, is the time when adults often use "reverse psychology" on the child to cope with oppositional and defiant behaviors. When a parent is directive and authoritative, a child will become oppositional and set off a power struggle between them. The child's independent behaviors can trigger the parents' unresolved drama triangle dynamics.

Family conflicts are complicated because two parallel levels of dynamics are happening simultaneously. The first is occurring between the child and parents in the present time; the second is occurring inside each of the parents in past time. Psychodynamic psychology recognizes that adults unconsciously regress to the chronological age of their child during a conflict (deMause, 1982, p.135). This psychological phenomenon, known as *regression-progression,* stimulates an unconscious restaging of the parents' own developmental trauma. This restaging provides the parents with a venue to unconsciously reprocess the trauma related to same-age experiences from their own childhood. In essence, these parent-child conflicts function as an unconscious "therapeutic" process for the parents.

Parents can be expected to replay their own developmental trauma through each stage of their child's development, particularly during the counter-dependent stage of development. Each parent becomes psychologically vulnerable to regression during family conflicts, especially when the other parent or caregiver is in conflict with the child. The parents' symbiotic bond and strong identification with the child triggers symptoms of post-traumatic stress, activating latent feelings and behaviors related to their own struggle for separation.

In other words, the boundaries between the parents' experiences of the past and the present become blurred. Similar to a post-traumatic flashback experience, the past feels as though it is still happening in the present. Parents experience exaggerated feeling states that relate more to their past than the present. For example, when the mother is in conflict with the child, the father may identify with the child as the Victim and perceive them as the Persecutor. This symbiotic identification with the child triggers Rescuer behavior in the father and activates the dynamics of the drama triangle between the two parents and the child.

Another common parent-child drama involves seeing the child as an enemy. For example, a father perceives that the mother is more attentive to the child than to him. This triggers the father's memories of developmental trauma related to sibling rivalry, stimulating him to criticize the mother for "spoiling" the child. Unable to identify his own unmet needs for nurturing, the father attempts

to diminish the strong bond between the mother and child. Parenting provides a stage where parents can unconsciously seek resolution to their unresolved developmental trauma. The recycling of trauma through family dramas is a major factor in causing intractable family conflicts.

Regression-progression is one of the most fascinating aspects of family conflict. While it sits on a foundation of love-based symbiosis between the parent and child, it can suddenly be transformed into a hate-filled incident in which the parent perceives the child as an enemy. The fact that a small child could appear threatening to an adult indicates the presence of a projection. Projections involving splitting between past/present, self/other, and us/them are prevalent in family conflicts. The adults' inability to separate the past from the present and self from other can suddenly transform a small conflict into a life-threatening episode of family violence involving the parents' deepest emotions. The parents' loss of reality indicates symptoms of PTSD, a critical factor in causing intractable family conflicts.

The problem with regression-progression is that it allows adults to unconsciously use children as projective or "therapy objects" to purge themselves of their feelings related to unresolved developmental trauma. Rather than working consciously on these issues through counseling or parenting classes, parents simply reenact their own trauma with their children. This reenactment creates intergenerational patterns of child use and abuse. The solution to regression-progression is conscious parenting that encourages adult family members to use external resources such as therapy or support groups to clear themselves of their unresolved developmental trauma. This recommendation applies not only to parents raising children, but all adults who provide custodial care for children, such as childcare personnel, school teachers and officials, athletic coaches, and church supervisors and teachers.

In working with the regression-progression phenomena in our classes and private practices, we have discovered a range of beliefs about the role past events play in current conflicts. This range is shown in Table 12.2.

Where people fall on this continuum typically correlates with their quantity and quality of undiagnosed symptoms of developmental trauma. Many people feel they do

Table 12.2
A Continuum of Beliefs Regarding the Role of Developmental Trauma in Causing Current Conflicts

People don't remember anything from childhood	People can remember their childhood but must put it behind them and go on	People can remember their childhood wounds but must rise above them	People can heal the wounds of their childhood and reclaim their true self	People can reframe their childhood wounds and use them as tools for becoming more conscious

not have the psychological resources to cope with reexperiencing or releasing any feelings related to post-traumatic stress. While many of the new trauma reduction therapies can provide rapid relief of post-traumatic symptoms without retraumatization, it is difficult to convince most people of this. Avoidance and the use of addictive and compulsive behaviors seems safer and more familiar. Notice that the word "familiar" contains the word "family." Coping mechanisms are an integral part of each family's intergenerational relational patterns.

Parents who learn to stop the practice of regression-progression generally fall into the two categories on the right side of the continuum. These individuals typically commit to extensive personal work via therapies that address the residue of their developmental trauma. Most significantly, however, these parents learn to redefine the nature of their wounds. Rather than seeing themselves as "broken," they reframe their problems as "developmental delay." This helps depathologize their dysfunctional behaviors and helps them learn to accept their projections and episodes of emotional overreactions as indicators of their own trauma. This reframing helps create a vision for complete healing of developmental trauma and the full realization of their potential.

WHAT IS THE ROLE OF FAMILY PATTERNS IN FAMILY CONFLICTS?

Parenting, unfortunately, is the last vestige of amateurism. Unless people take classes in parenting, they have only their own childhood experiences to guide them in parenting children. Parents tend to repeat the conflictual dynamics of the drama triangle from their family of origin. This intergenerational patterning is stored primarily through trauma-related memories activated by specific visual, auditory, olfactory, emotional, kinesthetic, and relational stimuli. The unconscious response to all resolved trauma is to reenact similar experiences in order to discharge the old, unexpressed feelings.

Patterns of family drama get reenacted through the "vicious cycle of cruelty" (Weinhold, 1991) because parents do not recognize or understand the harmful effects of their own developmental trauma. Rather than recognizing the cruelty present in their childhood experiences, parents repeat it while telling their children they are doing it "for your own good." Some typical social values that are passed on this way are:

- showing respect for elders at all times
- appearing modest and self-effacing
- never expressing strong feelings
- acting grateful, nice, or polite at all times
- loving parents out of duty
- learning to take shame or punishment without emotion

Acting out of regression-progression, some parents lay traps, lie, threaten violence, manipulate, withdraw their love, humiliate, distrust, scorn, ridicule, coerce, terrorize, and commit violence against their children. Doing these things to their children is a way of proving that their parents really did love them. This denial and repression of abusive and traumatic experiences is a major force in the replay of conflictual family patterns. The only way to break the cycle is to:

- reexamine your childhood experiences from an optimal parenting perspective that describes the needs of young children
- reframe any "for your own good" experiences as experiences of developmental trauma
- identify and meet your unmet developmental needs
- express any and all feelings that you did not express as a child
- repattern your relationship dynamics to eliminate trauma-related distortions

HOW CAN I WORK COOPERATIVELY TO RESOLVE FAMILY CONFLICTS AT THEIR SOURCE?

Psychoeducation is the first step in stopping regression-progression family dynamics. Adults who truly understand the nature of the regression-progression phenomenon become unable to participate in it. No longer able to participate in drama triangle dynamics, these adults commit to redefining themselves and reframing their life experiences. Breaking free from the regression-progression dynamic requires that adults become totally responsible for their residue of developmental trauma. Making this shift requires that they shift their whole reality base.

The primary goal of psychoeducation for family members is to help everyone develop an internal sense of object constancy and "I'm okay, you're okay" thinking. This allows them to keep their sense of worth even when they feel rejected or unworthy during family conflicts. When family members are not able to do this, it is an indication of unresolved issues from the splitting sub-phase of the counter-dependent stage of individual development that can best be resolved through individual counseling.

The Nurturing Program is a national program with a family-oriented, psychoeducational curriculum designed to teach effective parenting practices. Founded by Steven Bavolek, it was initially funded by the Kemp Center in Denver, Colorado, and field-tested at the University of Wisconsin at Eau Claire. It is now implemented through community-based programs offered via social service or community health departments around the nation. The Nurturing Program offers 23-week concurrent and interactive classes for parents and children involving four major constructs.

1. The development of empathy in parents.
2. Implementation of behavior management practices to eliminate corporal punishment.

3. Elimination of parentizing practices that involve parent-child role reversals.
4. Creating realistic parental expectations for children's behavior based on their developmental stages.

The Nurturing Program offers prenatal and school-age programs as well as parent–adolescent programs. While many participants are self-referred, most are referred through community social service agencies because they abused or neglected their children.

Family meetings are an important mechanism for implementing partnership relationships within a family structure. Here children learn to participate in group decision-making, to negotiate to get their needs met, to problem-solve, and to resolve conflicts effectively. Children who learn skills in family meetings can apply them outside the family setting. Emphasizing these kinds of learning can make implementing family meetings easier, as some members may not see the significance of family meetings.

When we work with couples who are transforming their family structures into a partnership system, we find that the children often resist their parents' attempts at reform. The children have learned how to function with secrets, triangulation, power plays, and other forms of dirty fighting and may fear losing their position of power in the family hierarchy. Once a new partnership structure is operationalized, the children usually like family meetings because the meetings support them in getting their needs met more directly. Figure 12.1 provides some guidelines for conducting family meetings.

HOW DO SOCIAL PROBLEMS CONTRIBUTE TO FAMILY CONFLICT?

Many social structures outside the family that once supported families are collapsing or in chaos. Cutbacks in aid to dependent families, the disintegration of the extended family, decreasing funding for school programs, the breakdown of the nuclear family, and the lack of quality childcare for young children can make parenting an extremely arduous task. Parents attempting to raise children in a culture that is neither family- or child-friendly feel challenged physically, emotionally, mentally, and spiritually. Every aspect of parenting becomes more difficult when social conditions undermine parents' attempts to provide a foundation for their children. Each family's attempt to counteract

---

1. *Start slowly.* It is best to initiate family meetings at a time when there are no crises in the family. Begin with short (15 to 30 minutes) meetings and hold them at convenient times for everyone, such as with dessert after dinner. Start with fun and easy issues such as planning a family outing. Stick to agreed time limits, eliminate outside distractions such as TV, music, or telephone calls (agree to not answer the phone during the meeting). Do not make the meeting a big production.

2. *Give equal time to everyone.* Ask everyone to contribute something to the discussion, even if it is, "I don't have anything to add at this time." The parents should encourage full participation by suggesting that each person propose an issue for discussion.

3. *Focus on solutions.* Avoid using meetings as gripe sessions. Present only problems and conflicts that cannot be worked out without full family input. Balance the presentation of problems with recognition of positive accomplishments by family members or positive issues such as planning menus for the coming week, where to go on a family vacation, and plans for birthdays and family celebrations.

4. *Be flexible about meeting times.* It's more important that the whole family be present at a family meeting than that it be at the same time each week. If it is a problem to get everyone together at the same time, ask family members to make meetings a high priority and rotate times to suit their schedules.

5. *Set clear ground rules.* Everyone needs to know the agenda of the meeting, how long it will last, and what is expected. Follow basic communication ground rules: each person is heard; feelings are acknowledged and accepted; no interrupting, using put-downs, or name-calling. Stick to issues and concerns that affect the entire family or several family members. If possible, avoid using meeting time for individual issues ("Can I go over to Joey's house on Saturday?"). These can be taken care of after the meeting.

6. *Avoid rescuing.* Rescuing is very common in families. It can be avoided in family meetings by having each person ask directly for what he or she wants. If everybody is aware of this rule, it is easier to support one another.

7. *Avoid using meetings as a soapbox.* Parents may be tempted to use family meetings to vent pent-up feelings or resentments or to assert their authority in the family. This can undermine positive outcomes.

8. *Break bread together.* A good way to make family meetings special is to serve popcorn, dessert, or other treats.

Figure 12.1
How to Conduct a Family Meeting

these social conditions requires a tremendous amount of energy, which is ultimately drained away from providing primary care for the children. The end result is an increase in child abuse, family violence, the collapse of the family as an institution, and more at-risk children.

THE ROLE OF PRIMARY PREVENTION IN RESOLVING FAMILY CONFLICTS

The systemic nature of family conflicts requires systemic interventions. The first level of intervention must be with parents via primary intervention programs that intervene prior to the appearance of a problem. There are a growing number of national, regional, and state organizations now focusing on primary prevention programs for children and families through psychoeducation. The expansion in interest in psychoeducational programs is the result of a growing awareness about how childhood experiences form the foundation for adulthood. Research repeatedly shows the critical role of childhood experiences in creating psychopaths and sociopaths.

Hawaii's *Healthy Start* home visitation program is a prototype of an effective early intervention program. The state of Hawaii provides three years of free, voluntary home visitation services to high-risk families. Screening to identify these high-risk families occurs prenatally at a clinic or in the hospital at the birth of a child. Two 5-year follow-up studies showed almost no reported child abuse or neglect among participants. Of families who did not accept these services, 5% had at least one reported incident of abuse after five years. At the beginning of the study, 15% of mothers were working and 85% were on welfare. After five years, 85% of the mothers were working and were off welfare. After seeing the results of the Hawaii study, Colorado Springs established its *First Visitor* program, which offers up to three years of free home visitation services to all parents who request them.

WHAT CHANGES ARE NEEDED IN SOCIAL AND FAMILY POLICIES?

The national and state governments and appropriate nongovernmental organizations need to adopt specific family friendly policies and practices that ensure, protect, and preserve democratic principles in families. The following list of recommendations will hopefully stimulate both discussion and action that supports families.

General Recommendations

1. Condemn all forms of violence and domination in families. Agree to take steps without delay and by all appropriate means to prevent, penalize, and eliminate all forms of violence and domination.
2. Develop coordinated governmental/nongovernmental action plans aimed at establishing effective presentation programs and services to protect family members from domination and abuse.
3. Review all existing national and state laws and policies to determine if they are fully supportive and protective of the rights of all family members.
4. Create stiffer penal and civil sanctions that penalize and also fully rehabilitate those who use domination and violence in families.
5. Provide mandatory free or low-cost public education on child development, parenting, conflict resolution, and communication skills to all people before they become parents or before the first birthday of their first child.
6. Reaffirm the federal government's role in the creation of an effective social and economic safety net for poor families and children.

Specific Recommendations

Specific social and family policy recommendations for changing the structural barriers and systemic bases of domination and violence in families are listed below. They are proposed as specific ways to strengthen and support democratic principles in families.

Social Assistance Programs and Services

1. Provide noncontributory social assistance for families who are ineligible for assistance under contributory programs such as Social Security or Medicaid.
2. Provide direct cash payments to women who are heads of households and who are needed to maintain the support system inside the family. Payments should be tied to participation in pre-and perinatal programs, parenting skill classes, or other supportive services designed to strengthen the woman's ability to help herself while also helping her family.

Social Services

1. Provide low-cost or sliding-scale counseling and support services for all couples and families designed to help family members deal with the symptoms of developmental trauma.
2. Provide free or low-cost services in parent education, nutrition and health support, pre- and perinatal care, childbirth education, family planning, medical care, family mediation, marriage counseling, and family therapy.
3. Provide classes in communication and human relationships, conflict management, sexuality, home economics, and child development.
4. Provide half-way houses for offenders who are returning from incarceration to assist them in the rehabilitation process.
5. Provide domestic violence centers and safe houses where survivors and their children can be protected from spousal abuse.
6. Provide free or low-cost individual and group therapy services for offenders and survivors.

Educational

1. Incorporate parenting and child development courses into the curricula of the public schools as early as fourth grade.
2. Revise educational curricula to better support the developmental stages of children.
3. Stop placing boys and girls of the same age in the same grade in schools (girls are developmentally more advanced than boys until age sixteen).
4. Eliminate competitive grading in schools.
5. Teach cooperative learning skills in schools.
6. Teach peer mediation and conflict management skills in schools.
7. Utilize neighborhood schools as family resource centers and adult education centers.
8. Teach sexual education and pregnancy prevention classes in schools.
9. Create low-cost, high-quality, public childcare facilities managed by school districts.
10. Reduce class size in inner-city schools so teachers can work more intensively with high-risk students.

Legislative and Family Policy-Making

1. Establish a cabinet-level position of Secretary of the Family to help develop national and state family policies and to review all legislation prior to its adoption to determine its potential impact on families.
2. Create a National Commission on the Family to look at social problems and policies from a cross-disciplinary perspective. This commission would then make solution-oriented recommendations to legislative bodies and policy-makers.
3. Adoption of the U.N. *Convention on the Rights of the Child.*
4. Adoption of the U.N. *Convention on the Elimination of All Forms of Discrimination Against Women.*
5. Adoption of laws that outlaw corporal punishment for children.
6. Adoption of laws that make domestic violence a felony crime.
7. Adoption of family leave policies that allow both men and women to interrupt their careers for childbearing, child care, or to care for aged parents or disabled family members.
8. Adopt and enforce laws prohibiting the genital mutilation of both girls and boys.
9. Adoption of laws guaranteeing equal pay for equal work for men and women.
10. Adopt stricter gun control laws that prevent the easy purchase of weapons by adolescents and would-be criminals.
11. Provide funding for free, voluntary home visitation services to all new parents.
12. Legalize midwifery and help establish standards for trained midwives.

Indigenous and Neighborhood Support Networks

1. Utilize kinship-based and non-kinship-based support networks to enhance the social safety net. Social welfare professionals can be used to identify, train, and coordinate the efforts of bartenders, teachers, bus drivers, ministers, beauticians, apartment managers, and neighborhood shop personnel, as well as family members.
2. Establish neighborhood associations and programs that provide regular and supportive contacts for all neighbors.
3. Provide funding to neighborhoods that are helping to prevent family violence and improving the quality of life for all residents.

Nongovernmental Organizations

1. Offer additional tax incentives to individuals and businesses who donate to nonprofit/nongovernmental organizations that can deliver high-quality, low-cost services such as family counseling, parent education classes, child care, neighborhood improvement programs, and recreational programs.
2. Open all government buildings after work hours to nongovernmental organizations so they can meet free of charge.
3. Help create neighborhood violence prevention boards that develop programs and services for all neighborhood families to help them deal with marital and family stress.

Private Sector and Businesses

1. Create workplace daycare facilities for parents.
2. Appoint management personnel to oversee employee child-care needs.
3. Create a company family leave policy along the guidelines suggested above.
4. Create flexible work schedules for parents.
5. Allow job sharing and job splitting options for couples with children.
6. Create benefit packages that include money for child care and paid family leave.
7. Allow part-time work or irregular work hours for parents of young children.
8. Allow scheduled days off that coincide with school holidays.
9. Help arrange work at home options for parents of young children.

Medical Services

1. Establish standards for trained midwives, and legalize and establish standards for lay midwives.
2. Provide accurate, up-to-date birthing information to mothers so they can make informed choices about their birthing options.
3. Establish birthing centers that allow rooming in and visits by siblings and family.

4. Provide breast feeding support programs for mothers who choose this option.
5. Cut the rate of cesarean births to a minimum and use only when there is great risk.
6. Reduce the use of epidural medications during delivery.
7. Allow father and other family support persons to be present at birth.
8. Create nonviolent birth practices (soft lighting, music, warm room temperature, infant massage, water births).
9. Advise pregnant women about the harmful effects of smoking, alcohol, certain diets, poor nutrition, and drugs on the fetus.
10. Advise mothers to eliminate swaddling of infants.
11. Eliminate male circumcision.
12. Eliminate routine use of ultrasound, enemas, pubic shaving, and episiotomies in pregnancy and childbirth.
13. Establish family violence as the number one public health problem in this country. Mobilize all public health agencies to campaign vigorously against family violence.

Environment

1. Establish more neighborhood parks and playgrounds, particularly in inner cities.
2. Design and build housing that promotes social relationships and cooperation rather than isolation and separation.
3. Plan work and home environments in close or adjacent areas to support family relationships.
4. Build bicycling and hiking paths in cities to reduce automobile pollution and serve as recreational resources.
5. Create auto-free zones in cities to maximize pedestrian and non-motorized traffic.
6. Plant more trees in inner cities to help clean the air.
7. Fund and build mass transit systems that reduce automobile use.

Media

1. Adopt even stricter regulations regarding the amount of graphic violence and explicit sex broadcast on television and shown in films.
2. Provide prime-time segments on commercial television stations for high-quality family life educational programs.

3. Produce high-quality programs that provide models of democratic principles for use in families.
4. Restrict the time periods when television stations can telecast materials containing graphic violence or explicit sex to late-night slots when children are usually asleep.
5. Produce and run regular locally focused anti-violence public service announcements.
6. Devote part of regular news programming to report good news stories about families.

Law Enforcement

1. Train police to better identify PTSD symptoms present in family disturbances. Make referrals for counseling of those suffering from PTSD symptoms.
2. Closely monitor family members who have a violent history.
3. Hold the violent person personally responsible for his or her violent actions and stress that the person is capable of changing.
4. Police and courts must express strong disapproval of violent spouses (including arrest and conviction, as appropriate) while accepting and demanding that the abusers change their abusive behaviors.
5. Refuse excuses for violent behavior.
6. Create in-depth counseling and regular leaves for law enforcement officers who have to deal with family or other forms of violence on a regular basis.
7. Take the lead in developing a community response team to help family members and neighbors deal with long-term effects of family violence.

Families can use the Partnership Way to address both common and more complex intractable conflicts that surface. Family relationships provide enough safety for members to reveal their unmet needs, making them the primary staging arena for unresolved conflicts. Parents who intervene in the regression-progression process by addressing the intergenerational patterns through psychoeducation, counseling, and other tools can learn to separate the present from the past in compassionate ways that foster increased family intimacy. By focusing on strengthening families and providing a framework for resolving intractable conflicts, the family system can be utilized as a way to resolve intractable conflicts at their source.

SELF-AWARENESS EXERCISE: WHAT IS THE DEVELOPMENTAL STAGE OF MY FAMILY?

Developmental Systems Theory Inventory–Form F© Barry Weinhold

Place the number in the column that best represents your perception of aspects of your family at this time.

In this family we:

_____ 1. Acknowledge each person's spiritual essence.
_____ 2. Accept and validate each person's feelings and needs.
_____ 3. Have appropriate mental, emotional, physical, and spiritual intimacy.
_____ 4. Engage in loving touch and find ways to show our appreciation for each other.
_____ 5. Express mutual trust and love.
_____ 6. Share common values, beliefs, and interests.
_____ 7. Separate nurturing touch from sexual touch.
_____ 8. Show respect and tolerance for any differences of values and beliefs.
_____ 9. Support each person's need to separately explore new ideas and activities.
_____ 10. Show respect for each other's psychological boundaries.
_____ 11. Ask and negotiate directly to meet our wants and needs.
_____ 12. Identify the underlying sources of our current unresolved conflicts.
_____ 13. Develop ways to fulfill our individual needs that do not involve others in the family.
_____ 14. Do things that break down cultural gender-role stereotypes regarding career and housekeeping activities.
_____ 15. Able to tolerate ambiguity and role diffusion in family relationships.
_____ 16. Recognize and do things to celebrate each person's unique qualities.
_____ 17. Encourage the development of individual self-identity.
_____ 18. Support each person's independent ideas and actions.
_____ 19. Use win/win methods to resolve our conflicts.
_____ 20. Shift from being close to being separate without conflict.
_____ 21. Keep our relationship agreements.
_____ 22. Help each other resolve unresolved conflicts from the past.
_____ 23. Make the relationship or family a priority over our careers.
_____ 24. Design and use regular spiritual practices with each other.

Scoring and Interpretation

This inventory yields four sub-scores and a total family score. The scoring procedures to obtain each sub-score are explained below, along with an interpretation of each sub-score and the total family score.

Codependent Stage (Items 1 through 6):   Add the numbers preceding these items to get the sub-score _____

Counter-dependent Stage (Items 7 through 12):   Add the numbers preceding these items to get the sub-score _____

Independent Stage (Items 13 through 18):   Add the numbers preceding these items to get the sub-score _____

Interdependent Stage (Items 19 through 24):   Add the numbers preceding these items to get the sub-score _____

Total Family Score: **Add the four sub-scores to get a total family score** _____

Interpretation of Sub-Scores

Check your score for each of the four stages and refer to the interpretation below.

21–24   Most of the important developmental tasks of the family have been completed.
15–20   A few important development tasks of the family have not been completed.(Check sub-scores to locate which ones.)
11–15   Some major developmental tasks of the family have not been completed. (Check sub-scores to locate which ones.)
6–10   Major problems exist because important developmental tasks of the family have not been completed. (Check sub-scores to locate which ones.)

Interpretation of the Total Family Score

79–96   Clear evidence of a partnership family.
60–78   Good progress underway toward the creation of a partnership family.
42–59   Evidence of major barriers to the creation of a partnership family.
24–41   Major problems and unresolved conflicts prevent the creation of a partnership family.

SELF-AWARENESS EXERCISE: BASIC RULES OF EFFECTIVE FAMILY COMMUNICATION

The following exercise illustrates the basic rules of effective family communication and can help family members learn these rules.

1. Form a group with two or three other people or family members. Depending on the ages of some family members, you may have to modify the language or explain each word that a family member doesn't understand.

2. Take turns discussing each rule of communication in the following way:
   a. Read aloud the seven rules listed below.
   b. Explain each rule in your own words: i.e., " I think this means...."
   c. Give others a chance to agree, disagree, or comment on the rule: i.e., "I agree, except that ...."
   d. Give an example of your own use or misuse of the rule: i.e., "Yesterday, I said _____instead of _____."

3. Proceed to the next rule and follow the same process.

4. Apply the ideas from each previous rule in discussing the next rule.

Rule #1. Say "I" when you are expressing an opinion or feeling instead of using "you," "they," and "people." For example, "I feel angry when that subject comes up."

Rule #2. Avoid asking questions unless you really need information or want to know something. Questions are often an indirect way of making statements without taking full responsibility for the statement. For example, "Don't you think that _____?" is an indirect way of making a statement without taking full responsibility for it.

Rule #3. Avoid discounting yourself or other people. The opposite of discounting is accounting, which means taking the feelings, thoughts, and desires of yourself and others into account. Some examples of discounting are :
   a. Interrupting when someone is speaking (discounting the situation and the person).
   b. Not speaking because you think you'll sound stupid (self-discounting).
   c. Not taking the other person's desires or feelings into account, i.e., deciding for other family members what your family will do on vacation (discounting the situation and the other family members).
   d. Saying things that put yourself down (self-discounting).

Rule #4. Avoid interpreting the thoughts and actions of others. An interpretation is telling someone what motivates them or why you think they are thinking, feeling, or acting the way they are. For example, saying, "You are an angry person," is an interpretation, which defines who he or she is. This form of communication usually produces defensive reactions in others. Instead, tell the person how you feel or what you think, making an "I" statement ("I believe that...") or describe what makes you think as you do. For example, "I perceive that you argue with or disagree with almost everything I say. This makes it difficult for me to talk to you. How do you see it?"

Rule #5. Although they are often confused, feelings and thoughts are two different things. For instance, saying, "I feel that you are wrong about that," is actually a thought, not a feeling. Use "I feel..." only when expressing feelings (anger, sadness, fear, shame, joy, and happiness).

Rule #6. Avoid using black-and-white language such as "always" and "never" or exaggerated language such as "incredible" or "the most _____ in the world." This may be a way of justifying your ineffectiveness, avoiding a problem, or avoiding responsibility for your behavior. For example. "I was so angry, I could not help myself." The fact is that you *could* help yourself.

Rule #7. Refuse to foster codependency. Codependency is when two or more people covertly agree to foster dependent behaviors in each other by doing things for each other that they can do for themselves. Here are some ways to break out of codependent communication patterns:
   a. Be willing to ask for what you want directly. For example, "Will you give me a hug?" instead of indirect complaining such as, "No one ever hugs me," or hinting at what you want, "I sure could use a hug."
   b. Don't agree with others just for the sake of being pleasant. Communicate your disagreement directly to the person involved: "I don't agree with what you just said."
   c. Avoid using the word "try." Say "I will do that" instead of saying, "I will try to do that."
   d. Negotiate differences. If you ask for what you want and the person says no, ask, "What are you willing to do?"
   e. When you have a point of view, state it loudly enough for everyone to hear you. Speaking too softly indicates a lack of self-confidence.

f. When you have a definite point of view, avoid words such as "I think," "I guess," or "maybe." If you feel confident or definite, say so.

g. Avoid saying, "I don't know," when you do know. Say instead, "I would rather not say."

h. Refuse to rescue. Rescuing is doing something for someone else that the person can do for himself or herself and has not asked you to do. Rescuing communicates to persons being rescued that you don't have confidence in their ability to do it themselves.

Rule #8. Avoid statements such as "I can't" or "I have to" unless that is really the case. People are rarely unable or incapable of doing something, and rarely do they have to do anything, unless someone is physically being forced. People actually choose how to behave in most cases. If they did not, they would suffer unpleasant consequences. Instead, say "I won't," "I choose to," or "I am willing to."

Rule #9. Confront other people's discounts or rescues. Confrontation is a way to care for yourself and to show respect for others. When you accept or ignore someone's rescuing, discounting, and so on, you are actually enabling ineffective behavior in that person. You can confront in a caring way without attacking the person or his or her behavior.

Rule #10. Take responsibility for how you feel, think, and behave. Don't say, "You made me angry." This makes someone else responsible for your feelings. Instead, say, "I am angry because..." (stating your reasons). Avoid saying, "That makes me feel...."

SELF-AWARENESS EXERCISE: WHAT WERE THE STRENGTHS IN YOUR FAMILY?

It is important to understand and identify family strengths. Research in this area identifies a clustering of six main variables or family strengths (Trivette, Dunste, & Deal, 1994). They are listed below with a brief explanation of each.

1. *Commitment*. This strength involves making a commitment to the family by spending quality time and energy in family-related activities. It means that the family as a whole agrees to support each member in reaching his or her fullest potential. Family members are not expected to suffer or deny themselves in some way so others can grow. Commitment involves a cooperative effort to insure that everyone gets what he or she wants and needs.

2. *Wellness*. Psychological wellness is built on a foundation of trust and love. It requires family members to focus on creating positive interactions with each other. This also means not denying or ignoring problems, but requires a collective effort to deal with these problems effectively.

3. *Communication*. Effective communication in strong families is clear and direct, with congruence between verbal and nonverbal behavior. A later exercise will help you learn the basic rules of clear, direct family communication.

4. *Appreciation*. Showing appreciation comes naturally as the result of a strong commitment to the family, a focus on family wellness, and good family communication. It involves giving and receiving compliments, helping to mirror for each other's individual strengths.

5. *Time together*. Spending quality time together as a family can be one of the most rewarding experiences for humans. In addition to quality time there also has to be a sufficient quantity of time together. This helps build the relationships that make the family strong.

6. *The ability to deal with stress, conflict, and crisis*. Strong families have developed effective ways to deal with individual as well as family stresses. They have built-in stress reduction mechanisms that include fun times, vacations, and nurturing activities. They also have developed effective ways to resolve conflicts when they occur in the family, particularly when they occur between family members. Strong families are also resilient enough to handle crises and possibly learn from them.

What Are the Strengths in My Family?

Look over the above list of family strengths and rate your own family of origin using the following scale:

1 = not present   2 = present only on rare occasions   3= present occasionally
4 = present most of the time   5 = present all of the time

If your total score is over 12, it is a good indication of the presence of family strengths. These strengths are resiliency factors that help mitigate the effects of any family dysfunction that may have been present.

SELF-INVENTORY & SKILL PRACTICE EXERCISE:
HOW TO WORK COOPERATIVELY TO RESOLVE FAMILY CONFLICTS AT THEIR SOURCE

Read over the list of common issues related to unresolved conflicts in the codependent and counter-dependent stages of development shown in Table 12.3. Indicate with a number from 1 to 10 (1 = not at all; 10 = all the time) how much that issue is of concern. Score and interpret your answers. Then look at the suggested way to resolve this issue at its source, using Worksheet #5 at the end of Chapter 10. Then contract with your spouse or a family member to resolve this issue.

Table 12.3
Common Issues from the Codependent and Counter-Dependent Stages of Family Development and How to Resolve Them at Their Source

Common Issue	Possible Source of Issue from Early Childhood Development	How to Cooperatively Resolve the Issue at Its Source
_____ 1. Fear of being consumed	Child was subjected to helicopter parenting where parent hovers over the child	Have your partner role-play the perpetrator and express any unexpressed feelings.
_____ 2. Addiction to activity	Conditional love and acceptance	Learn relaxation and meditation techniques. Have partner do them with you.
_____ 3. Victimization	Emotional, physical, and sexual abuse or shame-based discipline	Ask partner to role-play parents and give supporting messages for independent thoughts and actions.
_____ 4. Fear of influence from outside the family	Family secrets; an us-vs.-them attitude	Ask your partner to role-play a parent and give you lots of "yes" messages.
_____ 5. Secrets between family members	Shame-based parenting	Identify possible perpetrators and have your partner be with you while you express your feelings. Ask for nonsexual touch from your partner.
_____ 6. Unequal rights between adults and children	Authoritarian parenting style	Ask your partner to give you support for exploring new ideas and activities.
_____ 7. Rejects help from others even when needed	Neglect of needs, shame-based messages about expressing needs	Ask your partner to support you as you express your feelings about being shamed.
_____ 8. Control and manipulation used to get needs met	Conditional love and acceptance	Ask for unconditional strokes from your partner.
_____ 9. Lack of identified boundaries that are respected	No rights to privacy; children are seen as an extension of parents	Practice saying "no" as many ways as you can.
_____ 10. Unwillingness to assume responsibility for actions	Self-management skills were not taught effectively; personal boundaries not respected	Structure regular relationship meetings where agreements are considered contracts and written down. Each person decides on a consequence for breaking an agreement, if necessary.
_____ 11. Inability to handle time and money effectively	Little support for self-care	Invest in a time-management tool where all time is structured. Hire a financial advisor to teach you how to manage finances.
_____ 12. Intimidation or manipulation used to resolve conflicts	Not allowed to make own age-appropriate decisions	Create and enforce a "no-power-plays" contract. Learn to express feelings of shame directly.

Common Issue	*Possible Source of Issue from Early Childhood Development*	*How to Cooperatively Resolve the Issue at Its Source*
_____13. Suppression of feelings	Shame used to prevent development of independent ideas or actions	Use journaling to recover early memories of experiences. Contract with your partner to be with you while you express your feelings toward someone from your past.
_____14. Belief in scarcity	Lack of support and positive feed-back for efforts to be independent	Contract with partner to give you a specific kind and amount of positive feedback every day. Write positive affirmations.
_____15. Lack of personal accountability	Efforts to become separate either overtly or covertly sabotaged; failures were punished	Sign up for a wilderness experience to develop risk-taking skills.
_____16. Rebellious and acting-out behavior; testing limits	Lacked effective limit setting; raised with permissive discipline practices	Use limit-setting structures in your life (time, money, energy) as a focus for structuring realistic limits.
_____17. Indirect communication	Received messages that it was not safe to be a separate person; attempts to separate were punished	Take a public speaking or leadership development class. Explore some new activity that pushes you to risk.
_____18. Rebellious and/or violent behaviors	Possible unprocessed birth trauma or early abandonment experiences where bonding needs were not met	Use breathwork techniques with your partner present. Ask your partner to hold you and affirm you by offering unconditional love.
_____19. Addictive behaviors such as drinking, smoking, eating disorders, and drug use	No support for having feelings	Give each other body massages and other nonsexual touch.
_____20. Compulsive eating, smoking, drinking, or sex	Deprivation of nourishment and/or love; basic needs may have been neglected	Ask your partner to hold you and rock you, perhaps feed you a bottle.
_____21. Feeling unconnected to others or isolated in the relationship	Early abandonment by those charged with caring for you	Identify your unmet needs and ask your partner to role-play a caregiver providing you with those needs.
_____22. Trouble trusting, suspicious of the motives of others	Birth trauma and lack of attention to your needs at birth	Ask your partner to bathe you in a quiet room filled with soft lights and soothing music. Have your partner lead you on a trust walk.
_____23. Parents using children to make themselves look good to others	Not enough mirroring of your essence and positive responses from parents	Ask for reassurance from your partner in time of doubt or fear. Identify all the things you wish your parents had said and done during childhood and then ask your partner for them.
_____24. Unable to define wants and needs; expect others to just know how these needs should be met	Needs were anticipated and met prior to the expression of children's needs for feeding, affection, changing diapers; parents may have hovered and not waited for signals for needs to emerge	Ask your partner to role-play your parents and give you permission to identify your needs and affirm your right to get them met. Ask directly for things you want and need.

Common Issue	Possible Source of Issue from Early Childhood Development	How to Cooperatively Resolve the Issue at Its Source
_____25. Inability to shift from one-ness to separateness without difficulty	Rigid atmosphere where everything was either black or white; sometimes a traumatic experience between the age of one and two	Identify instances of trauma or repression and ask partner to support your expression of feelings about these experiences.
_____26. Unwillingness to negotiate to get needs met	Subjected to win/lose methods of conflict resolution; negotiation interpreted as losing	Enroll in a class in conflict resolution and learn win/win methods for conflict resolution. Express past feelings about situations where loss was experienced.
_____27. Avoidance of intimacy through workaholism or other compulsive activity	Abusive or invasive relationship with an adult during childhood that made intimacy unsafe	Identify instances of abuse or invasion and ask partner to support your expression of feelings about these experiences.
_____28. Resistance to developing spiritual practices	Spiritual trauma between the age of four and twelve; religious abuse	Identify instances of spiritual trauma and ask partner to support your expression of feelings about this experiences.
_____29. Fear of abandonment	Removed from mother at birth and taken to nursery; abrupt or extended separation from mother during the first year of life reinforced by later experiences of traumatic separation	Contract with partner for "I'm leaving now and I'll be back at ___" messages at times of separation; inner-child work to validate and release the feelings of loss and trauma during early childhood.
_____30. Breaking or forgetting relationship agreements	Unpredictability used as a way of avoiding abuse, invasion or punishment from care-givers	Create a commitment contract with partner about keeping agreements, with consequences for breaking them.
_____31. Unwilling to accept past conflicts as the source of current conflicts	Unprocessed rage from abusive and/or shame-based discipline and limit setting.	Identify instances of abusive and/or shame-based discipline and ask partner to support your expression of feelings about these experiences.

Scoring and Interpretation

30–90	A few codependent and counter-dependent issues in your family
91–180	Many codependent and counter-dependent issues in your family Therapeutic intervention may be useful.
181–310	A high level of codependent and counter-dependent issues in your family Therapeutic intervention is essential fora creating a partnershi family.

Chapter 13

~

How Can I Apply the Partnership Way in the Mental Health Profession?

Counselors and other mental health professionals have many opportunities—and therefore need many tools—to help their clients resolve conflicts. Unresolved intractable conflict is one of the most common reasons for seeking professional help. Most people are unaware of the intergenerational patterns of dysfunction in their families and do not understand how these patterns might be the cause of their intractable conflicts. For many people, it is a question of not being able to "see the forest for the trees" and needing someone outside the forest to articulate both the nature of the problem(s) and to help them identify possible solutions to the conflicts that seem unresolvable.

When your clients seem to be overreacting in the conflict situations they bring to you, it is important to remember that they are probably experiencing symptoms of post-traumatic stress. Rather than judging or criticizing them, try seeing them from a compassionate and understanding perspective. They are trapped in a cycle of conflict that they would gladly let go of if they knew how. If you find yourself getting triggered in response to the way they are handling their conflicts, develop a more compassionate attitude toward yourself while also looking for possible countertransference issues.

This chapter focuses on how to use the Partnership Way in the mental health profession to help clients resolve their intractable conflicts using a treatment modality called *developmental process work* (DPW). This chapter will also discuss the theory behind this approach, *developmental systems theory* (DST), and will discuss how to apply this modality to working with conflicts in seven different levels of human systems:

1. Individuals
2. Couples (intimate partners, friends, coworkers)
3. Families
4. Organizations
5. Cultural Subgroups
6. Nation-States
7. Humans as a Species

Each of these systems becomes increasingly more complex, which can make the treatment process increasingly more difficult. As a result, this chapter will focus mostly on treating individual clients who are dealing with intractable conflicts. Once you understand how to use this approach with individual clients, it is easier to use it in working with couples, families, and larger human systems.

CHALLENGES OF IMPLEMENTING THE PARTNERSHIP WAY IN THE MENTAL HEALTH PROFESSION

Mental health professionals are particularly vulnerable to being drawn into drama triangle conflicts in the role of rescuer. When an individual gets into an intractable conflict with another person, he or she often seeks out a third person with whom to align against the first person. For this reason, mental health professionals must be particularly aware of drama triangle dynamics to avoid participating in its inherent good/bad splits. When therapists are able to keep their own issues out of the way, it is easier to avoid rescuer and persecutor roles with clients. When therapists participate by agreeing with a client that another person is "bad," they make it impossible for their client to use the therapy situation to complete the individuation process. Many clients come to therapy in a crisis that was caused in part by them not being able to develop autonomy or emotional independence in their relationships. They frequently try to blame their problems on someone else to justify getting separate from them.

One cannot emotionally separate from another person by looking for fault, a form of splitting. If therapists have not achieved their own autonomy and emotional independence, they may inadvertently support their client's bad-making and rob them of an opportunity to complete this important milestone. The process of supporting clients' individuation process requires that therapists have completed much of this process for themselves so they can give careful attention to clients' attempts to get therapists to split and blame. The following guidelines may help therapists avoid being pulled into the drama triangle and becoming a professional rescuer.

Guidelines to Help Mental Health Professionals Avoid the Drama Triangle

1. *Verbally support the client's feelings.*
   "I can see and feel how sad you are."

2. *Encourage a full expression of these feelings in non-violent ways.*
   "Just close your eyes for a moment and let yourself really feel your sadness."

3. *Validate the reality of the client's experience.*
   "You have just experienced a deep loss, and it is natural to feel this kind of grief and sadness."

4. *Avoid taking sides and refuse to buy into any judgments or splitting by the client.*
   "I know that you feel sad and hurt that your wife left you and that you sometimes want to get revenge. This is also a natural feeling. Getting revenge and making her look bad might be ways of avoiding the feelings of sadness and grief you are feeling about the fact that she is not coming back to live with you. I want to encourage you to just keep feeling your feelings."

5. *Bring in the person(s) with whom the client has conflicts and offer to serve as a mediator in resolving them.*
   "It might be helpful to resolve this problem with your wife directly."

6. *Avoid rescuing the client or participating in secrets.*
   "Would you be willing to call your wife and ask her to come to our next session?"

7. *Encourage the client to work on his part of the conflict even if the other person is not willing to participate in a mediation.*
   "It takes two people to create a conflict. What part do you think you played in setting up this situation? Have you ever had this kind of conflict before, either with your wife or with other people?"

8. *Help the client identify the dynamics and patterns in his or her history of conflicts.*
   "I am hearing some similarities in the stories you have told me about the recurring conflicts you have had with your wife and the kinds of conflicts you had with your father when you were growing up. Are you aware of any of these similarities?"

Countertransference and Other Professional Issues

A second common professional pitfall for mental health professionals is countertransference, or contaminating the counseling process with their own issues. This is particularly possible when there are parallel issues between the therapist and client. A female clinician with a woman client having marriage or relationship problems, for example, must be very clear that her own marriage or relationship biases and experiences do not influence her treatment practices. It might be easy for the therapist to unconsciously attempt to resolve her own relationship issues through her clients. While countertransference is the natural result of an authentic therapeutic relationship, the therapist must address it consciously rather than trying to avoid it.

The transference/countertransference dynamic is seen as an essential component of object relations therapy, which actively seeks to reconstellate distorted relationship dynamics in the client-therapist relationship. Then the distortion can be corrected directly through the therapeutic relationship. This does not mean that the therapist is using the client to work on his or her own issues, only that there must be sufficient rapport between them to recreate the problem. Then the therapist can help the client create new, functional responses to their "common" problem. The clinician must be able to hold the functional relational dynamic steadfastly in the therapeutic relationship for this intervention to work effectively.

The experience of therapy is effective primarily because of the authentic relationship that develops between the client and clinician. This allows a psychological transfer to occur between them, which helps the client see more clearly his or her internal working model of reality and its degree of functionality. This model is created by the child during the first three years of life through an internalization of parent-child dynamics.

Through the interaction between client and therapist, any distortions in the parent-child relational patterns will emerge. The client-therapist relationship serves as a therapeutic "laboratory" where the client can practice and experience new relationship dynamics. Eventually these dynamics can be integrated into a more effective internal working model of reality. The therapist must stay sufficiently separate from the client's issues to hold the functional relationship dynamic if the client is to successfully modify his or her internal working model of reality. Unconscious countertransference and unresolved personal issues on the part of the clinician can sabotage this delicate process.

While effective therapy is based on clients transferring a certain amount of their unresolved issues onto the therapist, the unconscious countertransference of the therapist's issues back to the client creates an ethical problem. Professional ethical codes prohibit dual relationships between client and clinician. Unconscious countertransference can be considered a form of "using" the client to cathect or discharge the therapist's own unresolved parallel issues. In other words, the client provides an unconscious therapeutic experience for the therapist. From this perspective, professional ethical standards related to unconscious countertransference requires that therapists maintain an on-going program of personal development to address their own issues.

Another ethical issue related to countertransference is counselor codependency. It surfaces, for example, when clinicians keep their clients in therapy longer than they really need to or have them come more frequently than necessary in order to keep the counselor's practice filled. In this way the therapist may create a dual relationship where the client ends up serving the needs of the therapist. Making contracts to trade services or exchange services for goods can also create dual relationships that can confuse and distort the therapy dynamic. These kinds of abuses in the mental health profession were some of the primary factors in the rise of managed mental health care. At the end of this chapter, you will find a Counselor

Codependency Inventory to help you identify any of your professional codependency issues.

Another critical factor a clinician may face today is the interrelatedness in conflict situations between psychological, social, economic, political, racial, and ethnic issues. When working with conflict in complex systems, such as a community, organization, culture, or nation-state, it is helpful to understand some universal principles about human development and dysfunction that can be used to explain the nature of conflict in these larger systems. This provides a broader, more complete perspective to use in diagnosing the problem and in designing interventions.

USING DEVELOPMENTAL SYSTEMS THEORY AS A THEORETICAL FOUNDATION FOR MENTAL HEALTH PROFESSIONALS

Developmental systems theory is a systemic framework containing universal principles about human development and dysfunction that you can use to help resolve conflicts in all levels of human systems. Developmental systems theory explains the universal principles present in the development of an individual; principles that are replicated in the development of all larger systems such as couples, families, organizations, cultural groups, nation-states, and the human species. There are not only parallels in the way each system matures, there are also similarities in the kinds of problems and conflicts that appear in each system. Because of these parallels in both evolution and dysfunction, you can use DST principles to diagnose the nature of conflicts and, therefore, create more effective interventions.

In DST, understanding both the development and dysfunction of an individual provides a foundation for understanding the development and dysfunction of all other human systems. This chapter draws from conceptual material on developmental processes presented in earlier chapters on individual, couple, and family conflict and helps you understand how these same developmental processes occur in larger systems. In DST, all human systems move through four parallel stages of development: codependent, counter-dependent, independent, and interdependent. In every human system, the psychosocial tasks and developmental needs for each of these stages are similar.

DST uses inventories to help assess the impact of developmental trauma on the completion of essential psychosocial tasks for individuals, couples, families, organizations, cultures, and nation-states. You can use these inventories to "diagnose" the developmental stage of each of these systems. The data obtained from these inventories comprise a *developmental prescription*, or treatment plan for designing interventions to treat the client, whether an individual, a couple, family, or larger social system.

In DST, incomplete psychosocial tasks cause the delay of further development of the human system. For example, a child who does not sufficiently complete the important task of bonding and attachment during the codependent stage of development usually experiences difficulty in completing the task of separation during the counter-dependent stage of development. Each completed developmental task provides a foundation for the next task. This same principle applies to couples, families, organizations, and nation-states. Incomplete psychosocial tasks and their accompanying unmet developmental needs ultimately impede the psychological evolution of the human species. Moving human systems forward in their evolution requires unique clinical skills that recognize the similarities in development, dysfunction, and intervention in all seven levels of human systems.

Tables 13.1. 13.2, and 13.3 describe the seven levels of human systems and the key psychosocial tasks to be completed in each stage to insure ongoing psychological development. These tables also illustrate the correlation between each of the seven levels of human systems. You will find more complete descriptions of the developmental needs, psychosocial tasks, and the appropriate interventions for each level in chapters 10, 12, 13, 14, 15, 16, 17, and 18.

WHAT IS DEVELOPMENTAL PROCESS WORK?

Developmental process work (DPW), the applied technology of DST, is a systems-based therapy modality designed to help remove the impact of developmental traumas and conflicts in present time. By separating their behavior from their personal identity, DPW avoids "diseasing" clients. For example, the statement "I am an alcoholic" is

Table 13.1
A Developmental Perspective of Human Microsystems

Stage of Development	Psychosocial Tasks of an Individual	Psychosocial Tasks of a Couple	Psychosocial Tasks of a Family
Codependent	Bond with self Bond with parents Bond with immediate family Establish primal trust with parents Establish an identity as an individual	Bond with each other Establish primal trust in relationship Establish an identity as a couple	Bond between parents and children Establish primal trust in family Establish an identity as a family
Counter-dependent	Separate psychologically from the parents Bond with extended family Resolve internal conflicts between oneness and separateness	Separate psychologically from each other Resolve internal conflicts between needs of self and needs of others	Psychological separation between parents and children Resolve conflicts between needs of parents and needs of children
Independent	Master self-care Develop autonomy from parents Develop core personal values and beliefs Achieve object constancy as an individual Bond with nature	Master self-sufficiency within the relationship Develop autonomy within the couple relationship Develop core values and beliefs as a couple Achieve object constancy as a couple Bond with nature	Develop individual initiative within a family stricture Develop individual and couple autonomy within the family structure Develop core values and beliefs as a family Achieve object constancy as a family Bond with nature
Interdependent	Cooperate and negotiate Bond with culture Bond with person of the opposite sex Bond with children	Partner with each other Develop equity and equality in the relationship Develop each member's fullest human potential Utilize couple synergy in service to the community and the world	Partnership parenting Create rituals that sustain a spiritual dimension in the family Create divisions of labor based on individual interests and abilities

Table 13.2
A Developmental Perspective of Human Macrosystems

Stage of Development	Psychosocial Tasks of an Organization	Psychosocial Tasks of a Cultural Group	Psychosocial Tasks of a Nation-State
Codependent	Build trust Create organizational identity Provide for the basic needs of employees and managers Build esprit de corps	Build trust Create a group identity Provide for the basic needs of all group members Build esprit de corps	Build trust Create a national identity Provide for the basic needs of all citizens Build esprit de corps
Counter-dependent	Identify unique contributions of each employee Resolve internal conflicts between the needs of employees and the needs of management	Identify unique characteristics of the group Resolve conflicts of needs between group members	Identify unique characteristics of the nation in an international context Resolve conflicts of needs between cultural groups and between nations
Independent	Create an organizational culture with identified values and beliefs Provide specialized training and development for each employee to enhance individual contributions to the organization	Create a set of values and beliefs for the culture Provide opportunities for subgroups to form within the larger group Celebrate the unique characteristics of the cultural group and its subgroups	Create a national culture that honors diversity Provide opportunities for cultural groups to celebrate their uniqueness within a national context of cultural diversity
Interdependent	Team-building Consensus-building between teams	Build consensus between subgroup members	Build consensus between cultural groups and between nations

Table 13.3
A Developmental Perspective of the Human Species

Stage of Development	Psychosocial Tasks of the Human Species
Codependent	• Bonding with the world of nature • Establishing an identity as a species • Development of right-brain functions within the individual
Counter-dependent	• Separating from the world of nature • Establishing diversity in the species • Development of left-brain functions within the individual • Creation of nation-states • Resolving conflicts between nations
Independent	• Reuniting with the world of nature • Development of whole-brain thinking functions • Creation of civilizations • Celebrating the diversity between civilizations • Resolving conflicts of needs between civilizations • Providing for the basic needs of all citizens
Interdependent	• Establishment of a planetary culture • Development of the global brain

quite different from "I am addicted to alcohol." The first statement encourages shaming, splitting, and judging the self, while the second helps the client simultaneously hold the part that engages in dysfunctional behavior (drinking) and the part of the self that is more functional.

Diseasing is an orientation that implies the need for medical intervention (e.g., polio, diabetes, cystic fibrosis, bipolar disorder, schizophrenia). Encouraging clients to identify with their problems is disempowering and creates feelings of dependency, powerlessness, and helplessness. Diseasing also does not give people a vision for change or transformation but rather serves as a self-fulfilling prophesy. In DPW, the diagnosis becomes the prescription. That is, the very act of defining the problem creates the solution to it.

DPW is based on numerous operating principles that apply directly to the therapeutic process. These principles, which support the client in resolving intractable conflicts, are as follows:

1. *Trust the client's process.*
   - Recognize that clients know more about their process than the counselor will ever know.
   - See all client behavior as unconscious attempts to heal or complete something inside of them.
   - Look for the "rightness" of clients' problems and symptoms. This helps them reframe their experiences by removing the possibility of judgment that causes shame.
   - If you let them, through their unfolding developmental process, clients will show you what interventions will most likely be successful.

2. *The clinician must follow the client's process.*
   - Remember that you can't speed up a client's process but you can slow it down. Clients truly move at their own pace.
   - Consider that there is no such thing as client resistance, only poor timing on your part.
   - Hurrying clients often makes them skip important pieces of their learning process; this can require them to cycle through the issue again to pick up the missed pieces.
   - Put the client in charge of the therapy, including the speed of the process. This empowers the client and removes the counselor from the danger of acting out the perpetrator role in the drama triangle.

3. *Most intractable conflicts have their source in developmental traumas from the first three years of life.*
   - Recognize that memories of early traumas are difficult for clients to access via their declarative or conscious working memory because of the way the brain matures.
   - Look at reenactment behaviors for the elements of the original developmental trauma(s) causing the current conflicts.

- Recognize that the repetition compulsion activates the adrenal stress response and creates symptoms of post-traumatic stress disorder.
- Discover the patterns of developmental traumas that contribute to intractable conflicts by following the client's process.

4. *People split off aspects of themselves during conflict experiences that leave symptoms of developmental trauma.*
   - Help the client reclaim these split-off parts via object relations or attachment therapy.
   - Help the client identify and reclaim split-off parts of the self.
   - Help clients meet the unmet developmental needs that are related to the traumatic experience or conflict.
   - Help clients express core feelings related to the trauma that were split off or unexpressed.
   - Help clients reconnect split-off parts of themselves by creating a healthy client-therapist relationship.

5. *The client-counselor relationship serves as a therapeutic laboratory where the client can experience and practice new relationship dynamics.*
   - Utilize object relations therapy to help reconstellate and change the distorted parent-child relationship dynamics also present in the client-therapist relationship.
   - Provide nurturing, protection, and guidance for clients to help them heal developmental wounds and complete their psychosocial tasks.
   - Stay sufficiently separate from client issues and hold the functional relationship dynamic so that clients can successfully modify their internal working model of reality.
   - Avoid invasion, perpetration, and using or abusing the client via unconscious countertransference of the clinician's unresolved personal issues. To do otherwise qualifies as unethical clinical behavior.
   - Treat the client-counselor relationship as a sacred experience calling for integrity at the highest level.

6. *Each person contains an innate template that guides him or her toward wholeness.*
   - Remember that this innate template is always functioning at its highest (though often unskilled) level.
   - View your client's every behavior, whether it is effective or not, as an attempt to find wholeness.
   - Recognize that a client enters therapy carrying a healing process in progress that reveals core patterns of developmental trauma.
   - Look for those core patterns as they are expressed through body symptoms and relationship dynamics.
   - Help clients discover and modify behaviors created by developmental trauma.
   - View the client as evolving in this process, rather than as someone who is stuck in a particular psychological state.

- Adopt process-oriented thinking focused on wholeness rather than the state-oriented thinking that diseases the client.

7. *Clinicians attract clients with similar or parallel issues to their own.*
   - Utilize this mutual attraction to help both of you complete your unfinished business through the transference/countertransference dynamic.
   - Commit to your own ongoing personal growth to prevent countertransference.
   - Get regular clinical supervision.

WHAT ARE THE PRIMARY GOALS OF DEVELOPMENTAL PROCESS WORK?

A primary goal of DPW is to help clients move forward in their psychological development and become capable of interdependent relationships by successfully completing four essential developmental tasks: bonding, separation/individuation, autonomy/mastery, and cooperation. All human systems must successfully complete these tasks in order to reach the interdependent stage of development. This goal is achieved primarily through the relationship established between the therapist and the client, which is designed to reprocess and eliminate the adverse effects of developmental trauma, meet unmet needs, and complete psychosocial tasks.

The goals of DPW are to:

1. Identify the patterns of developmental traumas and conflicts that are the result of unmet developmental needs and incomplete psychosocial tasks that the client is reenacting.
2. Work cooperatively with the client to design interventions that change the reenactment patterns.
3. Desensitize and reduce the client's post-traumatic symptoms.
4. Reprocess distorted cognitions or beliefs.
5. Heal splits within the client's self.
6. Restructure skewed relationship dynamics.

The DPW clinician achieves the above goals by helping clients identify the patterns of developmental trauma being reenacted. The long-term clinical goal is to teach clients how to meet their unmet developmental needs and help them complete their incomplete developmental tasks so that they can break free of these patterns. In this way, DPW is growth-oriented. Rather than helping clients adjust to or cope with the impact of developmental trauma, DPW focuses on helping them correct the core problems that are creating intractable conflicts. At the end of the chapter, we will use a case example to describe how to use developmental process work as a therapy modality in more detail.

HOW ARE DPW THERAPISTS TRAINED?

Professionals trained in DPW first need to learn skills for counseling individuals and then, with some advanced training, move into working with larger systems such as couples, families, groups, organizations, and nation-states. They receive a strong foundation in psychodynamic, object relations, and attachment theories, systems theory, and process theory. They also receive a broad spectrum of skill training in various techniques drawn from object relations therapy, gestalt therapy, psychodrama, person-centered therapy, transactional analysis, cognitive-behavioral therapy, Jungian therapy, movement therapy, art therapy, and process therapy. In addition, they may learn various transpersonal techniques such as meditation, prayer, yoga, and breath-work therapy. Much skill development is learned via experiential training, where counselors work on identifying and healing their own developmental traumas. In addition, DPW counselors receive clinical training in integrating trauma reduction techniques into their practice and in resolving intractable conflicts.

Counselors who use DPW interventions to resolve intractable conflicts in complex systems such as organizations, cultural subgroups, and nation-states need additional training in chaos theory, cross-cultural psychology, large group dynamics, and cross-disciplinary team building. This broad background of theory and training provides the solid clinical and theoretical foundation needed to work effectively with larger systems.

What Skills Do DPW Professionals Need?

Mental health professionals who are helping their clients resolve intractable conflicts in both small and large systems need a set of basic skills to help them achieve the goals of DPW. These basic skills are:

1. *Contracting skills.* You must know how to establish a clear contract with your clients, whether they are individuals, couples, families, groups, or organizations. Both you and your client need to have clear outcome goals for both the duration of the therapy and for each session. You need to ask the client: "What would you like from our session today? Let's see how that fits with your therapy contract. What specifically would you like from me today related to your goals?" The contracting component of DPW solicits client participation in the intervention, which prevents you from acting out the rescuer role in the drama triangle. Contracting also creates safety for the client as it creates clear boundaries and teaches the client negotiation skills.

2. *Visioning skills.* Visioning is a critical component of DPW. A clear therapy contract requires that you help the client create a vision of the desired outcome. Without behaviorally based goals or clear vision of a positive outcome, counseling rarely produces positive change. Individuals and members of larger social systems need a

positive vision to focus their energies and create lasting change. Without a vision, the energy of the individual or system eventually stagnates or dissipates, preventing the successful completion of goals and objectives. A DPW clinician must also insure that the client does not present a negative therapy vision that focuses mostly on eliminating negative behaviors. Negative visioning ends up reinforcing the behavior or situation that is causing the problem. An example of this is "quitting smoking" or "giving up alcohol." Both of these goals focus on the undesirable behaviors and lack a positive vision such as "health" or "wellness."

An example of the power of a positive national vision is President Kennedy's dream of landing an American on the moon by 1970. At the time he articulated this vision, the technology did not exist to accomplish this dream. His vision helped focus the nation's collective energies toward completion of this seemingly impossible task. An example of a negative vision goal are attempts to reduce the size of the national debt. A more positive national vision might involve using our national resources to create a more humane and responsible society.

3. *Process skills.* The most important skill needed to use DPW effectively is learning how to follow the client's process as it unfolds. These include knowing how to:

* create a trusting, noninvasive relationship with clients
* give positive support for the client's presenting problems
* help the client reframe presenting problems to better understand their causes
* reflecting back aspects of clients' reality that appear to be unseen by them
* make appropriate interventions to change developmental trauma patterns
* desensitize the client's post-traumatic symptoms
* reprocess distorted cognitions or beliefs
* heal splits within the client's self
* restructure skewed relationship dynamics

4. *Diagnostic skills.* Clinicians need to learn to use system-specific inventories to assess clients' current functioning level. These inventories correlate with Tables 13.1, 13.2, and 13.3. Intake data from these diagnostic tools need to be combined with oral intake information from the client to create a profile of the client's stage of development.

5. *Intervention skills.* The diagnostic profile created in the previous step must be utilized to implement behaviorally based interventions that will interrupt the pattern of traumatic reenactment. These interventions also help clients get their developmental needs met and complete their psychosocial tasks so that they can move forward in their psychological development.

6. *Evaluation skills.* Both qualitative and quantitative tools must be used to evaluate the effectiveness of interventions. These include pre- and post-test quantitative measures such as the various DPW Systems Inventories

(included in this book), the Coolidge Axis II Inventory (see Resource Section under Professional Materials), and the Psychosocial Stressors Scale from Axis IV and Global Assessment of Functioning Scale from Axis V of *DSM-IV*. Feedback forms and follow-up interviews with clients also will provide post-intervention qualitative data that can be fed back into the design portion of the intervention process to insure more effective clinical work.

7. *Cross-disciplinary team building skills.* The systemic nature of DPW requires the development of skills for working in cross-disciplinary teams. Most traditional education, unfortunately, trains people as specialists with limited information and experience in other disciplines. DPW counselors who work with children, for example, learn very quickly that they must have skills in couple and family counseling as well. These services may require the development of a larger system of collaboration involving school officials, social service agencies, and the legal system. DPW counselors often serve on staffing teams that review the whole system of a client, requiring knowledge of the language and structure of a number of noncounseling disciplines.

8. *Large-group skills.* DPW counselors who do organizational consulting, or work with national or international groups organizations, also need large-group skills. In addition to public speaking and dialogue facilitation skills, they must be able to direct and/or understand group dynamics and synthesize and summarize complex group problems and thoughts. These skills are best learned through working with groups of increasingly larger size via a mentor or co-trainer.

9. *Cross-cultural skills.* DPW counselors may need to work with a variety of cultures to gain specialized cross-cultural skills. The term cross-cultural can apply to corporate cultures involving top managers, middle managers, and employees; ethnic, racial, religious, social, economic, and political groups within a community, state, or nation; and between nations-states. These skills include communication skills in values/beliefs clarification and specialized language and customs. These are best learned through immersion experiences in various cultures and training offered by groups or organizations that specialize in these areas.

HOW CAN HELPERS PREVENT BURNOUT?

If you are a DPW counselor with clients who are in crisis or experiencing post-traumatic symptoms, your work can be extremely stressful. Many helping professionals face the risk of burnout, a syndrome illustrated by the following statement made by a counselor:

> I love my work, but lately I find it contaminating my personal life. I have nightmares about the horrible things I hear from my clients, my sex life has deteriorated, I'm irritable and distractible, I'm afraid for my

kids and tend to overprotect them, and I don't trust anybody anymore. I don't know what is happening to me. (Courtois, 1993, p. 8)

Counselors who experience this kind of vicarious traumatization via their clients typically respond in two ways. They may start to avoid the traumatic content that their clients bring to them and begin a sort of empathetic withdrawal or emotional disengagement from the client or they may overidentify and engage in empathetic enmeshment with the client (Wilson & Lindy, 1994).

Helping the Helpers programs provide tertiary prevention services for those who work professionally with clients who have experienced human-induced victimization (child abuse, family violence, criminal assault, sexual violations) or catastrophic natural disasters. These professionals often suffer from *vicarious traumatization*, also known as countertransference, that appears as burnout and compassion fatigue.

There are specific debriefing protocols used by emergency disaster workers such as firefighters, policemen, and rescue workers after a crisis. You can protect yourself by implementing some of the following suggestions:

- Recognize that countertransference is highly likely when working with traumatized clients. Keep your eyes open to any signals and symptoms of vicarious traumatization.
- Create a balance between work and play in your life.
- Seek regular professional supervision, case consultation, and therapy if you experience symptoms of burnout.
- Limit your case overloads.
- Monitor the size of your caseload and number of trauma cases.
- Engage in self-care activities such as regular vacations, exercise, meditation, and regular massages.
- Bring inspirational objects into your office such as plants, pictures, artwork, and music.
- Recognize your limitations and adopt a positive outlook on life. Look for the healthy or "healing in progress" aspects in your clients' stories.
- Join a study group or attend conferences to learn more about how to deal with traumatized clients.
- Work on your own unhealed traumas. You may need individual therapy to help you uncover any hidden sources of internal conflict or trauma and to help you heal these wounds. If you have intractable conflicts that keep repeating themselves in your life, it is highly likely that you have hidden trauma that needs to be uncovered and healed.
- Learn all you can about treating PTSD.

DPW AS AN INDIVIDUAL THERAPEUTIC MODALITY

DPW provides a clinical lens for identifying a person's core patterns imprinted as the result of developmental trauma and designs appropriate interventions for healing the effects of these traumas when they surface through conflicts. The clinical session uses a process model to follow the client's signals and cues until the underlying clinical issues emerge.

DPW focuses on uncovering the dynamics in parent-child relationships during the prenatal, birth, infancy, and early childhood periods to find the sources of current conflicts and problems. Developmentally based inventories can help clients identify traumatic experiences that cause adult symptoms of post-traumatic stress and recurring conflicts. DPW also helps clients identify their internal working model of reality and change any relationship distortions that might be impairing their ability to maintain healthy relationships. DPW also uses behaviorally based treatment goals that stress the ability to establish safe, effective relationships, such as the ability to experience empathy, genuineness, and unconditional positive regard. DPW also seeks to find the causes of current relational difficulties in past relationship disturbances and help the client to revise their internal working model of reality by creating new patterns of self-other dynamics through the counselor-client relationship.

The process component of DPW focuses on following the client's verbal and nonverbal behaviors and tracking the manner in which the client processes information. This component utilizes channel theory and information from neurolinguistic programming (NLP). It recognizes two levels of processing: internal and external. The internal level is divided into four main channels:

1. auditory
2. visual
3. proprioceptive (a combination of emotions and physical sensations)
4. kinesthetic

Visually, the internal level of processing looks like Figure 13.1.

The primary task of the DPW counselor is to follow the information as it moves through the client's processing channels during the session and respond to the client in language that mirrors the channel that the client is using for processing. For example, when the client is recalling a past trauma through the visual channel ("I have this picture of the time my mother hit me and knocked me down"), the counselor might respond, "I can *see* how traumatic this was for you and how it must *look* to you now. It must have had a lasting effect on your ability to trust women." This response to the client also includes information regarding the impact of the trauma on the client's current female relationships.

The external channel is divided into two channels:

1. the relationship channel (two persons)
2. the family channel (three or more persons)

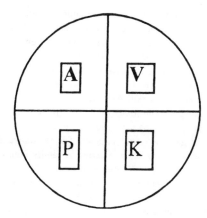

Figure 13.1
Internal Level of Processing

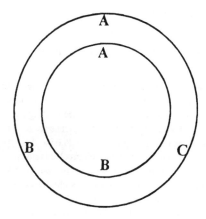

Figure 13.2
External Level of Processing

Visually, the external channels look like Figure 13.2. Together, the internal and external channels look like Figure 13.3.

During a DPW session, the counselor also assesses what intrapsychic parts of the client are visible and conscious and what parts seem invisible and unconscious. The visible or conscious parts of the client's self emerge in the client's presenting issues and are usually stated as though they have an identity of their own ("I am helpless when she yells at me like that"). The client is often more identified with parts that keep him or her defended, victimized, frozen, frightened, or wanting to flee. The relationship between the conscious mind and the unconscious mind might be conceptualized as in Figure 13.4.

The counselor helps the client approach the edge between the conscious and unconscious parts of the mind with the intention of identifying both the split-off or invisible intrapsychic parts and the unmet developmental need related to this unhealed trauma. The split-off part might be the inner protector, the assertive part, the nurturing part, the capable part, or the adult part of the person. The part containing the unmet need might involve the need for protection, the need for advocacy, the need for nurturing, or the need to feel capable and adult-like.

Once this assessment is made, the counselor affirms and supports the client's presenting identity and the parts of the self that are visible. This, again, involves using language that matches the client's channel:

visual channel = visual language
"I see why you might have this perception"

auditory channel = auditory language
"I hear what you are saying"

The exercises at the end of the chapter outline more specifically the steps in conducting a DPW session with an individual.

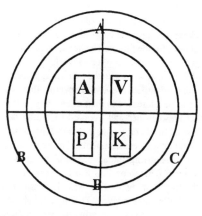

Figure 13.3
Internal and External Channels of Processing Together

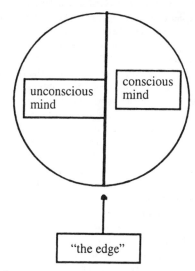

Figure 13.4
Relationship Between Conscious and Unconscious Mind

CASE EXAMPLE

The following example shows how we used Developmental Process Work and the Partnership Way in real life.

Leonard, a single professional father with five children, came to us with his fiancee, Melanie, for couples co-counseling. The two of them had been dating for about a year and were beginning to experience recurrent conflicts. Some of the conflicts were related to their couple relationship, but the most difficult involved family issues.

Leonard had been divorced for four years and recently had gained custody of his children through a lengthy custody battle. Their mother was unhappy about her loss of custody and was filing a countersuit for custody. Melanie, a single woman with no children, had been spending a lot of time with Leonard and his family and saw problems within the family system. The children, whose ages ranged from three to fourteen, were exhibiting signs of post-traumatic stress, including bedwetting, fighting, dependency, and poor academic performance at school. Leonard had hired a housekeeper to provide child care, cleaning, and laundry services for the family. The housekeeper sometimes brought her own two children to work.

Melanie actually made the therapy appointment for them and identified several concerns that she felt needed to be addressed in their counseling. First was a conflict between her and Leonard regarding the children's need for therapy to help them adjust to their new home and school environments. The second was the number of recurring intractable conflicts between the two of them. These conflicts had been present prior to the children coming to live with Leonard, but had increased after they arrived. The third involved problems with the housekeeper bringing her children with her to her job at Leonard's home and the regular conflict between her children and Leonard's. The fourth related to the attempt by Leonard's former wife to regain custody of the children.

This complex case involved several levels of work. After the initial session with Leonard and Melanie as a couple, we counseled them separately to look at the individual issues they were bringing into their relationship. We did an intake of their personal history and administered a series of diagnostic inventories to assess their individual development. After discussing the results of these assessments with them, we helped each of them understand the role of unresolved developmental traumas in their current intractable conflicts with each other, their children, and the housekeeper. This was a rather difficult task, as both Leonard and Melanie preferred to see Leonard's former wife and her parenting as the source of their family problems. It took a lot of patience and empathy to mirror and validate the impact of their rather significant childhood traumas on their current conflicts and problems.

Initially, we rotated between individual counseling with Leonard and Melanie and couples co-counseling. We also administered the diagnostic inventories for couples and helped them see how the conflicts in their relationship mirrored unresolved individual issues from their childhoods. We also spent a considerable amount of time helping them see the traumatized parts of each other and develop compassion for each other's wounds. This helped them see their childlike behavior that emerged when they regressed during conflicts. They began to work cooperatively to help each other resolve their developmental traumas and get some of their needs met. This skill increased the level of intimacy between them and strengthened their relationship sufficiently to make the next level of intervention.

We gave Leonard a number of books on parenting to read and then began a series of family counseling sessions. Because of the size of Leonard's family, we conducted these sessions in his home. We found home visits to be extremely effective. The children tended to behave spontaneously, without the kind of constraints that office visits create. This allowed us to see family dynamics very quickly. We helped Leonard design and implement a format for family meetings that would help build a more democratic family structure. This was the first experience for Leonard in parenting these children, as his former wife had been the children's primary caregiver. All the children were encouraged to present their perspective on the problems in the family, while Leonard took notes.

During these meetings, we were able to observe more closely the children's behavior and the relationships between them and with Leonard and Melanie. From these interactions, we were able to see their unmet developmental needs, incomplete psychosocial tasks, and determine their levels of development. The children participated in problem-solving family issues that involved them, such as conflicts between siblings, laundry, homework, and kitchen cleanup.

One of the most poignant moments of our family intervention came during a family meeting and involved the children giving Leonard feedback about how they appreciated his efforts to be a father and make a loving home for them. Leonard had just shared his feelings of discouragement about their fighting and lack of cooperation. While we saw how much the children loved their father, we also saw how he was seldom able to see beyond the negatives. We encouraged the children to speak their love and appreciation directly to him one at a time. As they did, Leonard's eyes welled. By the time the last one finished, he was sobbing uncontrollably. This authentic encounter with his children bolstered his sagging confidence as a father.

Once the family meeting structure was established to address their day-to-day problems, Leonard invited the housekeeper to attend a family meeting. As we observed the dynamics between her and Leonard's children, it was clear that her job in Leonard's home was very stressful for her. While she was able to perform the physical aspects of housekeeping, the child-care component was complicated by the presence of her own two children. We recommended that she find separate child care for them, which she did for a period of time. She eventually decided to terminate her position with the family, and Leonard hired a new housekeeper, who did not have children, to take her place.

The behavioral problems with Leonard's children continued, however, in spite of our efforts. We eventually recommended individual therapy for those exhibiting the most problems, including attachment therapy for one of the younger children. We consulted periodically with the therapists of these children regarding the family situation and gave them feedback after our family meeting sessions. On several occasions, we also went to school and consulted with the counselors regarding the developmental issues of the children who were not in therapy and made recommendations to their teachers regarding possible interventions. We also went to court and testified as expert witnesses during a custody hearing.

The complexity of the problems in Leonard's household overwhelmed Melanie. Though she struggled to ride the regular waves of family chaos and conflict, she found her experiences there kept her flooded with post-traumatic stress symptoms. She undertook an earnest program of personal counseling to help her cope. While she did free herself from many of these symptoms, she eventually decided that she was not physically or emotionally able to be a full-time stepmother to Leonard's children. She continued to be friends with Leonard and his children for a period of time and then entered a new relationship. Leonard continued in individual therapy for a while to help him adjust to this loss. He also continued to provide for some individual therapy for his children.

Our experience with this family has served as a "laboratory" for expanding our clinical skills in Developmental Process Work and for refining the Partnership Way. It illustrates the complexity of working with large systems and the amount of perseverance required to address this complexity. It also presents a realistic picture of the interface between individual development and couple, family, and social systems, as well as the limitations in changing larger systems when the individuals who comprise them are restricted in the resources that are needed for transformation. This case also helped us develop patience and realistic expectations about working with large systems. Change does not happen overnight and the effects of interventions are often not visible in the short term.

USING DEVELOPMENTAL INTERVENTIONS

DPW uses specific therapeutic interventions to help clients identify the sources of their conflicts, any regressive or dissociative residue of developmental trauma, and unmet needs related to traumatic experiences. The following questions can help clients identify both the source of their developmental traumas and what might be needed to heal them. Look over these questions and begin to see how you might use them to help a client identify his or her developmental traumas.

Questions You Can Ask to Help Clients Learn More About the Source of Their Trauma Patterns:

1. Have you had this kind of experience before?

2. What is the earliest memory you have of this kind of experience?

3. What is the most painful or intense memory you have of this kind of experience?

4. What is your most recent experience?

Questions You Can Ask Clients to Help Them Identify What Is Unfinished About This Trauma:

1. What is unfinished about this experience for you?
   * What words were you not able to say?
   * What feelings were you not able to feel?
   * What movements were you not able to make?
   * What goals were you prevented from fulfilling?

2. What are your unmet needs remaining from this conflict or trauma?
   * What did you need during this experience that you did not get?
   * From whom did you need it?
   * How can you get this need met right now?

3. How are you splitting in this trauma or conflict?
   * Who is right and who is wrong?
   * Are you withdrawing into yourself?
   * Are you pushing others away and making them "bad" and yourself "good" or vice versa?

4. What are the relational dynamics of this trauma or conflict?
   * I'm okay/you're not okay.
   * You're okay/I'm not okay.
   * I'm not okay/you're not okay.

SELF-INVENTORY: THE COUNSELOR CODEPENDENCY INVENTORY

Use this inventory to assess the level of codependency you may have with clients. Place the number of your response in the blank.

1 = Rarely   2 = Sometimes   3 = Usually   4 = Almost Always

Do you...

_____ 1. Avoid using written contracts that specify the number of sessions, specific goals, and agreed-upon methods for reaching these goals?

_____ 2. Dislike clients questioning your methods?

_____ 3. Have a hard time ending sessions on time?

_____ 4. Seem overworked and exhausted?

_____ 5. Do most of the talking in therapy sessions?

_____ 6. Give write-offs and fee reductions to "special" clients?

_____ 7. Find it hard to say no and set limits with clients?

_____ 8. Get defensive when given negative feedback by a client?

_____ 9. Take credit for your clients' progress in therapy?

_____ 10. Have trouble keeping good financial records and clear financial agreements with clients?

_____ 11. Answer phone calls during sessions with clients?

_____ 12. Worry a lot about your clients and what they think of you?

_____ 13. Share intimate details of your personal life that may not relate to the issues being discussed?

_____ 14. Get threatened when your clients want to talk to other professionals about their therapy?

_____ 15. Avoid working on your own codependency issues?

_____ 16. Avoid getting regular supervision on your tough cases?

_____ 17. Sit in your "special" chair while conducting therapy sessions?

_____ 18. Insist that clients talk to only you about their problems?

_____ 19. Allow clients to give you total credit for their success?

_____ 20. Find it hard to take time off just for yourself?

_____ **Total**

Scoring and Interpretation

Add up the numbers for each question to get your score. Check below for the interpretation of your score. If your score was between:

20–40   Some evidence of codependent patterns in your client relationships.

41–60   Moderate evidence of codependent patterns in your client relationships.

61–80   Strong evidence of codependent patterns in your client relationships.

Chapter 14

~

How Can I Apply The Partnership Way in Schools?

Conflicts between students, teachers, and other school personnel have long been a part of the school experience, but the tragic results of the recent shooting sprees by enraged students have brought that conflict more sharply into focus. One-half of all violence against teenagers occurs in school buildings, on school property, or on the streets in the vicinity of schools (NIDR, 1998). Rarely has the time been better for a school to institute conflict resolution methods and curricula. The Partnership Way, which was developed by the authors, is designed to address the psychological and social conditions that foster conflict. This model is unique in that it embraces conflict and encourages those involved to see themselves as partners who can help resolve conflicts at their source.

The Partnership Way can be used to help individuals, including children, develop skills to maintain an internal sense of "object constancy" and hold themselves as objects of worth even when feeling rejected or unworthy during conflicts. These skills include "I'm okay, you're okay" thinking that discourages splitting behaviors (which divide people or groups into "good" and "bad") and looking for three options or choices when resolving conflicts.

Professionals who work in school settings bring with them the residue of developmental trauma, such as incomplete psychosocial tasks and unmet developmental needs from their individual, couple, family, and work relationships. These unresolved developmental issues will eventually surface as conflicts containing drama triangle dynamics (persecutor, rescuer, and victim) within schools, neighborhoods, and community organizations. When people overreact during in-school conflicts they are probably experiencing symptoms of post-traumatic stress. (The Skill Practice Exercise with Table 14.2 at the end of the chapter is useful in identifying the impact of developmental trauma in school settings.) With the Partnership Way, that behavior is not judged; rather it is viewed from a compassionate and understanding perspective. The Partnership Way teaches individuals to avoid getting "triggered" in school or neighborhood conflicts and to develop a compassionate attitude toward themselves and their reactions to others and subsequent events.

THE NATURE OF SCHOOL CONFLICT AND HOW TO DEAL WITH IT

Although conflict has, unfortunately, become an accepted fact in public school life, most students do not know how to resolve conflicts in nonviolent or cooperative ways.

If students are taught to resolve conflicts effectively, they can live more productive lives, as well as avoiding the drastic and life-threatening action seen in the news. There are two ways to incorporate conflict resolution training in schools. The first is training students as conflict mediators to help other students resolve conflicts at school. The other is to offer a K–12 curriculum in conflict resolution for all students. A combination of these two approaches is the most effective way to insure that all students learn how to resolve conflicts nonviolently and from a win-win perspective.

Even with the trend toward teaching students conflict resolution skills, there seems to be a breakdown in civility among our young people and a sharp increase of peer violence. Student-to-student put-downs have become more cruel and hurtful, as well as more common. In addition, there is a growing group of children and youth who wish to dominate, intimidate, or bully other students, either to gain the attention of others or to pass on the vicious cycle of cruelty from experiences of being dominated, intimidated, or bullied by their parents or older siblings. Schools also become battlegrounds for rival gangs who vie for control in order to sell drugs to students. School officials often do not know how to cope with these challenges.

Public schools have become the largest purchasers of metal detectors. Many now hire guards to patrol their hallways. The most effective way to address these problems is mobilizing everyone in the school to work cooperatively to end the violence. Some schools have developed zero-tolerance policies that make it impossible for bullying and criminal behavior to exist in the schools. These same zero-tolerance policies can be extended into neighborhoods and communities.

HOW CONFLICT RESOLUTION CAN STEM THE RISE OF PEER VIOLENCE

The tremendous amount of peer violence and conflict in schools is often manifested as bullying and put-downs. Teachers and parents too often look the other way when children fight with each other. The tendency is to "let them fight it out." While this policy may prevent rescuing behaviors, "innocent" fighting, bullying and put-downs can severely traumatize a child. The average child receives 213 put-downs a week or 30 per day. Three out of four students report being bullied at school. Each month, 525,000 students are victims of attacks, shakedowns and robberies while at school (Fried & Fried, 1996). Getting away with bullying behavior doesn't bode well, for the perpetrator either. More than 50% of all schoolyard bullies end up in prison.

Peer violence is far more pervasive than youth violence in gangs and perhaps even more pervasive than domestic violence. Peer violence is first learned at home. Children who experience violence at home often go to school and treat their peers violently. Schools have become the battleground for releasing pent-up anger and rage. Violence, furthermore, can erupt over little things, such as the way one person looks at another. There are many different kinds of conflicts that occur daily in school: teasing, bullying, fighting, pushing, and shoving. Bullies often roam the schools looking for smaller kids to pick on, shake down, harass, beat up, or intimidate. Bullying behavior is one of the most destructive forms of school conflict.

ADDRESSING BULLYING BEHAVIORS IN SCHOOLS

The problem of bullying behavior in schools has been around for a long time and very little has been done to correct it. Children feel afraid to report it to school officials. Even when they do report it, adults usually fail to help them. Teachers and administrators often have difficulty distinguishing the boundary between true bullying behavior and normal peer conflict. Many teachers believe children should learn to resolve their own differences and are reluctant to rescue. Many children do not report bullying traumas because they fear they will be branded "snitches" and incite further retaliation by the bullies. These victims of violence and aggression feel isolated, fearful, and alone. Here are some facts about bullying behavior (Fried & Fried, 1996; Garrity et al., 1995):

- Three-out-of-four students from non-urban schools report being bullied during their school career.
- Ninety percent of all students felt that being bullied caused lasting social, emotional, or academic problems.
- Sixty percent of victims report being bullied by boys; 40% were bullied by girls.
- Bullying is reported as most severe in grades 7–9, followed by grades 9–12.
- Sixty-nine percent of all students believe that schools respond poorly to bullying and victimization.
- Ridiculing/teasing, verbal harassment, and practical jokes are the most frequently reported forms of bullying. Physical attacks are reported less frequently.
- Forty-four percent of teachers believe disruptive school behaviors are getting worse.
- Each month, over 525,000 students are victims of attacks, shakedowns, and robberies while at school.
- One out of five high school students report avoiding restrooms out of a fear for their safety.
- Ten percent of those who drop out of school do so because of repeated bullying.
- Both bullies and victims have problems later in life related to their experiences.
- Everyone plays a role in allowing bullying behavior to go on and everyone can play a role in helping to stop the problem.

The following strategies have proven to be effective:
- Teach the students effective strategies to stop bullying behavior.

- Train the faculty to recognize and effectively intervene in bullying situations.
- Establish school/classroom rules for reporting and eliminating bullying behavior.
- Develop programs for recognition of prosocial behaviors.
- Create peer mediation programs.
- Teach conflict resolution skills to all students and faculty.

PREVENTING SCHOOL CONFLICTS

Although most of the attention goes into trying to contain current conflict situations, it is just as important to work to prevent conflict. There are three basic kinds of prevention programs: primary, secondary, and tertiary. School-based intervention programs such as cooperative learning are an example of a primary prevention program. Cooperative learning has proven to be very effective in dealing with high-risk kids prone to violent conflicts. If begun early, children can learn quickly and effectively to use nonviolent means for resolving their conflicts. These skills help children feel safe and powerful without resorting to guns, gangs, and violence.

Primary Prevention

These programs encourage interventions prior to the appearance of a problem and provide a pleasurable experience as part of the intervention. When people are engaged in pleasurable or kind acts, the hypothalamus gland secrets endorphins that inhibit the release of "substance P," a brain chemical that communicates pain to the brain. Linking desired positive social behaviors with the biological secretion of a neurochemical can help build a new psychophysiological structure for behavior patterns (Kotulak, 1996). Primary prevention programs in schools provide supportive services to all members of the school community without focusing on a target group that has been identified as in conflict or at risk of conflict. Peer mediation programs, conflict resolution skills training for all K–12 students, and a cooperative learning curriculum are examples of primary prevention programs in schools.

Secondary Prevention

These programs intervene after a problem has begun and provide supportive services to target groups already identified as having conflicts or at risk of having conflicts. A program that offers support services to students who have been active in school fights is an example of secondary prevention. One such program assigns youths to community service rather than at-home suspension with the hope of giving them experiences that change their attitudes and behaviors. Other examples include the creation of zero-tolerance policies on bullying.

Tertiary Prevention

Services for those who have gotten into academic difficulty and can be rehabilitated are tertiary prevention programs. An example of this is alternative high schools for students who have dropped out of school and then decided to return.

SOME SUCCESSFUL PREVENTION PROGRAMS

This section identifies programs used by schools to help identify the source of conflicts, create direct communication dynamics, and prevent triangulation. These programs utilize components such as psychoeducation, individual empowerment, skill development. and peer mediation from the Partnership Way. Programs that focus on prevention are critical for teaching children to resolve conflicts nonviolently.

The growing problem of peer violence has been a catalyst for the expansion of conflict resolution and peer mediation curricula in schools. Over 8,500 schools in the United States are now using one or both of these kinds of programs (NIDR, 1998).

Peer Mediation

Peer mediation is designed to teach students how to help each other resolve conflicts nonviolently and effectively. One peer mediation program for resolving conflicts involves training a group of elementary-school or middle-school students to serve as the school's conflict managers. Peer mediators often wear a special sweatshirt, T-shirt, button, or some kind of tag to identify them. Peer mediators facilitate everyday school conflicts by bringing together the individuals in conflict to resolve the issues peacefully and honorably. A conflict manager who sees a conflict starting can approach the students involved and offer mediation services. The students in conflict are free to refuse this offer. If they do accept it, the peer mediator establishes ground rules for the students to use in working through their conflict.

Peer mediator training usually includes skills in conflict analysis, active listening, interest-based bargaining, and facilitation. Advanced training content includes more experiential activities, including structured experiences, role-playing, and simulations. Ongoing in-service training is also a part of this program. Peer mediators meet regularly with their trainers or coaches to discuss how they handled specific situations and get feedback on how they might improve their efforts.

Most schools that have adopted peer mediation programs believe they are effective. To get the most benefit from peer mediation programs, however, schools need to teach all students conflict resolution skills. Many large city school districts, including Chicago, New York, and Kansas City, have mandated teaching conflict resolution in their K–12 curricula. Teachers in school districts that have not yet mandated conflict resolution skills training can still do much to create a peaceful classroom (see the Skill Practice Exercises at the end of the chapter).

An Interview with a Trainer of Peer Mediators

The following is an interview with Martha Reed, a Colorado Springs middle-school trainer of peer mediators:

Q: *Martha, you have trained peer mediators at the elementary- and middle-school levels for some time. What is your approach?*

A: I work in the school system using a preventive model. The purpose of peer mediation is to prevent the kids from hurting themselves and each other. I teach practical skills to students that they can use both at home and at school.

Q: *How does your program work?*

A: When students come into the middle school from fifth grade, our team trains everyone in a conflict resolution curriculum we developed. It teaches them the skills through what we call an "enrichment program," which is taught the last half hour of the day. We identify the sixth-graders who we feel have the best skills in resolving conflicts and train them to become peer mediators.

These students are not allowed to resolve conflicts involving guns, drugs, or knives or anything involving risk. The peer mediators deal with situations where a fight erupts because one student says, "He looked at me wrong." Peer mediators are trained to prevent the escalation of a conflict. A lot of student conflicts start in the classroom or in the hallway. Peer mediators have "on call" periods where they are available should the social worker or the counselors need them. They also have rotating schedules where they are available in the counseling office. They may also be available at other times to students who want to sit down and work out their conflict through the mediation process.

Q: *What are peer mediators trained to do?*

A: Students often need a neutral party, which is the peer mediator. Students often respect their peers more than an adult who dictates, "You have to do this and this in order to resolve your conflict." We've found that using two mediators with two disputants is the most effective format. They help the students brainstorm all the possible solutions. Then they examine the solutions and choose the one that seems to work the best. Our model also teaches peer mediators a lot about problem solving. They also help students in conflict identify how they contribute to the conflict. Peer mediators also often discover they are learning more about their own conflicts while helping other students. It is amazing to see how student mediators learn about themselves through this program. We also require mediators to create an agreement that the students must complete and sign. If they don't, then they must go down to the office where they will have consequences, such as being suspended for three to five days. These consequences are also included in the agreement.

Q: *What other results have you found from your program?*

A: Our office referrals have declined significantly because of this program. It really seems to work. There have also been fewer fights. I feel amazed when I hear students say, "Wow! I can really resolve this conflict without fighting!" They feel proud they found their own solution and it makes an impression on them. Each of our grade levels now has trained peer mediators. When our students go on to high school, the teachers say that they see a difference in our students who had training in solving their own problems.

Q: *What kind of training do peer mediators receive?*

A: Middle-school students can choose any enrichment class they like. They have options such as chess and drama during this period. We also require all incoming sixth-graders to go through a six- to eight-week class in conflict resolution. Those students who demonstrate skill in conflict resolution are selected for the peer mediator training program that continues to meet during enrichment time. They receive a lot of skill training, such as role-playing typical situations they might encounter like fights and boyfriend/girlfriend conflicts. They experience many different role-plays so they can practice their mediation skills. Once they understand how peer mediation works through their role-plays, they love it and want to keep doing it.

A successful peer mediation requires staff buy-in. The staff and administration must commit to making it a top priority. I have found it takes two or three years for it to really take hold, so it is important to persevere and make a long-term commitment. We do in-service programs with our teaching staff, our social worker, and both of our counselors. They are really committed to it and believe in it.

Conflict Resolution Curricula

In his book, *Creative Conflict Resolution,* Kreidler (1984) lists the five qualities of a peaceful classroom:

1. Cooperation. Children learn to work together, trust and help each other, and share with each other.
2. Communication. Students learn to ask directly for what they want, rather than acting out or whining to get attention. They also learn how to listen sensitively.
3. Tolerance. Students learn to show respect and appreciation for differences. They learn to understand racial, religious, and other forms of prejudice and how to deal with it.
4. Positive emotional expression. Students learn to express feelings, particularly anger and frustration, in ways that are not aggressive or destructive. Students also develop impulse control.
5. Conflict resolution. In the peaceful classroom students learn win-win methods for resolving conflicts.

Kreidler is quick to point out that a peaceful classroom climate will not eliminate all conflicts, but will reduce them by providing effective methods of dealing with them when they arise. He also contrasts the peaceful classroom with one where conflict erupts on a regular basis. He groups the causes of conflict into six categories:

1. A competitive atmosphere. Students learn to work against each other rather than cooperate. They develop an attitude of everyone for himself or herself and do not learn how to work together in groups. They lack trust in the teacher and their classmates.
2. An intolerant atmosphere. Students are unfriendly, critical, unsupportive, and intolerant. Conflicts arise out of friction between cliques, from scapegoating, from intolerance of racial and cultural differences, because of resentment toward those who are successful, and from feelings of loneliness and isolation.
3. Poor communication. Students attempt to get their needs met by acting out and fighting and escalate incidents into conflicts because of misperceptions.
4. Inappropriate expressions of emotion. Students use conflicts as a way to express their feelings. They lack assertive ways to express feelings of anger and frustration and skills in impulse control.
5. Lack of conflict resolution skills. Students deficient in effective win-win conflict resolution skills are unable to respond effectively in conflict situations. Without skill training, students often resort to the aggressive or violent models of conflict resolution they see on television and at the movies.
6. The misuse of power by the teacher. Stressed-out teachers who feel out of control often misuse their power to cope with their stress and feelings of disempowerment. They may place irrational or unreasonable expectations on certain students who annoy them, create rigid rules, or use authoritarian methods that create an atmosphere of fear and mistrust.

A Curriculum to Prevent Violent Youth Conflicts

One of the most highly regarded conflict resolution curricula was developed in 1994 by the Education Development Center in Newton, MA, as the result of a collaborative study. Called Aggressors, Victims and Bystanders, (Slaby, Wilson-Brewer, & Dash, 1994) it is designed for grades 7 to 12 as part of a comprehensive school health curriculum. It is delivered in 45-minute class segments and contains a teacher's guide plus student activities and handouts. This curriculum has three main assumptions:

1. Fighting is not a viable way to resolve conflicts.
2. Adolescents can learn skills to resolve conflicts in nonviolent ways.
3. Conflict resolution skills will enhance the safety of students and help everyone maintain self-respect and the respect of others.

The backbone of the curriculum is a four-step "Think-First" model. It teaches students how to think, what to think, and how to develop a cool-headed approach in conflict situations. A unique aspect of this program is that it doesn't just focus on the aggressor's role in starting or preventing conflicts. It also emphasizes the roles of the bystander and the victim in preventing violent conflict. This approach correlates with the drama triangle aspect of the Partnership Way and its interchanging roles of persecutor, rescuer, and victim.

Bully-Proofing Schools

Other primary and secondary peer violence prevention programs have targeted bullying behavior. Aggressive and antisocial behavior is easy to spot and easy to treat, if caught early enough. One of the most effective programs to stop bullying behavior is the Bully-Proofing Program (Garrity et al., 1995) developed in Colorado.

This comprehensive curriculum targets elementary schools as early-intervention targets. Developed by a team of consultants in the Cherry Creek Schools in suburban Denver, the curriculum has three primary strategies:

1. Develop school-wide no-bullying policies.
2. Train the faculty and staff on effective implementation of the policy.
3. Train all the students in the school to deal with bullying behavior.

Olweus (1991) found that the single most effective way to stop bullying behavior in schools is to teach the adults to recognize bullying behavior and train them to stop it. Children look to adults for help in combating bullying. It is surprising how many teachers cannot recognize bullying behaviors or know when and where their help is needed. If they do recognize the problem, few know how to make effective interventions.

A key to teacher involvement in prevention programs is awareness of their own personal style of conflict resolution. This helps them correlate it with appropriate interventions for bullying situations. Teachers can quickly see how their style may not be effective in all conflict situations. For example, a teacher who is more of a compromiser or an accommodator might have trouble intervening in bullying situations such as physical fighting that requires a more directive approach. The Bully-Proofing Program suggests that teachers expand their personal style of conflict resolution and team up with other teachers whose style complements theirs.

The implementation part of this program involves developing classroom rules that parallel the overall school discipline policy and teaching students how to cope with bullying. In addition to these classroom interventions, the program also includes materials to help counselors work more intensively with students, either individually or in small groups, who are frequent victims of bullying. It also includes strategies for working directly with bullies to change their behaviors.

Dealing with bullying students themselves is another important intervention. Without intervention, these behaviors will get worse. In a study in Norway, Olweus (1991) discovered that 60% of the boys who were identified as bullies in the second grade were convicted of a felony by age 24. An American longitudinal study by Eron (1987) showed that aggressive behavior rarely changed over the course of his 22-year study. The more aggressive a boy was at age eight, the greater the chances he would be in trouble with the law as an adult. In addition, he was less likely to have finished college or secured a job. Aggressive girls were more likely to use aggressive methods of punishing their children when they became mothers. The children of these mothers were also more likely to become bullies. Eron says, "Early intervention is critical" (p. 14).

Samenow (1984, 1989) found that aggressive antisocial youth use faulty thinking to justify their actions. These thinking errors include the following:

1. "Life is a one-way street—my way."
2. "I should be number one immediately."
3. "It's not my fault."
4. "If someone disagrees with me, they are putting me down."

These kind of thinking errors are characteristic of people who are wounded by severe developmental trauma. These individuals probably suffer from unresolved abuse and neglect inflicted during early childhood that impacts their adolescent behavior. Table 14.1 identifies some of the common errors in thinking of people who haven't completed the counter-dependent stage of development. Teachers, counselors, and parents can confront children and adolescents in these errors in thinking in ways that can help correct these errors and promote responsible behavior.

Some of these errors in thinking are symptoms of Reactive Attachment Disorder and the presence of antisocial behavior. Many of these children are misdiagnosed with Attention Deficit Disorder. Studies show that the earlier these symptoms are addressed, the better the chances are that these disorders will not occur. Magid and McKelvey (1987) say that if a child is not treated by age sixteen it is difficult and perhaps impossible to reverse the effects of the early trauma. The only solution is to "warehouse" them. Many untreated youth and adults are already warehoused in our country's jails and prisons or locked residential adolescent treatment facilities.

As indicated in the research, bullying students can be identified early in their school years and given individual help. According to Lewis (1992), the early warning signals are impulsivity, hypersensitivity, and erroneous thinking. Garrity et al., (1995) list the following early warning signs that teachers can easily observe:

- Irritability, impatience, and moodiness from an early age.

- A tendency to perceive hostile intent of others even when it isn't there.
- A tendency to retaliate quickly for genuine or imagined threats.
- Trouble identifying feelings; acts them out rather than communicating them.
- Inability to recognize one's own pain or the pain of others.
- An abusive or neglectful home environment.

A Cooperative Learning Curriculum

The Partnership Way suggests that the school years between ages six and eighteen are the years to learn about cooperation and develop interdependence. This is the research finding of brothers David W. and Roger T. Johnson, pioneers in the development of cooperative learning curriculum materials and programs for the schools. The Johnsons have created theory, research, and application materials to develop interdependent thinking and behavior in students to facilitate social interdependence. They identify three key components for teaching social interdependence: competitive learning situations, individualistic learning situations, and cooperative learning situations. Their research, which reveals the limits of competitive and individualistic learning, indicates that cooperative learning produces:

- higher achievement
- more caring, supportive, and committed relationships
- greater psychological health, social competence, and self-esteem

In the 1960s, the Johnsons developed an effective conflict resolution model called the Teaching Students to be Peacemakers Program (Johnson & Johnson, 1995). It is a K–12 conflict resolution training program based on the principles of cooperative learning. The goal of the program is to teach all students to be peacemakers. They have implemented this program in the United States and other parts of the world. The program has six steps:

1. Create a cooperative context for resolving conflicts. Teach students to recognize the importance of their long-term interdependence when resolving conflicts. De-emphasize the need to win and emphasize the need to resolve the conflict for mutual benefit.
2. Teach students how to recognize what is and what is not a conflict. Many students hold misconceptions about conflict, based on what they see on television or in the movies. They do not see the positive gains from successful conflict resolution, such as laughter, insight, learning, and closer relationships.
3. Teach students a specific, concrete procedure for negotiating agreements. Students need a step-by-step method they can use to resolve conflicts without damaging their relationships. Telling students to "talk it out" or "solve your problem" is not enough.

Table 14.1
Common Errors in Thinking of People Who Have Had Developmental Traumas

Thinking Errors Related to Developmental Traumas	Healthy Ways to Deal with Students Who Have These Thinking Errors
"I am a victim." "He started it." " I couldn't help it." "It is their fault."	Do not accept these excuses. Focus on the individual, e.g., what he or she did that contributed to the problem.
"I can't do it." Tries to avoid responsibility by claiming it is impossible to accomplish anything.	Respond with, " 'I can't' usually means 'I won't.' " Ask why they are refusing to do this.
"I didn't know that would hurt you." They do not think how their actions affect others.	Say, "When you do this, I lose my trust in you and don't want to be with you. Will you change your behaviors" Ask, "How would you feel if someone did that to you?"
"I don't understand why you feel that way." They have little empathy for others. Very egocentric.	Ask, "How would you feel if someone did that to you?" Tell them your feelings.
"I'm bored" (and it's your fault).These people engage in self-pity, They may develop psychosomatic aches and pains as avoidance defenses.	Say, "Boredom is anger without enthusiasm." Ask what or who are the sources of blame and excuses. Point out natural consequences of their anger.
"I forgot to do it. So what!" Does not keep agreements, does not want to be held responsible for breaking them. Looks for excuses, blames circumstances for broken agreements.	Point out that people remember what they want to remember. Ask them to explain why they forget and to examine the real reasons. Give logical consequences. Ask how they feel when others break agreements.
"I am entitled to it, so if you don't give it to me, I'll take it." They expect others to do what they want them to do. No respect for property of others. Makes demands on others. Righteous attitude.	Give logical consequences for not respecting the property of others. Point out that they are not entitled to use the property of others without permission.
"You can't trust people." These individuals are emotional loners and have little trust or loyalty to anyone. Blame others for breaking trust but really are saying, "I can't trust you."	Give specific examples of behaviors that make it difficult to trust. Confront any betrayal of trust. Insist that trust be earned.
"If I think so, it will happen." Have unrealistic expectations and "magical thinking," which is often grandiose, with no understanding of how to accomplish goals.	Get them to provide a step-by-step plan and point out any missing steps. Help them to state their expectations, prepare for disappointment.
"I assumed you knew what I wanted." Make unwarranted assumptions and are angry when others don't agree. They don't find the facts or truth and blame others when things go wrong.	Point out their unwarranted assumptions and ask them to check them against the facts. If they don't know how to find the facts, help them learn.
"I am right and you are wrong." Prideful, refuse to back down, even on small points. Will not admit mistakes. Pride usually covers up shame. Egotistical.	Help them find a third alternative to black-and-white, either/or ways of thinking. Admit a mistake to them when you make one and request they do the same. Ask what they learned from their mistakes.
"I didn't know that would happen." They lack the ability to plan ahead or to make long-range plans.	Ask for a step- by-step plan and help them think ahead at each step. Show how advanced planning can prevent unpleasant events.
"If I do that, I will be a _____" Definitions of success and failure are grandiose. Failure is seen as something less than being first. Uses either/or thinking.	Help them see grades of success and failure. Teach that mistakes are just new kinds of learning. Help them define success and failure from a self-reference point.

Thinking Errors Related to Developmental Traumas	Healthy Ways to Deal with Students Who Have These Thinking Errors
"You are just trying to put me down." Feel put down if even the smallest things don't go their way. Personalizes feedback from others. Feels criticized by others.	Help them learn from mistakes. Show them how their behavior drew criticism and then how to evaluate the criticism.
"I'm not afraid of anything." Denial of fear. Uses false bravado to cover up fear. Sees fear as a weakness.	Tell them that acknowledging fear can be a sign of strength. Help them understand the sources of their fear.
"I don't get mad, I get even." Uses revenge to act out hurts. Uses attacks, intimidation, sarcasm, or threats to get their way. Anger may also be expressed passively or indirectly.	Help them realize that the function of anger is to let them know what they want. Also show how anger covers fear and help them identify their fears.
"I need to be in charge." These people try to dominate others through power and skills and control. They have to win at all costs.	Confront every attempt to use power over others. Help them learn partnering, show how dominating others doesn't get them what they really want.

4. Teach students to use a concrete and specific mediation procedure. Students need to be taught how to mediate their classmates' conflicts. They are given 30 hours of specific training on recognizing conflict, negotiation skills, and mediation skills.
5. Implement the program. Working in pairs, initially, student mediators help other students mediate conflicts. These roles are rotated so that all students get a chance to be a mediator.
6. Continue weekly training in negotiation and mediation procedures throughout the first through twelfth grades. This helps everyone refine and upgrade their skills. The students learn that to become competent in conflict resolution takes years of practice.

Unlike many similar programs, the Johnsons conducted extensive research, using ten different studies to document the effectiveness of their program in different schools. They found the following results (Johnson and Johnson, 1995):

1. In urban schools, most of the conflicts referred to student mediators involved physical and verbal violence. In suburban schools, most conflicts centered on possessions and access to resources, preferences about what to do, playground issues, and turn-taking.
2. Untrained students would almost always strive to win in a conflict situation, while those trained in peacemaking focused on maximizing joint outcomes.
3. The number of discipline problems dropped by 60% and referrals to the principal's office dropped about 95%.
4. Untrained students held generally negative attitudes toward conflict, while trained students held more positive attitudes toward conflict.

David and Roger Johnson's cooperative learning approach is now used widely in schools in this country to provide a counter-balance to the competitive and individualistic learning that is so prevalent in our public schools. There have been many criticisms of cooperative learning by some educators, who often do not understand the negative impact of competitive and individualistic models and who do not know how to facilitate effective cooperative learning activities. As many high-tech businesses adopt project team structures, the value of cooperative learning as an important job skill for the Information Age has increased. Schools are being encouraged to use more cooperative learning strategies to better prepare their students for living in a shrinking, increasingly more interdependent world.

They cite five causes of resistance to cooperative learning by educators and others:

1. Confusion about what makes cooperative learning groups work.
2. The patterns of isolation created by organizational barriers to cooperation.
3. A false social norm of "rugged individualism."
4. The risk that educators perceive because the groups might fail.
5. That using cooperative learning groups requires disciplined action by teachers for which they can be held accountable.

At the core of David and Roger Johnson's program on cooperative learning is the concept of positive interdependence (see the Self-Awareness Exercise: Positive Interdependence Brainstorming at the end of the chapter). The Johnsons' program of cooperative learning focuses directly on how to teach this vital skill. This program identifies and describes nine different types of activities that develop positive interdependence in children and youth. (Johnson, Johnson, & Holubec, 1993) These nine types of activities are described briefly below:

Positive Goal Interdependence: Activities are arranged so that students can achieve their learning goals only if all the members of their learning group also attain their goals. Members of a learning group develop their learning goals in a way that helps everyone achieve the goals.

Positive Reward Interdependence: Each learning group member receives the same reward for completing an assignment. A joint reward is given for a successful group effort.

Positive Resource Interdependence: Each group member is given only a portion of the information, resources, or materials needed to complete a task. The group members have to work cooperatively in order to complete their task.

Positive Task Interdependence: Learning tasks are arranged so that the actions of one group member have to be completed before the next group member can complete his or her part.

Positive Role Interdependence: Each group member is assigned complementary and interconnected roles that are necessary to complete a group task.

Positive Identity Interdependence: The learning group creates its own identity through a name, flag, motto, song, or poem.

Positive Outside Enemy Interdependence: Nothing will bring a group of people together more quickly than an outside force that they must overcome in order to be successful. Creating external opposition promotes this.

Positive Fantasy Interdependence: The group task is to imagine that they are in a life-or-death situation and must cooperate in order to survive.

Environment Interdependence: Group members are bound together by a physical environment in some way. For example, having to work in a confined area that they have to rearrange in order to work most effectively.

The Kindness Campaign: A Primary Prevention Program

The Kindness Campaign is a primary prevention program that reinforces empathic, prosocial rather than antisocial behaviors (Weinhold, 1996a & b). It is designed to create a positive school and community climate where antisocial behavior cannot thrive. The motto of the Kindness Campaign is "Spread Kindness—It's Contagious"©. The goals of the Kindness Campaign are:

1. To restore a sense of community and neighborliness that we seem to have forgotten and

2. To prevent the spread of violence that has taken hold in many parts of our schools, community, state, and nation.

Spreading kindness is up to everyone, and it can be fun and rewarding. Anyone can participate in this campaign to stop the spread of violence, hatred, and unkindness by remembering to do small daily acts of kindness for ourselves, our family, friends, neighbors, school mates, work mates, strangers, those who are sick or in need, and anyone else we meet.

This campaign reconfirms the important principle of interdependency and the responsibility to act kindly towards one's self as well as towards others. The attitude of kindness begins with first being kind to one's self because it is difficult to be kind to others when one's own heart is empty of kindness. True kindness comes from having a compassionate heart. It takes countless small daily acts of kindness to create an atmosphere of compassion necessary to transform a mass of separate individuals into a kind, caring community.

The Kindness Campaign is designed to provide simple recognition for daily acts of kindness. Many acts of kindness go unrecognized, while acts of violence are quickly recognized, perhaps even over-recognized by the media. The best way to eliminate violence is to reinforce its opposite: kindness. When you sign a pledge card, you are given a button that says "Spread Kindness—It's Contagious." A person who witnesses another person committing an act of kindness gives their button to this person to acknowledge this act. As they give away their button, they ask the recipient to pass on the button when they witness another act of kindness. In this way, kindness can spread quickly to help build a kind, caring school or community.

The Kindness Campaign is spreading rapidly in Colorado Springs schools. Many use *Spreading Kindness* (Weinhold, 1996a), a program guide developed for elementary and middle schools. Participating schools typically report an immediate 30% or more drop in discipline referrals after beginning the campaign. Longer term results show a 26% drop. Put-downs are also drastically reduced, with reports of up to 94% in several schools. Reports of bullying behavior and violent conflicts also drop sharply in participating schools.

Primary prevention programs that use kindness, mediation, and conflict resolution are slowly transforming the country's schools and providing more and more people with foundation skills in win-win conflict resolution skills. As the positive results of these efforts become more apparent to everyone, "Resolution" will literally become the "Fourth R" in our nation's schools.

SELF-AWARENESS EXERCISE: POSITIVE INTERDEPENDENCE BRAINSTORMING

1. Divide into small groups of five or six people.
2. Brainstorm as many ways as you can think of to teach each of the nine types of interdependence described earlier in this chapter.
3. Select what you as a group decide are your best ideas.
4. Each small group gives a report to the class on their ideas of how to teach the different types of interdependence.
5. As a variation, the large group could utilize one or more of the suggested activities to develop more interdependence in the class.

SKILL PRACTICE EXERCISE:
IDENTIFYING DEVELOPMENTAL TRAUMAS AS THE SOURCE OF STUDENT CONFLICTS

1. Study Table 14.2 and make sure everyone understands it.
2. Discuss how it could be used in a school or agency that deals with children and youth.
3. Divide into small groups of 4 to 6 persons. Take turns role-playing a student who is displaying one of the symptoms listed below. The rest of the group is asked to try different ways to confront this behavior.
4. Discuss each role-play situation and evaluate the effectiveness of the confrontation. Discuss the results in large group.

Table 14.2

SYMPTOMS OF DEVELOPMENTAL TRAUMAS	DEVELOPMENTAL ISSUES	SUGGESTED INTERVENTIONS
Clinging, an obvious need to touch or be touched, shy, regressive behaviors, whining, helplessness, watching others rather than participating, dependent in relationships with others, tendency to be lethargic and low energy	Incomplete bonding with another person Trauma during the first year of life that has damaged the child's ability to bond, including: premature separation from mother; repeated separation from mother; too many different caregivers	Spend extra time, recruit help with tasks, listen to and support feelings ("You look like you are sad"), give unconditional responses ("I like you"), provide mirroring ("I see you...")
Suspicious, sneaky, little self-disclosure, few friends, lying, secretive, belligerent, high-risk behaviors	Poorly developed sense of basic trust Impaired ability to trust due to abuse or threat of abuse, physical trauma such as surgery or medical procedures, particularly during the first two months of life	Encourage them to trust their own feelings and responses, teach them effective ways to determine the trustworthiness of others
Putting objects in their mouths, chewing pencils and erasers, talking incessantly, acting-out to get attention, smoking, drinking, using drugs, gum chewing, nail biting, excessive snacking	Unsatisfied oral needs Trauma during period between the ages of four and six months that disrupts the period of oral bonding between the child and mother	Confront inappropriate behavior, support "okayness" and problem solving, set reasonable limits, give positive reinforcement on appropriate behaviors
Not respecting property, feelings, and rights of others; not keeping agreements-, minor shoplifting; interrupting; name calling; not knowing who owns the problem; not taking responsibility but blaming others; touching others inappropriately	Lack of respect for personal boundaries, personal boundaries not respected by parents Lack of developmentally appropriate limits during the second year of life, inhibiting the child's abilities to accept external authority and to develop boundaries and consequences	Set reasonable, clearly defined limits that are enforced consistently; arrange logical and natural consequences

SYMPTOMS OF DEVELOPMENTAL TRAUMAS	DEVELOPMENTAL ISSUES	SUGGESTED INTERVENTIONS
Have trouble taking compliments, over-personalizing issues, moodiness, short attention span, attempting to be different in behavior and dress	Difficulty in separating self from others Trauma during period between six and eight months during the critical stage of symbiosis between the mother and child	Encourage independent thinking and acting, give feedback on personal uniqueness
Withdrawal from activities involving any physical risk, reluctance to try new things, fear of failure, perfectionism, procrastination, easily confused	Poor object constancy, weak self-image Trauma during period between two and four months of age that disrupts the first stage of self-development and inhibits building the foundation of self-esteem	Arrange safe exploratory learning activities, encourage risk-taking, reframe "mistakes" into "learning"
Exaggerations, grandiosity, black-and-white thinking, comparative thinking, daredevil acts, impulsiveness	Weak cause and effect thinking, stuck in the "splitting" stage of separation Trauma during period between 12 and 18 months of age when child is in the "splitting" stage of development, leaving a residue of narcissistic behaviors	Help arrange logical and natural consequences to behaviors, help with identification of good and bad qualities in situations and people
Denial, saying "I can't" and "I don't know," agitating, escalating, not thinking, reacting without thinking	Failure to develop effective ways to explore their world, lack of self-confidence Trauma during period between 8 and 10 months of age when the child typically begins exploring	Avoid rescuing, support problem solving, cheerlead ("You can do it"), encourage appropriate risk-taking
Use of control, intimidation, manipulation, and games to get needs met, blaming others, avoiding responsibilities, low tolerance for frustration, poor coordination, bullying younger peers	Lack of personal power, failure to develop skills in autonomy Trauma during period between 12 and 18 months of age when child is in the "splitting" stage of development, leaving a residue of narcissistic behaviors	Mediate disputes, positive support for independent action
Poor impulse control, inability to follow through, inability to delay gratification, poor personal hygiene, inability to handle resources such as time and money effectively, poor planning, last-minute cramming, sloppy or messy homework	Lack of self-management and mastery skills Trauma during the first year of life that inhibits the child's development of an internal regulating structure	Teach skills in structuring time and preparing budgets, encourage better self-care, empower by mirroring effective self-management behaviors

SKILL PRACTICE EXERCISE: THE PEER MEDIATION PROCESS

1. The Mediator Monologue:
   Intervene and ask if the parties would like some help
   in resolving their conflict.
   If the answer is "yes," explain the mediation process.
   Explain the mediator's role and confidentiality.
   Explain the ground rules:
   A. Parties agree to resolve the conflict themselves
      with the mediator's help.
   B. No name calling or put-downs.
   C. Do not interrupt and listen to each other.
   D. Tell the truth.
   E. Ask each student if they want to use mediation to
      help resolve their conflict.
2. Opening Statements:
   Ask student # 1 what happened and how they feel.
   Ask student # 2 what happened and how they feel.
   Use active listening to reflect back the content and
   feelings.
3. Reframe the Problem:
   Summarize the conflict in neutral terms.
   Get agreement on what the conflict involves.
4. Explore Interests:
   Ask student # 1 what is most important for them in a
   solution.
   Ask student # 2 what is most important for them in a
   solution.
   Ask student # 1 what would make them feel better or
   happier.
   Ask student # 2 what would make them feel better or
   happier.
5. Invent Options:
   Ask student # 1 to give possible solutions they would
   like.
   Ask student # 2 to give possible solutions they would
   like.
6. Choose the Best Option:
   Help the students pick what they agree is the best
   option.
   If the option they select is not clear to you, ask clari-
   fying questions.
   Write down the option they agreed to and have them
   sign it.
   Specify any consequences if they don't keep the
   agreement.

SKILL PRACTICE EXERCISE: WHAT IS THE ROLE OF THE PEER MEDIATOR?

The following skill practice exercise is designed to help
the students in this course better understand the role and
functions of a peer mediator operating in a school.

1. Divide into small groups of 4 to 5 students and brainstorm a list of typical school conflicts where mediators
   could be helpful in facilitating a win-win resolution.
2. Each small group reports on what they have found and
   a larger list is developed containing all the ideas.
3. The class then decides which of the typical conflicts to
   use in their skill practice session.
4. Using the mediation process in the previous exercise,
   review the steps to make sure everyone understands
   them.
5. Select two small group members to role-play one of
   the typical conflict situations and two other members
   to be the peer mediators. Any additional small group
   members should serve as process observers and give
   feedback after each role-play.
6. While the two students role-play the school conflict,
   the mediators need to follow the mediation process
   and attempt to get the students to resolve their conflict.
7. Rotate the roles so that each member of the small
   group gets to play all the roles.
8. Discuss the results in your small group and in the large
   group class.

SKILL PRACTICE EXERCISE: DEVELOPING CLASSROOM RULES TO DEAL WITH BULLYING BEHAVIOR

1. Discuss "what is bullying?" Get examples from the
   students.
2. Introduce the idea that if everyone sticks together, no
   one is left out and a bully can't isolate and pick on
   anyone.
3. Discuss the difference between tattling and getting
   adult help. Make sure they understand that it is not tattling when they help someone who is in danger.
4. Present and discuss the following classroom rules
   about bullying:
   a. We agree that no student in the class will be per-
      mitted to bully any other student.
   b. We agree that we will come to the aid of any stu-
      dent being bullied by telling a bully to stop and by
      getting help from an adult.
   c. We agree not to exclude any student from an activ-
      ity in school or on the playground and make sure
      to include all students in our activities at school.
5. Post the rules in the classroom.

Chapter 15

~

How Can I Apply the Partnership Way in the Workplace?

This chapter is designed to help you apply the principles of the Partnership Way in the workplace. The goal of these principles is to help people in work settings develop skills that maintain an internal sense of object constancy. These skills include "I'm okay/you're okay" thinking that discourages splitting behaviors and encourages looking for three options or choices when resolving conflicts. Such skills help people regard themselves as objects of worth even when feeling rejected or unworthy during conflicts.

Workplace conflict is complex because people unconsciously bring with them issues related to their unresolved developmental traumas. These unresolved issues leave a residue of unresolved conflicts that eventually surface as drama triangle dynamics during workplace conflicts. When you see people overreacting during workplace conflicts it is important to remember that they are probably experiencing symptoms of post-traumatic stress from previous unresolved conflicts or traumas. Rather than judging or criticizing them, try seeing them from a compassionate and empathetic perspective. If you find yourself getting triggered in workplace conflicts, develop a compassionate attitude toward yourself.

The systemic nature of these conflicts often make them difficult to resolve. Corporations, businesses, and other organizations are usually organized around a formal network of horizontal and vertical structures designed to accomplish the goals of the organization. Quantum theory and chaos theory suggest that it is the informal and invisible self-organizing structures that actually determine how the organization functions. Chaos theory says strange attractors, or organizing forces, help create fractals or predictable patterns that structure an organization. One of the most common strange attractors in many organizations is unrecognized and unresolved conflict.

In one company, where we served as developmental process consultants, we attended various executive committee meetings. During one of these meetings, we noticed that the group tended to discount the comments of the manufacturing vice president. Other members of this committee seemed to ignore him at breaks, cut him off in the meetings, or attempt to rescue him by trying to explain to others what he meant to say. The members saw him as weak and passive and then confirmed their perceptions by preventing him from speaking out very much in their meetings. They seemed to have him in a "category."

We voiced our observations regarding the categorization of this man in one of the committee meetings and then waited to see if it would reappear. After the third episode, we asked this vice president if he was aware of being ignored. When he said he was, we asked him how he felt about the situation. He took this opportunity to tell his colleagues how he felt ignored and hurt about the way they were treating him.

Once these feelings were expressed, the other group members began treating him differently. They encouraged him to speak more in their meetings. Once this happened, they learned that he had a lot of good ideas and that he was not weak and passive as they had previously believed. His colleagues began following his suggestions and found them to be successful. People began to gravitate to him at breaks and he was now perceived as a valuable resource in meeting discussions.

Unresolved conflict can affect the morale, productivity, and wellness of the workplace. When people work closely together for a period of time, unresolved conflicts from their families of origin begin to surface. One of the best ways to deal with this is to create a workplace structure that operates like a functional family. In her excellent book, *Family Ties, Corporate Bonds*, Paula Bernstein (1985) holds such a vision:

> Tomorrow's corporate family will be headed by a man or a woman—not necessarily in the old-fashioned father or mother role, but more an adult friend, a protector, and advisor to his or her adult children, cousins, siblings, and stepchildren. We will be grown-ups working with grown-ups, but still fulfilling our own individual, special emotional needs. (p. 176)

WHAT ARE THE STAGES OF DEVELOPMENT IN ORGANIZATIONS?

According to the tenants of developmental systems theory, the evolution of organizations follows a developmental process similar to that for individuals, couples, and families. The four stages of organizational development are *codependent, counter-dependent, independent,* and *interdependent.* The psychosocial tasks of each stage are listed in Table 15.1.

An organization that provides an environment where individual members can complete these psychosocial tasks can evolve to a higher, more effective stage of development. Some organizations create an organizational identity that helps its employees bond, but cannot provide ways for them to get their individual needs met. The company may have low wages or few benefits or is unable to create trust between employees and management. Employee turnover in this kind of company is usually high, which affects the corporate esprit de corps. Rapid turnover and the loss of friendships has a big impact on the emotional stability of employees. Most corporate environments, unfortunately, do not help people deal with these losses. Unprocessed losses in a work setting can trigger employees' post-traumatic symptoms related to previous losses, causing them to lose the present-time focus they need for productivity.

In order to facilitate steady movement to higher stages of organizational development, management must make a conscious effort to address employees' work-related experiences in functional ways. This includes processing traumatic events and resolving conflicts. Otherwise the drama triangle dynamics will get activated, employee morale will fall, productivity will decline, and the company will stagnate.

HOW DO UNRESOLVED CONFLICTS IN THE WORKPLACE AFFECT MORALE AND PRODUCTIVITY?

Most people spend over one-third of their life in workplaces where there are numerous ongoing conflicts. The only formal structure in place to resolve these recurring conflicts are grievance procedures. Most employees avoid using them because of their adversarial and confrontational nature. Without corporate endorsed structures that protect employees who are engaged in conflict, most people develop avoidant or indirect means such as the drama triangle to deal with their conflicts.

If all employees used partnership principles involving cooperation and win-win methods to resolve conflicts, a company could save enormous amounts of time and money and greatly increase its productivity. Why don't companies invest more in training employees in conflict resolution? Some enlightened ones do, but most of them do not understand the benefits of this action.

For example, a middle manager of a large high-tech company to which we proposed employee conflict resolution training said with great seriousness, "Our employees don't have any conflicts at work. They leave them all at the door." We wondered if the company's reported high level of alcoholism might be related to this no-conflict policy. We also wondered if employees carried home their work-related frustrations and dumped them on their families. Unfortunately, this example represents a still too common attitude among corporate leaders and managers who simply do not understand the economic impact of unresolved workplace conflicts.

Teaching employees how to effectively resolve their conflicts is a practice of good management. Bernstein (1985) writes that when she interviewed employees the conversation always returned to one theme: The lack of good management, the need for it, and how much the employees hungered for it. The employees she interviewed longed for fairness, leadership, and justice and for simpler, less convoluted, and more straightforward conflict-free relationships.

WHAT DETERMINES THE AMOUNT OF CONFLICT IN THE WORKPLACE?

The structure of an organization or company determines how much conflict is present in that organization. Litwak (1961) found that the potential for conflict is

Table 15.1
The Stages of Organizational Development

Stage of development	Primary psychosocial tasks of an organization	Methods for completing these tasks
Codependent	• Build trust • Create organizational identity • Provide for the basic needs of employees and managers • Build esprit de corps	• Provide fair wages and benefits • Acknowledge employee needs and take them seriously • Nurture trust relationships between employer and employee • Provide time and resources to build quality, relationships • Utilize regular group rituals to unify and inspire
Counter-Dependent	• Identify the unique contributions of each employee • Resolve internal conflicts between the needs of employees and the needs of management	• Offer differential workload policies • Offer training in conflict resolution to all employees • Encourage new and innovative ideas • Use a minimum of rules and regulations • Make decisions at the level of implementation • Reward speaking the truth • Maximize direct, face-to-face communication
Independent	• Create an organizational culture with identified values and beliefs • Provide specialized training and development for each employee to enhance individual contributions to the organization	• Create flexible job descriptions • Reward individual initiative • Regard mistakes as learning • Encourage direct communication of needs • Reward personal growth and professional mastery • Create flexible work hours and situations
Interdependent	• Build teams • Develop consensus between teams	• Determine goals and visions through collective processes • Practice partnership conflict resolution • Utilize team-learning experiences • Express and display concern for the welfare of all employees • Identify personal growth as a priority

greater in centralized, highly bureaucratic organizations than in organizations with less centralized structures. Likert and Likert (1976) developed a method for rating organizations on a continuum between rigidity and flexibility.

The most effective organizations are adaptable to changing conditions and needs. The following criteria, which we based on research on organizational systems theory and the work of the Likerts, are suggested for determining the flexibility and adaptability of an organization.

1. *A minimum of rules and regulations.* The openness of a system can be determined by identifying the number of rules and regulations and how long these have existed. Most open systems have very few rules and use a set of operating principles for each subsystem of the organization. These principles are determined by the group or team most directly involved.

2. *Decision-making at the level of implementation.* Another quick way to assess a system's openness is checking the number of levels a decision must pass through before it can be implemented. In an open system, all important decisions are made at the level of implementation.

3. *A minimum number of hierarchical levels.* An open system is relatively flat in organizational structure. The more levels that information and decisions must pass through, the more chances of error or misperceptions and the more opportunities for conflict.

4. *Maximum data flow with external systems.* To determine this, notice how the system exchanges information, resources, and data with the systems that are contiguous to it. In open systems, established methods insure a reciprocal flow of information, resources, and data.

5. *Collectively determined goals and purposes.* Identify how goals and purposes are determined. In an open system, they are determined collectively by those directly involved in the process. Input is also sought from members of the larger contiguous system to accommodate changing needs and purposes.

6. *Direct, wide-band, face-to-face communication.* In closed organizations, communication tends to become indirect (memos, voice mail, e-mail, etc.). Open systems use more direct, face-to-face, wide-band (information and feelings) communication. This offers some potential for group decision-making. By checking the transmission of information, it is possible to assess the openness of a system. There is also a need for structures that encourage the expression of both positive and negative feelings.

7. *Neutralized power.* Power plays are common in organizations. In open systems, power is distributed through all levels. There are no one-up/one-down power moves and no win-lose decision-making or conflict resolution. A good way to check the openness of an organization is to look for evidence of misuse of power.

8. *Flexible processes.* The processes (work schedule, flexibility of hours, curriculum, etc.) in open systems are very flexible and dynamic. They can easily be changed in response to the changing needs of those involved. In less open systems, curriculum guides or job tasks are rigidly enforced and time schedules have few opportunities to change them.

9. *Open, permeable, system boundaries.* Instead of operating as an enclave, the open system extends its boundaries into the next larger system. The goals, purposes, and processes of the organization are completely visible. Open systems seek to blend their information, resources, and data flow with the next larger system. Open schools, agencies, and corporations operate as integrated, rather than separate, systems that enfold the daily lives of the people involved.

10. *Flexible role definitions.* Job descriptions and rigid role definitions can affect the degree of openness in a school or agency. In an open system, the roles that people are assigned or choose to play are flexible and able to change.

The Openness to Change Inventory at the end of this chapter is also drawn from this research and may be used to assess the relative openness of your workplace.

The Likerts found that more rigid organizations tended to manage conflict poorly. They found that the personality and methods of the managers and supervisors also made a difference. Less defensive managers who could receive feedback and were naturally supportive of others tended to prevent conflict. The leadership style of the managers and supervisors generally set the tone for conflict management. Those managers and supervisors with good communication skills, supportive attitudes toward those they supervised, and the ability to facilitate the resolution of conflicts generally had fewer conflicts.

The culture of the organization can also play a part in conflict management. Organizations with competitive, win-lose, everyone-for-themselves cultures have more conflict than those with a spirit of cooperation for achieving the organization's goals. Some organizations unwittingly create a competitive climate because of punitive, petty, and divisive organization policies and procedures. These kinds of policies gnaw at morale, erode productivity, affect the health of employees, and ultimately impair the organization and its productivity.

The stability of an organization is an important factor in managing conflict. Organizations experiencing high levels of change are more vulnerable to internal conflict. The way in which an organization manages change can destabilize employee morale and increase conflict. Organizations experiencing rapid change can handle conflict effectively when the climate supports conflict resolution. When conflict is denied and/or avoided, any change can reverberate through the company and increase conflict.

HOW DO DRAMA TRIANGLE DYNAMICS APPEAR IN WORKPLACE CONFLICTS?

Bolton (1979) wrote about how dysfunctional employees may impact more functional employees. He said that some people carry an "emotional plague" that undermines the effectiveness of those who are working constructively in the organization. Dysfunctional employees use the drama triangle to process their conflicts or get their needs met by being a victim. It is important to recognize these dysfunctional dynamics in your workplace and refuse to participate. In most organizations, it isn't easy to recognize drama triangle dynamics until you are deep in the middle of them.

The Good Old Boy/Old Girl Drama Triangle

One of the most common ways the drama triangle gets played out in organizations is through the so-called "good old boy/good old girl" networks. These are based on codependent agreements that enable people in the areas where they have dependency. One person rescues another. This person is then obligated to rescue the first person at some point in the future. This contract of mutual rescuing creates ideal dynamics for each person to act out the traumatic elements of their personal psychodrama via the drama triangle.

The way the good old boy/girl network functions is that employee A finds out that he can do something to help out employee B. He hopes that employee B will then be dependent on him to perform this task. Employee B does not like to be this dependent, so he finds some favor he can do for employee A to get him dependent as well. This need/obligate system keeps both persons stuck in a dependent relationship. Both participants keep score to make sure that the tally comes out even. The problem with this system is that both parties end up feeling used by the other person at times.

For example, Sally is usually the first one at work because she gets dropped off by her husband on his way to work. She decides to make the coffee for everyone, even though it is Milly's job to do so. When Milly gets to work and finds that Sally has already made the coffee, she feels conflicted. She likes to make the coffee her way, which is a little stronger than how Sally makes it. She also feels as though she now owes Sally a favor. When Sally asks Milly to cover for her so she can leave work a little early to do some shopping, Milly doesn't want to do this but feels obligated to do so because Sally is making the coffee for her. This inability to be honest causes strained relations between the two coworkers. Then a conflict erupts over who got to the copy machine first. The conflict is not about the copy machine. Unless they can sort out the dynamics of the drama triangle and the need/obligate system, they will not be able to resolve it effectively.

Another common way many employees start the drama triangle is from the victim role. For example, an employee, John, is tardy or absent, but no one says anything so his behavior continues. A female employee complains to their mutual supervisor (triangulation): "I don't see why John is always late and nobody seems to care. Maybe I'll just start coming in late, too." The supervisor (persecutor) decides to come down hard on the tardy employee and issues an ultimatum to John: "If you are late one more time, you will be fired." John (victim) feels angry at his boss and asks one of his colleagues (rescuer) to intervene with his boss. The colleague defends John's behavior with his boss, discovers the name of the woman who complained about John's tardiness, and then confronts her for John (persecutes). The woman feels guilty when she finds out that John was given an ultimatum about his job. She then goes to their supervisor and pleads John's case (rescues): "But he was only late three times and then by just a few minutes." The supervisor (victim), who is tired of hearing about this problem, finally says: "Since you are the one who caused this problem in the first place, maybe I should fire you instead" (persecutes).

This game can go on forever until someone refuses to be a victim to get their needs met and begins asking directly for what he or she needs without any expectation from others. Remember, the best way to break the power of the drama triangle is by making agreements where everybody can get their needs met by asking directly for what they need and by negotiating any conflicts of needs.

The Gossip Mill: A Breeding Ground for Conflict

One of the most destructive forms of communication in organizations is the gossip mill, which typically involves drama-triangle dynamics. It usually involves triangulation. This is a form of splitting that creates divisiveness and a lack of trust in organizations.

It is tempting to engage in splitting in workplace conflicts. People often fear going directly to the people with whom they have conflict because they anticipate repercussions. Splitting transactions sound something like this: "Do you know what she did to me? Well, let me tell you." This indirect expression of anger during a conflict can cause repercussions that escalate into a major drama where you either become the organizational scapegoat or results with your sudden departure from the organization.

The best way to avoid these distorted relationship dynamics is to refuse to triangulate with other people and to resolve your conflicts directly with the people who are involved. If someone comes to you with information about another person, you can do the following:

- Refuse to get in the middle of their conflict. Ask them to deal directly with the other person involved.
- Refuse to hear about conflicts with other people unless they are willing to agree to deal directly with them at the earliest possible time.
- Warn them about how you will share everything you hear with the other person if they fail to follow through with their agreement to speak directly with him or her.
- You may also offer to help mediate the conflict if both people agree.
- Agree to serve as a mediator only if the two people involved ask you directly.

HOW CAN I AVOID DESTRUCTIVE CONFLICTS IN THE WORKPLACE?

The most effective ways to handle conflicts in the workplace are:

1. Teach everyone about the dynamics of the drama triangle.
2. Get a consensual agreement requiring each person to ask directly to get their needs met.
3. Educate the organization about the destructive power of triangulation and splitting.
4. Train everyone in conflict resolution. This training should be experiential and provide opportunity for skill practice.

The Partnership Way works well in the workplace because it provides skills in resolving conflicts of wants and needs, conflicts of values and beliefs, and resolving conflicts at their source. Unless your coworkers are trained in using the Partnership Way, it is best not to attempt to resolve your conflicts with them at their source. Resolving conflicts at their source is not appropriate at a workplace unless you have a supportive company structure and policies. It is best to use the model to identify your sources of the conflict and then work on them by yourself.

HOW DO UNRESOLVED FAMILY-OF-ORIGIN CONFLICTS IMPACT THE WORKPLACE?

Any time you find yourself in situations where you are interacting with three or more people, there is a high probability you may unconsciously act out your unresolved family issues. Why does this happen? The family shapes a person's attitudes, values, beliefs, feelings, and behaviors. When people leave their family of origin, they carry these formative experiences with them. It is natural for humans to recreate their family experience everywhere they go. This is why a boss may resemble your father or mother and the unresolved conflicts you had with them. This is why the things certain coworkers say or do may irritate you. They may be activating post-traumatic triggers related to traumatic family experiences involving a parent or sibling.

Organizations also have family patterns. It is quite common for the founder or president of the company to act out his or her family dynamics in the company. The workplace becomes a stage for reenacting family-of-origin issues, with the employees perceived as family members. An employee of one such large company perceived its dysfunction as the replay of the founder's alcoholic family dynamics. This employee saw how company policies, such as avoiding conflict, keeping secrets, rigidly defining the roles of subordinates, using unpredictable decision-making strategies, and throwing lots of parties where the alcohol flows freely, fit the profile of an alcoholic family.

Family patterns are a major factor in the failure of many small businesses. The dynamics can become so complex and intertwined that they create conflict that adversely affects corporate productivity and decision-making. The family patterns woven into a company structure can dictate the "story line" of the company's progress. The typical pattern of many small companies is a period of initial rapid growth, followed by a stabilizing and leveling off period, and then a decline in productivity that may lead to the company's demise.

Jongeward (1973) stated that a company story line "may depict a comedy, a saga, a tragedy, a farce, or a dull plodding drama going nowhere" (p. 6). She said that the family-patterned story line determines the company's cast of characters, their dialogue, the themes carried out, the dramatic actions taken, and the ultimate fate of the company.

Company policies are one of the most visible places to see family patterns and drama triangle dynamics in action, as the "rules" often resemble the structure from the founder's family of origin. For example, if the founder's family avoided conflict, it is likely that the company will also avoid conflict. In some companies, the founder runs the company like an authoritarian parent whose word is law and decisions are unquestionable. In a company with a noncollaborative leader, the boss is removed from the problems inside the business because employees are afraid to provide the boss with information about changing markets, the company's position in those markets, and other management issues.

HOW CAN I DIAGNOSE THE NATURE OF MY WORKPLACE CONFLICTS?

Employees often view their bosses as the "good parents" they always wanted, hoping the corporation or organization will compensate them for what was lacking in their family of origin. The family patterns of employees and those of the company are often remarkably congruent, providing a stage where everyone can trigger each other's unresolved developmental traumas. People seem to be unconsciously drawn to workplaces with compatible family issues.

Career choices are often made because of unresolved family patterns. Barry sees how they have influenced his career:

> I came from a post-depression family that had little financial stability during my early childhood. I felt a lot of tension in the house over money issues. I eventually saw how my decision to become a university professor was influenced by the need for predictability and financial security. As my awareness grew about the ongoing influence of developmental trauma, I saw how my supervisors and deans exhibited elements of my mother and father. Many of my conflicts with these people were reenactments of unresolved childhood conflicts with my parents.

You may choose a role at work that is different from the one you played in your family of origin; however, it is likely to be a role that was played out by someone else in your family. If you were persecuted by an abusive mother or father, for example, you may assume the persecutor role at work when you are promoted to a supervisory position. The reasons for doing this are always unconscious, but it is usually an attempt to resolve repressed feelings about being victimized. You may use your position at work to discharge repressed feelings of anger and resentment from your family-of-origin experiences. Some people find it safer to act out their repressed feelings in the workplace than at home. If you do find yourself reenacting your family-of-origin conflicts in your workplace, be compassionate toward yourself. Just focus on identifying what things triggered you so that you can identify the reenactment pattern and change it.

If you do have unresolved family-of-origin conflicts, they will surely appear at your workplace. If you can begin to identify the events that trigger your unresolved family-of-origin conflicts and use the tools from the Partnership Way for working through them, work could become an exciting forum for healing family-of-origin issues.

If your organization doesn't provide you with a forum for clearing your family-of-origin issues (and few do), you run the risk of reenacting these issues via workplace conflicts. This vulnerability can affect your job effectiveness. Without an awareness of the triggers that activate your post-traumatic responses, you are unable to prevent the replay of unresolved family issues at work. This can have a significant impact on your career, as it may promote an unstable employment history.

Perhaps the corporation of the future will discover the opportunities inherent in "functional family" policies. The traditional corporate model not only lacks the perspective of the family but often forces employees to sacrifice their family life for the good of the company. Some corporations understand that this policy is destructive in the long run. More employees are now demanding changes in corporate structures that make the workplace more humane and family-friendly.

In order to keep their employees, corporations have begun to provide benefits for employees that demonstrate appreciation. They are also providing more work-site policies and programs, such as flexible work hours, recreation programs, and on-site daycare facilities. These innovations facilitate a family-like atmosphere at work and provide a functional family structure. In this time of unsettled social conditions, rising divorce rates, and single-parent families, the workplace can be a stabilizing force for families.

At the end of this chapter are several exercises to help you identify your workplace conflicts. One instrument helps in the identification of family-of-origin patterns and unresolved childhood conflicts. Another diagnoses the developmental components of your workplace conflicts and helps you use the Partnership Way to resolve these conflicts.

The vision of the corporation of the future as a functional family can become a reality when you learn how to use your corporate or work-family conflicts as a valuable source of evolutionary information. When you do, you will be able to help create a healthy corporate family where you can grow and thrive.

HOW CAN I UTILIZE THE PARTNERSHIP WAY TO BRING ABOUT CHANGE IN MY ORGANIZATION?

At the core of the Partnership Way is the assumption that following the process of an organization will help you identify how and where it is developmentally stalled and design interventions to correct these problems. The various inventories at the end of this chapter provide some tools for assessing your company's development.

Another important assumption of the Partnership Way is that every person, couple, family, or organization is in a process of evolving. It is possible to move this process forward when people understand how it operates and know how to accelerate or redirect the process of evolution. With this information, people can identify the behaviors and beliefs that obstruct development and change them. Healthy organizations periodically review the effectiveness of their structures to determine how well they support their objectives. Individuals who are trained in the Partnership Way are able to facilitate this process.

The human interactions where developmental issues typically appear in an organization are:

1. Communication
2. Roles and functions in groups
3. Group problem-solving and decision-making strategies
4. Group norms and group growth
5. Leadership and authority
6. Intergroup cooperation and competition

Woven through all of these processes, however, is the presence of conflicts and policies for resolving them.

The person who uses the Partnership Way to make organizational changes is known as a *developmental process consultant* (DPC). This approach is an expansion of the process-consultation model long recognized in organizational development circles as an effective tool for changing organizations. The DPC helps members of an organization gain insight into the source of their conflicts and problems. Developmental process consultants teach managers, supervisors, and employees about the developmental principles inherent in their intrapersonal, interpersonal, and intergroup relationships and help them learn to use the Partnership Way for resolving conflicts.

The steps that a DPC might use when consulting with an organization are (Schein, 1969):

1. *Establish contact with the organization.* A member of the organization, usually an executive, seeks your help in addressing a specific problem. The most difficult part of this step is encountering a hierarchical "doctor-patient" orientation that gives you expert status as an outsider. This approach ignores the inherent wisdom of people who work within the organization regarding the causes of the problem and workable solutions for it. During a face-to-face meeting between you and a committee

of organizational members, advise them to consider a different approach. At this meeting, outline your alternative consultation approach and seek acceptance of it. In some instances, you may find a lack of compatibility regarding your approach and their goals. In these cases, you can decline their offer to retain your consulting services.

If you find the organization receptive to your ideas, then it is important to define your relationship via a formal contract stating how you will be paid, the exact nature of services you will provide, the time frame for providing services, and the outcome goals for the contract. It is very important to make the outcome goals as explicit as possible.

2. *Observe the organization's developmental process during key meetings.* It is best to attend key meetings to learn more about the organization and its processes. Here you can observe how the organization functions and what developmental components should be targeted for further study. Observe top-level meetings first, as these meetings reveal most about how the organization functions. Provide a context for your presence in these meetings to help people know you and you to know them. You may also choose to first interview some key people, not to gather data, but to help them know you better. Once they know and trust you, they are more likely to cooperate when you recommend interventions.

By attending key meetings, you can identify developmental processes for later follow-up. For example, we participated in a strategic planning process for a small company that was part of a large corporation. One activity asked employees to list their personal goals for the next year. These personal goals would be compared with the branch company's goals and with the goals of the overall corporation. One employee after another presented their personal goals written on a large piece of newsprint. It was interesting to discover that each employee actually presented not personal but organizational goals (e.g., "I am going to increase my attendance at supervisory meetings," or "I am going to work late to keep the paperwork from piling up"). Their goals did not focus on an outcome for themselves (e.g., "I am going to work for a promotion by the end of this year," or "I am going to join the company bowling team and spend at least one evening a week having fun").

We saw a "reversal" present in this company where employees felt that their primary task was supporting the company rather than supporting themselves inside the company. Through interviews and questionnaires, we confirmed that many employees came from families that had reversal patterns. These employees felt that they had parented their parents more than their parents had taken care of them. They were unaware that they brought this pattern to work with them. When we disclosed this in our reports from the data-gathering phase of our consultation, the management decided to implement policies that encouraged a balance between the welfare of the company and the needs of the employees.

3. *Conduct collaborative data-gathering activities.* Unlike other consultation models, that used by the DPC does not rely on the DPC's expertise to diagnose the organization's problem. Instead, the DPC suggests activities designed to actively involve everyone in the organization in discovering the nature of its problems. There are basically three kinds of data-gathering strategies: observation, interviews, and questionnaires. It is good to use a combination of the three. Having everyone fill out questionnaires will help reveal the problems and their developmentally related components that block the fulfillment of organizational objectives. There are two self-inventories at the end of this chapter that can be used in data-gathering activities.

In addition, the DPC should conduct structured interviews with key people who represent a cross-section of the organizational structure. Even in situations where the organizational objectives and goals have been jointly determined, it is best to have everyone identify the developmental processes that are needed to achieve corporate goals and objectives. These interviews should also identify what might prevent the organization from reaching its goals and objectives.

4. *Analyze the results of the data gathering and report back to the organization.* Once you have analyzed the results of your data-gathering activities, report your findings back to the organization. This prepares it for any interventions you might advise. All organizational members should have access to a written report of your findings. This step sets the stage for future developmental interventions. Your report should provide information about the six main processes of organizations identified earlier.

5. *Interventions.* There are three main ways to intervene as a developmental process consultant:

a. Observe key meetings and provide process feedback that can help people change dysfunctional behaviors and processes.

b. Train employees in key skills that can change the developmental patterns of the organization (i.e., conflict resolution training, counseling, or coaching individuals or groups). These interventions should be part of the contract you have with the organization.

c. Give process feedback to the groups you observe by allowing time for process analysis at the end of the meeting. You can focus this analysis through key questions. For example, if you observe some nonverbal reactions to a decision made during a meeting, you might ask: "How did all of you feel about how the decision was made about topic X? Did you feel that you had enough input into the decision in order to carry it out effectively?"

Giving process feedback to individuals or groups often leads to coaching or counseling sessions with the people involved. When given feedback about the ways their behavior is affecting others, people ask, "What can I do to change this behavior?" As a DPC, you can help key people identify how their family-of-origin patterns and unmet developmental needs may be reenacting and then help them find ways to address them more effectively.

Training should be built around the results of your data-gathering activities. Structure them around specific issues or problems, such as drama triangle dynamics, communication skills, and conflict resolution. Perhaps you offer basic training courses for everyone and more advanced methods for the key executives.

6. *Evaluation of results.* The goal of the developmental process consultant is to improve the effectiveness and functionality of the organization. The most important outcome as a DPC is to help people in the organization resolve their conflicts more effectively and to separate their personal history from events happening in the workplace. You may want to teach the members of the organization skills that enable them to diagnose and resolve conflicts at any level within the system: individual, couple, family, and group. One of the best indicators of this outcome is that the company begins allocating time to and creating structures for reviewing and analyzing itself.

SELF-INVENTORY: FAMILY PATTERNS IN THE WORKPLACE

Complete this self-inventory by placing a number in the blank preceding each statement to indicate how true it is for you.

1 = Almost Never   2 = Occasionally   3 = Usually   4 = Almost Always

_____ 1. My feelings about my boss remind me of those I had with a parent when I was growing up.
_____ 2. My boss says or does things that irritate me and reminds me of ways that my parents treated me.
_____ 3. My boss disapproves of things I say or do just the way my parents did.
_____ 4. I criticize myself and others the way I was criticized as a child.
_____ 5. Even though I don't want to, I find myself saying and doing things that hurt my coworkers the same way people hurt me while I was growing up.
_____ 6. When I get upset at myself at work, I say some of the same critical things to myself that my parents or others said to me when I was a child.
_____ 7. The way my boss relates to me reminds me of the way my parents related to me when I was a child.
_____ 8. I find myself acting weak and helpless so others at work will feel sorry for me or help me out.
_____ 9. I can see similarities between the way I relate to my colleagues and the way I related to my siblings.
_____ 10. I tend to feel uneasy when everything seems to be going well at work.
_____ 11. When I have conflicts with others at work, I tend to focus on what they did to cause the conflict.
_____ 12. I feel underpaid and unappreciated at work.
_____ 13. I feel so stressed by my job that I have no energy for play or exercise.
_____ 14. I am afraid to appear too successful at work.
_____ 15. I avoid taking risks at work and prefer to do what others expect of me.
_____ 16. I sacrifice myself and/or my family life for the sake of the company.
_____ 17. When asked, I have trouble thinking about or listing positive traits about my work responsibilities.
_____ 18. I cannot express my feelings the way I would like while at work.
_____ 19. I encounter people at work who tend to treat me like my parents treated me.
_____ 20. I feel controlled by the expectations of people at work.
_____ **Total Score** (Add the numbers in the column to get your total score.)

Scoring and Interpretation

Use the following guidelines to help you interpret the possible meaning of your score.

20–40　A few family patterns are likely sources of your present work conflicts.
41–60　Many family patterns are the likely sources of your present work conflicts.
61–80　Almost all of your present work conflicts have their source in unprocessed family patterns.

Review each item where you answered 3 = Usually or 4 = Almost Always. These items can offer clues to your family patterns present in any of your current work conflicts. For example, if you answered almost always to "I feel that I give more to my work than I receive back," explore the possibility that you were "parentized" in your family of origin and required to take care of others more than yourself. This might create work situations where you feel angry, unappreciated, and resentful. If this is true, it would be important to begin redirecting your anger toward family-of-origin members who expected you to deny your needs. Then learn effective ways to get your needs met in your current work relationships.

SELF-INVENTORY: THE OPENNESS TO CHANGE INVENTORY

Place a check in the column that best represents your experiences of living within your organizational culture.

Perception	Never	Sometimes	Usually	Always
1. The salary/wages I receive are fair for the work I provide.				
2. The benefits I receive meet my health care and other important needs.				
3. I trust that those who supervise me have my best interests at heart.				
4. My superiors listen to me and respect me as a person.				
5. When I have a problem or need, I know my superiors will respond seriously and effectively to my request for assistance.				
6. I have sufficient time to develop relationships with my coworkers.				
7. My superiors encourage me to contribute any new ideas I might have.				
8. There are few rules to restrict my freedom in this organization.				
9. I am consulted on decisions that directly affect me.				
10. Information and important decisions are shared in face-to-face meetings where I feel free to express my opinions and feelings.				
11. Important information and decisions are communicated in memos, policy letters, telephone calls, taxes, or e-mail.				
12. When I want an answer to something, there are many people with whom I have to check.				
13. I am encouraged to wear as many "hats" as the situation calls for.				
14. I am free to change what I am doing in response to my needs or the needs of my customers, clients, and coworkers.				
15. If I perform above my expected level, I will be praised by my superiors.				
16. Managers, super-visors, and employees work together toward common goals and objectives.				
17. I have the power to make the decisions that affect me most directly.				
18. My superiors support and/or reward my efforts toward personal growth and mastery.				
19. The approved procedures and schedules are loosely followed in this organization.				
20. The goals and purposes of this organization are determined through input from all those involved in the organization.				
21. When I have a conflict with a supervisor or administrator, I anticipate an equitable resolution.				
22. The opportunity exists in this organization for people to take cooperative and collective action to reach their goals and objectives.				
23. The basic attitude of everyone is to look out for themselves; looking out for each other is actively discouraged.				
24. A top priority of this organization is the personal growth and development of each employee.				

Scoring and Interpretation

This inventory yields four sub-scores and a total organizational score. Use the rating scale to obtain each sub-score, then refer to the interpretation of each sub-score and the total organizational score.

Rating Scale: Never = 4, Sometimes = 3, Usually = 2, Always = 1.

_____ Codependent Elements (Items 1 through 6)
_____ Counter-Dependent Elements (Items 7 through 12)
_____ Independent Elements (Items 13 through 18)
_____ Interdependent Elements (Items 19 through 24)
_____ **Total Organizational Score**

Interpretation of Sub-Scores

21–24	Most major developmental needs are being met in this organization.
15–21	A few major developmental gaps may be present in the structure of the organization.
11–15	Clear evidence of the presence of major developmental gaps in this part of the organization
6–10	Major reorganization of some of the basic structures of the organization may be necessary.

Interpretation of Total Organizational Score

79–96	Most major developmental needs are being met in this organization.
60–78	A few major developmental gaps may be present in this organization. (Check the lowest of the four sub-scores to locate the gaps.)
42–59	Clear evidence of the presence of major developmental gaps in this organization. (Check the lowest of the four sub-scores to locate the gaps.)
24–41	Major reorganization of some of the basic structures and processes of this organization may be necessary.

Chapter 16

~

How Can I Apply the Partnership Way to the Legal System?

When people fail to learn how to resolve conflicts in a partnership manner in their individual, couple, family, and workplace relationships, they often resort to the judicial system as a venue for resolving their intractable conflicts. Lacking strong skills in negotiation and cooperation, they may feel the need for support from legal professionals when they get into an intractable conflict.

A number of alternative programs to assist people in resolving intractable conflicts via the legal system now exist. The best of them encourage people to use partnership approaches to resolve their conflicts. The goal of these approaches is to help people involved in litigation develop skills that maintain an internal sense of object constancy. Such skills help people hold themselves as objects of worth even when feeling rejected or unworthy during conflicts.

WHAT IS ALTERNATIVE DISPUTE RESOLUTION (ADR)?

Many people with intractable conflicts involving litigation, such as divorce and personal or property damage, are now turning to alternative dispute resolution (ADR). ADR uses an outside party to help resolve intractable conflicts. Most people who use ADR could also benefit from working on the psychological aspects of the conflict (as described in Chapter 7) prior to working toward a settlement. While this may not resolve the intractable conflict, it will likely reduce any emotional charges related to the conflict. People can then enter into the legal process from a more stable psychological state, which could facilitate a quicker resolution.

Until recently, litigation and conflict resolution were seen as very different and very separate specialties. Litigation, the most common form of conflict resolution, uses either a judge or jury to resolve civil and criminal conflicts. In 1992, the Colorado Supreme Court and the Colorado Legislature adopted separate measures that brought litigation together with other forms of conflict resolution into the "Alternative Dispute Resolution Continuum" that includes negotiation, mediation, settlement conferences, early neutral evaluation, mini-trial, summary jury trial, med-arb, arbitration, and litigation. Many other states have adopted similar measures.

The Colorado Supreme Court modified its rules of conduct for attorneys to read: "In a matter involving or expected to involve litigation, a lawyer should advise the client of alternative forms of dispute resolution which might reasonably be pursued to attempt to resolve the legal dispute or to reach the legal objective sought" (Rovina, 1992). In addition, the legislature gave all courts of record the authority to refer cases that come before them to any ancillary form of ADR.

The United States legal system was designed as an alternative to the violent, revengeful forms of dispute resolution brought to this country by early European settlers. The "rule of law" has become part of our democratic foundation. In recent years, however, access to the legal system has become more time-consuming, expensive, and stressful, requiring additional methods of dispute resolution. Attorneys now must know how to help their clients determine which of these methods will best serve their needs.

The purpose of this continuum of conflict resolution options is to prevent further escalation of the conflict. For example, if everyone could effectively negotiate to get their needs met in conflict situations, it would significantly reduce the number of disputes and subsequently the number of legal cases. The creation of this continuum of options helps preserve the court system as a last resort option to be used only in civil disputes after all the other available methods fail. Some judges are reluctant to try civil cases that have not attempted the spectrum of alternative dispute resolution options.

The continuum in Figure 16.1, originally published by the Colorado Bar Association (1992), shows the main forms of alternative dispute resolution, followed by a description of each kind of alternative dispute resolution shown in the continuum. As a result of the crowded court system and the increased costs of litigation, many more people are turning to alternative dispute resolution. Negotiation and mediation are becoming the most popular forms of ADR.

Negotiation

Negotiation is the process most frequently used to resolve interpersonal conflicts. It involves direct interaction between the involved parties with no outside input.

Simple	Negotiation
	Mediation
	Settlement Conference
	Early Neutral Evaluation
	Mini-Trial
	Summary Jury Trial
	Med-Arb
	Arbitration
Complex	Litigation

Figure 16.1
The Alternative Dispute Resolution Continuum

Partnership Worksheet #2: An Eight-Step Method for Resolving Conflicts of Wants and Needs (found in Chapter 5) is helpful for people who want to use negotiation skills to find a win-win resolution to their conflict.

When negotiation is used as a form of alternative dispute resolution, many conflicts are resolved before they reach the litigation stage. The parties agree to talk directly with each other about their conflict and seek a mutually acceptable resolution. The costs of litigation plus the fear of the actual court proceedings often motivate people to settle their conflict out of court. In some cases, the parties involved may each employ an attorney to negotiate for them.

Negotiating a settlement gives people the most control over the outcome, as there is a better chance of finding a win-win resolution to the conflict. It is based on the voluntary disclosure of information and the good faith participation of those involved in the conflict. Negotiation has a higher probability of reaching a win-win resolution of a conflict than litigation, which usually results in a win-lose resolution. Whenever possible, negotiation should be tried before deciding to use other forms of resolution.

Mediation

Mediation is used when the parties' emotional state or rigid positions make negotiation impossible, but where the parties involved still want to retain their decision-making authority. Mediation uses a neutral third party, or mediator, to facilitate the negotiation of a conflict.

While it is private and confidential, the parties involved can also hire attorneys to represent them, to advise them on their rights during the mediation, and to inform them of the risks related to escalation of the conflict to litigation. Mediation is efficient and cost effective and increases the likelihood of reaching a win-win resolution of the conflict. The mediator's job is to help the parties involved reach a win-win resolution and to record the terms of their agreement once it is reached.

Settlement Conference

This is a legal action held before a judge who would not later be eligible to preside at a trial, should the conflict enter litigation. This form of alternative dispute resolution is recommended in cases where the disputants have strongly held positions about the outcome of the case. The main difference between mediation and settlement conferences is basically one of style. In a mediation session, the mediator uses interest- or need-based negotiating techniques; in settlement conferences, the judge uses more directive and reality-based techniques.

Settlement conferences help disputants analyze the issues involved in their case, review the facts, and evaluate their positions. It also allows them to review their case in a more informal and less costly setting than either a mini-trial or a full jury trial to determine the strength of their respective cases. Settlement conferences help narrow the issues, forcing both sides to reveal their trial strategies prior to litigation. This allows the other side time to prepare a counter-argument, if necessary. Settlement conferences can also encourage disputants to use mediation to resolve their conflict, rather than continuing to litigate it.

Early Neutral Evaluation

Early neutral evaluation (ENE) is a nonbinding, confidential review of the dispute by a neutral evaluator. The evaluator is chosen by the parties or appointed by the court to assist in settling the dispute. Both parties make short, informal case presentations and then the evaluator tries to streamline and simplify the case. After the presentation of the case, the evaluator prepares a written evaluation, which may be the equivalent to a judgment or may identify what is needed in order to render a judgment.

A neutral evaluator may also conduct settlement negotiations with the disputants before submitting a written report to the court. This gives them a chance to settle the dispute before going to trial. The evaluator may also conduct another round of settlement negotiations after submitting the report if there still seems to be a chance to mutually resolve the conflict.

Mini-Trial

The mini-trial uses elements of negotiation, mediation, and adjudication to try to reach a settlement of the case. In a mini-trial, the theories, strengths, and weaknesses of each side of the conflict are discussed in a nonbinding way before a three-person panel consisting of a neutral person and a person from each side who has the authority to settle the case. The neutral member of the panel then tries to facilitate settlement negotiations between the two representatives.

This is typically done in large and complex cases that would take considerable time to litigate. Cases that could take months to litigate can be presented in a few days. This process is far less expensive than litigation and still maintains the option for returning to the negotiation process to resolve the conflict.

Summary Jury Trial

This involves summary presentations of the case before a six-person jury impaneled to make a judgment on the case. The judgment may or may not be binding. This option is elected at the request of one or both disputants, who then select the six jurors from a panel of ten to twelve people. In order to use this method, the case must be ready for trial. Case presentations are limited to one hour, including rebuttal, although the time period can be extended if the case is complex.

The jurors are not informed of the advisory nature of their verdict until after it has been rendered. Then they are told it will be used to facilitate a settlement. This process can provide a low-risk method of getting feedback on the case to use in negotiating a settlement of the dispute and can drastically cut court time. It also provides feedback about how the case might be received by a jury and may be a catalyst for settlement of the dispute.

Med-Arb

This process involves a combination of mediation and arbitration. The disputants select a neutral third party to serve as both the mediator and the arbitrator in the conflict. This allows the parties to have the benefit of the techniques of assisted negotiations and discussion coupled with someone who will also make a binding decision. The risk in using this procedure is that the parties involved may be less candid, knowing that the mediator is also going to make a binding decision.

Another important difference is that arbitration requires that facts have to be proven, while in mediation information that both parties agree upon can be accepted as fact. Again, the goal of this procedure is to bring both parties to a win-win decision. This process can save time and money, as the same person can both mediate and arbitrate. Med-Arb should be used when a quick settlement or decision is needed.

Arbitration

This process involves the selection of one or more neutral, expert, and impartial third parties to hear the evidence and testimony and make a binding or nonbinding decision. Sometimes arbitration clauses are built into divorce or child-custody agreements, stating that if the parties cannot agree on some matter they will seek mediation and if that fails to produce an agreement, they agree to use an arbitrator to settle the dispute.

Although arbitration is typically less formal than court proceedings, it is adversarial and follows the same rules as a litigated court case. The parties can also agree in advance that the decision be nonbinding. If the decision is binding, it cannot be appealed. Limited court review is permitted after litigation only for special circumstances set forth by law.

Arbitration is private, relatively inexpensive, and speedy. It does have disadvantages, however: Only limited court review is permitted, the decision cannot be appealed (if arbitration is binding), punitive damages cannot be assessed, and, with the exception of labor arbitration, decisions have little or no precedential value.

As you can see from this list, there are many ways to resolve a conflict without using litigation. The courts are actually ordering that these methods be explored before using litigation, primarily because they are less costly to the parties involved and keep the court docket more available to try cases where these methods are not appropriate, such as those involving criminal offenses.

Litigation

This step uses a judge and/or jury to hear the case and to make a binding decision based on law and facts that is subject to appeal. Disputants may testify during the proceedings and participate in case presentations.

This option is chosen when disputants desire a public forum, when legal precedents related to their case are important, and when a final decision on the case is needed. The proceedings are the most adversarial of all the legal options and, therefore, have the highest direct and indirect costs. They generate the most publicity and the highest financial fees.

HOW IS NEGOTIATION USED IN ALTERNATIVE DISPUTE RESOLUTION?

Negotiation is often used in labor disputes to reach collective bargaining agreements. Negotiation is also used extensively to get the disputants to talk about the issues involved and to reach an agreement before seeking litigation. The negotiation process has all the benefits of mediation without the added expense of using a neutral third party. Negotiation is most effective when the parties involved can clearly identify their needs and are able to identify a solution that meets everyone's needs. When this is not possible, it is usually because of the presence of unresolved emotional issues from the past or a rigid adversarial attitude. There are a number of well-known approaches to negotiation, two of which are summarized below.

Fisher and Ury and the Harvard Negotiation Project

Fisher and Ury's (1981) best-selling book, *Getting to Yes*, suggested four steps for successful negotiations. The first is to separate the people from the problem. With group negotiations, such as labor-management disputes, they believe it is important to remember that both sides have strong emotions, deeply held values, different backgrounds, and disparate points of view. Some level of trust, understanding, respect, and maybe even friendship must be developed before these kinds of disputes can be successfully negotiated.

Their second step is to focus on common interests and not on positions. Any successful negotiation depends on reconciling conflicting needs, wants, or interests, but not positions. People can easily get locked into a position that is based more on a fear of losing than it is on their needs, wants, or interests.

The third step involves creating options for mutual gain. Fisher and Ury concluded that the most successful attorneys help generate solutions that have a high probability of meeting the needs of all parties involved, not just solutions that would benefit their own clients. The more that all parties seek solutions containing mutual gain, the easier the negotiation process becomes.

Fisher and Ury's final step is the use of objective criteria to determine a final solution. This approach prevents "positional" bargaining. Using objective criteria requires all parties to identify and apply fair standards, as determined by objective evidence. For example, in negotiating a divorce settlement, the parties might agree to use standard methods such as appraisals or blue-book figures for determining the value of property.

Fisher and Ury's bottom-line criteria asked, "Is this settlement satisfactory to all parties involved?" If one party feels victimized by the agreement, then there will likely be additional problems that emerge later, including attempts to sabotage the agreement.

Here is a summary of the general guidelines Fisher and Ury used:

- Define the conflict in terms of your needs or your beliefs, instead of trying to build an "objective case."
- Express your feelings in the context of your needs. Remember the normal functions of feelings, such as anger. Anger indicates you need something that you don't currently have.
- Offer solutions that would meet your needs. Then ask the other person if your solution meets his or her needs. State clearly what you want or need from the other person to resolve the conflict.
- Insist on fair and objective criteria for deciding on a solution. It must meet both your needs. Avoid win-lose solutions. Think about what you want vs. what you need. Consider solutions carefully to see if they meet your needs before dismissing them.
- Be sure to identify and state areas of agreement and then define any areas of disagreement about what must still be negotiated.
- Be easy on the person and hard on the conflict. Insist on finding a solution to which you both can agree. If possible, frame the conflict as being something outside of your relationship, as though you are observing it.
- Ask yourself if you fear "losing face" or feeling ashamed if you compromise on some of your points.
- Respond to objections with "and" rather than "but."
- Choose long-range solutions that support having an ongoing relationship.
- If possible, choose solutions that resolve the conflict rather than just managing it.
- Review your solution or agreement to make sure each person understands the terms.

The Highlander Center: Teaching Negotiation Skills

One of the most interesting and well-known places that teaches negotiation skills to grassroots groups is the Highlander Research and Education Center in New Market, Tennessee. This center has a unique approach to negotiation and conflict resolution. It does not offer formal training in anything, but provides a place where people can come to "live" their problems and be empowered to find their own solutions.

Located in one of the poorest regions of Appalachia, the center was started in 1932 by Myles Horton as the Highlander Folk School. During its history, staff members of the center have consulted with grassroots community groups, labor unions, civil rights leaders, educators and social activists. They discovered that bringing groups of people together to learn from each other helped them realize that they are not alone. Through their group experience, they become empowered, then take their skills back to their community or organization to create change.

Martin Luther King, Jr., and other members of the Southern Christian Leadership Conference met frequently at the Highlander Center to develop their civil-disobedience agenda, which eventually gave birth to the modern civil rights movement. The center's mission statement reflects a similar perspective: "Because we function in a racist society, as well as one suffering from discrimination based on gender, class, sexual preference, age and physical disabilities, we actively promote equity in our society." In 1982, the center was nominated for the Nobel Peace Prize for its historical role on behalf of human rights.

When critical conditions for negotiation, such as good faith participation and voluntary disclosure of information, cannot be met, the resolution of differences moves to mediation, a more complex form of ADR. At the end of this chapter is a skill-building exercise designed to help sharpen negotiation skills.

HOW IS MEDIATION USED AS A PART OF ALTERNATIVE DISPUTE RESOLUTION?

Mediation is a process that uses a neutral and impartial third party (the mediator) to settle a conflict. The mediator has no decision-making authority and can give legal information but not advice. Mediation is recommended when the situation involves intense feelings on the part of one or both parties, when both parties want to preserve their ongoing relationship, or when they want to terminate an existing relationship in the least adversarial way. It is an efficient and cost-effective method for resolving either simple or complex cases and increases both the likelihood and quality of a settlement.

A mediator may ask the disputants to generate a list of possible solutions and then helps them evaluate each until they can agree on one. Attorneys may attend the mediation sessions with their clients and can advise them on legal matters related to the possible solution they generate, but cannot make any decision for their clients. Everything that is discussed in the mediation session is held confidential and cannot be used in court, even if the mediation process fails.

Couples who seek a divorce in many states are now required to seek mediation first. It is also being used more widely to settle neighborhood disputes and, as discussed in Chapter 15, it is used in schools to settle conflicts by trained peer mediators.

Mediation and negotiation work best when people are not able to look for the source of their conflict or to resolve it at the source. The disputants may, in fact, desire to continue the conflict rather than resolve it. The goal of the mediator is to discover a force that is greater than the client's refusal to resolve the conflict.

The continuum of ADR gives individuals a series of decision points where the persons on each side of the conflict can feel the risks and emotional impacts of their refusal to settle. Each step toward litigation increases disputants' level of risk, the emotional impact, and the costs. This step-by-step progression provides a series of opportunities to choose between settlement or increasing the stakes. Each step toward litigation should increase the pressure on both parties to settle. This increasing pressure helps to avoid long, drawn-out law suits that cause not only stress on the parties involved but also clutter the legal system.

Below is a list of important guidelines to remember when doing third-party mediation.

- Be objective and neutral. You have to represent both sides equally and fairly, even if you favor one over the other.
- Be supportive of both parties in finding a win-win resolution to their conflict.
- Discourage disputants from judgments about who is right or wrong. Don't ask questions like, "Why did you do that?" Instead, ask, "What happened?"
- Create a nonthreatening environment where people feel safe to open up. Get them to agree to resolve their conflict in a nonviolent, win-win way.
- Interfere as little as possible. Encourage them to talk directly to each other, not to you.
- If you are talking to only one of the parties involved, be sure not to take sides. Do not agree with their position, just communicate understanding of their position. "I understand that you are upset with your neighbor over this."

Steps in the Mediation Process

There are well-established steps to follow in conducting a mediation session.

Step 1: Set the stage for mediation. Explain why you are there, what your expectations are, and what agreements are possible.

   a. Clarify your role and explain the ground rules, including the need for a win-win outcome.

   b. Be clear that you will remain neutral and that you are not going to resolve the conflict for them.

   c. Explain that your role is to help them come to their own win-win resolution.

   d. Reflect back to them the content and feelings you hear to help build empathy and understanding.

Step 2: Identify the conflict. It is important to get agreement from the parties involved on the exact nature of the conflict.

   a. Have each person tell their perspective of the conflict.
   b. As they do this, reflect back the important issues and feelings you hear from each person.
   c. Periodically summarize what you think are the main points each side is making.
   d. Make sure each person understands how the other person sees the problem.

Step 3: Decide how to resolve the conflict. It is useful to ask each person how they would like to see this conflict resolved. This gives you an idea of how close or far apart they are.

   a. Solicit possible solutions from each person about how to resolve the conflict.
   b. Support ideas that move the disputants toward resolution.
   c. If they get stuck, ask them to repeat what they think they heard the other person say. Help clarify their understanding.

Step 4: Identify areas of movement and agreement. After some discussion has taken place, propose a resolution.

   a. Ask them if they are ready to develop an agreement that resolves the conflict.
   b. Summarize the points of agreement, no matter how small, such as pointing out that they both hurt or that they both want the conflict to be resolved.
   c. Help both sides identify any remaining issues that need to be negotiated.

Step 5: Negotiate the agreement and make a contract to carry it out. If you see they are close to an agreement, you may want to suggest one that grows out of what you have heard them say. Once a resolution has been agreed to by the parties involved, you will need to encourage them to make a contract to carry out the agreement.

   a. Ask disputants to offer suggestions on how they would like the conflict resolved.
   b. Only offer your ideas if asked or if you perceive that they are stuck, then be tentative with your suggestions.
   c. Encourage them to trade points on each side: "If Jack were willing to do _____, what would you be willing to do?"
   d. Make sure each issue is discussed and agreed upon by the disputants.
   e. Summarize the agreement. Ask each person to commit to making it work.
   f. Write up the agreement and have each person sign it. Make a copy of the agreement for each person.

Step 6: Close the mediation session. Discuss the future and test how solid the agreement feels to everyone.

   a. Congratulate both parties for being willing to resolve their conflict directly with each other.
   b. Ask them how they feel about your role as mediator and the agreement they reached. This will test the sincerity of the disputants in keeping it.
   c. Talk about the future. Ask them what is going to be different between them now that they have resolved their conflict.

Neighborhood Justice Centers: Mediation of Neighborhood Disputes

One of the most common places where mediation is used to help citizens peacefully resolve conflict is through neighborhood justice centers. They provide free mediation services for neighborhood conflicts that need quick action. These centers not only keep neighborhood disputes from overloading court dockets but bring the conflicts to a timely conclusion before they can escalate into a larger conflict. Usually run out of the district attorney's office, neighborhood justice centers are staffed by trained mediators who volunteer their time or are paid a small stipend for their services. They mediate cases referred to them by the courts, the police and sheriff's departments, community agencies, schools, or walk-in clients who file a complaint and request mediation.

For example, two neighbors were involved in repeated shouting matches with each other because of barking dogs. A woman had accused the man who owned the dogs of purposely keeping her awake at night, as well as disturbing her daytime hours when she was in her yard. The two agreed to mediate their dispute. At the end of their mediation session, they agreed that the man could keep the dogs outside but would put them inside if he was gone during the day. He also agreed to bring them in the house at night. The parties agreed to try this arrangement and if it wasn't working to either person's satisfaction they would get back together for further mediation before filing a complaint.

Another example involved a tenant who withheld a portion of his rent payment to his landlord because he claimed that a number of needed and promised improvements had not been completed by the landlord. After a mediation session, the disputants reviewed the list of complaints and agreed to prioritize them. The landlord would begin with the one needing immediate attention. The mediator allowed both parties to explain their problems as a tenant and as a landlord. They reached an agreement stating that the landlord would fix the high-priority items by a certain date. When this work was completed, the tenant would pay the full amount of his rent.

An Interview With a Professional Mediator

The following is an interview with Philip Pierce, a professionally trained mediator, who works mostly with divorce mediation and neighborhood dispute resolution in Colorado Springs, Colorado.

Q: *What makes mediation work?*

A: I think the premise of dispute resolution is that conflict is a neutral and natural part of life. When people are in conflict, unfortunately, they don't see this. This is the unique perspective that a mediator can bring to their conflict situation. The perspective of the mediator has the potential for creating a better atmosphere for problem solving. I really try to facilitate problem solving between people who are putting up various kinds of walls between them and refusing to talk to each other in ways that might produce a solution. I try to show them the common ground that they're both standing on. Often, they just don't realize it because they're too emotionally involved in the situation. I first try to help them find common ground and then help them construct a solution to the problem that comes from that common ground."

Q: *What are some of the areas where you use mediation?*
A: Besides divorce mediation, I also mediate all kinds of disputes at the Neighborhood Justice Center. For example, two students get into a fight at the bus stop while waiting for the school bus to come. The school bus shows up just as one student kicks a second in the chest. The second student falls down, the bus driver comes out and breaks it up. The second student says, "I can't breathe," so the bus driver calls the office, the office calls 911, and they take the student in an ambulance to the emergency room to be checked.

When these students are referred to us, they say, "We're not going to fight anymore, so what's the big deal?" Unfortunately, the injured student's parents now have a bill for $1,100 from the emergency room. They have had to use promissory notes to cover these expenses and feel very upset. This is a mediation situation that requires the ending agreement be very specific regarding who is going to do what and by when it will be done.

Specific agreements are also very important in divorce mediation, particularly if children are involved. We use the term "blowing on the house of cards" as a measure of the strength of the settlement. With really strong settlements, it is possible to "blow hard on them" and they remain standing. About 99.9% of these kinds of settlement agreements do not resurface. The mediator's focus on the execution of the conditions of the final agreement is crucial in creating strong agreements. If, for example, a final agreement includes a promissory note, there may be a small-claims-court issue involved that needs follow-up attention. A lack of follow-through on this detail could create another legal offshoot that perpetuates the conflict.

Another thing I'm interested in doing is called offender/victim mediation, which creates a forum for the offender and the victim to talk to each other. This new form of mediation is important to help heal the issues that often remain after the court has rendered a verdict. Restitution can be part of this form of mediation as well.

Q: *I understand that mediation is confidential. How does that work?*
A: Because mediation is an agreement between the parties and the mediator, there can be no recording equipment present. People have this obsession about recording each other. I've had people say, "I brought my tape recorder here to make sure they tell the truth." Frequently, the parties involved in the mediation have been video- and audiotaping each other in an attempt to prove guilt and innocence. One of the elements of confidentiality to which I personally adhere is to destroy all of the notes and records that I take during mediation. At the beginning of the mediation session, I pledge to destroy everything at the conclusion.

Mediators are required to maintain confidentiality except under certain conditions. If we believe one party poses a significant danger to the other or if children are in need of protection, we are required to report this, as are other human service professionals such as teachers and physicians. If I unsuccessfully mediate a conflict and it goes to litigation, I can't be subpoenaed to testify. Because the legal system wants to promote settlements, anything that is said during a mediation session becomes privileged communication. Like therapists, I hold therapist-client privilege of confidentiality.

One interesting thing about mediation settlements is that they prevent the creation of records for the disputants. Negotiating positions are protected and can't be introduced in a jury trial. The agreement itself states what is confidential and cannot be revealed. Regardless of the letter of the law, a contract can prevent the facts from being revealed. For example, if someone originally attempted to mediate settlement of a case for $25,000 but then asked for $100,000 in a jury trial, I couldn't reveal this to a jury.

Most cases I see at the Neighborhood Justice Center end with the legal charges being dropped. This is written into the final settlement. Both parties also sign a request for dismissal of charges. This is all forwarded to the judge and the prosecutor, who always cooperate. The bottom line of the settlement is that charges are dismissed as long as these promises are substantially performed as per the contract. It is not possible to completely drop the charges unless the terms of the contract are completed. The agreement has to be approved by the prosecutor and the judge.

It's important to emphasize the need for clear mediation settlements. A skilled mediator must look for any area of the agreement that might fail and then inform the parties of this possibility. One important area I monitor is the level of feelings remaining between the disputants at the conclusion of the agreement. If one person still displays escalated feelings, I might say, "Now that you have come to this agreement, can you let go of these feelings? If you can't, say so now and let's modify our settlement agreement." I work to get a commitment that addresses the level of feelings. I have also developed a knack for identifying an ineffective settlement.

WHAT ARE RELEVANT AND CRITICAL PROFESSIONAL ISSUES FOR THE FIELD OF MEDIATION?

One of the greatest professional risks for attorneys, mediators, arbitrators, and judges is avoiding getting caught up in countertransference while defending a client or prosecuting the opposition. Most individuals involved in the legal profession are unaware of the influence of their own unresolved conflicts or residue of developmental trauma and the danger they pose. These professionals may inadvertently become a part of the problem rather than being part of the solution.

Because of the level of high professional skill that is needed, many states now certify and license mediators. It is important to check with your state regulatory agencies to determine what training or licenses are required to be a mediator. Mediators are generally people with counseling, social work, or psychology backgrounds with special training in the legal aspects of mediation. Many mediators are also attorneys who left the legal field because of their frustration with its adversarial nature and subsequently sought special training in alternative dispute resolution techniques.

Mediators need to design a mediation session so that an agreement can be finalized at the meeting. This means it may be necessary to have attorneys present or to structure the agreement using draft language. Another option is to schedule a second meeting to finalize the agreement. Most mediators prefer the first option, as the contestants may decide to escalate during the interim period and force a second round of mediation. At the end of this chapter are exercises designed for help in practicing mediation skills.

HOW IS LITIGATION USED TO STOP RACIAL AND ETHNIC CONFLICTS?

Litigation is the last and most extreme method our legal system offers to resolve conflict in a civilized fashion. When either disputant prefers the win-lose option of litigation, the remaining option is a judge and/or jury trial that involves witnesses and testifying.

Maintaining the rule of law requires the presence of a strong system of litigation for those who refuse to resolve their conflicts directly. Litigation may be employed to stop the use of force or intimidation to discriminate against certain minority groups. The history of this country is full of examples of hate groups that tried to force their agendas on racial, ethnic, and cultural minorities.

The civil rights movement is one example of how the rule of law has been used to protect certain groups from hate crimes. Federal civil rights legislation was enacted to protect the rights of minority groups from legal discrimination and attempts to invalidate the basic rights guaranteed by the Constitution.

The Southern Poverty Law Center in Montgomery, Alabama, is a private, nonprofit organization that stands out in its efforts to protect the rights of minority groups. The Center, headed by attorney Morris Dees, has used civil litigation against the Ku Klux Klan and other white supremacist and hate groups when they attempted to discriminate against blacks and other minority groups.

Through its Klan Watch Project and Militia Task Force, the Center keeps close tabs on all hate groups in the United States and files civil suits against their leaders to keep them from spreading their hatred and fear. In a landmark decision before the U.S. Supreme Court, Center attorneys won a civil judgment against the United Klans of America that ordered them to pay $10 million to Rosa Mae Donnell, the mother of a black man slain by the Klan. Because the Klan organization did not have $10 million in assets, they were forced to deed over their national headquarters to Mrs. Donnell. The Center also sued the state of Alabama, forcing it to integrate the Alabama State Police, once a bastion of white power. The tireless efforts of the Center have overturned many other white power bases.

Hate groups so feared the Center that in 1985 they fire-bombed its headquarters, totally destroying it. It was rebuilt through the contributions of thousands of Americans who valued its work in protecting the rights of all minorities. In 1996, the Center helped uncover a second plot to fire-bomb its headquarters in Montgomery. Three members of a patriot group known as the Oklahoma Constitutional Militia were eventually tried and convicted of conspiracy. In December 1994, Morris Dees wrote a letter to U.S. Attorney General Janet Reno, warning her that the "mixture of armed groups with those who hate is a recipe for disaster." Six months later the truth of those words was confirmed in the bombing of the federal building in Oklahoma City.

Since the Oklahoma City bombing in 1995, the Center staff has created a Militia Task Force to keep watch on patriot groups. It also wrote a national report called "False Patriots: The Threat of Antigovernment Extremists." It is available by writing to the Center at 400 Washington Ave., Montgomery, AL 36104. Morris Dees has also written *Gathering Storm*, a book warning the country about the threat of domestic terrorism posed by antigovernment groups. Dees, in a letter to Attorney General Reno in June 1996, requested the formation of a joint state and federal task force of attorneys general to develop a plan to deal with possible domestic terrorists. The Center's most recent victory was to bring an end to chain gangs in state prisons. They have become known as tireless fighters for social and racial justice and operate solely on donations from private citizens. They do not charge any legal fees for their work.

The Center also has an outreach program designed to teach tolerance to the nation's schoolchildren. It publishes and distributes *Teaching Tolerance*, a magazine containing articles and lesson plans for teachers to use in classroom discussions. It offers three curriculum kits, *The Shadow of Hate: The History of Intolerance in America*,

Starting Small: Teaching Tolerance in Preschool and the Early Grades, and *America's Civil Rights Movement*. The latter contains an Academy Award-winning video, *A Time For Justice*. All kits are distributed free to school principals and to college history department chairs upon written request from the Center at the above address. The Center has also produced another award-winning video, *The Klan: The Legacy of Hate in America*, about their Klan Watch work. It is also offered free of charge to educators.

SKILL-PRACTICE EXERCISE: NEGOTIATION SKILLS

Use Worksheet # 2: The Partnership Model for Resolving Conflict of Wants and Needs with a partner to role-play a resolution of a current conflict of wants and needs.

1. Find a partner who also has a conflict. Decide who is going to go first. This person explains the conflict to the other person, who then role-plays the other person in the conflict.
2. The role-play starts with the first person practicing negotiation skills with the second person.
3. After completing the role-play, both of you fill out the Negotiation Skills Checklist below. Discuss your performances and your reactions to each other.
4. Repeat the process, with the second person presenting a conflict and practicing negotiation skills with the first person role-playing the conflict. Again, using the Negotiation Skills Checklist, evaluate your performance and discuss your interaction.

SELF-AWARENESS ACTIVITY: NEGOTIATION SKILLS CHECKLIST

Using the above skill-practice exercise, you and your partner need to respond to the questions below.

1. Did you achieve a win-win resolution to your conflict?
2. What ideas did you get to use with the actual person involved in the conflict?
3. Were you able to negotiate from a cooperative, instead of a confrontational, stance?
4. Were you able to create trust between you? If so, how did you do that?
5. Were you able to get the conflict defined in terms of each person's needs?
6. Were you able to keep the focus on areas of agreement and identify areas of disagreement to negotiate? How did you do that?
7. Were you able to handle objections from the other person without ignoring them or trying to discredit them?
8. Were you able to be soft on the person and be hard on the conflict? Were you able to be assertive about your needs while being respectful of the other person's needs?
9. How realistic was the second person's role-play of the person with whom you have the conflict? In what ways?
10. What contributed the most to your success or failure to reach a win-win solution?

SKILL PRACTICE EXERCISE: MEDIATION SKILLS

Take a current conflict of wants and needs and again using Worksheet #2 attempt a role-play where you use a third-party mediator to help resolve the conflict. In addition, make use of the guidelines and steps in the mediation process listed earlier in this chapter.

1. Form groups of three. One agrees to be the mediator, one presents a conflict, and the other role-plays the other person in the conflict. Rotate roles so that each of you gets an opportunity to practice mediation skills.
2. After each practice round, stop to evaluate the effectiveness of the mediation skills being used. Have each person involved fill out the Meditation Skills Checklist that follows and discuss the results.

SELF-AWARENESS EXERCISE: MEDIATION SKILLS CHECKLIST

Using the skill-practice exercise above, you and your partner need to answer and discuss the questions listed below.

1. Was the mediator able to stay objective and represent both sides fairly?
2. Was the mediator able to be supportive to both sides without taking sides? How was that done?
3. Was the mediator able to avoid making judgments about who was right or wrong?
4. Was the mediator able to create a safe nonthreatening environment? How?
5. Was the mediator able to facilitate a win-win resolution of the conflict?
6. Did the mediator allow the two parties to make their own decisions?
7. Was the mediator able to get the parties to be soft on each other and hard on the conflict? How was that done?
8. Was the mediator able to help the parties maintain respect for each other's needs? How?
9. Did the mediator help the parties evaluate the solidness of the resolution at which they arrived? How?
10. What was the most effective thing the mediator did to facilitate the process?

Chapter 17

~

How Can I Apply the Partnership Way in Larger Social Systems?

We all carry the residue of our unresolved developmental traumas and conflicts from our individual, couple, family, school, and work experiences into larger social systems. These community, cultural, and nation-state systems provide a large collective stage where our unresolved issues can be reenacted through athletic contests, economic and social competitions, and ethnic, religious, and national wars.

When people overreact during community, cultural, and national events they are probably experiencing symptoms of post-traumatic stress related to their own unresolved personal conflicts. Rather than judging or criticizing people when this happens, try seeing them from a compassionate and empathic perspective. If you find yourself getting triggered by these events, develop a compassionate attitude toward yourself and work on discovering the roots of your own reaction to these events.

National and worldwide events, as the O.J. Simpson trials, the death of Princess Diana, and the scandals of the Clinton presidency bring forth enormous reactions from millions of people all at once and provide many people with an opportunity for "collective therapy." Actually, many counselors and psychotherapists reported a very large increase in people coming to them for therapy immediately after Princess Diana's death. Many of them were dealing with overwhelming grief that was making it hard for them to function effectively. Highly visible people such as Princess Diana and President Clinton serve as collective role models that people can use to project either positive or negative aspects of themselves.

THE DEVELOPMENTAL STAGES OF COMMUNITIES AND CULTURES

There are many kinds of cultures within a community, state, or region, including religious, ethnic, political, economic, social, academic, athletic, and environmental, as well as groups with special needs or interests involving sexual preferences, disabilities such as deafness or blindness, athletic teams, and academic specialties. People belong to numerous communities and cultures, all of which combined give them a unique identity, such as: "a Caucasian male with a mid-western farm background, who graduated from Northwestern University with a degree in chemical engineering, is a member of the Methodist Church, is a fan of the Chicago Cubs and Chicago Bears, and lives in Las Vegas, Nevada."

Each aspect of this man is linked into a base of information, values and beliefs, and behaviors that allow him to participate in specific activities within a community. If the Cubs win the World Series (however unlikely), this Cubs fan along with all other Cubs fans would be screaming "We're #1." The team actually won the games, but through their identification with this team they all claim a vicarious victory that makes them feel more important or special.

The evolution of communities and cultures follows a developmental stage model similar to that of individuals, couples, families, and organizations. These stages of development are: *codependent, counter-dependent, independent,* and *interdependent.* The evolution of a community and culture correlates with the level of development within all these smaller subsystems. For example, if a majority of individuals, couples, families, and organizations in a community are operating primarily at a codependent level, then the community will likely be operating at the same codependent level. The degree to which these subsystems have resolved the residue of developmental trauma and intractable conflict determines how far a community or a culture can evolve. The psychosocial tasks of each stage of development are shown in Table 17.1.

In order to facilitate steady movement to higher stages of community and cultural development, leaders must make a conscious effort to model how to resolve conflicts effectively and to find functional ways to help meet the individual, couple, family, and organizational needs of its citizens. Otherwise the community or culture gets caught in drama triangle dynamics, obstructing its evolution.

HOW DOES DEVELOPMENTAL HISTORY IMPACT COMMUNITIES AND CULTURES?

Communities and cultures create civilizations with specific ideologies related to a cluster of common components such as religious and philosophical orientations and collective historical experiences based on their experiences in couple, family, school, work, and social relationships. This perspective is validated through the work of two historians. The first is Samuel Huntington (1993), who studied the civilizations of Europe. He identified a line of cultural demarcation that divides Eastern and Western Europe, which he called the "Velvet Curtain of Culture." This dividing line developed as the result of very different social structures that eventually created different religious and political structures.

Table 17.1
The Developmental Stages of a Community and Culture

Stage of Development	The Psychosocial Tasks of a Culture	Methods for Completing These Tasks
Codependent	• Build trust • Create a group identity • Provide for the basic needs of all group members • Build esprit de corps	• Provide meaning through community or cultural identity • Identify common values and beliefs • Utilize group song, dance, and ritual to unify and inspire
Counter-Dependent	• Identify unique characteristics of the group • Resolve conflicts of needs between group members	• Encourage creativity regarding the expression of values and beliefs • Offer conflict resolution to all members
Independent	• Create a set of values and beliefs for the culture • Provide opportunities for subgroups to form within the larger group • Celebrate the unique characteristics of the cultural group and its subgroups	• Create forums to encourage the interfacing and interweaving of diverse expressions of values and beliefs • Acknowledge and honor the presence of cultural subgroups • Teach divergent and convergent thinking • Encourage direct communication between members of cultural subgroups
Interdependent	• Build consensus between subgroup members	• Identify common goals and visions through collective processes • Utilize subgroup interactions for learning experiences • Create humanitarian organizations to serve the needs of members

Huntington saw this line of demarcation as more closely representing the boundary between East and West than the ideological line known as the Iron Curtain. His geographic division follows the five-hundred-year-old eastern boundary of western Christianity. The map in Figure 17.1 shows how, according to Huntington, this line divides the major cultures of Europe.

According to Huntington, the countries on the western side of the Velvet Curtain share a common history of feudalism, the Renaissance, the Reformation, the Enlightenment, the French Revolution, and the Industrial Revolution. More influenced by Rome, it is traditionally Catholic and Protestant Christian in religious orientation. Human systems in this culture tend to have more democratic family structures that influenced the development of social and governmental structures built on the values of freedom, individual initiative, and personal responsibility.

The countries on the eastern side of the Velvet Curtain make up what Huntington calls the Slavic-Orthodox culture. Created from the Ottoman and Tsarist Empires and more influenced by Byzantium, it is traditionally Orthodox and Muslim in religious orientation. These countries did not go through the Renaissance, Reformation, and Enlightenment, but remained under the primary influence of feudalism. Hence, the family structures in this culture influenced the creation of more socialistic governmental systems that value collective initiative and collective responsibility. It is interesting that Huntington's dividing line between these two civilizations runs directly through the former Yugoslavia, where conflicts regarding cultural values and mores have created wars for hundreds of years. Huntington believed that the divergent nature of these two civilizations are responsible for much of the intractable conflict in this region of the world.

A similar phenomenon in the United States is the contrast between the cultures of the North and the South. The line of demarcation between them is considered to be the Mason-Dixon Line that divided the country between states that did and did not allow slavery. This line of demarcation also separates the country linguistically, as the groups speak slightly different dialects of American English.

The second person who studied the evolution of Western civilization is psychohistorian Lloyd deMause (1982). He identified psychological lines of demarcation between the people of the United States and Western Europe. He contends that the people who came to the United States are a unique group of people who asserted their "counter-dependency from mother-England" (p. 113) and from the established cultures and religions of Europe. This group of people who physically separated from the "motherland" developed a new form of mother-child relationship that changed the structure of the family. This influenced the development of new social structures and ultimately created a nation of people who

Figure 17.1
Boundaries Between Cultures of East and West

value independence and autonomy. He described Americans as a new "psychoclass" of humans who were not subjected to the hazards of infanticide, flogging, swaddling, and wet-nursing typical of European parents. According to deMause, European visitors to colonial America often complained that the children were "spoiled and indulged," which made them "petty domestic tyrants."

The deeply rooted aspects of human experience that comprise communities and cultures make it very difficult to resolve conflicts between them. Conflicts of values and beliefs repeatedly ignite philosophical, ethical, religious, and value-based conflicts and wars in an effort to prove once and for all who is right and who is wrong or to determine whose rules will ultimately prevail. The inability to resolve these conflicts deepens the divisions between individuals and groups, reinforcing cultural biases, prejudices, projections, and hatred.

HOW DO UNRESOLVED DEVELOPMENTAL ISSUES IMPACT COMMUNITIES AND CULTURES?

Huntington suggested that the characteristics of family structures strongly influence the structure of communities and cultures and the subgroups contained within them. Members of communities and cultures raised in families with hierarchical structures, for example, become conditioned to inequities in power and feel comfortable with hierarchical social, political, and cultural structures. They learned first to relinquish their individual needs to the needs of the family and then to subjugate them to the culture. Hierarchical family structures go hand-in-hand with hierarchical cultural structures. Conversely, individuals raised in families with egalitarian structures that value team-building, collaboration, and negotiation skills help to create cooperative, partnering, and democratic social, political, and cultural structures. The differences between these cultures are outlined in Table 17.2.

Communities and cultures that provide effective support for their smaller social subsystems to process unresolved developmental trauma and conflict and complete their psychosocial tasks eventually evolve to higher stages of development. Some communities and cultures are good at creating strong social and economic foundations for their members but do not provide enough ways for members to meet their unique psychological and emotional needs. Communities and cultures with political, economic, religious, social, and ethnic policies that promote unity more than diversity often have high levels of social unrest.

Table 17.2

Characteristics of Dominator and Partnership Communities and Cultures

Dominator Communities and Cultures	Partnership Communities and Cultures
Value the good of the whole culture over the good of its subgroups	Value both the good of the whole culture and the good of its subgroups
Use force or threat to enforce domination within the culture	Use negotiation and cooperative linking to work for the common good of all members and subgroups
Create inequalities in power, money, and decision-making	Create equal opportunities or money and use knowledge as shared power for joint decision-making
Value violence and exploitation	Value cooperation and harmony
Utilize rigid gender roles	Utilize flexible gender roles
Have competitive interactions	Have cooperative interactions
Use fear to create separation	Use hope and high ideals to create unity
Are more materially oriented	Are more spiritually oriented
One subgroup is usually dominant	All subgroups share power
Support codependent and counter-dependent behaviors in members and subgroups	Support independent and interdependent behaviors in members and subgroups
Use control, manipulation, and deception in communicating	Use truth, empathy, and directness in communicating
Value the needs of the culture more than the needs of subgroups or individual members	Value both the needs of the culture and the needs of subgroups and individual members

DRAMA TRIANGLE DYNAMICS IN CONFLICTS INVOLVING LARGE SOCIAL SYSTEMS

Joan Lachkar (1993) applied psychodynamic theory to the ongoing cultural conflicts between Arabs and Israelis. She examined the collective group myths and defense mechanisms of both cultures and found the behavioral dynamics were similar to the codependent/counter-dependent model we used in Chapter 10 for resolving intractable relationship conflicts. Cultures that utilize these polarized dynamics in their microcosmic social structures, particularly couple and family relationships, often find that they show up as well in their macrocosmic social structures. In addition, the drama triangle dynamics that play out in individuals, couples, families, and organizations are also present in cultural conflicts.

Cultures with primarily codependent characteristics, such as the Israelis, typically act out the victim role on the drama triangle, while more counter-dependent cultures, such as the Arabs, act out the persecutor role. Third parties such as the United States and the former Soviet Union were usually drawn into drama triangle dynamics in the rescuer role. Table 17.3 illustrates how the codependent and counter-dependent roles mesh exactly and create the ideal dynamics for the drama triangle to be played out at all levels of human systems.

Mediators and organizational consultants who work with intractable conflicts in large social systems can utilize many of the same tools used to resolve conflicts in couple and family relationships. A culture must be seen as a client with a presenting problem that is rooted in its developmental history. The cultural client needs similar kinds of support that individuals, couples, and families need in resolving conflicts that involve any residue from developmental traumas, completing psychosocial tasks, and meeting developmental needs.

Mediators and organizational consultants involved in conflict resolution need to help their clients develop skills that foster an internal sense of object constancy. These skills include:

1. "I'm okay, you're okay" thinking that discourages splitting behaviors that divide people or groups into good and bad.
2. Looking for three options or choices when resolving conflicts.

Such skills help people develop the ability to hold themselves as objects of worth even when feeling rejected or unworthy during conflicts.

Interventions that deal with conflicts involving large systems are similar in philosophy but somewhat different in practice than those used in couple, family, school, and organizational conflicts. Resolving large-group conflicts usually involves group processing of collective issues. Table 17.4 provides guidelines for healing collective psychological splits between communities or cultural groups.

Table 17.3
Comparison of Codependent and Counter-Dependent Roles

Codependent Role	Counter-Dependent Role
Use "I'm not okay/you're okay" defenses in conflict situations	Use "I'm okay/you're not okay" defenses in conflict situations
Play victim and/or rescuer roles in the drama triangle	Play persecutor and/or rescuer roles in the drama triangle
Lacks structure and boundaries to contain self	Has artificial structure containing false self
Immobilized by feeling states	Cut off from feelings
Other-directed	Self-centered
Use oral and "downer" addictions	Use anal and "upper" addictions
Exhibit poor self-esteem	Inflated self-esteem
Act dependent	Act counter-dependent
Have depressed behaviors	Have manic behaviors
Feet ashamed of having needs	Feet guilty about having needs
Are people pleasers	Are people controllers
Accept responsibility for everything	Accept responsibility for nothing
Blame self	Blame others

Table 17.4
How to Heal Codependent and Counter-Dependent Splits in Community and Cultural Conflicts

Codependent Behaviors	Counter-Dependent Behaviors
Confront the dysfunction of their defenses and behavior	Empathize with the wound under their defenses. reflecting how they use defenses to protect themselves
Provide support, empathy and, truth to mobilize client out of feeling state into action	Provide mirroring interpretation of their vulnerability to help client access feelings
Develop skills in autonomy	Develop skills in intimacy
Develop problem-solving skills needed to mobilize out of intense feeling states	Identify body signals related to experiencing and expressing feelings
Move quickly to provide structure	Move slowly to remove defenses
Master the outer world of work and self-care	Master the inner world of relationships
Set behavioral limits	Expand behavioral responses
Develop defenses against projections	Identify projections used as defenses against feelings and memories
Diminish personal over-committing	Expand range of personal commitments
Separate nurturing and sexuality	Separate power and sexuality
Develop compassion for wounds to the self	Develop compassion for wounds of others

PROGRAMS DESIGNED TO PREVENT CONFLICT IN COMMUNITIES AND CULTURES

Primary, secondary, and tertiary prevention programs designed to prevent conflict in communities and cultures are essential. Primary prevention programs make interventions prior to the appearance of a problem and are usually psychoeducational in nature. Secondary prevention programs are designed to intervene after a problem has begun. Tertiary prevention programs provide services for those who have gotten into trouble within society and can be rehabilitated. Following are some examples describing prevention programs known to be effective within communities.

Individual intervention programs provide primary prevention services in partnership conflict resolution models to anyone who wants it. These programs are mostly experientially based or educational and offered via private or public organizations such as churches or businesses. Conflict resolution training for all students in schools is an example of this kind of program.

Family intervention programs can also provide primary prevention services. It is interesting that economics is the major force driving the implementation of primary prevention programs. Statistics from pioneering programs such as Healthy Start in Hawaii indicate that these programs produce significant savings in the cost of social services such as foster care, youth detention services, and alternative education programs. In addition, this program virtually eliminated reported child abuse and neglect as a

major family and social problem. Two follow-up studies showed that there was virtually no reported child abuse and neglect among the high-risk family population that received voluntary home visitation services for three to five years (Healthy Start, 1992).

Community-based intervention programs use peer influence to change behaviors that are deemed socially unacceptable. Anti-smoking campaigns are an example of a secondary prevention program. Over a period of years, the medical community released increasingly stronger statements about the dangers of smoking. As these reports were released, public opinion demanded nonsmoking sections in restaurants, airplanes, airports, and other public facilities. When the research on the dangers of second-hand smoke were released, a number of individuals brought legal action against employers and others responsible for their exposure to secondhand smoke. Their success in court quickly persuaded policymakers to ban smoking in most public buildings. The private sector quickly followed suit and banned smoking at the workplace. Public awareness regarding the dangers of smoking became quite high. Individuals who smoked soon became regarded as "polluters," facing the contempt of nonsmokers. This peer pressure and public policies within the community were major forces in the significant reduction of smoking around the country.

The success of community-based intervention programs is supported by the premises of the Community Reinforcement Model, which relies heavily on the use of peer pressure to treat alcoholism. This systemic model, developed by Sisson and Azrin (1986), also includes other components, such the use of antabuse, marital counseling, job skills training, social skills training, advising on appropriate social and recreational activities, and counseling to help control urges to drink.

Four controlled studies found that the Community Reinforcement Model was significantly more effective than the more traditional methods. For example, a six-month follow-up study found the control group spending one-third of their days unemployed and intoxicated and the treatment group with nearly total sobriety (Sisson and Azrin, 1986).

There are three other programs designed to strengthen families and neighborhoods by generating meaningful interactions among neighbors while also building positive assets in individuals. The first is Communities That Care (Hawkins, Catalano, et al., 1992), which is designed to reduce the risk factors associated with adolescent problems. The Communities That Care program is a neighborhood leadership-training program that teaches a step-by-step approach to mobilization and planning based on a risk and resource assessment model. It was developed by David Hawkins and Joseph Catalano and field-tested in Washington and Oregon. Their research showed that the most effective way to reduce children's' risk is to strengthen their bond with positive, prosocial family members, teachers, or other significant adults and/or prosocial friends. They cited studies indicating that children who live in high-risk neighborhoods but have strong bonds with a caregiver are not nearly as likely to get into trouble as adolescents.

Another program, the Developmental Assets Model (Benson, 1995), utilizes a shared responsibility approach for addressing community issues. The Developmental Assets Model emerged out of a pilot project by the Search Institute, located in a Minneapolis suburb. Based on survey research, the Search Institute has identified forty internal and external developmental assets that children and adolescents need to have in order to succeed (Benson, Galbraith, & Espeland, 1995). Over 100,000 children and adolescents in grades six through twelve were surveyed to determine how many of these developmental assets kids need to be successful. Each asset has a behavioral definition of how to know whether or not the asset is being met. The Search Institute recently produced a longer list of developmental assets they believe predict success starting at birth and extending to age eighteen (Leffert, Benson, & Roehlkepartain, 1997). This promising effort still needs outcome research to determine the effect of focused family and community efforts to develop the assets of our children and youth.

The Kindness Campaign is a community-based, primary-prevention, anti-violence program that has been implemented in Colorado Springs, Colorado, and Omaha, Nebraska (Weinhold, 1996b). The main goal of this program is to recognize and reinforce prosocial behaviors in order to reduce the recognition given to family violence, gang activity, and other antisocial behaviors. The school-based part of this program is described in Chapter 14.

The community-based component of the campaign utilizes the media to promote the campaign. To get it started in a community, a grass-roots coalition of social service agencies typically teams with a local television station to provide coverage of positive human-interest stories on the nightly news. In addition, the station airs daily public service announcements and covers special events like Kindness Week and Recognition Awards events. Research by the local television station in Colorado Springs that serves as its cosponsor shows that after one year of sponsorship over 70% of viewers were aware of the goals of the Kindness Campaign and 75% of those believed it was having a significant impact on this community (Weinhold, 1996a).

During Kindness Week each February, churches and neighborhoods get involved in the campaign via special events such as Interfaith Celebrations of Kindness. Neighborhood associations involve different segments of the community via special kindness projects. Schoolchildren nominate adults for Community of Kindness Awards. Kindness Awards also are given to companies, churches, or organizations that enroll 50% or more of their employees or members. These events recognize the unsung heroes and heroines in the community and reinforce prosocial behaviors throughout the community. The goal of the campaign is to inform and enroll a critical mass of community members (usually 20% of the population).

Here are some suggestions for spreading kindness:

- Make a list of things you can do to bring more kindness to your self, your family, neighborhood, school, workplace, or community.
- Return your shopping cart to its appointed space in the parking lot.
- As you walk through your neighborhood, pick up any trash on the sidewalk or in the gutter.
- Send a letter to a teacher or minister letting them know what a difference their acts of kindness made in your life.
- Make an anonymous donation to a local charity that is actively helping young people or start a fund-raising drive in your office for such organizations.
- Organize your friends or work mates to gather used clothing and give it to homeless shelters.
- Ask your children to go through their toys and donate some of them to children who are less fortunate.
- Offer to baby-sit for a neighbor's children so they can take a break from parenting.
- Welcome new people into your neighborhood by visiting them and taking them food.

WHAT ARE THE POTENTIAL COSTS AND BENEFITS OF PREVENTION PROGRAMS INVOLVING LARGE SOCIAL SYSTEMS?

The policies and practices of local, state, and federal governments have long adhered to a band-aid approach for fixing problems after they have developed, while largely ignoring prevention efforts. Politicians who are elected for short two- to six-year terms are not usually interested in long-term solutions. They typically seek short-term and often short-sighted solutions to problems such as youth conflict and violence. Prevention, particularly primary prevention, has been shown to be extremely cost and human effective.

Kotulak (1996) cites neuropsychiatrist Dr. Bruce Perry, whose studies show that every dollar spent on early childhood development programs translates into $5 of savings later in social services, mental health services, prisons, and other programs intended to deal with the aftermath of aggression and violence. Early developmental experiences also determine the brain's capacity to function. According to Perry, negative developmental effects to the brain's hardware are a major factor in the need to build more prisons for developmentally traumatized individuals.

It is now possible to use psychological tests and predictive measures to identify potential future criminals by the time a child is eight years old. Unless there are interventions in his life, these measures perfectly predict the same kind and degree of aggressive and antisocial behavior in that child when he becomes a thirty-eight-year-old adult. About 50% of aggressive and antisocial eight-year-olds will grow up to become criminals. The others may never end up in jail but will nevertheless abuse, bully, and intimidate their children, spouses, and friends.

Primary prevention programs could prevent up to 50% of those aggressive-eight-year olds from growing up to become criminals. The potential cost-benefit ratio of this kind of primary prevention is enormous, without even factoring in the human life cost and benefits. For example, in El Paso County, where Colorado Springs sits, there are currently about 90,000 students. Research tells us that about 5%, or about 4,500 students, will engage in serious bullying behavior. As indicated by the research cited above, 50% or 2,250 of these bullies will become incarcerated as adults.

If primary prevention programs could avert bullies from becoming criminals, it would save millions of tax dollars each year. According to the Colorado Department of Corrections, the current minimal cost of housing a criminal in state facilities is $19,300 a year. This means that the potential savings from a prevention program aimed at reducing bullying behavior could be over $43 million per year if it just involved people from El Paso County. To put this in a state perspective, there are currently over 10,000 people in prisons in Colorado. At $19,300 per inmate, the state spends at least $193 million just to house these individuals. The 1992 statistics for the El Paso County jail show that 15,000 criminals were housed for short stays at an annual operating cost of $10,954,000.

These county and state budget figures do not include the costs of capturing, trying, and convicting these criminals or the costs related to losses by their victims and their families. These figures also do not include the cost of building and remodeling jails. If you factored in these additional costs, you can see that taxes could be reduced significantly if more primary prevention program could be started. Finally, and most importantly, these figures do not include the costs of wasted human lives.

EXAMPLES OF CULTURAL INTERVENTIONS USING THE PARTNERSHIP WAY

We field-tested the Partnership Way through several projects in Central and Eastern Europe. One project involved a seven-month residency in Bratislava, Slovakia (the Czech and Slovak Republics were partitioned in 1993), where we worked as consultants for the United Nations. Our task was to establish an International Centre for Family Studies in Bratislava and to begin the affiliation process with the United Nations. This experience afforded us a rare opportunity for in-depth study of a system just emerging from its codependent stage of development with the Soviet empire. While the people were freed of the external chains of communism, they initially retained much of the oppressive totalitarian thinking that limited their freedom. The people still followed the Soviet cultural maxim that "the nail that sticks out gets pounded," a cultural contrast to the Western adage that the "squeaky wheel gets the grease." Many people still felt afraid to do anything that might call attention to themselves.

Neither family nor governmental structures supported people in developing exploratory behaviors and independent thinking during the communist era. Children typically remained psychologically and economically dependent on their families and on the state. Housing shortages often made it necessary for young people to continue living with one of the couple's parents after their marriage.

Intervention in the Slovak Ministry of Labor, Social Affairs, and Family

As the Slovak people split from communism, they tended to make everything from the old system bad and looked at the free market economy ideas of the West as all good. This was a reversal from their communist days when everything from the West was bad and everything in the East was good. These tendencies to split and reverse contained the potential for adopting another governmental system that also might not serve the needs of the people.

Our responsibilities as consultants to the Slovak Ministry of Labor, Social Affairs, and Family was to advise government policymakers and human development professionals on social and family policies during the economic and political transition. In our numerous talks with the Minister of Labor, Social Affairs, and Family and with her staff, we used the theme, "don't throw the baby out with the bath water." We developed a number of specific interventions to address the psychosocial task of separation:

- We validated the social value of some policies from the old system to help them see the good in their culture.
- We spoke about policies of western systems that might not be useful in their culture and why.
- We suggested the policymakers always seek a third option when weighing policy proposals to develop policies and government structures that synthesized the best of East and West.

When we addressed groups of Slovak family-life professionals, we applauded the great support that families give their children in the codependent stage of development and spoke about how Western cultures could learn much from them in this area. Under communism, for example, women received three years of paid maternity leave that encouraged mothers to stay home during their children's critical formative years. We hypothesized that this period of early stability, the slower pace of life, and the fact that families often spaced their children about three years apart might be factors in the calmness many of the young children exhibited. We saw very few children with hyperactive behaviors.

We also validated the Slovak people's feelings of frustration and anger about the difficulties they experienced in their rapid process of individuation and encouraged them to learn this skill from Westerners. We encouraged Slovak people to synthesize the strengths from both East and West to prevent them from reenacting the dynamics of the drama triangle in the future.

Interventions in the Partition of Czechoslovakia

During our assignment with the United Nations we witnessed the Czechs and the Slovaks going through their "velvet divorce." These two countries have very different root cultures. The Czechs are more Bohemian, Germanic, and more connected to the West, while the Slovaks come from Slavic roots on the Eastern side of Huntington's Velvet Curtain of Culture. Once they were free to choose, the Czechs moved quickly to align with the Germans and the West, while the Slovaks moved toward the East and their former Soviet partners of Russia and Ukraine.

This national partition activated a codependent/counter-dependent dynamic between the Czechs and the Slovaks. Perceiving their Czech partners as abandoning them, the more agrarian and economically vulnerable

Slovaks acted out the counter-dependent role. In a fit of "abandonment rage," the Slovak leader threatened to leave their federation if his Czech partner didn't take Slovak needs into account in political and economic decision-making. The Czechs, who saw the Slovaks and their antiquated industrial structures as a burden, called the Slovaks' bluff and pushed for separation, even though neither side was realistically prepared for independence. Each side acted out culturally influenced roles that activated dynamics of the drama triangle.

We observed the separation of Czechoslovakia into the Czech and Slovak Republics with great interest. Having counseled numerous couples, their partition dynamics reminded us of a divorcing couple. The Czechs played out the traditional male role during the partition. As part of the property settlement, they got most of the country's desirable economic and social resources, such as the light industries and educated people and experienced politicians. The Slovaks played out the traditional female role. Their property included dirty industries, such as steel-making and munitions plants, nuclear reactors, and a more agrarian, less educated, and less politically experienced populace. While we did not serve as official advisors to government officials or agencies regarding the separation, we did talk informally with many people about the partition. During these conversations, we used interventions that supported the Slovaks in completing this partition without splitting:

- We validated the aspects of their federation with the Czechs that had been useful.
- We acknowledged the policies and structures that they believed had not served their needs.
- We suggested that they synthesize new policies and government structures utilizing the best of the old and the best of the new.

WHAT ARE THE DEVELOPMENTAL STAGES OF NATION-STATES?

Nation-states are an assimilation of cultures that contain numerous subsystems, each carrying unresolved developmental traumas and conflicts, incomplete psychosocial tasks, and unmet developmental needs. The evolution of a nation-state correlates with the degree of development of its subsystems. The degree to which individuals, couples, families, organizations, and cultural groups have completed their important psychosocial tasks and met their developmental needs determines the stage of evolution of a nation-state. Nation-states that encourage individuation and psychological development will have social structures that are more independent and interdependent, while nation-states that discourage individuation and psychological development will have social structures that are more codependent and counter-dependent in nature.

The evolution of nation-states follows a developmental model similar to that for individuals, couples, families, schools, communities, and organizations.. The psychosocial tasks of each stage (codependent, counterdependent, independent, and interdependent) of nation-state development are listed in Table 17.5.

Nation-states that provide effective methods for helping their subsystems complete their essential developmental tasks evolve to a higher stage. Some nation-states can create strong national identities for their members but have difficulty providing a strong psychological foundation that helps their citizens get their individual needs met. For example, a nation-state may have political, economic, religious, social, and ethnic policies that value unity more than diversity. Differences get stifled, creating undercurrents of unrest, as occurred in the former Soviet Union.

In order to facilitate the steady movement of nation-states toward the higher stages of development, leaders

Table 17.5
The Developmental Stages of Nation-States

Stage of Development	The Psychosocial Tasks of a Nation-State	Methods for Completing These Tasks
Codependent	• Build trust • Create a national culture and identity • Provide for the basic needs of all citizens • Build esprit de corps	• Provide meaning through history • Identify common values and beliefs • Provide and protect basic human rights • Provide for the welfare of the poor and disabled • Provide equal education for all • Protect the rights of minorities • Utilize group song, dance, and ritual to unify and inspire
Counter-Dependent	• Identify unique characteristics of the nation in an international context • Resolve conflicts of needs between cultural groups and between nations	• Encourage creativity regarding the expression of values and beliefs • Establish freedom of press and speech • Offer freedom of choice in work, religion, and residence • Establish laws to protect rights and property of all people • Permit freedom to travel and work without restraint • Guarantee the right to petition the government • Offer conflict resolution to all members
Independent	• Create a national culture that honors diversity, initiative, responsibility, and freedom • Provide opportunities for cultural groups to celebrate their uniqueness within a national context of cultural diversity	• Create forums to encourage the interfacing and interweaving of diverse expressions of values and beliefs • Create laws protecting minorities and cultural subgroups • Acknowledge and honor the presence of cultural subgroups • Teach divergent and convergent thinking • Encourage direct communication between members of cultural subgroups
Interdependent	• Build consensus between cultural groups and between nations • Support full development of all members of the nation-state • Develop transnational perspective	• Identify common goals and visions through collective processes • Utilize subgroup interactions for learning experiences • Create humanitarian organizations to serve the needs of members

must create structures that help citizens resolve conflicts effectively and create policies designed to support individual initiative, cooperative living, and basic freedoms.

HOW DO YOU DIAGNOSE DEVELOPMENTAL ISSUES IN NATION-STATES?

As in cultures, nation-states operate on a set of values, beliefs, and practices that may be different from those espoused in their laws or ideals. A change in the perceptions of the majority of the citizens can cause the leaders of the country to either look seriously at changing an unpopular belief or practice or ignoring the plea of its citizens and risking deeper conflict. The system of checks and balances present in the United States makes change more difficult and protects its citizens against rapid or destabilizing changes. It can also lead to frustration in the citizenry if they feel their views are not being taken seriously.

DRAMA TRIANGLE DYNAMICS IN CONFLICTS BETWEEN NATION-STATES

The characteristics of family structures strongly influence the social and political structure of nation-states. In her book, *Prisoners of Childhood*, Alice Miller (1983) correlated the rise of Nazism in Germany to the dominator structure of German families. Her brilliant analysis of Adolf Hitler's childhood describes how his mother did not bond with him and how his stepfather repeatedly beat him. In an effort to find a safe outlet for his feelings, according to Miller, Hitler became a bully, played violent war games, and expressed hatred toward Jews and other minorities that he had heard from his stepfather. Hitler undoubtedly suffered from PTSD and identified with the aggressor in his family, acting out the "fight" adrenal stress response.

Hitler became a totalitarian leader who was able to mobilize a whole nation to help him replay his family's drama triangle dynamics. In his family, Hitler was the victim, his stepfather was the persecutor, and his mother did not rescue him. The collective reenactment of this family dynamic is known as the Holocaust, where Hitler was able to recreate his family experiences. Hitler and the Third Reich played the persecutor role; the Jews, Gypsies, and other minorities were the victims, and the Allies acted out the rescuer role. The persecutor in the Holocaust used this large conflict as a form of collective therapy for releasing their feelings related to child abuse and other kinds of developmental trauma and family conflict.

Many of the people who participated in Nazi war crimes questioned, in retrospect, how they got sucked into it. It is possible that post-traumatic stress played a significant role in their participation. Hitler's extreme rhetoric and aggressive, dominator behavior might have triggered symptoms of post-traumatic stress reactions stemming from their own family experiences that activated the adrenal stress response in them, as in Hitler, became a fight reaction.

Once German citizens became adrenalized, they may have suffered a loss of reality that catapulted them into a mass reenactment of their childhood memories. In this altered state, they were no longer able to make rational, logical decisions. The strong undercurrent of repressed emotions from a nation of adults who grew up in dominator family structures created the resonant field of energy needed to create a dominator nation-state. Hitler became a collective father figure (der Führer) who provided individuals with a stage where they could collectively act out the persecutor role in a national drama triangle.

The pervasiveness of drama triangle dynamics in human systems became shockingly clear at a Soviet-American conference on citizen diplomacy that we attended in 1989 in Washington, DC. We became quite friendly with a few of the Soviets we met and began to talk about each other's perceptions and experiences from the Cold War era.

One Soviet colleague said that he viewed the United States as a persecutor, attempting to dominate and victimize developing countries (Vietnam, Afghanistan, Nicaragua, Cuba) and convert them to capitalism. He perceived Soviets as the rescuer of these countries and the Soviet Union as the force stopping the whole world from becoming capitalist. We shared with them our perceptions of the Soviet Union as a persecutor, attempting to dominate and victimize developing countries so that they would convert to communism. We saw the United States as the rescuer of these countries (Vietnam, Afghanistan, Nicaragua, Cuba) and the force preventing the whole world from becoming communist.

It was clear how Mother Russia and Uncle Sam had been locked in a conflict that might end in divorce (nuclear war) and destroy the global family. The children (the developing countries) were afraid and decided to act out, as adolescents often do in family systems. Uncle Sam seems to have won this war and now seeks to dominate the world. Unless we Americans can move forward in our psychological development, it appears that the whole world will be Americanized. This would destroy the diversity that exists in the world and ultimately will create high levels of social unrest at a global level. Table 17.6 compares the characteristics of dominator and partnership nation-states.

International mediators and peacemakers who work with intractable conflicts between nations can adapt the tools used for resolving conflicts between individuals, couples, and families. First of all, they should see a nation as a "client" with a presenting problem that is rooted in its developmental history. The "client" needs similar kinds of support for dealing with developmental traumas and conflicts, completing its essential psychosocial tasks, and meeting its developmental needs, as do those in the other levels of the system. The interventions that are needed

Table 17.6
Characteristics of Dominator and Partnership Nation-States

Dominator Nations	Partnership Nations
Use force or threat to enforce domination	Use the vision of higher consciousness to encourage linking for the common good
Create inequalities in power, money, and decision-making	Create equal opportunities or money and use knowledge as shared power for joint decision-making
Value violence and exploitation	Value cooperation and harmony
Utilize rigid gender roles	Utilize flexible gender roles
Competitive interactions	Cooperative interactions
Use fear to create separation	Use hope and high ideals to create unity
Are more materially oriented	Are more spiritually oriented
One culture is dominant	All cultural groups share power
Support codependent and counter-dependent behaviors	Support independent and interdependent behaviors
Follow a path of fear and protection	Follow a path of learning and discovery
Use control, manipulation, and deception in communicating	Use truth, empathy, and directness in communicating
Value the needs of the nation more than the needs of subgroups or individual members	Value both the needs of the nation and the needs of subgroups and individual members

will be similar in philosophy, but different in practice, as they will likely require group processing of collective issues. At the end of this chapter, Self-Inventory: DST Inventory Form N-S can be used to assess perceptions of the prevailing values and beliefs about the United States.

EXAMPLES OF NATIONAL INTERVENTIONS USING THE PARTNERSHIP WAY

In 1990, Janae began working collaboratively with Ukrainian psychologists to train them in applied psychology. During this period, the Soviet empire began collapsing into a cluster of new nations. Almost immediately, she saw the codependent/counter-dependent dynamics of drama triangle emerge between the Ukrainians and the Russians. The Russians played out the counter-dependent/persecutor role and the Ukrainians assumed the codependent/victim role. The splitting phenomenon emerged very quickly as the Ukrainians pushed for independence. Their projections of the persecutor role onto Russia would be an integral part of the unfolding of Ukrainian nationhood and an undercurrent of conflict that would resurface periodically, blocking Russian efforts to rebuilt the USSR.

Janae recalled her first intervention with a group of Ukrainian mothers:

Drama triangle dynamics first emerged in my work with a group of twelve Ukrainian women from families that had been relocated from the Chernobyl region to Kiev. Housed in an isolated, large gray development at the edge of the city, these women had been waiting five years for the Soviet government to provide them with social support and medical assistance for their exposure to radiation. I sat with them for several hours during my visit, helping them reprocess some of their post-traumatic stress symptoms related to the explosion of the reactor and their subsequent evacuation from their homes. These women also described how their children's health had steadily degenerated since their exposure to the high levels of radiation. In their stories, they placed the Soviet government in the persecutor role and themselves in the victim roles. Clearly they wanted me to play the rescuer role by mobilizing a large humanitarian effort for them from the West.

Initially, I just expressed my concern and compassion regarding their life-threatening trauma and supported their feelings of fear and anxiety about their children's health. I also spoke to them about the unknown effects of radiation on the long-term health of them and their families, acknowledging their horrible reality of exposure to radiation and validating their perceptions about the gravity of their situation. I emphasized that I was just one person working independently as a citizen diplomat in their country, without resources for large humanitarian efforts. I concluded my first visit with a short lesson on the rights and responsibilities of democratic life. I emphasized the remote possibility of government representatives miraculously knocking at their doors with solutions for their problems. I particularly stressed that their children's lives depended on them taking assertive individual and group action to bring their problems to the attention of the Ministry of Health.

I still remember the stunned looks on the faces of these women as they stood on the curb waving good-bye as I drove away from our meeting. Shortly after my reality therapy session with them, they began to mobilize themselves out of the victim role. Within six months, they had formed a parents' support group within their school. This group had conducted a massive letter-writing campaign to the Minister of Health requesting medical and nutritional support for their sick children (which they eventually received); organized health camps for the children in Crimea and southern Ukraine during the summers; organized a Chernobyl Children's Choir that began singing regularly in the region to publicize their plight; and wrote letters to U.S. families that eventually created a family-to-family humanitarian aid network that now supplies these families with important nutritional supplements and nonprescription remedies to support their weak immune systems.

HOW CAN THE PARTNERSHIP MODEL BE USED IN INTERNATIONAL DIPLOMACY?

During our five years of field-based research in Central and Eastern Europe, we discovered firsthand the parallels between the development of large and small human systems. One of the most significant things we learned during this period was how to help people without rescuing them. Professionals in Central and Eastern Europe responded enthusiastically to our training sessions in developmental systems theory and developmental process work. These approaches provided people with a cognitive framework and experiential intervention tools that addressed their problems in transitioning to democracy and free-market economies. Functioning as trainers and limiting our assistance to providing information and consultation helped us avoid the rescuer role and helped empower the people to make their own choices and to create their own solutions to their problems.

Our journey into cultural and national affairs gave us opportunities to network with many individuals and nongovernmental organizations (NGOs) whose programs and philosophies contain elements similar to the partnership way. We endorse the work of the two below.

The Institute for Multi-Track Diplomacy

Located in Washington, DC, the Institute for Multi-Track Diplomacy has developed a multidisciplinary view of peace-building with nine specific tracks:

- governmental
- professional conflict resolution
- business
- private citizen
- research, training, education
- activism
- religious
- funding
- public opinion

This model recognizes that individuals and organizations are more effective in working together than separately and that ethnic and regional conflict situations involve a large and intricate web of parties and factors requiring a systems approach. Each track in the system brings with it its own perspective, approach, and resources, all of which must be called upon in the peace-building process.

Headed by Dr. Louise Diamond and Ambassador John McDonald, the Institute for Multi-Track Diplomacy has been active in providing:

1. Training and consultation on conflict situations in Cypress and the Middle East.
2. Developing diplomacy skills for the Tibetan government in exile in India.
3. Conducting a consortium and teaching peace-building skills in Liberia.
4. Teaching dialogue skills to the Tibetans and the Chinese and in Ethiopia.

The institute also offers training and education for professionals in the many fields of activity related to peacemaking and peace-building through its professional development programs.

The Carter Center

Founded in 1982 by former President Jimmy Carter and his wife, Rosalynn, the Carter Center is a nonprofit, nonpartisan, public-policy institute dedicated to fighting disease, hunger, poverty, conflict, and oppression. The center is a separately chartered and independently governed member of the Emory University, Atlanta Georgia, community. Programs are directed by resident experts, many of whom hold academic appointments at Emory University.

The center develops collaborative initiatives in the areas of democratization and development, global health, and urban revitalization, and manages thirteen core programs active in 65 countries. Its conflict resolution program, which operates out of its International Democratization and Development program, marshals the experience of peacemakers to address suffering caused by armed conflicts around the globe. Through its 25 member International Negotiation Network (INN), the program monitors conflicts weekly and, upon request, offers advice and assistance to resolve disputes. Chaired by Jimmy Carter, the INN includes world leaders, experts in dispute resolution from international organizations, universities, and foundations who seek peaceful ways to prevent and end civil conflicts.

DEVELOPMENTAL SYSTEMS THEORY INVENTORY – FORM N-S

Use the rating scale to indicate your perceptions of prevailing values, beliefs, and practices of the country you call home.

4 = Almost Never   3 = Occasionally   2 = Usually   1 = Almost Always

_____ 1. People receive salary/wages that are fair for the work they provide.

_____ 2. The government provides benefits that meet the health care and other important needs of its people.

_____ 3. People trust that the government has their best interests at heart.

_____ 4. People trust that the government will listen to them and respect them as persons.

_____ 5. When they have a problem or need, people know their government will respond seriously and effectively to their request for assistance.

_____ 6. People are encouraged to develop relationships with their neighbors and coworkers.

_____ 7. People are encouraged by their government to contribute any new ideas they might have.

_____ 8. There are few rules in government that restrict people's freedom.

_____ 9. People are consulted by their government on decisions that affect them directly.

_____ 10. Information and important decisions by the government are shared in face-to-face meetings where people feel free to express their opinions and feelings.

_____ 11. People learn about government information and decisions that affect them from the media.

_____ 12. When people want an answer to something, there are many people in the government with whom they have to check.

_____ 13. People are encouraged by the government to "wear as many hats" as the situation calls for.

_____ 14. People are free to change what they are doing in response to their needs or the needs of their government.

_____ 15. If people perform above their expected level, they will be praised by their government.

_____ 16. The government encourages people to work together toward common goals and objectives.

_____ 17. The government gives people the power to make the decisions that affect them most directly.

_____ 18. People receive support and/or reward from the government for their efforts toward personal growth and mastery.

_____ 19. The established government rules and regulations are loosely followed.

_____ 20. National goals and purposes are determined through input from all citizens.

_____ 21. When people have conflicts with the government, they can anticipate an equitable resolution.

_____ 22. The opportunity exists for people to take cooperative and collective action to reach their goals and objectives.

_____ 23. The basic attitude is "everyone should look out for each other."

_____ 24. A top priority is the personal growth and development of each citizen.

Scoring and Interpretation

This inventory yields four subscores and a total nation-state score. Check your score for each of these four elements and refer to the interpretation below.

_____ Codependent Elements (Items 1 through 6)

_____ Counter-Dependent Elements (Items 7 through 12)

_____ Independent Elements (Items 13 through 18)

_____ Interdependent Elements (Items 19 through 24)

_____ **Total Nation-State Score**

Interpretation of Subscores

21–24   Most major developmental needs are being met in this country.

15–21   A few major developmental gaps may be present in the structure of this country.

11–15   Clear evidence of the presence of major developmental gaps in the structure of this country.

6–10   Major reorganization of the basic cultural values and beliefs may be necessary in order for this country to evolve. (Check the lowest of the four subscores to locate the gaps.)

Interpretation of Total Nation-State Score

79–96   Most major developmental needs are being met in this country.

60–78   A few major developmental gaps may be present in this country.

42–59   Clear evidence of the presence of major developmental gaps in this country.

24–41   Major reorganization of the basic values, beliefs, and practices of this country may be necessary.

Chapter 18

~

How Can the Partnership Way Be Applied to the Evolution of the Human Species?

One of the most critical dynamics that must be transformed to accelerate the social and psychological evolution of the human species is that of the drama triangle. As we developed the Partnership Way, it became clear to us that drama triangle dynamics, imprinted via family-of-origin experiences, are the predominant relationship dynamic in all human social systems. Adults who have not completed their own psychological development cannot help their children achieve emotional independence, which should be completed by age three. Parents and other adults need to be able to model and support the completion of this vital developmental task. Without a critical mass of role models who have achieved this state of emotional independence, intergenerational patterns of developmental "stuckness" will penetrate all social systems. The dysfunctional substitute becomes the drama triangle that permeates all social systems.

The missing piece in the evolutionary stuckness of humans as a species could also be described from a mythic perspective. Contemporary humans are isolated in time; that is, their perspective of human evolution is still very narrow from a temporal viewpoint. When information from prehistory, the era prior to recorded history, is added to human history, a much bigger picture of human development emerges. This larger perspective on human history provides the missing mythic piece needed to more fully understand the evolution of humans.

For example, including prehistorical information in the developmental history of humans brings a new dimension of awareness of global problems. Youth and family violence, global conflicts, and environmental problems might be considered symptoms of systemic stuckness. Contemporary history, which reaches back to approximately 2500 B.C.E., tells the story of the patrifocal period of human history that emphasized masculine values. During this era, humans developed agriculture, domesticated animals, established nation-states, and created technology for industrialization.

Although much of what happened during prehistory (prior to 2500 B.C.E.) is not written, archeological evidence has helped scientists piece together a fairly complete picture of life during this time. This evidence brings us the story of a matrifocal era of human history that emphasized feminine values. People lived in tribes as hunters and gatherers and there were few wars or other large-group conflicts. For example, there was a period of over 1500 years (3000 to 1500 B.C.E.) where the Minoan culture on Crete flourished without war. Many of their family and social practices also emphasized more feminine or partnership values. Even earlier, from 7000 to 3500 B.C.E., archeological evidence shows that small settlements in parts of Asia Minor practiced equal gender relations and peaceful relations with neighboring settlements (Eisler, 1987). When these two periods are combined, they give us a more complete story of our human evolution. In other words, "his-story" + "her-story" = "our-story."

Using this larger perspective on human history, it is possible to show how human evolution parallels the development of the individual. The prehistorical or matrifocal period parallels the codependent stage of individual development, the more recent patrifocal period of human development parallels the counter-dependent stage of human development, and contemporary history brings us to the edge of the independent stage of human development. The next stage of human evolution might parallel the interdependent stage of development. Table 18.1 illustrates stages of human evolution and the psychosocial tasks of each stage.

The next section summarizes some of the findings related to the prehistoric period or codependent stage of human development. The following section shows how this missing mythic piece impacts contemporary development.

THE CODEPENDENT OR MATRIFOCAL PERIOD OF HUMAN EVOLUTION

The matrifocal period of human development was studied extensively by Maria Gimbutas (1982) mostly through prehistoric mythology, archeology, and art. Her research revealed that these early societies were governed primarily by feminine values, beliefs, and deities. Some societies were matrilineal, meaning that property and lineage came through the women. Others were also matriarchal, governed by women. The critical factor during the matrifocal period of history, however, was its emphasis on feminine values such as inclusion, life-giving, nurturing, partnering, and cycles or circular thinking.

During the Paleolithic and Neolithic eras of prehistory, humans existed in a symbiotic relationship with nature. Living as hunters and gatherers, their consciousness was still undifferentiated from the primitive energies of the biomaterial world of animals, rocks, and other climatic and natural forces. This undifferentiated consciousness, or flock mentality, kept them lost in oceanic spheres of existence, unable to separate their individual world from the world of other people or organisms. There was no sense of self and other.

Humans were able to find food without great effort as they moved from one campsite to another. Wild fruits, grains, and game were plentiful as nature supplied everything they needed. This symbiotic relationship between humans and the Earth during the matrifocal period parallels an infant's symbiotic experiences with its human mother during the codependent stage of individual development.

Table 18.1
A Developmental Perspective of the Human Species

Stage of Development	The Psychosocial Tasks of the Human Species
Codependent (prehistory)	Bond with the world of nature Establish an identity as a species Develop the right brain functions of individuals
Counter-Dependent (recent history)	Separate from the world of nature Establish diversity in the species Development of left-brain functions within individuals Creation of nations-states Resolving conflicts between nations
Independent (contemporary history)	Reunite with the world of nature Develop unified, whole-brain thinking functions in individuals Creation of civilizations Celebrate the diversity between civilizations Resolve conflicts of needs between civilizations Provide for the basic needs of all citizens
Interdependent (future history)	Establish a planetary culture Develop the global brain

These prehistoric societies used tribal rituals related to hunting activities as a stage for resolving internal conflicts and elements of unresolved developmental traumas. These ritualized dramas, which contained good-bad splits such as hunter-hunted and other mythic or archetypal themes, might be called "tribal therapy." Specific rituals were created for tribal events, such as births and the change of seasons, to provide continuity and security in the tribe. How these prehistoric people evolved from the codependent stage to the counter-dependent stage of development is an interesting question.

James DeMeo (1992) postulates that environmental and climactic changes may have influenced the developmental history of humans. Prehistoric peoples' relationships with nature varied due to differences in climactic conditions. In the region known as Old Europe (Canaan, Babylonia, Egypt, and Anatolia), climactic patterns during the Neolithic period provided humans with a fairly constant environment where agriculture flourished. Early hunting-and-gathering societies living in these regions found a steady supply of native crops. The fertile soil quickly produced food from seeds and provided fodder for animals. The region provided a steady, predictable environment where people had "good mother" experiences. According to DeMeo, the more constant relational experiences with Mother Nature may have stimulated positive relationship patterns that created the good mother archetypes within this culture.

In other parts of the world, such as the steppes of East Asia where weather and climactic patterns were uncertain, humans experienced a lack of constancy in their relationships with nature. DeMeo links harsh environmental conditions with the development of patriarchal social structures, such as rigid social roles for men and women, the sexual subordination of women, the equation of masculinity with toughness and warlikeness, and the repression and/or distortion of sexual pleasure. These behaviors were characteristic of patrists who came from Saharasia, an area including the Russian steppes of western Asia and the Arabian desert. Gimbutas (1982) identifies a similar group, the Kurgans or "barrow" people, whom she believed were from the steppes between the Dnieper and Volga rivers in what is now Eastern Ukraine. These patrists, who were aggressive and violent, worshiped sky gods and wielded the thunderbolt and the ax, emphasized masculine values such as war-making, life-taking, domination, and hierarchy.

DeMeo hypothesizes that negative feedback from the environment in the Saharasia region may have fostered splits in people's thinking that separated their perception of Mother Earth into good and bad. His interpretation of the relational dynamic between humans and the Earth's environment corresponds with object relations theory and developmental psychology, which recognize that a human must have an "other" in order to develop a sense of self.

The varied climatic conditions in different parts of the world during prehistory, interspersed with natural disasters involving volcanic eruptions and earthquakes, may have been factors in the creation of polarized civilizations—one with a good mother archetype and the other with a bad mother archetype. On the whole, however, human consciousness remained undifferentiated during the prehistoric stage of evolution until Old Europe was invaded between 4500 and 2300 B.C.E. by several waves of the patrist marauders from Saharasia. These invasions appear to have gradually fragmented both the tribes and the consciousness of cultures in Old Europe, ending the codependent stage of human development.

The widespread destruction inflicted by the patrists on the matrifocal culture of Old Europe gave the civilization its first experiences of conflict, separation, and trauma. The patrist paradigm set the stage for the eventual emergence of the counter-dependent stage of development and the "bad father" archetype.

While the prehistoric matrifocal cultures worshiped images of the goddess and divine feminine, they did not have images of male divinity nor value the male principle. The invasions of the patrists helped catalyze both individual and collective development of humans from matrifocal to patrifocal. The patrifocal era helped humans become separate from Mother Earth and created a contrast between male and female values.

The transition to a patrifocal stage of development, which took several thousand years, was the beginning of the process of individuation in both humans and in their social systems. In order to establish a good father archetype, women got saddled with the bad mother archetype.

THE COUNTER-DEPENDENT OR PATRIFOCAL STAGE OF HUMAN EVOLUTION

This stage of development can be characterized as a reverse of the codependent social structures of prehistory. Patrifocal structures and values worshiped images of a male god and the divine masculine and forbid the worship of the goddess and the divine feminine. Over a period of a few thousand years, images of the goddess and the feminine principle and its values were systematically destroyed. One answer to why there is such a bias toward masculine values and a prejudice against feminine values in our global family structure lies in understanding more fully the role of the splitting stage of the counter-dependent stage of development. Below are notable quotations that describe the depth of the bad mother split (Curran, 1990).

"One hundred women are not worth a single testicle."

Confucius (551–479 B.C.E.)

"There's nothing in the world worse than women—save some other woman."

Aristophanes (488–380 B.C.E.)

"A woman should be covered with shame at the thought that she is a woman"

Clement of Alexandria (109–203 A.D.)

In Lyons, France, in 584 A.D. a group of 63 Catholic bishops, after a lengthy debate, decided by one vote that women were human.

Council of Macon, France

"Woman is defective and accidental...a male gone awry...the result of some weakness in the father's generative power.... . The voice of a woman is an invitation to lust and therefore must not be heard in the church."

St. Thomas Aquinas, 13th century A.D.

"The souls of women are so small that some believe they're not at all."

Samuel Butler (1612–1680)

"Man shall be trained for war, and woman for the recreation of the warrior: All else is folly."

Nietzsche (1844–1900)

"Sensible and responsible women do not want to vote."

President Grover Cleveland (1837–1908)

"Women are simple souls who like simple things.... . Our family Airedale will come clear across the yard for one pat on the head. The average wife is like that."

Episcopal Bishop James Pike (1968)

"I want to remind women that motherhood is the vocation of women.... . It is women's eternal vocation."

Pope John Paul II (1979)

Splitting has many negative connotations, such as judgment, separation, alienation, and projection. There are more positive connotations, however, from psychological and neurological perspectives that support its rightness. As humans perceived more clearly the differences between the principles of maleness and femaleness, their brains simultaneously developed more specialized capacities. The five-thousand-year patrifocal era has been a time of accelerated development in left-hemispheric brain functions such as analysis, differentiation, logic, rationality, and compartmentalization. All of these capacities are necessary for the next step in human evolution: full individuation, or the process of separating self from other, especially the mother.

Humans' emergent psychological capacities for perceiving differences, creating personal boundaries, and distinguishing self from other also stimulated new social behaviors. People began establishing villages, city-states, and nation-states constructed to protect them from the forces of nature and the invading hordes. This shift from hunting and gathering tribes to cities and states marks the beginning of the counter-dependent stage of development for humans as a species. It has been said that when the plow penetrated the soil of Mother Earth, the process of separating from Mother Nature began.

The increased capacity of the human brain to differentiate also facilitated the development of specialized languages and cultures containing unique values, beliefs, and social mores. As the differentiating function of the human brain accelerated, so did humanity's capacity for assessing, evaluating, and discriminating. The development of these brain functions had both positive and negative outcomes. On the positive side, humans became more capable of comparison and discernment. On the negative side, these same abilities also fostered competition, separation, and splitting that eventually led to violence and war against those perceived as different and therefore, bad.

Splitting was an important aspect of early Judaism, one that helped people develop left-hemispheric functions of the brain. Much of Hebrew mythology, for example, is framed as a battle between Yahweh, the masculine god, and the ebbing goddess culture of the Canaanites. When disasters struck Israel, the Hebrews blamed the Israelites for having regressed to goddess worship (Baring & Cashford, 1993).

Splitting served a similar purpose in early Christianity during the several centuries after Christ's death. When the Christian community in Jerusalem disbanded following the Jewish Revolt in 66–74 A.D., there was no authoritative version of Christianity that could claim to be the only authentic faith. Christianity fragmented into numerous sects that struggled for control of church doctrine. In 325, the Council of Nicaea established a creed for the orthodox Christian empire and sent missionaries out to convert the pagan tribes of the goddess cultures to its dogma (Birdsong, 1993).

Christianity was gradually institutionalized as the Catholic Church and it served as the collective ego structure for humans during this fragile transitional from the matrifocal to the patrifocal period. The Great Father of Christianity, the Buddha of Buddhism, Mohammed of Islam, Lao Tse of Confucianism, and Quetzecotal of the Mayan teachings all replaced the Great Mother of prehistory as collective parent figures. As patrifocal values deepened within European cultures during the Middle Ages and left-hemispheric functions became more highly specialized, technology began to emerge.

Many of the first products of technology were tools of war and violence created to intimidate people and force patriarchal values and Christianity on the civilizations of Old Europe. Remnants of the goddess culture in this region were systematically defaced and destroyed in humanity's unconscious attempt to separate from the Great Mother. As with the human toddler, emerging humanity made its mother "bad" to justify its drive to separate from her and to sublimate any residual feelings of dependency.

As the masculine principle that dominated European cultures spread via Catholic Christianity, the feminine principle receded into underground streams of esoteric Christianity known as the Cult of the Black Virgin. The period of the institutionalization of Christianity, known in European history as the Dark Ages, lasted until the 12th and 13th centuries when an awakening began in the Provence region of what is now France.

This region, home of the Cult of the Black Virgin, was an area of relative enlightenment and markedly free from the oppressive dogmas of the Roman Catholic Church. Marked by egalitarian relationships between men and women, progressive ideas, and science, this region exhibited an openness to cultural diversity unmatched in the northern and eastern regions of continental Europe. Here, where the appreciation for feminine values was never quite obliterated, Mary Magdalene was the established patron saint of gardens and vineyards throughout the region, the mediatrix of fertility, beauty, and the joy of life who reclaimed the ancient domains of the Great Mother of antiquity (Birdsong, 1993).

This remaining vestige of the ancient matrifocal culture was fertile ground for growth of esoteric groups such as the Cathars, the Knights Templar, and the troubadours extolling the virtues of their "Lady," a cultural projection of the good mother. Early in the 13th century, the Catholic Church began furiously attacking this remnant of the goddess culture with vicious, repeated campaigns designed to remove the last vestige of the Great Mother. The tenaciousness of these esoteric groups infuriated Church authorities, as they threatened the ever-expanding and strengthening structures of patriarchy. Some historians estimate that up to nine million men, women, and children were systematically tortured and murdered as witches or heretics during these campaigns in the 12th and 13th centuries (Sjöö & Mor, 1987).

After the Cathar Crusades in the 13th century, the Church in Rome drafted a document to accelerate its war against the feminine. This document, the *Malleus Maleficarum,* literally translated means "witches hammer." Collaboratively written by Heinrich Kramer and Jakob Springer and first published in 1484, the manual was a literary expression of patriarchy's primal fear of the bad mother. Making the mother bad, however, placed men in a quandary, because they also needed the presence of the good mother archetype in order to be sexual. To alleviate the internal dissonance between the need for oneness via sexuality and the need for psychological differentiation, patriarchy also made sexuality and the physical body bad. The only good woman was a virgin (the Virgin Mary).

The *Malleus* repeatedly stated that women are inferior, lustful, and depraved with weak minds, polluted bodies, and susceptible to becoming evil incarnate (i.e., witches). Pope Innocent VIII's Papal Bull, which accompanied the *Malleus,* was written in the gravest possible language. His endorsement "...gave the book enormous weight and prestige, inferring that whoever defied the work would bring down the wrath of God and his Apostles on his own head" (Hitchcock, 1994, p. 214).

The *Malleus,* ignored by virtually all contemporary historians, became the law of the land in Christendom for over two hundred years. Its threads, woven so deeply into the fabric of contemporary cultures, made its institutionalized animosity toward women and the feminine archetype virtually invisible. The *Malleus* presented women as "predators, abortionists, and killers of fetuses and speaks to the vilest aspects of the subconscious in no uncertain terms" (Hitchcock, 1994, p. 217). Here the Catholic Church clearly reinforced not only the bad mother archetype but also utilized humans, natural tendency to split to help obstruct humanity's drive for individuation.

From the 12th to the 17th centuries, Christianity reinforced the good mother–bad mother split by portraying women either as virgins in the light of Mother Mary or as whores such as Mary Magdalene. Neither of these extreme female archetypes provided women with a balanced model for their growth nor encouraged healthy relationships with men. Christianity also fostered a parallel split in male archetypes by portraying Jesus as chaste and Father God as judgmental, punitive, and aggressive. Because neither gender could achieve the high standards of behavior needed in order to embody the good archetypes, they typically perceived themselves as bad. Priests further reinforced splitting and badness in humans' relationships with God when they established themselves as religious intermediaries and drew upon patrist language from the Old Testament of the Bible to reinforce their role.

As bad as all this was, there were some positive connotations of splitting related to the concept of duality. Splitting provided people with opportunities for making choices, which is essential for accelerated consciousness. The ability to have a separate self and to make choices during the counter-dependent stage of development stimulated the development of more complex wiring in the brain. A contemporary example of this would be the outcomes of the split between the Soviet Union and the Eastern Block Countries in 1990. As the result of this split there has been an incredibly rapid growth of brain function and social systems in this region. During the Communist era, people were given few, if any, choices in their daily lives as everything was designed and regulated by the government. Since that time, post-Communist culture has been inundated with new ideas and products that have given people many new choices.

Splitting is a natural behavior, characteristic of individuals, couples, families, groups, organizations, and nations-states when they are in the counter-dependent stage of development, and they must be mastered as part of our evolutionary journey. We must accept splitting behaviors as an essential aspect of our humanness, an important step in our collective evolutionary journey toward wholeness.

THE INDEPENDENT AND INTERDEPENDENT STAGES OF HUMAN EVOLUTION

The cumulative effect of the five-thousand-year patrifocal era is a deep split in the human psyche that is reflected in all our social, economic, and political systems. Eliminating the good mother archetype, particularly in Western cultures, has effectively made patriarchal humanity into a single-parent family. Just as the toddler child needs to have two parents, each with both good and bad qualities, to complete its psychological birth or separation, so does "toddler humanity." Children from single-parent homes often become stuck in their psychological individuation process. The human species, without seeing its collective parent figures as having both good and bad qualities, became stuck in its evolutionary process as well. The constant recycling of developmental trauma, particularly during the splitting behaviors from the counter-dependent stage of development, creates regional and national wars as stages for collective reenactment.

Unresolved developmental trauma is the primary obstacle to the evolution of the human species. While this developmental stuckness is evident in all subsystems, primary relationships seem to offer the best place for resolution. While the war between patrists and goddess worshippers continues in battles at the collective or archetypal levels, intimate relationships have become the everyday battlegrounds where male/female, good/bad, mine/yours, and other splits seek resolution.

Androgyny and the Union of Opposites

Androgyny, or the union of the masculine and feminine energies, has mythic and archetypal elements. Its principles can be found in the mandorla figure shown on the cover of this book. Found in the art of many ancient cultures, such as the Chalice Well in Glastonbury, England, it symbolizes the binding together of that which has been torn apart and made unwhole (unholy). It helps people shift from a mundane cultural life to a spiritual life and offers the most profound spiritual experience available to humans. It helps the soul know that the fire of transformation and the flower of rebirth are one and the same (Johnson, 1991).

The mandorla is also a symbol of the partnership resolution of conflict, of the bringing together of dark and light, the conscious and unconscious, so that opposites, duality, and splits in consciousness can be healed. Whenever there is a clash of opposites and neither will give way to the other, it is certain that Spirit is present. All the great transformational teaching stories are mandorlas, because they bring together good and evil and the two become one. You create a mandorla in your mind each time you say something that is true (Johnson, 1991).

Creating a mandorla or story that balances maleness and femaleness at mythic levels calls for a new vision of history. This vision must include the knowledge, wisdom, and values of the feminine archetypes from the matrifocal era. Some consider this a revolutionary act, as it challenges the legitimacy of a patriarchal reality and those who govern it. Technological society's exclusion of the prehistoric mother from the everyday consciousness of humans has had an enormous impact on contemporary civilizations. Being cut off from our earlier history prevents us from understanding our deep, unconscious drive to travel in space, to escape the confinement of Mother Earth, and to rebuild our own versions of nation and culture in the imagined total freedom of a space colony (Thompson, 1981). We have forgotten that we are locked in an archetypal struggle to separate from the mother.

Larger social systems provide a grand stage for reenacting humanity's archetypal effort to separate from the mother. Here they reenact this biological drive through collective activities containing the dynamics of the drama triangle. Most people find transforming large systems too complex and too difficult. It may truly be a monumental task. The place to begin to resolve this archetypal struggle is in relationships where people are committed to working cooperatively to resolve conflicts in a partnership way.

Here we see the shadow forces of maleness and femaleness erupting into escalating levels of conflict, domestic violence, and divorce. Men and women project their dark aspects on each other in the most personal and destructive ways imaginable without an awareness of the archetypal nature of their battle. Mythic elements of human evolution enter into time and space, seeking resolution between opposites through men and women. Because the mythic elements are unconscious and men and women personalize their battle, there has been little hope for uniting opposites.

The information that could help committed couples work cooperatively to resolve this split has been available for many years and from many sources. For example, it can be found in the following excerpts from the Gospel of Thomas:

> Simon Peter said to them, "Let Mary leave us, for women are not worthy of life."
>
> Jesus said, "I myself shall lead her in order to make her male, so that she, too, may become a living spirit resembling you males. For every woman who will make herself male will enter the Kingdom of Heaven." (Robinson, 1977, p. 130).

Jesus does not mean that women should become like men but that, in the process of psychological growth, each gender must also take on the character of the opposite before wholeness can be achieved. This is revealed in a third excerpt from the Gospel of Thomas.

> Jesus said to them, "When you make the two one, and when you make the inside like the outside, and the outside like the inside, and the above like the below, and when you make the male and the female one and the

same, so that the male be not the male nor the female; and when you fashion eyes in place of an eye, and a hand in place of a hand, and a foot in place of a foot, and a likeness in place of a likeness, then you will enter [the Kingdom]." (Robinson, 1977, p. 121)

A New Vision of the Future

Couple relationships can foster androgyny in both people, whether it is a heterosexual or homosexual relationship, by using the partnership tools described in this book, especially in Chapter 10. By learning to resolve conflicts in a partnership way, shadow aspects can be integrated in a safe, committed, and loving relationship. The divine masculine and divine feminine can enter into family structures where children are welcomed into a divine triangle. This divine family structure, capable of meeting children's physical, mental, emotional, and spiritual needs, eliminates the dysfunctional drama triangle dynamics, and helps to create a new social structure for humanity.

In this new structure, feminine values such as nurturing, diversity, inclusion, life-giving, cooperation, sharing, and creating sustainable cultures are valued equally with masculine values related to discrimination, autonomy, individuation, and independence. Rescuers are transformed into mediators, and people can take responsibility for their behaviors, feelings, and problems. Family members can negotiate in partnership ways to get their needs met and resolve differences when they appear.

If you want to achieve these evolutionary tasks as an individual and help the human species move in this direction, you need a number of important elements. First, you need maps that outline the process of human evolution. Second, you need a shift in consciousness that helps you understand how developmental, mythic, and archetypal elements are being processed through your conflicts. This shift requires an upgrade in the wiring of your brain that helps you think multidimensionally. Third, you need to make a personal commitment to accept responsibility for owning your shadow aspects and not projecting them onto others. This means that you must stop projecting your shadow and "eat it" instead, as Robert Bly suggests in Chapter 10. Fourth, you must develop compassion for yourself and others during conflict situations by seeing escalated behaviors as evidence of post-traumatic stress. Fifth, you must commit to serving as a change agent, bringing your skills and awareness into other social systems where you are a member.

This is a large vision, one that is supported by a wealth of new tools that can foster human potential beyond any level previously known in the history of the human species. This book can help you move forward in your own evolution and allow you to become the catalyst for the growth of those around you. Bon voyage!

SELF-INVENTORY: THE INTERDEPENDENT LIVING INVENTORY

In the process of evolution, it can be helpful to inventory how your personal choices impact other levels of society. Use the following inventory to become more aware of the choices you have and of the choices you are currently making. Place a number before each statement to indicate the degree to which this statement is true for you.

1 = Never   2 = Occasionally   3 = Frequently   4 = Almost Always

_____	1.	I use natural ventilation instead of air conditioning in my home.
_____	2.	I conscientiously turn out lights when not in use.
_____	3.	I avoid buying and using unnecessary electrical gadgets such as toothbrushes, carving knives, and electric can openers.
_____	4.	I use mass transit or a bicycle whenever possible.
_____	5.	I own a car that gets 25 miles per gallon or more.
_____	6.	I eat less meat and more vegetables and grains.
_____	7.	I grow some of my own food.
_____	8.	I separate and recycle newspapers, glass, aluminum, and plastic.
_____	9.	I avoid prepackaged and processed food.
_____	10.	I compost my leaves, grass, and kitchen wastes.
_____	11.	I avoid using herbicides and pesticides on my yard and garden.
_____	12.	I grow drought-resistant landscape plants and avoid extensive lawn watering.
_____	13.	I actively support organizations such as the National Audubon Society and Greenpeace that help preserve the natural ecology.
_____	14.	I do not smoke.
_____	15.	I vote at local, state, and national elections.
_____	16.	I attend personal-growth seminars and workshops.
_____	17.	I am a member of a 12-step group or self-help support group that provides mirroring and acts as a catalyst in my growth.
_____	18.	I participate regularly in family meetings.
_____	19.	I volunteer or contribute to a nonprofit, social-service organization.
_____	20.	I participate in citizen diplomacy activities such as home stays in other countries or having guests from other countries.
_____	21.	I speak a foreign language.
_____	22.	I write to my state and/or national senator or representatives about my concerns.
_____		**Total**

Scoring and Interpretation

Add your numbers to get a total score, then use the following guidelines to interpret your score.

75–100	High degree of participation as an interdependent citizen.
50–74	Moderate degree of participation as an interdependent citizen.
25–49	Some participation as an interdependent citizen.
0–24	Little participation as an interdependent citizen.

Chapter 19

~

How Can I Integrate the Elements of the Partnership Way?

Just as this book opened your journey through the mysteries of conflict with the circular metaphor of the Medicine Wheel, it ends with another metaphor designed to help you integrate this journey. The skills and understanding you developed during this journey can guide you for many years to come. You will be tested on everything you have learned from using this book as you continue on your life journey. As you integrate your learning into daily life and gradually change the way you resolve conflicts, you will continue to sharpen your skills for resolving conflicts of values and beliefs. You will learn to use the strong feelings that accompany conflicts to help you get your needs met, and you will discover the sources of your intractable conflicts. As you do these things, you will experience a journey of personal and professional transformation.

While the journey of transformation may seem strange and scary, know that others have traveled this road and created maps to guide you. One ancient map of transformation was discovered by Joseph Campbell (1968) and described in his book, *The Hero with a Thousand Faces*. One of the world's leading authorities on mythology, Campbell studied myths and fairy tales of the Western world and the Orient that had been part of an oral teaching tradition for over 25,000 years. Throughout the history of the human race, myths and fairy tales have been used to teach people the simple and profound truths of life needed to grow and change. Embedded in these teaching stories, he discovered keys to the universal journey of transformation.

WHAT IS THE JOURNEY OF TRANSFORMATION?

While there seems to be a larger journey of transformation that covers each person's lifetime, there are also numerous mini-journeys. Each time you decide to resolve a conflict at its source, you move through a mini-journey. Each of the stages of development in each human system is like a larger journey of transformation. You, like most people, are probably in the midst of several concurrent journeys of transformation that involve yourself, your intimate relationships, your profession, and your special interests or hobbies.

You can get caught in your mini-journeys, trapped by fears about changing your life circumstances or an inability to remove yourself from the victim role. Some people fear looking deeper into their conflicts and exploring their developmental history. According to Campbell, you can change your patterns and break through your fears at any moment in your life. The decision to break free of the past and forge a new future requires spiritual courage and a determination to evolve as a human being.

Figure 19.1 shows the journey of transformation. Notice that it, like the Medicine Wheel, is circular. The beginning and the end of the journey come together.

Below is a description of each of the separate steps on the transformational journey. We use stories from our lives as examples to help you apply the map to your life. A self-awareness exercise at the end of this chapter will also help you chart your journey of transformation.

The Call to Awaken

This call usually comes as the result of an external event or some inner awareness that asks you to examine your life and the direction it is heading. This call can

appear as an opportunity to do something new or as an obstacle that prevents you from living the way you have been. It can come at any time in your life, a fork in the road where you can choose a new direction or pattern for your life. It can be precipitated by an illness or accident that interrupts your usual routine and gives you time to reflect. The call can be the result of losing one job or finding another job that requires moving. It also can come from reading a book, seeing a movie or play, losing a loved one, or the breaking up of a relationship.

Barry remembered getting his first call to awaken when he was in his mid-twenties and working as a junior-high-school counselor:

> Although I had never traveled further west than Pittsburgh from my small Eastern Pennsylvania hometown, I decided to get my master's degree in counseling at the University of Minnesota, which meant moving to the big city of Minneapolis. This decision drastically

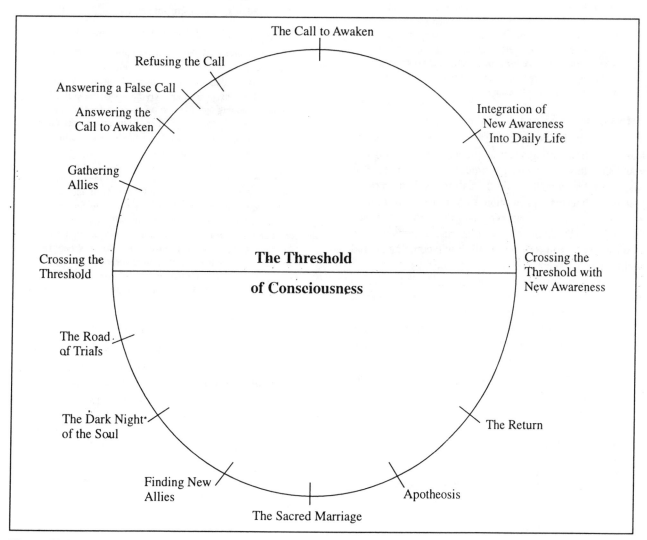

Figure 19.1
The Journey of Transformation

altered my life path, as I stayed on there for five years and completed my Ph.D. This move set the stage for subsequent calls to awaken that led me into deeper levels of consciousness.

Janae remembered her first call to awaken:

I was enrolled at the Merrill-Palmer Institute for Family Development in Detroit between my junior and senior years of college. Here I was exposed to many new and exciting ideas and people who were leaders in the field of human growth and development. My fellow students, who were from all over the country, helped me broaden my perspective and exposed me to many different cultural values and beliefs. Many of these experiences were in stark contrast to the conservative, repressive home environment of my native Midwestern farm culture.

One particularly expansive experience awakened me to some new dimension of spirituality. It happened at a Methodist church near the institute. During one particularly inspiring church service, the heavens seemed to part and I had a brief experience of being at one with God. It was such a profound moment, I didn't know what to do with this experience and had no one with whom I could talk about it. It gave me a glimpse of a deeper way of experiencing myself in relationship to something much larger than myself. This experience awakened in me a feeling of optimism about my future and a strange sense of destiny.

Refusing the Call

You may decide not to answer the call to awaken. At least not at first. Perhaps fear dominates your thinking and you decide this is not the right time to make changes. It is easy to find reasons to avoid the call to awaken. Perhaps you are in line for a promotion, or you decide to build a house or buy a car or boat. Whatever the reason, you may feel unable to break out of your roles and responsibilities. Don't worry. If you refuse the call, it will come again and again, ringing louder and louder each time.

Some people spend a lifetime being stuck at this step of the journey. They receive the call, refuse to answer it, and go back to business as usual. As the calls keep coming and getting a little louder, you may find life getting more and more intense until you realize what is happening. Perhaps a family member gets sick, you get passed over for a deserved promotion, or get fired from your job. Something forces you to answer the call.

Janae observed:

After graduating from college I was offered a teaching position at the Merrill-Palmer Institute that would have allowed me to begin graduate work with an outstanding staff at a prestigious school. I refused this tremendous opportunity and the call to awaken because I was afraid to risk moving alone to Detroit.

Answering a False Call

You may answer a false call by agreeing to do something that asks you to ignore your own needs and feelings, such as rescuing others. You may believe you are doing what is expected of you, but you are really setting yourself up to be a victim again. Perhaps old loyalties or debts pull at you, asking you to give up your own needs. You may become the chair of a committee at church, run for public office, or take a job you didn't want. Only later do you realize you have answered a false call.

Barry recalled doing this a number of times:

I became involved in causes to help others in the community. Each time I would find myself losing my focus and then losing interest in the cause and moving on to another cause. Recently, I was asked to chair a committee in the community that was creating new primary-prevention programs for infants and children. I put in increasing amounts of time on this project until I found myself feeling resentful that I did not have time for myself. As I became increasingly more critical of the project and the people involved, I could see that I was becoming a negative force at committee meetings. Fortunately, Janae noticed what was happening and encouraged me to extricate myself from this obligation and spend more time nourishing myself.

Janae remembered doing the same thing herself:

Instead of answering the call to awaken and risk opening myself to unknown challenges, I refused the call for something safe and known. I married during my first year of teaching and we quickly had our first child. I stopped teaching and focused on making my marriage succeed. Having lost my mother at the age of thirteen and spending my adolescence in a single-parent family, I wanted to create a happy and stable home.

During the years after my first son's birth, my marriage grew increasingly conflictual. Each time my marriage faltered, I tried even harder to make it succeed, but nothing seemed to work. To avoid feeling my despair, I became a workaholic housewife. By the time my oldest son was three years old, it was clear that my husband and I had deep incompatibilities. When I looked at the options related to divorce, however, I couldn't see any. I buried my fears and feelings of despair and decided to have another child.

Answering the Call to Awaken

This usually involves some kind of risk, such as trying something entirely new, discovering your own inertia, or identifying family patterns. Answering the call can be very difficult if you have refused it many times and feel backed into a corner. In any case, this decision usually involves a conscious choice to open yourself up to new growth and awareness. This decision is irreversible, although you may not realize until much later that you cannot go back to being unconscious.

When Barry answered his first call to awaken by attending graduate school in a big city far from his home, he didn't realize the impact this decision would have in awakening him to life:

While the challenges of graduate school and big-city life were new and exciting, one event changed my life forever. One day in a group therapy class, my professor, who was leading a practice group of graduate students, suddenly turned to me and said, "Barry, I don't think you are close to anyone." He saw through my mask, and I was terrified. Where could I hide? I was furious at him for seeing through me, but something told me that he was right and that it was time for me to answer the call to awaken.

Deciding to answer this call did not mean that things immediately got easier for me. First, I confronted the unresolved conflicts in my marriage, and then started therapy. As a result of taking these risks, I began to feel more and more alive. It took several more years of hard work before my decision to become alive bore fruit. I had refused so many calls to awaken that my whole life needed to shatter so that I could rebuild it.

Janae recalled how difficult it was for her to finally awaken:

My marriage did not improve. Rather, I sought ways to avoid facing the truth about my unhappiness. As my children got older and began to develop their own lives, I allowed myself to admit how much I missed the mental stimulation and challenge of teaching. One semester, I took a maternity-leave teaching position that renewed my zest for life but terrified my husband. He was adamant that my desire to teach was in direct conflict with his need for me to be a full-time homemaker and mother. He became critical of my interests and jealous of any time that I took away from him and our children. We eventually hit an impasse in our relationship that left me feeling hopeless and depressed.

One day I realized that I was dying. I knew deep inside of me that if I continued in the marriage, I would either get some catastrophic disease or I would have some kind of fatal accident. Once this realization hit me, I knew that I needed outside help. I entered therapy and discovered how much unresolved trauma from my childhood was replaying in my relationship with my husband and children. One of the first self-preserving things I did as a result of my counseling was to return to graduate school.

Gathering Allies

At first, the new challenges related to answering the call to awaken can seem overwhelming. It is often necessary to gather allies for support during your journey. The word *ally* comes from the Greek word meaning "silly or fool," so we may see our allies as silly or foolish in the beginning. Allies may also find you, rather than you having to look for them. Books may fall off the shelf into your hands in a bookstore, someone may give you a book to read or a tape to listen to, or you may have a chance meeting with an interesting stranger. You may also consciously seek allies by joining a support group or getting into therapy. These allies help us realize that we are on the right track and encourage us to become more awake.

The process of gathering allies was an ongoing process for Barry:

I found several books that really impacted me during this period and helped me see that I was on the right

track. I also developed several transforming friendships as well. While attending the American Humanistic Psychology conference in Berkeley, California, in the late 1970s, I encountered two new allies that eventually helped me change my life.

The first was Leonard Orr, who was one of the keynote speakers. Leonard is the founder of rebirthing, a breathwork process for releasing old traumas from the body. I tape-recorded his speech and as he spoke I noticed that the audience was laughing at him. Both his delivery and the content of what he was saying seemed to make many people in the audience very uncomfortable. After the conference, I listened to that tape many times because, in spite of the laughter, his message had a profound effect on me. I finally recognized the truth in what he was saying and a few months later I was headed back to California to be trained as a rebirther. As part of the training, I had to be rebirthed myself. I experienced tremendous energy releases from my body during this process and the whole training experience seemed to give me more confidence to move forward in my life both personally and professionally.

The other ally I encountered at this conference was Jean Houston, who was also a keynote speaker. When I heard her speak, I was filled with awe. Never before had I heard anyone speak so eloquently; what she said penetrated me to my core. It was as if she were speaking just to me that evening. I knew then that I wanted to study with her and this decision led me to sign up for several of her extended trainings in the next five to six years. I could feel myself heading in a new direction in my life, even though I didn't know at that time it would also open up some painful life events.

Janae found an ally almost the moment she decided to enter a master's program in psychology:

I felt old beside many of the students in my classes. In one of my classes, I met Molly, a woman about my age and we began a friendship. She was divorced and her husband had custody of her four children. I was absolutely stunned when I discovered that her children lived next door to me with their father and stepmother. Molly understood my struggle to make my marriage work, my desire to have a life and interests of my own, my feelings of guilt about neglecting my children, and my experience of feeling lost and lacking an identity as a person.

Molly and I spent many hours together talking about ourselves, our lives, and our dreams. For the first time since college, I felt as though I had a friend with whom I could share everything. She also invited me to join a therapy group to which she belonged, which expanded my circle of support while I was deciding what to do about my failing marriage. This circle of allies reflected back my feelings and validated my need to become an independent person. Molly was a great role model for me in believing that my children could survive a divorce and that I could repair any damage to them that might result. I felt really grateful to have Molly's support during this difficult period. She is still my friend today.

Crossing the Threshold of Consciousness

When you have gathered enough allies, you must risk crossing the threshold of consciousness into the unknown. This usually requires a leap of faith, a belief that you are doing the right thing. This step involves crossing a number of smaller thresholds before you can take that leap of faith into the unknown. The first is the *silliness* threshold, which involves the fear of looking foolish to others. Another is the *sanity* threshold, or fearing you might go crazy if you leap into the void or that you will fall into a black hole and never return.

The *knowledge* threshold involves a fear of discovering something new that might invalidate your way of seeing yourself or the world. The *trust* threshold reflects your vulnerability and fear of being hurt. You may also experience a love threshold, where you fear that you will lose the love of friends and family if you cross the threshold. Finally, you may find a *survival* threshold looming in front of you, fearing death or abandonment.

Barry continued his story:

I felt stuck in my relationship with my first wife for a long time, but I seemed to lack the courage to do anything about it. I finally decided to tell her about my feelings. We sat up that night and talked for about four hours. At the end of our talk, we decided to get a divorce. We had been having marital difficulties for a long time and it became clear to both of us that we were headed in different directions. While I had an internal feeling of rightness about this decision, I felt really scared. This was the most risky thing I had ever done in my life and I didn't have a pattern for what I had decided to do. It truly felt like a leap into the unknown.

Janae:

It became increasingly clear over a period of several months that my marriage was not transformable. This realization emerged slowly as the result of many long conversations with my husband. I was very clear that I wanted a relationship based on partnership and he did not. I wanted desperately to change my "mousewife" existence and to do it in a way that preserved our family.

My husband wanted me to be a traditional housewife and to give up my need for interests outside him and our children. His expectations, which mirrored the patriarchal, Midwestern farm culture that I grew up in, asked me to move backward in my growth and development. It was clear that I would have to sacrifice myself, my interests, and my need to become an individual in order to preserve my marriage and our family.

At some point, I decided to end our interminable discussions and begin divorce proceedings. This decision was an act of independence and self-preservation, an indication of my growing sense of self and need to be more conscious about the way I lived.

The Road of Trials

After the decision to cross the threshold into the unknown is made, you are immediately faced with the road of trials. These tests of your courage and commitment force you to rely on your internal resources to handle the tests you encounter. There is no time to look back, to consult your notes, to think it over, or talk to a trusted friend. The decisions must be made quickly and decisively.

Barry:

After our decision to divorce, I found myself moving into a new home, building new relationships with my children, dating for the first time in over 25 years, and daily meeting new challenges I never thought I would ever have to face. Within a year, I married Barbara.

My happiness was short-lived because our closeness brought up a new wave of family patterns for both of us. Barbara began to be critical of me in ways that reminded me of my mother, and I began to act in ways that reminded Barbara of her father.

Janae:

In the period of the time during my separation and divorce, I moved three times. I did not want to buy a home because I did not have any idea where my journey would take me. I decided to invest in myself and, after completing one year of graduate school, enrolled in the Mystery School, a year-long, human-potential training program in New York led by Dr. Jean Houston. I used the money from my divorce settlement to retool and began envisioning a new life for myself. Of course, my children and old friends thought I was crazy to do something so risky, but I knew that it would take some radical experiences to revitalize my life.

The Dark Night of the Soul

Sometime during the road of trials, you may have to endure the dark night of the soul when the bottom literally drops out of the world. This might involve the death of a loved one, the end of a career, a serious illness, or an accident that tests you beyond anything you have ever experienced. You usually emerge from this experience feeling much stronger and more integrated.

Barry related his dark night of the soul:

It was the day before Easter in 1983. Barbara and I had plans to go skiing and stay overnight at a ski resort. That morning as we packed to leave, Barbara seemed distant and suggested that we not go. Because of my eagerness, she finally agreed. Early that afternoon, as we were skiing together down an intermediate level slope, we hit an unmarked patch of sheer ice. I was ahead of her and went tumbling down the hill. After I stopped sliding, I looked around for Barbara. She was lying in a heap about thirty feet to my right. When I got to her she was unconscious and was bleeding through her ski pants. For the next twenty hours she clung to life as I stayed by her side in the hospital. Finally at eleven o'clock on Easter morning she died.

The bottom fell out of my life. For months after her death, I also wanted to die. I could not find much reason to live, except to console our children and friends. Slowly, I began to piece together the fragments of my life. I realized that if it had been my time to die, I would have died with her that day. I made the choice to continue living.

Janae related one dark night of her soul:

Shortly after my divorce was final, my oldest son left for college and my youngest son decided to live with his father. For the first time in my life, I was alone. I was faced with focusing on myself, my own needs, and my purpose in life. I read a lot of spiritual books, prayed, continued my graduate studies in transpersonal psychology and participation in the Mystery School training. Even with all my newfound freedom and expanded interests, I still felt lost. Finally, I admitted that I was experiencing a spiritual crisis.

Finding New Allies

The kind of life-altering events around a dark night of the soul often attract new allies. The friends from before your shift in consciousness will probably seem shallow and unable to understand your despair. This step gives you an opportunity to go deeper into yourself to seek the meaning of your Dark Night of the Soul experiences. Some people return to therapy, travel, or develop new interests and activities.

Barry recounted his efforts to find new allies:

After Barbara's death, I began doing things I had never tried. I traveled to Europe for a vacation. I began speaking more directly about my feelings, wants, and needs. I found new teachers to help me move deeper into myself. I had difficulty relating to the old friends I had had with Barbara. I would talk about Barbara's death to anyone who would listen, mostly trying to understand it and talk my way through the enormous grief I felt. This became too much for most old friends to handle and they just stayed away.

Janae recalled how quickly she found new allies:

I decided to look around me for help. I began meeting with my housemate's group of spiritual friends, learning more about their nontraditional beliefs. I also began dating a man deeply involved in Eastern forms of spirituality who taught me to meditate and introduced me to vegetarian eating. His respectful and loving nature helped me heal the deep wound in my femininity from my failed marriage. I also joined a meditation circle and began reading teachings from a body of materials known as the Ageless Wisdom teachings. These experiences broadened my perspective about the meaning of life and opened friendships with a whole new variety of people. It gradually became clear that I must find a way to focus myself and begin living more purposely.

The Sacred Marriage

This very special step in your journey starts when you begin reclaiming your projections. You develop a sense of inner unity between your masculine and feminine parts that helps you integrate your power and your love.

In many sacred traditions, this step was ritualized and celebrated as a major step toward deeper consciousness.

Barry remembered his sacred marriage experience:

The twelve months following Barbara's death were a time of tremendous healing and growth for me. I realized that codependency had been a strong dynamic in our relationship. I had projected my ideal feminine image on Barbara and she had done her best to fulfill it. Conversely, I saw how Barbara had projected her ideal masculine image on me and I had done my best to fulfill it as well. When Barbara died, it was as though my feminine side had died with her. I felt like half a person and my first impulse was to try to find someone to replace that part of me.

I had been developing a much greater appreciation for myself and decided not to search for another woman who would carry my projected feminine aspect. I knew I could now care for myself and began feeling complete and whole for the first time in my life. I was developing a new kind of relationship with myself and vowed not to get into another serious relationship until I had completed the process of building a solid relationship with myself.

In order to reclaim and integrate my feminine part, I began to nurture myself and pursue some of my creative interests. I also read many books, especially those about the process of recovering shadow parts. I attended workshops with people who specialized in helping men integrate lost or split off parts of themselves and I began therapy again.

Janae remembered her sacred marriage experiences:

I first participated in a sacred marriage ritual during a human-potential workshop with Dr. Jean Houston. This workshop exercise, which occurred during the period when I was separating from my first husband, was a very powerful transcendent experience. I had my first understanding of what it meant to have an internalized male part. It seemed clear to me that I had always projected it onto my father or my husband. Once I began to reclaim my own inner male, I no longer felt such a dependency on my husband. This experience prepared me for a period of living independently and for restructuring myself and my life so that I could live in partnership.

The Apotheosis

This step involves casting off the false self, which you developed earlier in life in order to please others, so that your higher and lower selves can merge. At this point, you have sufficiently dealt with your residue of developmental trauma and feel compassion for yourself and your parents. This is a time of inner healing, a time to move out of old victim or rescuer roles and build healthy boundaries with friends and loved ones.

Barry shared how this process is moving in him:

I have had many transcendent or transpersonal experiences in my life where I connected with my higher self. Some took me years to fully understand. I have felt blessed by my relationship with Janae. I can share these moments of deep connection to myself with her. One of my greatest challenges, however, is to "re-member" who I really am and to live every day out of my higher self. I have been able to experience periods of feeling this connection but have difficulty sustaining it. My goal in life is to be able to sustain a deep connection with my higher self and remember who I really am.

Janae remembered her experiences of apotheosis.

In retrospect, I have had several experiences of apotheosis, beginning with my call to awaken in the Methodist Church in Detroit while I was in college. This was followed by a long period of spiritual emptiness. During the first months of my relationship with Barry, I began experiencing episodes of transcendence that helped me connect to my higher self. Sometimes they happened during our lovemaking or other times when we were feeling close. Another occurred while standing on the bank of the Dneiper River during a trip to Ukraine. These experiences each felt uplifting, inspiring, and left me experiencing myself and life at a higher plane of existence.

In 1996, it became clear that it was time to deepen spiritually. I felt it was time to seek lost parts of my eternal self and went to New Mexico to do past-life regression work. These transcendent experiences opened me up to a new level of connection with my higher self and stirred my desire to live fully in this state of awareness.

I spent the following summer immersed in the teaching of Agni Yoga and began meditating another hour to two hours daily. I found that meditating early in the mornings when my mind was fresh and the world was quiet to be an excellent doorway to my higher self. Then I went on a month-long retreat to deepen even more and had a peak experience of what I would call rapture that lasted about two hours. Since this experience, I have continued my practice of extended meditations and committed more deeply to living out of my higher self at all times.

The Return to Consciousness

The transformational journey often seems complete at this stage, but actually this is only the halfway point. Your task in the next stage of the journey is to be able to take all that you have learned during your inner journey and integrate it into your everyday life. In other words, to get on with it.

This is not an easy task, for the everyday world still contains all the traps and family patterns that can lull you back to sleep again or pull you off-center. There are also unexpected costs for gaining access to your depths. Your friends and loved ones may not understand your experience or you may be tested and criticized by your peers about your beliefs and visions for yourself. They may work very hard to get you to return to the old drama-triangle dynamics. You also may find that the world that was once comfortable to be common, ordinary, banal. You may wish to return to the comfort and safety of your rich inner world. To put it simply, it becomes incredibly difficult to live in the everyday world after living in depth.

You must bring the knowledge from your inner depths back to the everyday world and learn how to integrate the inner and outer worlds. Crossing back over the threshold of consciousness into the outer world can activate some of the same fears that you had when you took your leap of faith into the unknown. You may fear that people will think you are weird or silly for wanting to pray, spending an hour a day in meditation, writing in a journal, or doing some daily spiritual practices. You may also fear that the split between your inner and outer worlds will drive you crazy.

Barry related his experiences of bringing his new awareness of wanting to live again after so many months in his inner world after Barbara's death:

I decided to follow my passion as things unfolded for me. If I was to stay single the rest of my life, that was okay. If I found a person with whom I felt compatible, I was open to a new relationship. I finally just surrendered to the flow of life. My decision to return to the outer world took place while I was attending Jean Houston's Mystery School in New York. One Friday evening during our dance and movement period, I literally bumped into an attractive woman named Janae who was attending the training.

When I went to apologize to her again the next day, I felt a strong attraction to her. Before I returned to Colorado at the end of the weekend, I took a bold step. I told her that I was attracted to her and, although I knew that she lived in Illinois, invited her to come to Colorado. On the plane back to Colorado, I had second thoughts about my boldness. I decided to write her a letter and explain why I had risked being so bold and about my decision to follow my passion.

Janae wrote back quickly and told of her plans to come to Colorado in the next month. We agreed to spend some time together getting to know each other at our next weekend of the New York training. When she came to Colorado to visit me, it took us only four days to recognize that we were meant to be together. The connection we felt for each other was so deep and so complete that we could hardly believe it. On Thanksgiving Day in 1984, Janae and I were married legally in Colorado, and in January 1985, Jean Houston performed our spiritual wedding ceremony at the Temple of Isis and Osirus at Abydos, Egypt.

Here our stories merged. Janae:

It seemed that I had spent most of my life focused on meeting the needs of others and had attracted people to me who liked my dependency. This dependency was not an issue in my relationship with Barry. My return to the outer world happened quite quickly after a few short months of intense bonding during our short courtship and honeymoon.

The day after our return from Egypt, Barry was scheduled to teach his class in group counseling at the university. He returned, unfortunately, with a case of King Tut's revenge and was not able to get out of bed. I had been a substitute teacher many times and knew it was not a difficult job, so I volunteered to go in his place. He gave me the preliminary information I needed to get the students oriented to the class and I went as his substitute. I gave out all the course outlines, explained the requirements of the class, and then shared with the group where we had been and why Barry was sick. This began a dialogue with the group that was very stimulating for me. I discovered quickly that the students were quite attuned to what I was sharing and I realized how comfortable I felt with them. My love of teaching had been rekindled and it was exciting to feel its energy again.

I returned home and gave Barry a report of my evening with the students. I remember saying, "It was one of my best experiences ever, as I could feel the excitement of relating with students and how easy it was for me. It was also one of my worst experiences in front of a class. I realized they were ready to work with me and I realized I didn't know what to do next. It was awful!" Barry looked at me with a little grin on his face and said softly, "Well, why don't you get your doctorate." I looked at him in total shock. After a moment or two, I said, "Okay, I will." Three months later I left for a ten-day entry colloquium and began my doctoral work. Two years and one month later it was finished. I felt elated. I finally had some tools and skills to enter the outer world.

Becoming the Master of Both Your Worlds

The last step on the circular journey is to become the master of both your inner and outer worlds. This means developing a "passport" that allows you to travel back and forth over the threshold between them. Then you can enter your rich inner world, harvest your riches, and bring them with you back into your everyday world. It means being able to navigate the interdependent world between oneness and separateness, free of major splits in your consciousness, and free of your developmental traumas and the traps of the drama triangle. As for our parallel journeys:

> This is the purpose of all our inner work. We continue to live and work together cooperatively, which brings to the surface pieces of our patterns that we help each other clear. Each conflict that we have is like a mini-journey of transformation. Looking at the source of our conflict forces us to cross the threshold of consciousness again and look within. As we discover split-off parts of ourselves, we go through the apotheosis and sacred marriage again and again.

> We feel grateful that we found tools and metaphoric maps to guide us into our depths. Without them, we probably wouldn't take the risks we do in pushing through our conflicts. We find our relationship stimulating and spiritually invigorating. It seems to have no end; it keeps us spiraling into more self-awareness and appreciation for life's complexity and more awe regarding the depth of the human psyche. We know that we will have many more adventures together and separately as we grow and become more conscious of who we really are.

SELF-AWARENESS EXERCISE: HOW DO I MAP MY OWN TRANSFORMATIONAL JOURNEY?

Below is an exercise designed to help you map your own transformational journey. As was mentioned, if you look closely at the major events of your life you can begin to see patterns, and if you have a map for organizing these patterns, you should be able to chart your life journey of transformation and determine where you actually are on that journey. By using this same map, you will probably be able to discover a number of mini-journeys that are also part of the larger life journey. Take a look at Figure 19.1 and read the short descriptions of the steps in the transformational journey below, thinking about the events in your life that parallel each of these steps.

1. *The Call to Awaken*: The time in your life when you felt that things must change for you, often caused by some kind of life crisis or a sense of impending crisis.
2. *Refusing the Call or Answering a False Call*: The call is refused, or you choose to do something that will help you avoid waking up to something you need to do or know. What events in your life can you identify with as fitting these circumstances?
3. *Answering the Call to Awaken*: The call to make changes in your life is so strong that you cannot refuse to listen to it. When you answer the call to awaken you make a conscious choice to awaken.
4. *Gathering Allies*: You search for friends or resources to help you, to provide you with information or skills, and to support you while you take the risks to change.
5. *Crossing the Threshold*: After getting up your courage and collecting enough information, you decide to take action. You cross into the unknown (perhaps quitting a job, ending a relationship, returning to school, entering therapy). It makes you encounter all your worst fears and limitations. You (or others) may think you are going crazy. You may be afraid that you will lose your relationship with loved ones or family (the familiar). It is a very scary time.
6. *The Road of Trials*: Tests of your courage and determination challenge your decision to make changes in your life. Are you really ready to do this? Self-doubts may cloud your perceptions but you must go on.
7. *The Dark Night of the Soul*: During this time in your life you face great difficulties and challenges that become a crisis for you. It may be the death of a loved one or a betrayal.
8. *Finding New Allies*: Friends and allies who have been helpful in the past may now be replaced by new ones who are further along on their own journey. You may have to say good-bye to old friends and safe situations as you journey onward.
9. *The Sacred Marriage*: At this halfway point of your journey you need to connect your inner masculine and feminine energies. You balance yourself through an inner marriage that allows you to take charge of your life without feeling guilty and helps you receive what you want and need without resistance.
10. *The Apotheosis*: Another kind of union, where the higher and the lower selves unite. You begin to know your own divineness and can begin to live out of a deeper sense of who you are and what your life purpose is.
11. *The Return*: You may experience a long voyage back to the daily, external world where you can use and apply things you have learned on your internal journey. This can mean letting go of the old ways of relating or resolving conflicts and replacing those ways with your newly developed skills and information.
12. *Master of Both Worlds*: The world of your inner journey and your external world work together so that you can live a life that is fulfilling and satisfying.

SKILL PRACTICE EXERCISE: MAPPING YOUR OWN TRANSFORMATIONAL JOURNEY

List below the events in your life that correspond to the various steps on the transformational journey. Consult the preceding descriptions and examples in the chapter for ideas.

1. My call(s) to awaken:
2. The calls to awaken that I refused:
3. False calls I have answered:
4. The allies I gathered to help me were:
5. The thresholds that I had to cross were:
6. On the road of trials I encountered the following obstacles:
7. During my dark night of the soul, I experienced:
8. The new allies that I found while on the road of trials were:
9. During my sacred marriage/apotheosis, I:
10. As I returned from my inner journey, I brought the following ideas or visions with me:
11. The ways that I now master my inner and outer worlds are:

RESOURCES

INSTRUCTIONAL MATERIALS

Curriculum Guides, Videos and Books

CURRICULUM GUIDES

Alternatives to Violence (1986) by Kathy Bickmore and the Northeast Ohio Alternatives to Violence Committee. Akron, OH.

Children's Creative Response To Conflict Program (CCRC). Fellowship of Reconciliation, Box 271, Nyack, NY 10960. 914-358-4601.

> They provide specially designed activities around the themes of cooperation, communication, affirmation, conflict resolution, problem solving, mediation and bias awareness. Involves parents and teachers in the creating of a safe, supportive classroom atmosphere.

Conflict Management: A Middle School Curriculum by Elizabeth Loescher, 2564 South Yates St., Denver, CO 80219. 303-936-3286. $20.

> Contains twelve lessons, designed to fit any classroom. Tested in urban schools. You and your students will learn: Your own conflict resolution style, strategies for win-win outcomes, processes that solve the conflict and build relationships, how to fight fair and violence prevention skills that work.

Coordinators' Student Mediation Manual: High School (1995). (Elementary and Middle levels available) by Colorado School Mediation Project. CSMP 3970 Broadway, Ste. B3, Boulder, CO 80304.

Creating the Peaceful School: A Comprehensive Program for Teaching Conflict Resolution. (1994). Research Press, Dept. 110, PO Box 9177, Champaign, IL 61826. 1-800-519-2707.

> Creating the Peaceful School includes two books: a Program Guide and a Student Manual. Recommended for elementary grades but adaptable for use in middle schools.

Creative Conflict Solving for Kids 4-9 (1985) by Fran Schmidt and Alice Friedman. Grace Abrams Peace Education Foundation, Miami Beach, FL.

Fostering peace. Iowa Peace Institute, Grinnell, IA. 515-236-4880.

> A comparison of nine different conflict resolution approaches for use with both elementary and high school-aged children.

Games Children Should Play: Sequential Lessons for Teaching Communication Skills in Grades K-6 (1980) by Mary Cihak and Barbara Jackson Heron. Good Year Books, Scott Foresman and Co., 1900 E. Lake Ave., Glenview, IL 60025.

Learning the Skills of Peacemaking: An Activity Guide for Elementary-Age Children on Communicating, Cooperating, Resolving Conflict (1987) by Naomi Drew. Jalmar Press, Rolling Hills Estates, CA.

> A creative activity guide for elementary-aged children to learn self-awareness, understanding of others, and mediation skills.

Opposing Viewpoints Pamphlets. (1997). Greenhaven Press, Inc., PO Box 289009, San Diego, CA 92198-9009. 1-800-231-5163.

> Presents opposing viewpoints on 80 of the important controversial issues. Good to use to help students practice resolving conflicts of values and beliefs.

Peacemaking Made Practical: A Conflict Management Curriculum For the Elementary School. (1991). Elizabeth Loescher. The Conflict Center, 2564 South Yates St., Denver, CO 80219. $25.

> A practical curriculum with over 50 lesson plans in developing awareness of feelings of self and others, social skills and problem solving. All of the content is designed for the elementary level student and many clever applications of

conflict resolution are included for the K-3 classroom.

Peer Mediation: Conflict Resolution in Schools. (1996). Fred Schrumpf, Donna K. Crawford and Richard J. Bodine. Research Press, Dept. 110, PO Box 9177, Champaign, IL 61826. 1-800-519-2707.

> A revision of a widely used resource that contains a Program Guide and a Student Manual. Provides step-by-step instructions on implementing a successful program.

Personal Development, (1990) Vicki Phillips, Personal Development, PO Box 203, Carmel Valley, CA 93924.

> This is a one semester curriculum designed to promote self-esteem, communication skills, goal setting and problem solving. Gershen, and Raphael, Lev., Minneapolis, MN: Free Spirit Publishing.

Student Mediation Manual: High School (1995) by Colorado School Mediation Project. (Elementary and Middle levels available). CMSP 3970 Broadway, Ste. B3, Boulder, CO 80304.

Teaching kids to care. (1987). Charlene Trovato. Instructor Books, Cleveland, OH.

> A guide to understanding and developing a pro-social environment both within the classroom as well as within the home. Specifically focuses on ages 2 to 6 with special chapters on disabilities, handicaps, and ethnic differences.

Teaching Young Children in Violent Times: Building a Peaceable Classroom (1994) by Diane Levin. New Society Publishers, Philadelphia, PA.

The Friendly Classroom for a Small Planet (1988). Priscilla Prutzman; Lee Stern; M. Leonard Burger; and Gretchen Bodenhamer. New Society Publishers, Philadelphia, PA.

> Techniques for nonviolence, cooperation, and problem solving in grades K through 6 developed by the Reconciliation Quakers and used by more than 20,000 teachers and parents.

Training and Implementation Guide for Student Mediation (1990) by New Mexico Center for Dispute Resolution. (elementary, secondary, and youth detention). Albuquerque, NM.

The Vortex: Conflict, Power and Choice! A play and follow up workshop for secondary schools written, developed and performed by the Metro State College of Denver Touring Theatre Company. Play and workshop are each 45 minutes in length. Contact: Deb O'Donnell 303-494-7470.

We Can Work It Out!: Problem Solving Through Mediation (1993) by Judith Zimmer and the National Institute for Citizen Education in Law. Social Studies School Service, Culver City, CA.

VIDEOS

Alternative to Violence: Conflict Resolution and Mediation. A two part video series produced by Chariot Productions and United Learning. $150. (Available from the Colorado School Mediation Project, 303-444-7671.)

Broken toy. (1992). Summerhill Productions, 846 1/2 McIntire Ave., Zanesville, OH 43701. Price $50.

> A 25-minute video that depicts a number of realistic scenarios in the life of a 12-year old boy who is ridiculed and physically assaulted at school. Not only is the home life of the victim portrayed but the main bully's family is also depicted. While the story builds empathy for the victim, the content is dramatic. The ending, however, restores hope. The goal of this video is to build awareness and compassion in the bullies by showing them how much emotional damage their behavior can cause. Grades 4 and up.

Bully. (1973). National Instructional Television Center, Box A, Bloomington, IN 47401.

> A 20-minute video that presents a new boy in a classroom who is resented for his academic success. He is taunted and harassed by a bully who follows him after school. No violence or overly dramatic content is shown. While the classroom setting and dress of the boys appear dated, the film effectively presents the frightened feelings of being singled out by a bully. Grades 2 to 6.

Bullying at school. (1992). BV Project, Dan Olweus, University of Bergen, Oysteinsgate 3, N-5007 Bergen, Norway. Price $250.

> A 20-minute video that shows scenes from the lives of two bullied children, a 10-year-old boy and a 14-year-old girl. Designed as a basis for discussion amongst students and teachers. The video does use English subtitles. Grades 4 and up.

Bus discipline. (1992). Teaching Strategies, PO Box 5205, Eugene, OR 97405-9929. Price $299.

> A four-tape set that presents information on setting policies that are positive, trains drivers in management, shows teachers how to support safe policies,

and gives a step-by-step process for solving behavior problems.

Conflict Resolution: CR Essentials. (1995). The Conflict Resolution Network, PO Box 1016, Chatswood, NSW 2057, Australia (02)419-8434. Purchase: $325 plus postage (discount price available to schools and community groups).

This video introduces basic conflict resolution skills in a high quality, viewer-oriented production. Deals with win/win approach, assertiveness, active listening, mapping, developing options and creative response. A comprehensive workbook accompanies the video and includes handout sheets with background information, pre-and post-viewing questions, discussion issues, follow-up activities and timelog.

Coping with Bullying. (1991). James Stanfield Company, Drawer G, PO Box 41058, Santa Barbara, CA 93140. Price $249.

A 3-video set with a teacher's guide to help students understand and recognize bullying behavior. Various assertive responses are demonstrated as ways to respond to bullying. Grades 6 and up.

Different and the Same. (1995). Available from the CSMP, 3970 Broadway, Ste. B3, Boulder, CO 80303.

This multi-cultural awareness series is designed to help children and teachers talk about, understand and combat racism. Animal puppet figures represent children whose experiences reflect situations involving prejudice and lead to discussion of ways to resolve situations. A teacher training video is also available to help teachers effectively use the series with children. This is a nine-part series and training video.

Freedom from Violence. (1995). Available from the CSMP, 3970 Broadway, Ste. B3, Boulder, CO 80303.

This four-part staff development program provides teachers and staff with the skills to help youth avoid violence. Experts demonstrate effective techniques that students can practice to resolve conflicts, recognize and avoid behavior, manage anger, stay out of gangs and more. Guidelines for creating a safe school and tips for an emergency plan in case of violent situations will provide staff and students with the security they need to teach and learn.

Get straight on bullies. (1988). National School Safety Center, 4165 Thousand Oaks Blvd., Ste. 290, Westlake Village, CA 91362. Price $50.

An 18-minute video that presents the story of a young boy victimized by a bully. The video is designed to educate faculty and students that bullying is a problem and one that adversely effects everyone within a school environment that tolerates it. Does not tell how to institute a program but convincingly presents the problem.

Hopscotch-Revised. (1987). Churchill Media. Price $195.

An animated story of a boy who wants to make friends and tries showing off his prowess, parading possessions, being noisy and disruptive, acting tough, and flattering. Finally, he stops playing roles and is accepted. Available as a video or film. Grades K to 6.

Michael's story: The no blame approach. (1990). Lame Duck Publishing, 71 South Road , Portshead, Bristol BS20 90Y. Price 40 Francs.

Produced in England, this video introduces a step-by-step, teacher-led program that has been successful in the English schools in helping the victims and stopping the perpetrators.

Peace on the Playground. (1997). Films for the Humanities & Sciences, PO Box 2053, Princeton, NJ 08543-2053. Tele.: 1-800-257-5126. Purchase $129; Rental $75.

This program, hosted by a father and his young son, teaches children and parents how to deal with the problems of violence and the proliferation of guns. Kids suggest ways to deal with anger and tips for parents on dealing with violence on television. Also discusses the danger of guns in the home and at school.

Peer Mediation in Action (1996). A four "scenario" videotape for training students to be mediators and to educate staff and parents on the mediation and negotiation process. For the middle school level. $125. (Available from the Colorado School Mediation Project, 303-444-7671.)

Playground discipline. (1991). Teaching Strategies, PO Box 5205, Eugene, OR 97405-9929. Price $249.

A two-video set that trains the teaching and playground staff in setting up a safe playground environment, designing consistent and effective expectations and clear procedures. Specific playground scenes very effectively show how to interact with the students, deal with crises, implement consequences and deal with fighting. A very effective, helpful video for training playground aides.

Right Turns Only. (1995). Available from CSMP, 3970 Broadway, Ste. B3, Boulder, CO 80303.

This middle school drug education series targets students in urban and suburban school systems and focuses special attention on African-American and Hispanic youth. This series examines substance abuse, self-esteem, critical viewing, conflict resolution and peer relationships.

Secret Shame: Bullied to Death. (1997). Films for the Humanities and Sciences, PO Box 2053, Princeton, NJ 08543-2053. Tele.: 1-800-257-5126. Purchase $129; Rental $75.

The video tells a tragic story of a 13-year-old who took his own life after being bullied viciously by peers. (28 min. color).

Standing up for yourself. (1986). Coronet Films and Video. Price $250.

Part of the "Taking Responsibility" series of tapes. This video reminds the viewer that some attempts to be assertive will not be successful and that sometimes it is necessary to get help from adults. Grades K to 6.

Stamp out bullying. (1990). Lame Duck Publishing, 71 South Road, Portshead, Bristol BS20 90Y Price 40 Francs.

Produced in England, this video follows a training workshop in a school, which was the result of a 14-year old girl's suicide attempt following a bullying incident.

Student Workshop: Solving Conflicts. Hands on workshop in conflict resolution skills for grades 2-4. Sunburst Video, 1-800-431-1934.

The choice. (1981). Phenix Films and Videos. Price $225.

The story of how three boys struggle with their relationship when a new boy attempts to enter their group. The film is a good example of bully/victim relationships and of how the silent majority can be helpful. Unfortunately, this is not available as a video but only as a film.

Violence: Inside/Out. United Learning, 1-800-424-0362. $150. (Available from the Colorado School Mediation Project, 303-444-7671.)

BOOKS

Alexander, Martha. (1981). *Move over twerp*. Dial Books, New York.

An enchanting story showing the resourcefulness of a young boy who employs humor to solve a bullying problem.

Bavolek, Stephen. (1994). *Red, white & bruises*: *Spanking in the U.S.A.; What to do instead*. Family Development Resources, Inc., 3160 Pinebrook Road, Park City, UT 84060. $1 plus postage. 1-800-688-5822.

This little 18 page booklet offers an overview of the problem and possible consequences plus practical discipline suggestions to parents that do not involve spanking.

Beale and Fields. (1989). *The win/win way*. Harcourt, Brace; New York.

Bach, George and Goldberg, Herb. (1974). *Creative Aggression: The Art of Assertive Living*. Anchor Press, Garden City, NY.

Bennett, William J., Ed. (1993). *A Treasury of great moral stories*. Simon and Schuster, New York.

This book is a collection of stories and excerpts that relate to: self-discipline, compassion, responsibility, friendship, work, courage, perseverance, honesty, loyalty and faith.

Borba, Michele, (1989). *Esteem builders*. Rolling Hills Estates, CA: Jalmar Press.

A Self-esteem book designed for grades K to 8, which presents specific ideas for improving student achievement and behavior as well as the school climate.

Bosch, Carl. (1988). *Bully on the bus*. Parenting Press, Inc., Seattle.

A terrific book that allows the reader to select from different options in how to handle a bully encountered on the school bus. For example, the victim can decide to fight back or to ask a friend for help by turning to different pages to learn the outcome. Children eventually read all the options, curious to find out which one proves the most effective.

Bush, Robert and Folger, Joseph. (1994). *The promise of mediation*. San Francisco, CA: Jossey-Bass.

Brookfield, Stephen. (1987). *Developing critical thinkers: Challenging adults to explore alternative ways of thinking and acting*. Jossey-Bass, San Francisco.

Brown, Marc. (1990). *Arthur's April fool*. Little, Brown & Co., Boston.

Bush, Robert and Folger, Joseph. (1994). *The promise of mediation*. Jossey-Bass, San Francisco.

Byers, Betsy. (1981). *The 18th emergency*. Puffin Books, New York.

> A twelve-year old boy is tormented by the school bully for belittling him. His parents are of no help nor is his best friend, who is also frightened of the bully. Eventually he is beaten up by the bully.

Carlson, Nancy. (1983). *Loudmouth George and the sixth grade bully*. Puffin Brooks, New York.

> How George, with the help of his friend Harriet, thwarts an older and larger boy from stealing his lunch.

Carrick, Carol. (1983). *What a wimp!* Clarion Books, New York.

> Story of a fourth-grade boy who moves to a new school following the divorce of his parents. He is harassed daily by a bully as he walks home from school. Finally, he decides to just let the bully beat him up. Surprisingly, the bully does nothing.

Cohen, Richard, (1995). *Students resolving conflict: Peer mediation in schools*. (Grades 6-12). Goodyear Books, Glenview, IL.

Colorado Bar Association. (1992). *Manual on alternative dispute resolution*. Colorado Bar Association, 1900 Grant St., Ste. 950, Denver, CO 80203-4309.

> In 1992 the Colorado Supreme Court and the Colorado Legislature adopted separate measures to open up alternatives to litigation. This manual describes the various alternatives and their appropriate uses.

Coombs, Karen. (1991). *Beating bully O'Brien*. Avon Books, New York.

> A fifth-grade boy is physically assaulted by a girl bully on his way home from school. His dad makes him feel like a sissy for not defending himself, but the boy is a viola player and he does not want to hurt his hands. When the bully's older brother attacks the boy, the girl bully intervenes and helps him. He later learned that she gets beaten up on at home by her older brother.

Covey, Steven. (1994). *The seven habits of highly effective people*. Simon and Schuster, New York.

> This is a best selling book and prescription for success which develops the psychological aspects of success.

Crum, Thomas. (1987). *The magic of conflict*. Simon and Schuster, New York.

Dinkmeyer, Don and McKay, Gary. (1989). *Parents' handbook for systematic training for effective parenting*. Random House, New York.

Drew, Naomi. (1987). *Learning the skills of peacemaking*. Jalmar Press, Rolling Hills Estates, CA.

> A creative activity guide for elementary-aged children to learn self-awareness, understanding of others, and mediation skills.

Etzioni, Amitai. (1993). *The spirit of community*. Crown Publishers, New York.

> This book has a chapter on character-building and moral conduct.

Faber, Adele & Mazlish, Elaine. (1980). *How to talk so kids will listen and listen so kids will talk*. Avon Books, New York.

Faber, Adele & Mazlish, Elaine. (1987). *Sibling rivalry: How to help children live together so you can live too*. Avon Books, New York.

Goleman, Daniel. (1995). *Emotional intelligence*. Bantam Books, New York.

> Goleman offers a new vision for excellence and a vital new curriculum for life. Emotional intelligence has as much or more to do with success in life than I.Q. Lack of emotional intelligence can sabotage the intellect and ruin careers. Emotional intelligence includes self-awareness, impulse control, persistence, zeal, self-motivation, empathy and social deftness. Goleman shows that emotional intelligence is not fixed at birth and how it can be nurtured.

Greenbaum, Stuart; Turner, Brenda; and Stephens, Ronald. (1989). *Set straight on bullies*. Malibu, CA: Pepperdine University, National School Safety Foundation.

> Statistics on bullying in the schools as well as recognition of bullies and victims. Prevention strategies for changing the attitudes and actions of adults and students alike.

Greer, Colin and Kohl, Herbert. (1995). *A Call to Character - A family treasury of stories, poems, plays, proverbs, and fables to guide the development of values for you and your children.* Harper Collins Publishers, New York.

This book is an annotated collection of stories, poems and excerpts from literature on the topics of courage, self-discipline, integrity, creativity, playfulness, loyalty, generosity, empathy, honesty, adaptability, idealism, compassion, responsibility, balance, fairness and love.

Hans, William. (1988) *Tyrone the horrible.* Scholastic, Inc., New York.

A small dinosaur is picked on repeatedly by a larger dinosaur. In the end the dinosaur tricks the bully, who never bothers him again.

Henkes, Kevin. (1991). *Chrysanthemum.* Greenwillow Books, New York.

A kindergarten-aged mouse is teased upon entering school because of her unusual name. Resolution is weak but story is engaging and definitely builds empathy for the victim.

Huffman, Henry A., (1994). *Developing a character education program: One school district's experience.* ASCD, Alexandria, VA. This book has an extensive bibliography covering recent journals, publications, books and organizations that cover the growing network of Character Education.

Iowa Peace Institute. (1992). *Fostering peace.* Grinnell, IA. (515) 236-4880.

A comparison of nine different conflict resolution approaches for use with both elementary and high school-aged students.

Kaufman, Gershen, and Raphel, Lev. (1990). *Stick up for yourself-teacher's guide.* Minneapolis, MN: Free Spirit Publishing.

A comprehensive guide to a ten-part course that correlates with the book by the same title. Blends self-esteem and assertiveness with activities for a full year in the classroom. Grades 4 to 8.

Kilpatrick, William and Wolfe, Gregory and Suzanne M. (1994). *Books that build character.* Simon and Schuster, New York.

This book includes an annotated bibliography of stories that teach moral values.

Kolb, Deborah, et al. (1994). *When talk works: Profiles of mediators.* Jossey-Bass, San Francisco.

Kottler, Jeffrey. (1994). *Beyond Blame: A new way of resolving conflicts in relationships.* Jossey-Bass Publishers, San Francisco.

Kreidler, William. (1984). *Creative conflict resolution.* Glenview, IL: Scott Foresman and Co.

Techniques for creating a caring classroom environment. Exercises for assessing the students' behavior as well as concrete activities for promoting cooperation are specifically presented. Grades K through 6 are covered.

Kritek, Phyllis. (1994). *Negotiating at an uneven table: Developing moral courage in resolving out conflicts.* Jossey-Bass Publishers. San Francisco.

Lamme, Linda Leonard, Krough, Suzanne Lowell and Yachmetz, Kathy A. (1992). *Literature-based moral education.* Oryx Press, Phoenix, AZ.

This book includes an annotated bibliography of books, stories and activities for teaching responsibility, self-esteem, sharing, truthfulness, peaceful problem-solving, respecting and appreciating others, ecological values, diligence, perseverance, patience and unconditional love in the elementary school.

Lickona, Thomas. (1991). *Educating for character: How our schools can teach respect and responsibility.* Bantam Books, New York.

McGinnis, Ellen; Goldstein, Arnold; Sprafkin, Robert; and Gershaw, N. Jane. (1984). *Skill streaming the elementary school child: A guide for teaching prosocial skills.* Champaign, IL: Research Press Co.

Detailed behavioral techniques for teaching children the necessary behaviors for social engagement and interaction. A similar guide is available from the same publisher for the preschool-aged child and for the adolescent.

Moore, Chas. (1986). *The mediation process: Practical strategies for resolving conflict.* Jossey-Bass, San Francisco.

Moser, Adolph. (1991). *Don't feed the monster on Tuesday.* Landmark Editions, Kansas City, MO.

A wonderful book that presents valuable information to children about understanding the importance of self-esteem. Practical approaches are presented that children can use to evaluate and strengthen their sense of self-esteem. Very practical guide to thinking in small steps toward success. Grades K to 5.

Millman, Dan. (1991). *Secret of the peaceful warrior.* H.J. Kramer, Inc., Tiburon, CA.

An older mentor teaches a school-aged boy how to thwart a bully by hiding his fear and side-stepping his physical advances. Somewhat unrealistic, as the boy and the bully end up friends in the end.

National Institute of Justice (NCJ149549). (1995). *Building the peace: The resolving conflict creatively program (RCCP)*. U.S. Dept. of Justice, Washington, DC 20531.
A report on this successful program available from the National Institute of Justice.

Naylor, Phyllis. (1991). *Reluctantly Alice*. Atheneum, New York.
Story of a seventh-grade girl who is made fun of in class, tripped in the halls, and hit by flying food in the cafeteria by another girl and her cohorts. When each student in class must select someone to interview, the girl chooses the bully. The girls eventually come to know each other better and the bullying stops.

Nelsen and Lott. (1990). *I'm on your side: Resolving conflicts with your teenage son or daughter*. Prima Publishers, Rocklin, CA.

Paley, Vivian Gussin. (1992). *You can't say, you can't play*. Howard University Press, Cambridge, MA.
An experimental year in the kindergarten classroom of Vivian Paley, an innovative teacher and educator, who introduces the rule "You can't say, you can't play." Not only are the voices of the children heard as they adapt to this new order, but those of the older fifth graders observing the process are shared as well.

Petty, Kate, and Firmin, Charlotte. (1991). *Being bullied*. Barron's Books, New York.
A young school-aged girl encounters a girl bully who calls her names, teases, and scribbles on her papers. She tells her mom about her problem and she gets help from her teacher, who protects her from the bully.

Prutzman, Priscilla; Stern, Lee, Burger, M. Leonard; and Bodenhamer, Gretchen. (1988). *The friendly classroom for a small planet*. New Society Publishers, Philadelphia.
Techniques for nonviolence, cooperation, and problem solving in grades K through 6 developed by the Reconciliation Quakers and used by more than 20,000 teachers and parents.

Schindler, Craig and Lapid, Gary. (1989). *The great turning: Personal peace, global victory*. Bear & Co., Santa Fe, NM.

Schmidt, Fran. (1994). Mediation - *Getting to win-win*. Grace Contrino Abrams Peace Education Foundation, Inc., 2627 Biscayne Boulevard, Miami, FL 33137.

Schmidt, Fran & Friedman, Alice. (1989). *Fighting fair for families*. Grace Contrino Abrams Peace Education Foundation, Miami Beach, FL.

Stolz, Mary. (1963). *The bully of Barkham Street*. Harper Collins Children's Books, New York.
The main character in this story is the bully. He is a sixth-grade boy who is the oldest and biggest in his classroom. His family rarely listens to him and often threatens to take away his only friend, his dog.

Stone, Karen F. and Harold Q. Dillehunt. (1978). *Self science: The subject is me*. Goodyear Publishing Co., Santa Monica, CA.
This book contains Character Development research and curriculum.

Tillett, Gregory. (1993). *Resolving conflict: A practical approach*. Oxford University Press, Oxford.

Trovato, Charlene. (1987). *Teaching kids to care*. Instructor Books, Cleveland, OH.
A guide to understanding and developing a pro-social environment both within the classroom as well as within the home. Specifically focuses on ages 2 to 6 with special chapters on disabilities, handicaps, and ethnic differences.

Ury, William. (1991). *Getting past no: Dealing with difficult situations*. Bantam Books, San Francisco.

Webster-Doyle Terrence. (1993). *Operation warhawks: How young people become warriors*. Atrium Society Publications (Education For Peace Series), PO Box 816, Middleburg, VT 05753.
Helps raise consciousness in youngsters 12-15 about war and the military. It presents realistic and frank view of what creates warriors and war in hopes that they will not glorify war, but understand it. Also shows how to direct that energy toward peaceful conflict resolution.

Wells, Rosemary. (1973). *Benjamin and tulip*. Dial Books, New York.
A charming little animal story in which the bully is a girl and the victim is a boy. The situation resolves when they encounter a bigger problem that affects them both.

PROFESSIONAL MATERIALS

Professional Organizations, Journals and Resource Catalogues

PROFESSIONAL ORGANIZATIONS.

Academy of Family Mediators
4 Militia Dr., Lexington, MA 01273
Phone: 781-674-2663; Fax: 781-674-2690
E-mail: afmoffice@mediators.org

> The Academy of Family Mediators was established in 1981 as a non-profit educational membership association and is the largest family mediation organization in existence. Our members are mediators working in a variety of settings including private practice, courts, schools, and government in the United States and Internationally.

Aiki Works, Inc.
PO Box 251 PO Box 7845, Victor, NY 14564, Aspen, CO 81612
Phone: 716-924-7302 970-925-7099; Fax: 716-924-2799 970-925-4532

American Bar Association, Standing Committee on Dispute Resolution
1800 M St., NW, Washington, DC 20036

The Arias Foundation for Peace and Human Progress
Apdo. 86410-1000 Costa Rica
Phone: 506-255-2955 or 255-2885; Fax: 506-255-2244

> The Arias Foundation for Peace and Human Progress is a not-for-profit organization whose mission is to build just and peaceful societies in Central America. In order to accomplish its mission, the Arias Foundation operates through three Centers: the Center for Organized Participation, the Center for Human Progress and the Center for Peace and Reconciliation.

Aspen Systems Corporation
1600 Research Blvd., Rockville, MD 20805

Association for the Treatment of Sexual Abusers
10700 SW Beaverton Hillside Hwy., Ste. #26, Beaverton, OR 97005-3035
Phone: 903-643-1023

> Membership organization with a journal, *(Sexual Abuse: A Journal of Research & Treatment)*, and a newsletter, "The Forum".

California Center for Civic Renewal
Dave Diamont, PO Box 307, Santa Barbara, CA 93102
Phone: 805-864-1973; Fax: 805-564-4260

> The Public Conversations Project was founded in 1989 to explore the possibility that family therapists have ways of working with hot and costly conflict that can be fruitfully applied in the political arena. Since then, using action-research methods, the project has developed principles and tools for fostering dialogue which they have used in a variety of settings on a variety of public issues. Many of the project's general principles were developed through designing, facilitating, and following up eighteen dialogue sessions on abortion. One recent subproject involved national leaders on issues of population, women's health, the environment and development. Another involved facilitating dialogue among stakeholders in the Northern Forest of New England and New York.

The Carter Center
Attn: Office of Public Information, One Copenhill, 453 Freedom Parkway, Atlanta, GA 30307
Phone: 404-331-3900
E-mail: carterweb@emory.edu

> The Carter Center is a nonprofit, nonpartisan public policy institute founded by former U.S. President Jimmy Carter and his wife Rosalynn, in 1982. The Center is dedicated to fighting disease, hunger, poverty, conflict, and oppression through collaborative initiatives in the areas of democratization and development, global health, and urban revitalization. At present, the Center operates 13 core programs, which have touched the lives of people in 65 countries, including the United States.

Center for Dispute Settlement
918 16th St., NW, Washington, DC 20006

Center for Policy Negotiation/Common Ground
Thomas Scott, 20 Park Plaza, #520, Boston, MA 02166

Center for Study & Prevention of Violence
Institute for Behavioral Sciences, University of Colorado-Boulder
Campus Box 442, Boulder, CO 80309-0442
Phone: 303-492-8465

> Operates a free database service on violence topics. Included under the VIOPRO section, is a category for conflict resolution programs. VICEO-SOURCE contains information on resource materials on violence and violence prevention. Includes curricula, videos, manuals and guidebooks.

Center for Teaching International Relations
University of Denver, Denver, CO 80208
Phone: 617-482-8660; Fax: 617-482-4972

> The Center for Policy Negotiation/Common Ground serves as a third party to facilitate interaction among government, non-government organizations, industry, and citizens' groups. With offices in Boston and in the Washington, DC area, CPN has specialized in public policy conflicts related to energy, air and water pollution, and development since 1974.

Center Source Publications
305 Tesconi Circle, Santa Rosa, CA 95401

City at Peace Guidebook. (1994)
A Creative Response to Communities in Crises
9502 Lee Highway, Fairfax, VA 22031
Phone: 703-385-4494

> This organization also publishes a "City of Peace School Kit" that helps bring young people together to address the violence they face in their lives, their schools and their communities.

Cleveland-Marshall College of Law
1801 Euclid Ave., Cleveland, OH 44115

Colorado School Mediation Project
3970 Broadway, Ste. B3, Boulder, CO 80304-1995

Common Ground Network for Life and Choice
Mary Jackstelt, Director
1601 Connecticut NW, Ste. #200, Washington, DC 20009
Phone: 202-265-4300; Fax: 202-232-6718

> The Common Ground Network for Life and Choice offers a "meeting place" for pro-choice and pro-life people to come together to dialogue in a non-adversarial manner and to explore ways to address issues of shared concern, such as teenage pregnancy and inadequate resources for women and children. The Network staff offers facilitation, training, and resource materials. The new ground breaking work of the Network has received national attention. The project is sponsored by Search for Common Ground, an independent, non-profit organization dedicated to finding workable solutions to divisive national and international problems.

Common Ground Productions
John Marks, President
1601 Connecticut Ave. NW, Ste. 200, Washington, DC 20009
Phone: 202-265-4300; Fax: 202-232-6718

> Common Ground Productions, a division of the Search for Common Ground, produces video programming that promotes creative collaborative dispute resolution, to bring about a shift in how international domestic issues are resolved. CGP is currently working on a monthly magazine TV series called Search for Common Ground that, unlike mainstream media, which focus on chronicling conflict, will explore workable solutions to deep-seated personal, community, national, and worldwide problems.

Community Board Program, Inc.
Terry Amsler, 1540 Market St., Ste. 490, San Francisco. 94102
Phone: 415-552-1250; Fax: 415-626-0595
E-mail: cmbrds@igc.apc.org

> The Community Board Program is a non-profit organization which provides free community mediation services in San Francisco and offers conflict resolution-related program development and training assistance to schools, juvenile correctional facilities and other agencies nationwide. Volunteer mediator handbooks are available in both English and Spanish. Community Boards also provides on site training, and program implementation assistance to schools and communities starting conflict resolution programs.

The Conflict Center
2564 So. Yates St., Denver, CO 80219
Phone: 303-936-3286

> Conduct training in conflict resolution and publish curriculum materials for schools.

The Conflict Resolution Network
PO Box 1016, Chatswood NSW 2057, Australia
Phone: (02) 419-8434

> The Conflict Resolution Network was founded by the United Nations Association of Australia. Works closely with the

Centre for Conflict Resolution at Macquarie University. Its purpose is to research, develop, teach and implement the theory and practice of Conflict Resolution. They produce training videos, curriculum materials and books on conflict resolution. They also publish a newsletter highlighting their activities.

Conflict Resolution and Confrontation Skills Training is offered by ETC with Career Track
3885 Center Green Dr., Boulder, CO 80301-5408
http://www.careertrack.com

Conflict Resolution Center International, Inc.
2205 E. Carson St., Pittsburgh, PA 15203-2107 USA
Phone: 412-481-5559; Fax: 412-481-5601

> The Conflict Resolution Center International, Inc. is a resource center assisting everyday people who are working on resolving conflict in their own communities. Specifically, it is concerned with neighborhood disputes and racial, ethnic and religious conflicts. One of the primary means of reaching people like you is through their journal Conflict Resolution Notes. You can send for a sample copy at the e-mail below. If you have a direct access to ConflictNet you will find this publication in the conference cn.crnotes. A hard copy subscription is available at a $25 annual rate. Student rate is $20. Back issues are available for $1.50 each of $25 for a complete set.

Consortium on Peace, Research, Education and Development
George Mason University, 4400 University Dr., Fairfax, Virginia 22030

Cornerstone: A Center for Justice and Peace
940 Emerson St., Denver, CO 80218

CPR Institute for Dispute Resolution, Panel Management Group
366 Madison Ave., New York, NY 10017
Phone: 212-949-6490; Fax: 212-949-8859

> CPR is a nationwide nonprofit resource for alternative dispute resolution for significant public and corporate disputes. CPR members include 500 general counsel of major corporations, leading law firms and prominent legal academics in support of private alternatives to the high costs of litigation. CPR's panel members are among the country's preeminent former judges and lawyers who are particularly well-qualified to resolve

disputes of a public character and to facilitate large complex disputes. CPR's operations also include a research, counseling, and customized training service to meet an organization's unique needs.

Dispute Resolution Services
2830 Pico Boulevard, Santa Monica, CA 90405

Educators for Social Responsibility
23 Garden St., Cambridge, MA 02138

Family Institute of Cambridge
Public Conversations Project, Laura Chasin, Director
51 Kondazian St., Waertown, MA 02172
Phone: 617-924-4400; Fax: 617-924-5111

> The Public Conversations Project was founded in 1989 to explore the possibility that family therapists have ways of working with hot and costly conflict that can be fruitfully applied in the political arena. Since then, using action-research methods, the project has developed principles and tools for fostering dialogue which they have used in a variety of settings on a variety of public issues. Many of the project's general principles were developed through designing, facilitating, and following up eighteen dialogue sessions on abortion. One recent subproject involved national leaders on issues of population, women's health, the environment and development. Another involved facilitating dialogue among stakeholders in the northern forests of New England and New York.

First Visitor Program
Linda Harroun, MSW, Director
1939 S. El Paso Ave., Colorado Springs, CO 80906
Phone: 719-578-6120

Florida Growth Management Conflict Resolution Consortium
Bob Jones, 325 John Knox Rd., Building G, Ste. 100, Tallahassee, FL 32303-4161
Phone: 904-921-9069; Fax: 904-921-9066
E-mail: Haylor@mailer.fsu.edu

> The Florida Growth Management Conflict Resolution Consortium is a university-based public service program that serves as statewide neutral problem solving resource for those involved in land-use, environmental and growth-related community conflicts. It assists parties in convening collaborative dispute resolution processes and in selecting mediators and facilitators from its directory of over

100 professionals. The Consortium offers conflict resolution, problem solving and facilitative leadership training and education and sponsors evaluation of dispute resolution initiatives.

Grace Contrino Abrams Peace Education Foundation, Inc.
PO Box 19-1153, Miami, FL 33139

Hawaii Healthy Start
Hawaii Family Stress Center
1833 Kalakua Ave., Ste. 1001, Honolulu, HI 96815
Phone: 808-944-9000

Highlander Research and Education Center
Jim Sessions, Director
1959 Highlander Way, New Market, TN 37820
Phone: 615-933-3443;Fax: 615-933-3424

> The Highlander Research and Education Center helps organizations analyze their problems, test their ideas, and learn from other organizations. The Center offers residential workshops and educational training sessions for social activists, educators and grassroots leaders. The Center also provides a library and resource center which houses thousands of materials on community development, social and educational issues.

International Alliance of Holistic Lawyers
PO Box 753, Middleburg, VT 05753

> This is a membership organization designed to support its members in approaching conflict and other legal issues consistent with principles of integrity, fairness and personal responsibility. Also aid to educate members on holistic ways of working within our legal institutions. Publishes a newsletter "The Whole Lawyer".

International Association for the Study of Cooperation in Education
136 Liberty St., Santa Cruz, CA 95060

Keystone Center
Robert Craig
Box 8606, Keystone, CO 80435
Phone: 303-468-5822; Fax: 303-262-0152

> The Keystone Center is a national, non-profit organization that provides neutral conflict management and mediation services in international, national, regional, state and local public policy disputes in several areas, including: environmental quality; natural resources; health; energy; and science and technology. In addition,

the Center provides training and organizational development services and assists organizations with strategic planning and the design of conflict-specific processes.

Massachusetts Advocacy Center
76 Summer St., Boston, Massachusetts 02110

Moral Education Resource Fund
Harvard Graduate School of Education
Larson Hall, 12 Appian Way, Cambridge, Massachusetts 02138

National Association for Community Mediation (NAFCM)
1726 M St., NW, Ste. 500, Washington, DC 20036
Phone: 202-467-6226; Fax: 202-466-4769
E-mail: nafcm@nafcm.org.

> The National Association for Community Mediation (NAFCM) is a membership organization comprised of community mediation centers, their staff and volunteer mediators, and other individuals and organizations interested in the community mediation movement. Membership benefits include funding possibilities, networking, research, publications, a membership directory, and more. From coast to coast and beyond, NAFCM enjoys a unique position as the only national non-profit organization dedicated solely to community-based mediation program.

National Center for Neighborhood Enterprise
Robert Woodson
1367 Connecticut Avenue NW, Washington, DC 20036
Phone: 202-331-1103; Fax: 202-296-1541

> The National Center for Neighborhood Enterprise provides technical and financial assistance to self-help strategies and projects for urban neighborhoods. NCNE networks corporations with "neighborhood executives," represents low-income people in social policy debate, and empowers people and communities to develop their own solutions to local problems.

National Institute for Dispute Resolution
1726 M St., NW, Ste. 500, Washington, DC 20036
Phone: 202-466-4764; Fax: 202-466-4769

> The NIDR fosters the development of innovative conflict resolution processes. Their goal is to provide those in conflict with the skills and understanding to productively solve problems. NIDR focuses special attention on underpresented ethnic,

economic, and cultural groups. The Institute's services include workshops, research and evaluation, and publications. NIDR's grant program for innovation funded these projects:

Center for Social Gerontology, Inc., Ann Arbor, MI

The Sounding Board, Boise, ID

Forsyth County Board of Commissioners, Winston-Salem, NC

The Parent Educational Advocacy Training Center, Alexandria, VA

Institute for Judicial Administration, New York, NY

Squaxin Island Tribe Shelton, WA

Open Adoption and Family Services, Eugene, OR

Pension Rights Resource Center, Washington, DC

Geoff Ball and Associates, Los Altos, CA

New Foundations Nonviolence Center
1615 Ogden St., Denver, CO 80218-1413
Phone: 303-861-5303

> They conduct trainings for trainers of alternatives to violence program. They conduct their workshop at various prisons and have participants work one-on-one with prisoners.

New Mexico Center for Dispute Resolution
Mediation in the Schools Program
510 Second St., Ste. 209, Albuquerque, NM 87102

New York State Forum on Conflict and Consensus
Allen Zerkin, Chair
244 Hudson Ave., Albany, NY 12210
Phone: 518-465-2500; Fax: 518-465-2500

> The New York State Forum on Conflict and consensus is a non-profit membership organization whose mission is to explore and promote the appropriate use of collaborative problem solving and conflict resolution techniques to improve public policy decision making at all levels of government in New York. Some specific aims of the Forum are to establish a clearinghouse for information about applications of dispute resolution approaches in New York and increase the public understanding of the potential benefits of such approaches.

Northern California Mediation Association (NCMA)
Joan Kelly, 100 Tamal Plaza, Ste. 175, Corte Madera, CA 94925
Phone: 415-927-1422; Fax: 415-927-1477

The Northern California Mediation Association (NCMA) is an organization of professional and volunteer mediators, established in response to the rapidly growing interest in non-adversarial methods of dispute resolution. NCMA offers educational programs and networking opportunities for anyone interested in mediation.

The Nurturing Program, Family Development Resources
Stephen Bavolek, President and Founder
3160 Pinebrook Road, Park City, UT 84060
Phone: 800-688-5822

Ohio Commission on Dispute Resolution and Conflict Management
Chris Carlson, 77 South High St., Columbus, OH 43266-0124
Phone: 614-752-9595; Fax: 614-752-9682

> The Ohio Commission on Dispute Resolution and Conflict Management assists Ohioans with ways to deal with disputes and conflict. Working in partnership with communities, schools, and state and local government, the small staff of the Commission acts as a resource center, consultant, catalyst, trainer, and evaluator. Its mission is to disseminate information about constructive ways to manage conflict and to help them build the foundations for making conflict resolution a part of social institutions as well as individual lives.

Peaceful Schools Project, New Foundations Nonviolence Center
PO Box 18030, Denver, CO 80218-0030
Phone: 303-861-5303

> They conduct training workshops for professionals on conflict resolution using the Children's Creative Response to Conflict (CCRC) model.

Public Conversations Project
Lauren Chasin, Director

Family Institute of Cambridge
51 Kondazian St., Watertown, MA 02172
Phone: 617-924-4400; Fax: 617-924-5111

> The Public Conversations Project was founded in 1989 to explore the possibility that family therapists have ways of working with hot and costly conflict that can be fruitfully applied in the political arena. Since then, using action-research methods, the project has developed principles and tools for fostering dialogue

which they have used in a variety of settings on a variety of public issues. Many of the project's general principles were developed through designing, facilitating, and following up eighteen dialogue sessions on abortion. One recent subproject involved national leaders on issues of population, women's health, the environment and development. Another involved facilitating dialogue among stakeholders in the Northern Forest of New England and New York.

Social Sciences Education Consortium, Inc.
Educational Resources Center, 855 Broadway, Boulder, CO 80302

Society of Professionals in Dispute Resolution, International Office
815 15th St., NW, Ste. 530, Washington, DC 20005
Phone: 202-783-7277; Fax: 202-783-7281

Sojurn House
PO Box 5667, Weybosset Hill Station, Providence, RI 02903

Southeast Negotiation Network, Center for Planning & Development, G.I.T.
Michael Elliot, Georgia Institute of Technology
Atlanta, GA 30322-0155
Phone: 404-894-2351; Fax: 404-894-1628
> The Southeast Negotiation Network (SNN) assists policymakers and community leaders to resolve complex or controversial public policy issues. SNN provides negotiation and mediation services on issues related to development and infrastructure policy, environmental and resource management, and planning. Clients include local communities and all levels of government. SNN also provides training in negotiating and managing public conflicts.

Southern Echo
Hollis Watkins, President
PO Box 10433, Jackson, MS 39289
Phone: 601-352-1500; Fax: 601-352-2266
> Southern Echo is a non-profit state-wide organization which seeks to make the political, economic, educational, and cultural systems accountable to the needs and interests of the African-American Community. Southern Echo offers training sessions and workshops to educate community leaders with the skills necessary to build a strong community. In addition to training community organizers,

Southern Echo offers training in conflict resolution and for youth leadership.

Stanford Program on International and Cross-Cultural Education
International Security and Arms Control Project, Stanford University
200 Lou Henry Hoover Hall, Stanford, CA 94305

Study Circles Resource Center
697 Pomfret St., PO Box 203, Pomfret, CN 06258
860-928-2616
> Offers dialogue training circles on critical social and political issues.

The Foundation for the Prevention & Resolution of Conflict (PERC), 75 East 55th St., New York, NY 10022
Phone: 212-421-0771; Fax: 212-856-7814
> PERC's objective is to help individuals and organizations, as an advisor, consultant, facilitator or representative, to prevent conflicts from arising in the first place, to counsel them on how best to resolve conflicts that do arise and to assist them in understanding, selecting and using the various techniques of Alternative Dispute Resolution (ADR).

The Mediation Center, Inc., 440 East Broadway, Ste. 340, Eugene, OR 97401, 941-345-1456
> Offers training in conflict resolution and mediation.

The Southern Poverty Law Center
400 Washington Ave., Montgomery, AL 36104
> Publish free CR materials to schools ("Teaching Tolerance"), closely monitor Klan and Militia groups and provide litigation services to individuals or groups whose civil rights have been violated.

The UVic Institute for Dispute Resolution (IDR)
Begbie Building, Room 123, University of Victoria
PO Box 2400, Victor, British Columbia, Canada V8W 3H7
Phone: 250-721-8777; Fax: 250-721-6607
> The UVic Institute for Dispute Resolution (IDR) was founded at the University of Victoria in 1989 as an interdisciplinary, university-based research centre focused on effective dispute resolution and alternative dispute resolution (ADR) theory and practice. The mandate of the Institute is to work toward fair, effective and peaceful dispute resolution locally, nationally and internationally.

Triune Arts, 517 Wellington St. West, Ste. 207, Toronto, Ontario, Canada M5V 1E9

Triune Arts, a non-profit, charitable institution established in 1981 has produced award-winning educational programs on a variety of subjects including alternative dispute/conflict resolution, restorative justice, cross-cultural communication, employment training for youth and international development.

Victim Offender Mediation Association (VOMA)
c/o The Restorative Justice Institute, PO Box 16301, Washington, DC 20041-6031
Phone: 703-404-1246

Working for Alternatives to Violence through Entertainment (WAVE)
105 Camino Teresa, Santa Fe, MN 87505
Phone: 505-982-8882; Fax: 505-982-6460
   Dennis Weaver, Martin Sheen, Edward James Olmos, Arun Gandhi (grandson of Mahatma Gandhi) and others concerned about the culture of violence plaguing our society serve on the Board of Advisors. Founded by film Producer Arthur Kanegis, WAVE is developing feature films with new kinds of heroes and heroines weiling techniques and strategies more advanced than violence. If violence is a learned behavior—learned partly through the entertainment media—then alternatives to violence can also be learned best through entertainment.

JOURNALS

Mediation Quarterly. Published by Jossey-Bass, Inc.
350 Sansome St., San Francisco, CA 74104
   This journal is sponsored by the Academy of Family Mediators but covers the whole emerging mediation field.

The Fourth R: The Newsletter of the National Association for Mediation in Education
c/o NIDR, 1726 M St. NW, Ste. 500, Washington, DC 20036-4502
Phone: 202-466-2772

Journal of Emotional and Behavioral Problems. 3:1, Breaking Conflict Cycles
1610 W. 3rd St., Bloomington, IN 47402

RESOURCE CATALOGUES

Childswork/Childsplay: A catalog addressing the social and emotional needs of children and adolescents
c/o Genesis Direct, Inc., 100 Plaza Dr., Secaucus, NJ 07094-3613
Phone: 800-962-1141

Colorado School Mediation Project
3970 Broadway, Ste. B3, Boulder, CO 80304
Phone: 303-444-7671; Fax: 303-444-7247

Colorado Educational Theater—Building Bridges
3490 Cripple Creek Square, Boulder, CO 80303
Phone: 303-499-6061

CRN Resources Catalogue, The Conflict Resolution Network
PO Box 1016, Chatswood NWS 2057, Australia
Phone: 02-419-8434 or 02-419-8500
   This catalogue describes the books, videos, audio tapes and curriculum materials produced by the CRN and other conflict resolution books and materials.

Education Development Center, Inc.
55 Chapel St., Newton, MA 02169
Phone: 800-225-4276
   Catalogue of materials on violence prevention. Produce Teenage Health Teaching Modules that include violence prevention modules with videos and curriculum materials.

Interaction Book Company
7208 Cornelia Dr., Edina, MN 55435

Jossey-Bass Inc., Publishers
433 California St., San Francisco, CA 94104

Kendall/Hunt Publishing Company
2460 Kerper Boulevard, PO Box 539, Dubuque, IA 52001

Martindale-Hubbell: Dispute Resolution Directory (1996)
   Over 55,000 listings of dispute resolution practitioners. Contains information, practice areas, geographic scope, licenses, education, services provided, experience, languages spoken and affiliations. Also included is information on federal arbitration acts and key state statutes as well as professional standards and ethical codes for alternative dispute resolution.

MTI Film and Video
420 Academy Dr., Northbrook, IL 60062

National Association for Mediation in Education
c/o NIDR, 1726 M St. NW, Ste. 500, Washington, DC 20036-4502
Phone: 202-466-2772

New Society Publishers Catalogue
New Society Educational Foundation

4527 Springfield Ave., Philadelphia, PA 19143
Phone: 800-333-9093
   Describes books and curriculum materials on various topics including conflict

resolution, non-violence, sustainable economics and environmental action.

Parenting Press, Inc.
7744 31st Ave. NE, Seattle, WA 98115

Program for Young Negotiators – The Consensus Building Institute Inc.
131 Auburn St., Cambridge, MA 02138
Phone: 617-492-7474; Fax: 617-492-1919

Resolution Resources of Colorado
102 S. Tejon, Ste. 1100, Colorado Springs, CO 80903
Phone: 719-471-0970
Roots and Wings Educational Catalogue

PO Box 3348, Boulder, CO 80307
Phone: 303-494-1833

Scott, Foresman and Company
Good Year Books Department
1900 East Lake Ave., Glenview, IL 60025

Sopris West Catalogue of Programs
1140 Boston Ave., Longmont, CO 80501
Phone: 303-651-2829

Sunshine Series
2715 Purgatory Dr., Colorado Springs, CO 80918

Teaching Peace
PO Box 190, Hygeine, CO 80533
Phone: 303-772-5788

The Conflict Center
2626 Osceola St., Denver, CO 80212
Phone: 303-433-4983
The Mediation Information & Resource Center (MIRC)
Offers online mediation information for the public http://winwin.mediate.com/resolution.cfm, locate a mediator at http://www.mediate.com/mediator/searc

h.cfm, and mediator resource at http://www.mediate.com/medspage. cfm. An interactive electronic magazine "Resolution" has been added to the public section of MIRC.

The National Center for Drug Abuse, Violence & Recovery (1997-98)
PO Box 9, 102 Hwy. 81 North, Calhoun, KY 42327-0009
Phone: 800-962-6662
A catalogue of videos, books, software, CD-ROMS, displays, games and posters for middle school and high school students on various topics including conflict resolution.

The National Center for Elementary Drug & Violence Prevention (1995)
PO Box 9, 102 Hwy. 81 North, Calhoun, KY 42327-0009
Phone: 800-962-6666
A catalogue of videos, books, software, displays and games on various topics including conflict resolution.

The Safer Society Press (1996)
PO Box 340, Brandon, VT 05733-0340
Phone: 802-247-3132
Catalogue of publications, tapes and videos

Sunburst Communications Catalogue
Dept. TG96, 101 Castleton St., PO Box 40, Pleasantville, NY 10570
Phone: 800-431-1934
A catalogue of videos, games, posters and K-12 curriculum modules on a variety of timely subjects including conflict resolution and character education.

REFERENCES

Alternative Dispute Resolution Committee of the Colorado Bar Association. (1992). *Manual on alternative dispute resolution.* Denver: CO: Colorado Bar Association.

American Psychiatric Association (APA). (1994). *The diagnostic and statistical manual* (4th ed.) (DSM-IV). Washington, DC: American Psychiatric Association Press.

Associated Press. (1997). Something to stress out about: Pressure can destroy brain cells. *The Gazette,* Colorado Springs, CO, Oct. 29, A9.

Babcock, D., & Keepers, T. (1976). *Raising kids ok.* New York: Grove Press.

Bach, G. R., & Wyden, P. (1968). *The intimate enemy: How to fight fair in love and marriage.* New York: Avon.

Baring, A., & Cashford, J. (1993). *The myths of the goddess.* New York: Penguin Books.

Bateson, G., Jackson, D. D., Haley, J., & Weakland, J. (1956). Towards a theory of schizophrenia. *Behavioral Sciences, 1,* 251–264.

Belsky, J., & Rovine, M. (1988). Nonmaternal care in the first year of life and infant-parent attachment security. *Child Development, 59,* 157–167.

Benson, P. (1995). *Uniting communities for youth.* Minneapolis: Search Institute.

Benson, P., Galbraith, J., & Espeland, P. (1995). *What kids need to succeed: Proven ways to raise good kids.* Minneapolis: Search Institute.

Bernstein, P. (1985) *Family ties, corporate bonds.* New York: Henry Holt.

Birdsong, M. (1993). *The woman with the alabaster jar.* Santa Fe: Bear and Company.

Blake, R. R., & Moulton, J. (1983). *Consultation: A handbook for individual organization development* (2nd ed.). Menlo Park, CA: Addison-Wesley.

Bly, R., & Woodman, M. (1993). *Facing the shadow in men and women* (audiotape). Pacific Grove, CA: Oral Tradition Archives.

Bohm, D. (1987). *Science, order and creativity.* New York: Bantam.

Bolton, R. (1979). *People skills.* New York: Simon & Schuster.

Borysenko, J. (1996). *Seventy times seven: On the spiritual art of forgiveness* (audiotape). Boulder, CO: Sounds True Audio.

Bowen, M. (1971). Family therapy and family group therapy. In H. Kaplan & B. Sadock (Eds.), *Comprehensive group psychotherapy.* Baltimore: Williams and Wilkins.

Bowen, M. (1978). *Family therapy in clinical practice.* New York: Jason Aronson.

Bowlby, J. (1969). Attachment and loss, Volume 1. In J. Bowlby, *Separation: Anxiety and anger.* New York: Basic Books.

Bowlby, J. (1973). Attachment and loss, Volume 2. In J. Bowlby, *Attachment.* New York: Basic Books.

Bowlby, J. (1975). Attachment theory, separation anxiety and mourning. In S. Arietya (Ed.), *American handbook of psychiatry.* New York: Basic Books.

Bradshaw, J. (1988). *Healing the shame that binds you.* Deerfield Beach, FL: Health Communications.

Bradshaw, J. (1990). *Homecoming: Reclaiming and championing your inner child.* New York: Bantam.

Briggs, J., & Peat, F. (1989). *The turbulent mirror.* New York: Harper & Row.

Buckley, W. (1968). *Sociology and modern systems theory.* Englewood Cliffs, NJ: Prentice Hall.

Callahan, R. (1997). A Thought Field Therapy: The Case of Mary. *Traumatology: An Electronic Journal of Innovations in the Study of the Traumatization Process and Methods for Reducing or Eliminating Human Suffering, 3,* Article 4. URL:http://www.rdz.stjohns.edu.trauma/traumaj.html.

Cameron-Bandler, R. (1978). *They lived happily ever after.* Cupertino, CA: Meta Publications.

Campbell, J. (1968). *Hero with a thousand faces.* Princeton, NJ: Princeton University Press.

Camus, A. (1980). *Neither victims nor executioners.* New York: Continuum Publishing Co.

. Carbonell, J., & Figley, C. (1996). A systematic clinical demonstration methodology: A collaboration between practitioners and clinical researchers. *The International Electronic Journal of Innovations in the Study of the Traumatization Process and Methods for Reducing or Eliminating Related Human Suffering,* 2(1), Article 1. URL: http://www.rdz.stjohns.edu:/trauma/traumaj.html.

Cashdan, S. (1988). *Object relations therapy: Using the relationship.* New York: W. W. Norton.

Chamberlain, D. (1996). Past and future birth. *The APP-PAH Newsletter.* Summer, 1-2.

Clarke, J. (1978). *Self-esteem: A family affair.* New York: Harper & Row.

Clarke, J., & Dawson, C. (1989). *Growing up again: Parenting ourselves, parenting our children.* Minneapolis: Hazelden.

Cole, N. (1997). The impact of trauma on infancy and early childhood: Treating the adult survivor from a developmental perspective. Presentation given by the Colorado Springs Chapter of the Colorado Society for Clinical Social Work, Colorado Springs, Colorado, September 12, 1997.

Courtois, C. A. (1993). Vicarious traumatization of the therapist. *NCP Clinical Newsletter, 3,* 8–9.

Curran, D. (1990). *Traits of a healthy family.* New York: Random House.

deMause, L. (1982). *Foundations of psychohistory.* New York: Creative Roots.

DeMeo, J. (1992). The origins and diffusion of patrism in Saharasia c. 400 BCE, *World Futures,* March–May, 247–271.

Diamond, J. (1989). *The adrenaline addict: Hooked on danger and excitement.* Willits, CA: self-published.

Diamond, J. (1994). *The warrior's journey home: Healing men, healing the planet.* Oakland, CA: New Harbinger Publications.

Dickstein, L. L., & Nadelson, J. (Eds.). (1989). *Family violence: Emerging issues of a national crisis,* Clinical Practice Series No. 3. Washington, DC: American Psychiatric Association Press.

Dunn, P. (1985). Ninth European Congress of Perinatal Medicine. *ObGyn News, 19,* 24.

Eggert, L.L. (1994). *Anger management for youth: Stemming aggression and violence.* Bloomington, IN: National Educational Service.

Eisler, R. (1987). *The chalice and the blade.* San Francisco: Harper & Row.

Ellis, A. (1995). Rational emotive behavior therapy. In R. J. Corsini & D. Wedding (Eds.), *Current Psychotherapies* (5th ed.). Itasca, IL: Peacock.

Erickson, E. (1959). *Psychological issues.* New York: International Universities Press.

Eron, L. (1987). Aggression through the ages. *School Safety.* Fall, 12–16.

Fenell, D., & Weinhold, B. (1997). *Counseling families* (2nd ed.). Denver: Love Publishing.

Finkelhor, D. (1990). Early and long-term effects of child sexual abuse: An update. *Professional Psychologist,* 21, 329–330.

Fisher, R., & Ury, W. (1981). *Getting to yes.* New York: Penguin.

Framo, J. (1981). The integration of marital therapy with family of origin sessions. In A.S. Gurman & D.P. Kniskern (Eds.), *Handbook of family therapy.* New York: Brunner/Mazel.

Framo, J. (1982). *Explorations in marital and family therapy.* New York: Springer.

Freyd, J. (1994). Betrayal trauma: Traumatic amnesia as an adaptive response to childhood abuse. *Ethics & Behavior, 4*(4), 307–329.

Fried, S. (1995). Personal communications.

Fried, S., & Fried, P. (1996). *Bullies and victims: Helping your child survive the schoolyard battlefield.* New York: Evans and Company.

Garbarino, J., et al. (1991). *No place to be a child: Growing up in a war zone.* New York: Lexington/Macmillan.

Garbarino, J., et al. (1992). *Children in danger: Coping with the consequences of community violence.* San Francisco: Jossey Bass.

Garbarino, J. (1993). *Raising children in the midst of a war zone: A plenary address* (audiotape). 10th National Conference on Child Abuse and Neglect, Pittsburgh. Tape available from Chesapeake Audio/Video Communications, Inc., Elkridge, MD.

Garrity, C., et al. (1995). *Bully proofing your school: A comprehensive approach for elementary schools.* Longmont, CO: Sopris West.

Gimbutas, M. (1982). *The goddesses and gods of old Europe Ñ 6500-3500 BC.* Berkeley and Los Angeles: University of California Press.

Gladding, S. (1979). The creative use of poetry in the counseling process. *Personnel and Guidance Journal, 57,* 285–287.

Gladding, S. (1996). *Counseling: A comprehensive profession.* Englewood Cliffs, NJ: Prentice Hall.

Gleick, J. (1987). *Chaos: Making a new science.* New York: Penguin.

Goleman, D. (1997). *Emotional intelligence.* New York: Bantam.

Goulding, M., & Goulding, R. (1978). *The power is in the patient: A Gestalt approach to psychotherapy.* San Francisco: TA Press.

Grof, S. (1985). *Beyond the brain.* New York: State University of New York Press.

Gyatso, T. H. H., 14th Dalai Lama (1997). *Harmony in diversity* (videocassette). Broomfield, CO: Conscious Wave.

Havighurst, R. (1972). *Developmental tasks and education.* New York: David McKay.

Hawkins, J. Catalano, R., et al. (1992) *Communities that care: Action for drug abuse preventions.* San Francisco: Jossey-Bass.

Healthy families america: Critical elements for effective home visitor services, (1995). Unpublished paper. Chicago: NCPCA. WWWURL: http://www.child-abuse.org/elements.hfa.html.

Healthy Start. (1992). *Report to Hawaii State Legislature* (unpublished paper). Honolulu, HI: Hawaii Department of Health. WWWURL: http://www.tyc.state.tx.us/prevention/hawaii.html.

Herman, J. (1992). *Trauma and recovery.* New York: Basic Books.

Hitchcock, J. (1994). *The witches hammer.* New York: Dutton.

Hillman, J. (1975). *Loose ends: Primary papers in archetypal psychology.* New York: Spring Publications.

Hills, C. (1980). *Creative conflict.* Boulder Creek, CA: University of the Trees Press.

Houston, J. (1980). *Life force: The psycho-historical recovery of the self.* New York: Delta.

Hunsaker, P. & Alessandra, A. (1980*). The art of managing people.* New York: Simon & Schuster, Inc.

Huntington, S. (1993). The clash of civilizations. *Foreign Policy,* Summer, 22–48.

Jackson, D. (1965). Family rules: The mantel quid pro quo. *Archives of General Psychiatry, 12,* 589–594.

James, B. (1994). *Handbook for treatment of attachment-trauma problems in children.* New York: The Free Press.

Jeffries, A. (1997). Personal conversation.

Johnson, D. W., & Johnson, R. T. (1987). *Creative conflict.* Edina, MN: Interaction Book Company.

Johnson, D. W., & Johnson, R. T. (1995). *Teaching students to be peacemakers.* Edina, MN: Interaction Book Company.

Johnson, D. W., Johnson, R. T., & Holubec, E. J. (1993). *Circles of learning: Cooperation in the classroom* (6th ed.). Edina, MN: Interaction Book Company.

Johnson, R. (1991). *Owning your own shadow: Understanding the dark side of the psyche.* San Francisco: Harper.

Jones, C. (1995). *Childbirth choices today.* New York: Citadel Press.

Jongeward, D. (1973). *Everybody wins: Transactional analysis applied to organizations.* Menlo Park, CA: Addison-Wesley.

Kaplan, L. (1978). *Oneness and separateness: From infant to individual.* New York: Simon & Schuster.

Karpman, S. (1968). Fairytales and script drama analysis. *Transactional Analysis Bulletin, 7,* 39–43.

Katz, N. H., & Lawyer, J. W. (1985*). Communication and conflict resolution.* Dubuque, IA: Kendall/Hunt.

Keen, S. (1991). *Fire in the belly.* New York: Bantam.

Kegan, R. (1994). *In over our heads: The mental demands of modern life.* Cambridge, MA: Harvard University Press.

Kernberg, O. (1976). *Object relations theory and clinical psychoanalysis.* New York: Jason Aronson.

Klaus, M. (1995). *Forum: Importance of post-natal relationships.* Speech given at the 7th International Congress, Association for Pre and Perinatal Psychology and Health. San Francisco, CA, September 30, 1995.

Klaus, M., & Kennell, J. (1976). *Maternal-infant bonding.* St. Louis: C.V. Mosby Co.

Klaus, M., Kennell, J., & Klaus, P. (1993). *Mothering the mother: How a doula can help.* Reading, MA: Addison-Wesley.

Klaus, M., Kennell, J., & Klaus, P. (1995). *Bonding.* Reading, MA: Addison-Wesley.

Kotulak, R. (1996). *Inside the brain.* Kansas City, MO: Andrews and McMeel.

Krause, A., & Haverkamp, B. (1996). Attachment in adult child–older parent relationships: Research, theory and practice. *Journal of Counseling and Development, 75,* 83–75.

Kreidler, W. J. (1984). *Creative conflict resolution.* Glenview, IL: Scott Foresman and Company.

Lachkar, J. (1993). Marital and political conflict. *Journal of Psychohistory, 20,* 275–286.

LeBoyer, F. (1975). *Birth without violence.* New York: Knopf.

LeDoux, J. E. (1994, June). Emotion, memory and the brain. *Scientific American,* 50–57.

Leffert, N., Benson, P., & Roehlkepartain, J. (1997). *Starting out right: Developmental assets for children.* Minneapolis: Search Institute.

Leiva, J. (1995). *Misogyny in the birth room: Primal violence against women and children.* Speech given at the 7th International Congress, Association for Pre- and Perinatal Psychology and Health. San Francisco, CA, September 30, 1995.

Levin, P. (1988a). *Becoming the way we are.* Deerfield Beach, FL: Health Communications.

Levin, P. (1988b). *Cycles of power.* Deerfield Beach, FL: Health Communications.

Lewis, D. O. (1992). From abuse to violence: Psychophysiological consequences of maltreatment. *Journal of American Academy of Child and Adolescent Psychiatry, 31,* 383–391.

Likert, R., & Likert, J. (1976). *New ways of managing conflict.* New York: McGraw-Hill.

Litwak, E. (1961). Models of bureaucracy which permit conflict. *American Journal of Sociology, 67,* 177–184.

Magid, K., & McKelvey, C. (1987*). High risk: Children without a conscience.* New York: Bantam.

Mahler, M. S. (1968). *On human symbiosis and the vicissitudes of individuation, Vol. 1, Infantile psychoses.* New York: International Universities Press.

Mahler, M. S., et al. (1975). *The psychological birth of the human infant.* New York: International University Press.

Maslow, A. (1971). *The farther reaches of human nature.* New York: Viking Press.

McKay, M. (1994). The link between domestic violence and child abuse: Assessment and treatment considerations. *Child Welfare League of America, 73*, 29–39.

McWilliams, J. M., et al. (1992). *Manual on alternative dispute resolution*. Denver: Colorado Bar Association.

Meichenbaum, D. (1994). *A clinical handbook/practical therapist manual: For assessing and treating adults with post-traumatic stress disorder (PTSD)*. Waterloo, Ontario: Institute Press.

Metnick, D. (1966). *Traumatic incident reduction: Specialized treatment for rapid emotional healing*. URL: http://www.tir.org.

Miller, A. (1981). *The drama of the gifted child*. New York: Basic Books.

Miller, A. (1983). *For your own good*. New York: Farran, Straus & Giroux.

Miller, A. (1986). *Thou shalt not be aware*. New York: New American Library.

Miller, A. (1988). *Banished knowledge*. New York: Doubleday.

Miller, A. (1991). *Breaking down the wall of silence*. New York: Dutton.

Miller, J. G. (1978). *Living systems*. New York: McGraw-Hill.

Mindell, A. (1983). *Dreambody*. Santa Monica, CA: SIGO Press.

Mindell, A. (1985a). *Rivers way*. Boston: Routledge and Kegan Paul.

Mindell, A. (1985b). *Working with the dreaming body*. Boston: Routledge and Kegan, Paul.

Mindell, A. (1987). *The dreambody in relationship processes*. Boston: Routledge and Kegan, Paul.

Mindell, A. (1989). *The year one: Global process work*. New York: Arkana.

Murray, J. C. (1985). *We hold these truths: Catholic reflections on the American proposition*. Kansas City, MO: Sheed and Ward.

Myss, C. (1996). *Anatomy of the spirit*. New York: Three Rivers Press.

National Institute for Dispute Resolution (NIDR). (1998). *Conflict resolution education facts*. URL: http//www.CREmet.org.

Ney, P. G. (1987). The treatment of abused children: The sequence of events. *American Journal of Psychotherapy, 41*, 390–401.

Ney, P. G. (1988). Transgenerational child abuse. *Child Psychiatry and Human Development, 18*, 151–168.

Ney, P. G. (1992). Transgenerational triangles of abuse: A model of family violence. In E. C. Viano, *Intimate violence: Interdisciplinary perspectives* (pp. 15–25). Bristol, PA: Taylor & Francis.

Odent, M. (1984). *Birth reborn*. New York: Pantheon.

Olds, D., & Henderson, C. R. (1994). Does prenatal and infancy nurse home visitation have enduring effects on qualities of parental care-giving and child health at 25 to 50 months of life? *Pediatrics, 93*, 80–98.

Olweus, D. (1991). Bully/victim problems among schoolchildren: Basic facts and effects of a school-based intervention program. In D. Peple and K. Rubin (Eds.), *The development and treatment of childhood aggression*. Hillsdale, NJ: Lawrence Erlbaum.

Orr, L., & Ray, S. (1977). *Rebirthing in the new age*. Milbrae, CA: Celestial Arts.

Paul, J., & Paul, M. (1989). *From conflict to caring*. Minneapolis, MN: Comp Care Publishers.

Peck, S. (1987). *A different drum: Community making and peace*. New York: Simon & Schuster.

Perry, B. (1996). ÒIncubated in terror: Neurodevelopmental factors in the cycle of violence,Ó in J. Osofsy (Ed.), *Children, youth and violence: Searching for solutions*. New York: Guilford Press.

Piaget, J. (1951). *The child's conception of the world*. New York: Humanities Press.

Reber, K. (1996). Children at risk for reactive attachment disorder: Assessment, diagnosis and treatment. *Progress: Family Systems Research and Therapy, 5*, 83–98.

Robinson, J. (Ed.). (1977). The gospel of Thomas, trans. T. O. Lambdin, in *The nag hamamadi in english*. New York: Harper & Row.

Rogers, C. (1986). The Reist workshop: A personal overview. *Journal of Humanistic Psychology, 26*, 23–45.

Rogers, C., & Ryback, D. (1984). One alternative to nuclear planetary suicide. In R. F. Levant & J. M. Shlien (Eds.), *Client-centered therapy and the person-centered approach: New directions in theory, research and practice*. New York: Praeger.

Rovina, L. (1992). A letter to Colorado attorneys. *In Manual on alternative dispute resolution*, Colorado Bar Association, 1900 Grant St., Denver, CO 80203-4309.

Russell, P. (1979). *The brain book*. New York: Hawthorne.

Sager, C. J., et al. (1971). The marriage contract. *Family Process, 10*, 311–326.

Samenow, S. (1984). *Inside the criminal mind*. New York: Random House.

Samenow, S. (1989). *Before it's too late: Why some kids get into trouble and what parents can do about it*. New York: Random House.

Satir, V. (1988). *The new peoplemaking*. Palo Alto, CA: Science & Behavior Books.

Schein, E. (1969). *Process consultation: Its role in organizational development*. Reading, MA: Addison-Wesley.

Schiff, J. (1970). *All my children*. New York: Pyramid.

Schiff, J., et al. (1976). *The cathexis reader*. New, York: Harper and Row.

Senge, P. (1990). *The fifth discipline*. New York: Doubleday.

Shapiro, F. (1995). *Eye movement desensitization and reprocessing: Basic principles, protocols, and procedures.* New York: Guilford Press.

Sheets, C. (1997). *Thought field therapy: Rapid resolution for intractable problems.* Level I training, March 7-8, Colorado Springs, CO.

Sisson, R. W., & Azrin, N. H. (1986). Family-member involvement to initiate and provide treatment of problem drinkers. *Journal of Behavior Therapy and Experimental Psychiatry, 17*(1), 15–21.

Slaby, R., Wilson-Brewer, R., & Dash, K. (1994). *Aggressors, victims, and bystanders: Thinking and acting to prevent violence.* Newton, MA: Educational Development Center, Inc.

Slotkowski, E., & King, L. (1982). The incidence of neonatal circumcision in Illinois. *Illinois Medical Journal, 162,* 421–426.

Sjöö, M., & Mor, B. (1987). *The great cosmic mother: Rediscovering the religion of the earth.* San Francisco: Harper & Row.

Sroufe, A., & Rutter, M. (1984). The domain of developmental psychology. *Child Development,5,* 17–29

Stolt, D. (1973). Follow-up study from birth on the effects of prenatal stresses. *Developmental Medicine and Child Neurology, 15,* 770–787.

Storm, H. (1972). *Seven arrows.* New York: Ballantine.

Straus, M., & Gelles, R. (1988). How violent are American families? Estimates from the national family violence survey and other studies. In G. Hotaling et al. (Eds.), *Family abuse and its consequences: New directions in research* (pp. 770–787.) Newbury Park, CA: Sage.

Taub-Bynum, E. (1984). *The family unconscious.* Wheaton, IL: Theosophical Society Publishing House.

Thompson, R. A. (1996). *Counseling techniques.* Washington, D . C.: Accelerated Development.

Thompson, W. (1981). *The time it takes falling bodies to light.* New York: St. Martin's Press.

Trivette, C., Dunste, C., & Deal, A., (Eds.) (1994). *Supporting and strengthening families: Methods, strategies and practice.* Cambridge, MA: Brookline.

United Nations. (1992). Families: Forms and functions. *Occasional Papers Series I.* Vienna: United Nations Office.

van der Kolk, B. (1988). The trauma spectrum: The interaction of biological and social events in the genesis of the trauma response. *Journal of Traumatic Stress, 1,* 273–290.

van der Kolk, B., Greenberg, M., Orr, S., & Pitman, R. (1989). Endogenous opioids and stress induced analgesia in post traumatic stress disorder. *Psychopharmacology Bulletin, 25,* 108–112.

van der Kolk, B., McFarlane, A., & Weisaeth, L. (Eds.) (1996). *Traumatic stress: The overwhelming experi-ence on mind, body and society.* New York: Guilford Press.

van der Kolk, B., Roth, S., Pelcovitz, D., & Mandel, F. (1993). *Complex PTSD: Results of the PTSD field trails for DSM IV.* Washington, DC: American Psychiatric Association.

van der Kolk, B., & van der Hart, O. (1989). Pierre Janet and the breakdown of adaptation in psychological trauma. *American Journal of Psychiatry, 146*(1), 530–1540.

van der Kolk, B., & van der Hart, O. (1991). The intrusive past: The flexibility of memory and the engraving of trauma. *American Imago, 48,* 425–454.

van der Kolk, B., van der Hart, O., & Burbridge, J. (1997). *Approaches to the treatment of PTSD.* Trauma Website.

Verny, T. (1981). *The secret life of the unborn child.* New York: Dell.

Viano, E. C. (1992). *Intimate violence: Interdisciplinary perspectives.* Bristol, PA: Taylor & Francis.

von Bertalanffy, L. (1968). *General systems theory: Foundation, development, applications.* New York: Brazillier.

Violato, C., & Russell, C. (1994). *Effects of nonmaternal care on child development: A meta-analysis of published research.* Poster presentation at 55th Annual convention of the Canadian Psychological Association, Penticton, BC, July 1, 1994.

Wallenstein, E. (1985). Circumcision: The uniquely American medical enigma. *Symposium on Advances in Pediatric Urology: Urology Clinics of North American, 12,* 123–132.

Weiner, N. (1954). *Cybernetics, or control and communication in the animal and the machine* (2nd ed.), Cambridge, MA: MIT Press. (Original work published in 1948.)

Weinhold, B. (1991). *Breaking free of addictive family relationships.* Walpole, NH: Stillpoint.

Weinhold, B. (Ed.) (1996a). *Spreading kindness: A program guide for reducing youth violence in the schools.* Colorado Springs, CO: The Kindness Campaign.

Weinhold, B. (1996b). *Building a community of kindness: A community organizer's guide to the kindness campaign.* Colorado Springs, CO: The Kindness Campaign.

Weinhold, B., & Andresen, G. (1979). *Threads: Unraveling the mysteries of adult life.* New York: Richard Marek Publishers.

Weinhold, B., & Fenell, D. (1997). *Student manual for counseling families.* Denver: Love.

Weinhold, B.., & Hendricks, G. (1993). *Counseling and psychotherapy: A transpersonal approach* (2nd Ed.) Denver, CO: Love Publishing Co.

Weinhold, B., & Weinhold, J. (1989). *Breaking free of the co-dependency trap.* Walpole, NH: Stillpoint.

Weinhold, J., & Weinhold, B. (1992). *Counter-dependency: The flight from intimacy.* Colorado Springs, CO: CICRCL Press.

Weinhold, B., & Weinhold, J. (1993). Building partnership families: A psychosocial approach. *Family Counseling and Therapy, 1,* 1–20.

Weinhold, B., & Weinhold, J. (1993). Conflict resolution: The partnership way in schools. *Counseling and Human Development, 30,* 1–12.

Weise, D., & Daro, D. (1995). *Current trends in child abuse reporting and fatalaties: the results of the 1994 annual fifty state survey.* Chicago: NCPCA.

Weiss, L., & Weiss, J. (1989). *Recovery from co-dependency.* Deerfield Beach, FL: Health Communications.

Wheatley, M. J. (1992). *Leadership and the new science.* San Francisco: Bennett-Koehler.

Wilber, K. (1980). *The Atman project: A transpersonal view of human development.* Wheaton, IL: Theosophical Publishing.

Wilber, K. (1996). *A brief history of everything.* Boston: Shambhala.

Wilson, J., & Raphael, B. (Eds). (1993). *International handbook of traumatic stress syndromes.* New York: Plenum Press.

Wilson, J. P., & Lendy, J. D. (1994). *Countertransference in the treatment of PTSD.* New York: Guilford.

Winnicott, D. W. (1965). *The maturational process and the facilitating environment.* New York: International Universities Press.

Winnicott, D. W. (1975). *Through pediatrics to psychoanalysis.* New York: Basic Books.

Zohar, D., & Marshall, I. (1994). *The quantum society.* New York: William Morrow.

INDEX